The Human Dimension of Cybersecurity:

Cultivating a Protective Organizational Culture

Asif Iqbal Hajamydeen
https://orcid.org/0000-0002-5034-1781
Management and Science University, Malaysia

Asmaa Mahfoudh Alhakimi
https://orcid.org/0000-0002-4038-5203
Management and Science University, Malaysia

Md Gapar Md Johar
Management and Science University, Malaysia

I. Wayan Budi Sentana
Bali State Polytechnic, Indonesia

IGI Global
Scientific Publishing
Publishing Tomorrow's Research Today

Vice President of Editorial	Melissa Wagner
Director of Acquisitions	Mikaela Felty
Director of Book Development	Jocelynn Hessler
Production Manager	Mike Brehm
Cover Design	Jose Rosado

Published in the United States of America by
IGI Global Scientific Publishing
701 East Chocolate Avenue
Hershey, PA, 17033, USA
Tel: 717-533-8845 | Fax: 717-533-7115
Website: https://www.igi-global.com E-mail: cust@igi-global.com

Library of Congress Cataloging-in-Publication Data

LCCN: 2025032426 (CIP Data Pending)
ISBN13: 9798337341545
Isbn13Softcover: 9798337341552
EISBN13: 9798337341569

British Cataloguing in Publication Data
A Cataloguing in Publication record for this book is available from the British Library.

Table of Contents

Detailed Table of Contents

Technological and human factors synergistically decrease information security levels while increasing information security breaches. Argumentation supported ideas that complex, adaptive, socio-technical systems have needed to be contemplated with differing analysis perspectives. Several frameworks for understanding, measuring, mapping, or improving organizational cybersecurity culture have been previously presented. his chapter explores central issues regarding organizational cybersecurity culture and its measurement and suggests a model and examples that should help broaden the exploration of cybersecurity culture as a technical-based organizational structure and a significant human factor.The primary objective is to investigate the evolving fields of behavioral and human factors, as well as the recent convergence of social science and engineering approaches in this context. Given the complexity of adaptive socio-technical systems, this chapter will detail the necessity of diverse analytical perspectives in understanding these challenges.

As government organizations increasingly use digital tools in smart cities, employees must understand cybersecurity properly. This chapter introduces a practical model to improve institutional handling of cybersecurity and privacy by combining education, awareness, and readiness into a clear approach supporting safer digital governance. The model, based on Protection Motivation Theory (PMT), examines employees' understanding of digital tools, perceived cyber risk, exposure frequency, system complexity, privacy concerns, and the usefulness of cybersecurity tools affecting their readiness. It includes AI-based awareness tools and structured training like the SETA program to foster safer habits. The focus is on human responses, learning, and how management shapes cybersecurity culture. This chapter targets leaders, IT staff, and public managers aiming to build responsibility toward cybersecurity in smart city institutions or those transitioning into them.

As 2030 approaches, the digital landscape is evolving rapidly and so are cyber threats. Once viewed as purely technical challenges, these threats are now deeply intertwined with human behavior. This chapter explores the evolving role of cyber hygiene in higher education, reflecting the diverse digital habits of students, faculty, and staff. It examines how behavioral patterns, cognitive overload, and trust in digital systems shape vulnerabilities, and what can be done to build stronger defenses. Emphasizing the need for smarter awareness programs, cultural shifts, and user-informed policies, the chapter provides practical, real-world insights into people-centered cybersecurity. Higher education institutions emerge as early test beds for organizational readiness. Ultimately, achieving cyber resilience by 2030 requires more than advanced tools, it demands empowered individuals who are not the weakest link but the first and strongest line of defense.

Many small and medium-sized businesses (SMEs) now rely heavily on online platforms like Open Journal Systems (OJS) as a result of the digital transformation of academic publishing. However, because cybersecurity resilience and operational efficiency are inextricably linked, this reliance poses serious risks. In order to examine the operational disruptions brought on by cybersecurity threats aimed at

This chapter presents a framework for integrating cryptographic technologies with organizational culture to build sustainable cybersecurity resilience. It examines how core mechanisms such as encryption, digital signature, and key management must align with leadership, policy design, and workforce engagement to protect data and ensure compliance. Drawing on practices from finance, healthcare, and government, the chapter highlights how successful organizations embed cryptography into governance and operations. It also addresses barriers such as user resistance, poor usability, and fragmented implementation that weaken security controls. The final section explores future directions, including blockchain-based trust systems, post-quantum cryptography readiness, and the need for crypto literacy across roles. By connecting technical controls with human and institutional factors, the chapter emphasizes that cryptography should be viewed not as an isolated IT function but as a strategic cultural asset essential for trust, continuity, and resilience in evolving threat environments.

Data security strategies in the digital age rely on cryptography, yet human behavior remains the most critical and unpredictable factor. This chapter explores the intersection of corporate culture and cryptographic implementation, highlighting how user habits, training gaps, and weak cybersecurity cultures can undermine even the most robust encryption. Using real-world examples from healthcare, finance, and IT, the chapter emphasizes the need for leadership engagement, staff training, and policy clarity. It examines behavioral models like PMT and TAM, advocating for gamified training and maturity assessments. As quantum computing and cloud complexities rise, the chapter underscores the importance of cryptographic agility and future readiness. Ultimately, it argues that cryptography must be embedded into organizational culture to ensure resilient, human-aligned digital security.

In an increasingly interconnected world, the confidentiality, integrity, and authenticity of digital information are critical to individual privacy, institutional trust, and national security. This paper explores the essential role of cryptographic techniques in protecting data across storage, transmission, and processing layers. It provides a comprehensive review of symmetric and asymmetric encryption algorithms, hash functions, digital signatures, and key management protocols. Particular emphasis is placed on the comparative strengths, computational costs, and use-case suitability of algorithms such as AES, RSA, ECC, and SHA variants. The paper also examines emerging challenges—including quantum computing threats, side-channel attacks, and secure multi-party computation—and discusses post-quantum cryptography as a forward-looking solution. By bridging theoretical principles with practical implementations, this work underscores cryptography's indispensable role in shaping secure digital ecosystems.

The Border Gateway Protocol (BGP), known also as an Exterior Gateway Protocol (EGP), is used frequently by Internet networks to exchange routing information among various autonomous systems (ASs). BGP is divided into two variations. The internal variation exchanges the data between two neighbours in the same an AS, while the external BGP is responsible for exchanging packets among different ASs. BGP has path-vector protocols that are used to select a path to a remote network based on routing policy. This research aims to investigate and implement BGP protocols in different attributes by using GNS3 software. The second goal is delivering a good tutorial with no complexity that would lead to comprehensive understanding of the BGP routing features with different attributes. In this dissertation, Graphical Network Simulator version 3 (GNS3) emulator software is used to design the practical network. Students in MSc networking professional and one MSc Advanced Computer Network course student were chosen to test the implementation and were interviewed for feedback used to improve the work

Foreword

In an era of digital transformation, cybersecurity has become a critical pillar of organizational integrity and national resilience. However, amidst the rapid innovation of technologies and automated defense systems, one constant remains at the heart of every security framework — the human factor. "The Human Dimension of Cybersecurity: Cultivating a Protective Organizational Culture" emphasizes this truth, highlighting that sustainable cybersecurity starts not with technology, but with people, leadership, and culture.

This volume offers a compelling exploration of how organizations can adopt a human-centric approach to cybersecurity governance. It examines the interplay between leadership, ethical responsibility, behavioural awareness, and technological innovation in creating resilient digital ecosystems. By integrating human factors into cybersecurity strategies, organizations can foster trust, enhance accountability, and improve their capacity to adapt to evolving threats.

The chapters present diverse perspectives on leadership models, workforce awareness, artificial intelligence, cryptography, and organizational readiness, collectively demonstrating that effective cybersecurity is as much a social and cultural process as it is a technical one. The text advocates for a paradigm shift — from viewing cybersecurity as a reactive technical task to recognizing it as an embedded organizational value that informs decision-making, operations, and human behaviour.

This book is a timely and valuable addition to contemporary cybersecurity discourse. It provides scholars, practitioners, and policymakers with a comprehensive understanding of how digital trust, ethical leadership, and informed human actions together form the foundation of a protective organizational culture. By reminding us that while technology may defend, it is people who protect, this work reinforces the essential role of the human dimension in securing our shared digital future.

Warusia Yassin
Universiti Teknikal Malaysia Melaka, Malaysia

Preface

The twenty-first century of cybersecurity has evolved beyond technological advancements and has become a human, cultural and ethical practice. Even though the most sophisticated systems and artificial intelligence are helping to build online defences, human behaviour and organizational values, as well as leadership, are still the greatest weaknesses and strengths.

The Human Dimension of Cybersecurity: Cultivating a Protective Organizational Culture presents a holistic exploration of cybersecurity from a human-centred perspective. It investigates the connection of governance and culture, trust, and education, and innovation in order to establish safe digital environments. Conceptual, behavioural, and technical perspectives are incorporated in the book through eleven chapters in explaining how organizations have to establish and sustain protective culture of cybersecurity in the digital age.

CHAPTER OVERVIEW

Chapter 1: Leadership and Cybersecurity Governance — Building a Human-Centric Protective Culture in the Digital Age: Empowering Digital Trust and Leadership Strategies for Cultivating a Human-Focused Cybersecurity Culture

The first chapter introduces the grounds that the effective cybersecurity is initiated in the leadership. It talks about governance structures and leadership approaches that foster accountability, transparency, and empowerment concerning the cybersecurity of organizations. The emphasis is made on the development of digital trust, matching human values with technological innovation, and the establishment of the environments in which all stakeholders can play their part in the process of security culture.

Chapter 2: Fostering a Cybersecurity-Aware Workforce in Smart Public Institutions — A Framework for Privacy Innovation and Organizational Readiness

This chapter discusses the way intelligent, public organizations may make their cybersecurity preparedness better through building awareness-based workforces. It gives a systematic approach to privacy innovation, digital ethics and implementation of policies. The discussion identifies training programs, behavioural reinforcement and organizational strategies as a way of creating a culture of active cybersecurity responsibility.

Chapter 3: Cyber Hygiene in Higher Education — Organizational and Human Lessons in Cyber Defence

The chapter focuses on the institutions of higher learning as creators and consumers in the digital ecosystem. It highlights both human and procedural weaknesses in universities and the need to practice cyber hygiene. The chapter presents the best practice towards creating resilient, security conscious academic settings through real-life experiences.

Chapter 4: Future Science Press as an Example of Operational Optimization and Cybersecurity Resilience in Academic Publishing

The case study has vividly explained the manner in which Future Science Press has streamlined its operations and made its cybersecurity more resilient. The chapter outlines the strategic digital transformation efforts, infrastructure modernization policies, and policies on risk management that added up to strengthening academic publishing processes against cyber disruptions.

Chapter 5: Strategies for Proactive Threat Detection — From Monitoring to Intelligence

In this chapter, the author moves away with traditional security monitoring and introduces proactive cyber threat intelligence. It describes how companies should use behavioural analytics, risk assessment based on context, and correlation of data on predicting and mitigating incidents before they occur. The focus is on changing passive defence to the strategic foresight.

Chapter 6: Navigating the Human Factor in Cloud Transformation — Adapting Roles, Behaviours, and Mindsets for Secure Cloud Adoption

This chapter, centred on the cloud era, explores the human challenges associated with cloud migration. It highlights the importance of employee adaptation, redefining roles, and fostering cultural transformation to ensure successful cloud adoption. Additionally, the chapter offers practical insights for aligning technical migration efforts with behavioural readiness and compliance awareness.

Chapter 7: Securing Data with Cryptography — Bridging Technical Excellence and Organizational Culture for Enterprise Resilience

This chapter connects advanced cryptographic practices with enterprise governance. It emphasizes the necessity for technical proficiency to align with ethical culture and organizational leadership in order to achieve comprehensive data protection. The narrative stresses that encryption alone is insufficient; organizational culture must also support its effectiveness.

Chapter 8: Securing Data with Cryptography — Bridging Human Behaviour and Organizational Culture in Cybersecurity

This section explores the behavioural dimensions of cryptography, focusing on employee awareness, compliance, and responsible data handling as essential for encryption success, framing cybersecurity as a collective organizational commitment rather than just a technical function.

Chapter 9: Cryptography and the Human Firewall — Building Resilient Data Practices

Here, the "human firewall" metaphor comes alive. The chapter argues that human awareness, accountability, and education are as essential as cryptographic tools. It outlines strategies for cultivating security-minded employees who can actively prevent breaches through informed behaviour and disciplined data practices.

Chapter 10: Designing a Comprehensive Network Topology Using BGP Attributes in GNS3

This technical chapter emphasizes practical network defence architecture. It guides readers in designing comprehensive network topologies using Border Gateway Protocol (BGP) attributes within GNS3 simulation environments. The chapter illustrates how effective topology planning enhances resilience and routing security across digital infrastructures.

Chapter 11: A Parallel Ensemble Machine Learning System for Android Mobile Endpoint Malware Detection

The final chapter introduces an advanced machine learning approach to mobile security. It proposes a parallel ensemble model for Android endpoint malware detection, demonstrating how artificial intelligence improves threat identification accuracy, operational scalability, and user protection within mobile ecosystems.

These eleven chapters collectively demonstrate that cybersecurity transcends a purely technical framework; it is an evolving social system where leadership, awareness, innovation, and ethics intersect. This book emphasizes that genuine resilience emerges when organizations integrate security consciousness into their culture, empower their workforce with knowledge, and align technology with human intent.

The Human Dimension of Cybersecurity: Cultivating a Protective Organizational Culture ultimately advocates for a paradigm shift—from perceiving cybersecurity as a technological challenge to recognizing it as a human responsibility. Through this comprehensive perspective, the book envisions a future in which secure behaviour becomes instinctual, trust becomes ingrained, and digital resilience is embraced as a shared organizational value.

Asif Iqbal Hajamydeen
Management and Science University, Malaysia

Acknowledgement

This work has been made possible through the dedication, collaboration, and intellectual generosity of numerous individuals and institutions. I extend my deepest gratitude to all the contributing authors whose expertise, research, and commitment have influenced this work into a comprehensive exploration of the human aspects of cybersecurity. Their collective insights provide diverse perspectives that bridge leadership, technology, and human behaviour.

I would like to offer special thanks to the editorial and review teams for their meticulous efforts in refining the chapters and ensuring the scholarly quality of this publication. Their professionalism and attention to detail have significantly enhanced the clarity, coherence, and academic rigor of this work.

I am also grateful to the organizations, universities, and research institutions that supported the contributors throughout the development of their chapters. Their encouragement and commitment to advancing cybersecurity knowledge have made this project both meaningful and impactful.

To the publishing team, your ongoing support, patience, and technical guidance have been instrumental in bringing this book to completion.

Finally, I acknowledge the wider cybersecurity community—researchers, educators, practitioners, and policy advocates—whose continuous efforts to integrate human understanding with technological innovation inspire and shape the future of digital trust and resilience.

This book is dedicated to all who believe that the strongest defense in cybersecurity lies not only in machines or algorithms but in the minds and values of people working together toward a safer digital world.

Chapter 1
Leadership and Cybersecurity Governance:
Building a Human-Centric Protective Culture in the Digital Age

Manisha Singh
https://orcid.org/0000-0003-1741-0148
VIT Bhopal University, India

Sonali Srivastava
https://orcid.org/0000-0003-0551-8442
Jaypee Institute of Information Technology, India

Rajendra Mahanandia
VIT Bhopal University, India

ABSTRACT

Technological and human factors synergistically decrease information security levels while increasing information security breaches. Argumentation supported ideas that complex, adaptive, socio-technical systems have needed to be contemplated with differing analysis perspectives. Several frameworks for understanding, measuring, mapping, or improving organizational cybersecurity culture have been previously presented. his chapter explores central issues regarding organizational cybersecurity culture and its measurement and suggests a model and examples that should help broaden the exploration of cybersecurity culture as a technical-based organizational structure and a significant human factor.The primary objective is

DOI: 10.4018/979-8-3373-4154-5.ch001

to investigate the evolving fields of behavioral and human factors, as well as the recent convergence of social science and engineering approaches in this context. Given the complexity of adaptive socio-technical systems, this chapter will detail the necessity of diverse analytical perspectives in understanding these challenges.

1. INTRODUCTION

This academic inquiry investigates the impact of leadership on crafting a human-centric cybersecurity culture aligned with governance mandates in digital organizations. Organizations increasingly rely on digital frameworks, platforms, and infrastructure, confronting sophisticated cyber-threats that demand effective governance structures supported by leadership across all levels. A structured model delineates the stages and mechanisms governing information security practice, underpinned by the complementary roles of operational, digital, and security maturity. (Alauthman et al.2025)

Cybersecurity governance is defined as an enterprise-level framework that articulates leadership, organizational structures, and processes designed to safeguard information assets in compliance with stakeholder requirements. Globally recognized standards and frameworks—ISO/IEC 38500, ISO/IEC 27014, NIST Cybersecurity Framework, COBIT, COSO, CIS, TOGAF, and ITIL—tribute best practice and frequently cite the imperative of executive cyber-leadership. (Faruq, 2025; Quinn et al., 2024)

Leadership is conceptualized as an assumed position of power and influence over individuals and groups. Human characteristics inherent in leadership—capability, personality, empowerment, vision, communication, coaching, involvement, and ethical climate—directly affect corporate governance efficiency. Effective cybersecurity governance encompasses the strategic evaluation, direction, and supervision of an organization's security risk management, executed by the board and top executives. (Agarwal & Shah, 2024; Mızrak, 2023)

Workforce members perform daily organizational, operational, and security functions for which they often lack training or motivation. Consequently, leaders are encouraged to regard information security as a social as well as technological concern that requires both knowledge and engagement to yield informed, committed participants. A comprehensive training programme elevates individual and organizational security awareness, motivating diligent conduct and encouraging spontaneous proactive contributions. Sustained education and training, disseminated gradually and reinforced through exercises and workshops, are vital to embedding corporate information security parameters and requirements within the operational day. (Tejay & Winkfield, 2025)

Organizational security culture can be defined as the collective knowledge, attitudes, and behaviour of individuals and groups within the context of information security. A shared acceptance of the importance of compliance with expected codes of conduct develops a strong, internally enforced culture, significantly reducing business risk (Huang & Pearlson, 2019). Instilling a supportive security culture shapes an adaptive organization that embraces change and acts as a catalyst for the continuous improvement of cybersecurity governance.

2. UNDERSTANDING CYBERSECURITY GOVERNANCE

Cybersecurity governance has evolved in response to the changing threat landscape. Once the scope of a few specialized practitioners, these responsibilities have gradually increased their scope to the entire social and organizational fabric of organizations (Huang & Pearlson, 2019). Studies show that the human factor is where 85 percent of breaches and cyber incidents occur, influenced by deliberate attacks, insider threats, and unintentional lapses in employee protocol. Organizational cybersecurity requires all members to act to reduce risk, with leaders responsible for shaping and aligning organizational beliefs and values with security goals. Managers need practical solutions for dealing with the human side of cybersecurity. Understanding cybersecurity governance not only involves deploying secure technologies but also establishing an organizational culture that integrates governance measures across all organizational levels. (Yeo and Banfield2022; Ahmed et al.2024)

2.1. Definition and Importance

When an organization moves away from relying predominantly on formal rules and regulations, which are difficult to customize to rapidly changing information security risk environments and require a monoculture of exceptional rule-following, "organizational cybersecurity culture" emerges as the pattern of complex social interaction and sensemaking behavior that shapes the beliefs and attitudes influencing how the organization manages its cybersecurity risk environment (Huang & Pearlson, 2019). Given that every individual within the organization can significantly affect risk by their actions, addressing only the human element will not mitigate risk. An organizational approach that involves all members, necessitating that the organization's fundamental beliefs and attitudes are aligned to reduce risk, is required. The essence of organizational cybersecurity culture is the ability of all members to independently make security-oriented decisions that positively impact and reduce risk for the organization while continuing to show the flexibility needed to effectively respond to an ever-changing environment. (Iyer and Raji2025; Sutton & Tompson, 2025).

Cybersecurity Culture is broadly understood as the collective values, beliefs, and behavioral norms that influence how individuals within an organization perceive, approach, and act toward information security risks (Huang & Pearlson, 2019; Sutton & Tompson, 2025). It emphasizes attitudes, awareness, and compliance behaviors that collectively determine the level of organizational resilience.

Protective Culture, by contrast, focuses on embedding defensive behaviors and routines that ensure the safeguarding of digital and organizational assets. It is an operational extension of cybersecurity culture, emphasizing *how beliefs are translated into consistent protective actions and practices* (Syed, 2024; Iyer & Raji, 2025).

2.2. Frameworks and Standards

Numerous frameworks and voluntary standards provide organizational guidance on governance, risk management, and control in the realm of cybersecurity. In the course of developing a new 'higher-level' premium framework, the Information Security Forum identified a conceptual gap—addressing the intermediate organizational level between the protection of individual information assets and enterprise-level governance (Taherdoost, 2022). The formulation of this premium framework involved evaluating and synthesizing 28 key voluntary cybersecurity standards, guidelines, and authoritative sources from around the world to extract commonalities and discern emerging trends (Huang & Pearlson, 2019).

Developed upon the considerations specified in the inaugural chapter, the premium framework offers authoritative guidance intended to assist senior managers and their teams in cultivating a robust cybersecurity strategy, vision, and culture, mitigating the risks of unsuccessful projects, and accelerating the adoption of sound cybersecurity risk management practices. The framework encapsulates the accumulated wisdom of leading global practitioners and serves as a valuable input to the leadership cycle. (Edwards, 2024)

3. THE ROLE OF LEADERSHIP IN CYBERSECURITY GOVERNANCE

Organizational cybersecurity governance is a leadership responsibility. The leader of an organization needs to establish the vision, mission, and strategy, develop guides, set priorities, and place decision rights to implement cybersecurity (Huang & Pearlson, 2019). Cyber risks start at the top and the tone at the top sets the cultural value; leaders must invest in protecting information assets and create a human-centric protective culture to influence people to behave correctly in cyber situations. People are the most vulnerable link in cybersecurity and behaviours drive human risk in sophisticated ways that accumulate and connect risks between groups and industries. Cybersecurity leaders cannot control all technical mechanisms, but they are responsible for establishing a human-centred defensive culture (Syed2024).

Leaders must clearly communicate goals and strategy, develop trust and recognition, and build a cyber protected mindset that governs everyday behaviour. When articulate and demonstrable, the protective culture aligns beliefs, values, and attitudes with organizational objectives that then guide behaviour amid uncertainty and stress. (Patel & Sable)

3.1. Leadership Styles and Their Impact

Appropriate leadership styles remain absolutely vital when it comes to effectively developing a robust and sustainable cyber-protective culture within an organization. Extensive research that has been conducted in the fast-evolving technology sector indicates that the chosen leadership style profoundly and significantly impacts both employee engagement levels and the intentions of subordinates to operate securely in a digital work environment. For example, it has been found that a task-oriented leadership approach often contributes not only to the establishment but also to the reinforcement of a less cyber-protective culture (Mahlatje, 2022). In stark contrast, a relationship-oriented leadership style evidently enables the development and nurturing of a much more comprehensive and enduring cyber-protective culture within an organization of any size. This type of leadership is characterized by the way leaders actively encourage, support, and motivate secure behavior among their team members, fostering a sense of collective responsibility. Consequently, leaders may find it highly valuable and beneficial to momentarily set aside their regular, habitual leadership style when the circumstances call for it. Instead, they can adopt a more relationship-oriented approach specifically when the primary goal is to enhance cybersecurity measures or to significantly progress in developing a strong cyber-protective culture as an important initial step in the overall process of organizational development. This deliberate shift in approach and perspective can ultimately lead to a stronger, more resilient foundation for cybersecurity practices and create a more engaged, aware, and security-conscious workforce, thus ensuring a safer organizational environment. (Huang & Pearlson, 2019)

3.2. Strategic Decision Making

Strategic decision making concerning cybersecurity highlights the critical role that executive functions within the business infrastructure play in establishing and maintaining systemic cybersecurity measures. A common feature of research in this domain is that the topic is often approached through the lens of the business as a whole, rather than being limited to specific, finite subdisciplinary departments, such as those focusing exclusively on information security or information systems (Al-Hashem and Saidi2023). In other words, the process of strategic decision making as it relates to cybersecurity encompasses all areas of the enterprise, necessitating that high-level executives across various functions, including finance, operations, and compliance, be actively engaged in order to ensure that informed and effective decisions are made. Several comprehensive academic investigations have thus sought the input of business executives to gain a deeper understanding of the holistic decision-making process. Furthermore, the topic of strategic decision making can also be examined from a cultural perspective, which adds another layer of understanding. When looked at through this cultural lens, the interplay between decisions and organizational culture becomes apparent: each element serves to inform and influence the other, creating a dynamic interplay that shapes the overall cybersecurity posture of the organization. Thus, it becomes essential to recognize that the intersection of strategy, culture, and executive oversight is foundational to achieving robust cybersecurity outcomes. (Abubakari, 2024; Mızrak, 2023)

4. HUMAN-CENTRIC APPROACHES TO CYBERSECURITY

The successful development of cybersecurity depends not only on effective technology, but also on human factors and leadership approaches. A human-centric perspective emphasizes the awareness, capability, motivation, and opportunity of individual members in the system. Cyber risk remains high because vulnerabilities of the cyber-protective system continue to be exploited by cyber attackers (Yaacoub et al.2022; Li & Liu, 2021). Digitally vulnerable assets are susceptible to increasingly sophisticated attacks, and despite the widespread recognition of cyber threats, security breaches continue at an alarming pace.

Much of the current literature on cyber risk reduction places attention on the technology component in the cyber-protective system. Although technological protection remains necessary to the cyber-protective system, it cannot alone provide adequate protection. The cyber-protective system is comprised of three distinct components: (1) technology, (2) process, and (3) people (Hossain et al., 2023). The relative vulnerabilities of the system therefore reflect the weakest component, which in the case of cybersecurity remains the people component. Solutions and policy prescriptions that focus on technology exclusively cannot and will not protect organizations from cyberattack. The cyber-protective system must be built and maintained around a human-centric architecture in order to survive the onslaught of attacks that are enabled by the advances in digital technologies. A human-centric architecture is characterized by the following features: Awareness (the understanding of potential problems), Capability (the knowledge and skills needed to address potential problems), Motivation (the willingness to act), and Opportunity (the enabling conditions to act). Among these, leadership plays a significant role in influencing the motivation of system members (Hossain et al., 2023; Halbouni et al.2022)

4.1. Culture of Security Awareness

A positive, engaged culture of security awareness serves as a first line of defense—and a shield—against potential cyberattacks. This culture actively reduces risk by cultivating such a mindset throughout the organization.

Cybersecurity guidance shapes the collective attitude toward security, effectively forming a state of resilient awareness. Establishing a well-defined and straightforward plan empowers personnel to act promptly during incidents. By anchoring in clear instructions, individuals develop a robust mindset even when confronted with unfamiliar situations.

In the digital era, organizations generate and store substantial amounts of information on computers and servers. They increasingly connect these systems to the internet or provide mobile access, thereby exposing networks to greater vulnerability (Huang & Pearlson, 2019). The digital transformation era introduces new tools and capabilities but also increases cyberattack exposure. Organizations must respond effectively to human factors shaping overall cybersecurity hygiene. Key to this is cultivating a culture that recognizes the seriousness of cyber risks and encourages everyone to mitigate them. Maintenance of cybersecurity involves continuous assessment of risks, threats, and vulnerabilities, supported by well-documented policies, training programs, and detailed response and recovery plans. Because then-CEOs were 23 times more likely than other employees to become phishing victims, senior management demonstrate a commitment to cybersecurity by completing phishing qualitative measurements. Drawing on collective expertise, frontline information security workers—both within and beyond the organization—collaborate to anticipate, identify, and neutralize emerging threats. Without such a culture, security efforts become a wasted investment (Alaaraj & Yassin, 2024; Alhumud et al., 2023).

Similarly, an informed security architecture, grounded in a comprehensive understanding of a sector's changing threat environment, illuminates where organizations should concentrate initial and subsequent transformations. It identifies those investments with the greatest potential to cease the exploitation of a missing control or a flawed business process. The model further refines gaps by isolating them to specific elements of the defensive stack, providing precise guidance on the architectural components to enhance (Judijanto et al.2023).

4.2. Training and Development Programs

Leadership plays an undeniably dominant role in developing, reinforcing, or even eroding a robust culture of cybersecurity within an organization. Senior executives, in particular, hold significant power to set the ethical example for others to follow, advocate for key demonstration projects that underline the importance of a secure environment, and provide ongoing support crucial for reinforcing desired behaviors. Understanding various aspects of organizational culture and the multifaceted roles that leadership can play enables organizations to manage their culture in a more deliberate and intentional manner. Leaders who are attuned to the nuances of their organizational culture can readily recognize when particular elements undermine the principles of cybersecurity, allowing them to focus resources strategically to encourage and amplify positive cultural aspects that contribute to security. Additionally, they possess the capability to shape the organization's culture in ways that effectively protect against an evolving landscape filled with increasingly sophisticated cyberthreats. One tangible method to foster a resilient cybersecurity culture was successfully implemented through the Responsible Defender™, a dynamic platform designed with engaging messaging, structured rewards, and interactive participatory activities (Aksoy, 2024; Willie). The Chief Information Security Officer (CISO) and their dedicated team established a vital leadership role known as the Product Owner for Cybersecurity Awareness. This role is instrumental in creating effective messaging and influencing beliefs regarding data protection practices throughout the organization. To promote positive cybersecurity behaviors, a range of incentives—including both rewards and punishments—was put into practice, primarily facilitated through simulated phishing exercises that aimed to motivate employees to enhance their cybersecurity vigilance. Performance evaluations were carefully crafted to incorporate discussions surrounding cybersecurity practices, whereby continued failures in phishing tests would adversely influence evaluations, whereas employees demonstrating proactivity by assisting their peers in strengthening cybersecurity measures received well-deserved recognition. The culture leader firmly asserted that continuous learning constitutes the most effective and enduring approach to cybersecurity training, fostering a mindset of adaptability and vigilance among all employees. (Huang & Pearlson, 2019) .

5. BUILDING A SECURE ORGANIZATIONAL CULTURE

Leaders confront information technologies, such as social media, cloud computing, sensors, algorithms, and big data, which promise new capabilities but introduce significant security and privacy risks (Huang & Pearlson, 2019). Technology alone cannot protect organizations from adverse consequences; nor can senior managers delegate cybersecurity responsibility to other personnel. Instead, all organizational members must contribute to risk reduction. A primary leadership task involves shaping shared security priorities and conventions—ethical standards—among organizational members. These conventions are often embodied in an organization's culture, way of doing things, and ways of relating to colleagues and customers. Cybersecurity culture guides the behavior of each member within an organization and determines its resilience in the face of threats and vulnerabilities. Cultural change is therefore a central problem in leadership and a necessary condition for effective cybersecurity. A secure organizational culture underlies practices, procedures, policies, and written and unwritten rules through which employees carry out their work. Attitudes, norms, and shared understandings regulate everyday behavior and provide ready-made scripts for reaching a negotiated order. Persistent insider threats driven by human behaviors—accidental or deliberate—are difficult to control through managerial and technical means (Sutton & Tompson, 2025). Even organizations with robust cybersecurity programs cannot preclude deliberate insider threats or recurring errors due to negligence, frustration, or carelessness. Cybersecurity culture has consequently become high on the executive agenda: a single act of carelessness can erase years of sophisticated interventions. The problem is that cybersecurity culture is hard to identify, build, and measure, and there are few academic or practical resources to offer guidance. Prior academic efforts assessing cybersecurity culture are conceptually thin and disaggregated into multiple terms with unclear boundaries (Creese et al.2021). A reliable foundation rests upon an understanding of established models of organizational culture that predate the term "cybersecurity culture" and explicitly address the origins, consequences, and drivers of common beliefs and attitudes.

5.1. Engagement and Communication Strategies

The 'people' factor has increasingly come to dominate the landscape of contemporary cybersecurity, as it plays a critical role in determining the success and effectiveness of various security measures. In this context, investment in shaping human-centric governance is not merely beneficial but essential, requiring well-devised engagement and communication strategies that prioritize the involvement of individuals and communities. This approach has become vital for enhancing overall cyber resilience in organizations and systems. Within a collective-security framework, sensitivity to cyber risks is increasingly seen as a natural and necessary response to the actionable concerns that arise from the possibility of a compromised system. It is important for organizations to understand that messages reiterating the threat of a breach may not be sufficient on their own to solicit the intended generic defensive posture among users and stakeholders (Zaid & Garai, 2024). This is especially true without explicit and clear statements outlining the collective-security implications that would result from a successful attack, which can lead to widespread consequences. These factors highlight the need for a multifaceted approach that integrates human behavior into the strategies aimed at bolstering cybersecurity efforts across sectors.

5.2. Rewarding Positive Cybersecurity Behaviors

AA relatively straightforward and effective approach to encouraging secure behavior in the realm of cybersecurity involves recognizing and rewarding the positive actions taken by individuals within an organization. Following the popular adage, “a little genuine appreciation goes a long way,” managers who observe proactive cybersecurity measures can build on positive reinforcement practices to foster continued engagement and motivation among staff members. Rewards for such behavior do not necessarily require a significant financial expenditure (Moustafa et al., 2021; Mashiane and Kritzinger2021). Instead, they can take many forms such as public acknowledgment during team meetings, electronic badges, trophies, certificates, or similar tokens of appreciation. This form of recognition effectively introduces an experiential benefit to individuals who actively align their behavior with the core ideals of the organization, creating a culture of security awareness and responsibility. By highlighting and celebrating these positive actions, organizations can cultivate an environment where secure behavior is not only encouraged but becomes ingrained in the daily practices of all employees. (Hubbart, 2024; Radu, 2023)

6. CHANGE MANAGEMENT FOR CYBERSECURITY MATURITY

Navigating the Complex Landscape of Organizational Change and Human Factors in Enhancing Cybersecurity Culture and Resilience. Leading change within an organization stands as one of the most challenging aspects of the leadership responsibility. This familiar aphorism highlights a truth that resonates especially in the realm of cyber defence, where the human factor, alongside a strong organisational cyber security culture, plays a pivotal role in significantly enhancing overall organisational resilience. Cyber security culture is not merely a collection of security practices or policies; it transcends those elements and encompasses the values, knowledge, and actions that are directed toward the protection of vital information assets, all with a keen focus on information security management. A well-planned approach that integrates a thorough understanding of the characteristics inherent in the information security culture can empower the workforce to effectively adapt and change behaviours necessary for transitioning to the desired cyber security stance. It is imperative that this culture change culminates in a state of awareness where employees are not only educated but are also equipped to adhere rigorously to the established security policies. In this scenario, information security is perceived as being intrinsically vital, and trust is effectively built and maintained with customers and stakeholders. However, if this change is not guided by strategic change management, there is a significant risk that inappropriate assumptions will be perpetuated, leading to misallocations of resources and ineffective expenditure. Creating and sustaining an effective cyber security culture is an ongoing process that involves a meticulous management of the organisational information security culture, underpinned by robust culture measurement techniques. Such measurements not only assist in identifying existing strengths and weaknesses but also provide a roadmap for continuous improvement, ensuring that cyber security remains a priority within the organisational framework. Ultimately, fostering this kind of culture is essential for any organisation aiming to navigate the complexities of the modern digital landscape.

Organizational change ranks among the most demanding leadership challenges. The imperative of leading change is particularly evident in cyber defence, wherein the human element, supported by a strong organisational cybersecurity culture, decisively enhances resilience. Cybersecurity culture extends beyond mere assemblages of practices or policies; it embodies the constellation of values, knowledge, and actions oriented toward protecting critical information assets within the framework of information security management (Da Veiga, 2018). A carefully schemed intervention, grounded in a comprehensive understanding of information security culture characteristics, equips the workforce to modify behaviours congruent with the targeted cybersecurity posture (Huang & Pearlson, 2019). The requisite cultural shift culminates in an awareness whereby personnel are not only instructed but also prepared to comply stringently with prescribed security policies. Within such a milieu, information security assumes intrinsic indispensability, and trust with customers and stakeholders is effectively cultivated and preserved. (Aksoy, 2024; Andronache2021)

Absent strategic change management, organisational endeavours run the risk of perpetuating flawed assumptions, resulting in misdirected resource allocation and inefficient expenditure. The creation and perpetuation of an effective cybersecurity culture constitute an ongoing endeavour necessitating meticulous oversight of information security culture supported by rigorous measurement instruments (Aksoy, 2024; Ferreira et al.2025). These mechanisms facilitate the identification of extant strengths and vulnerabilities and inform continuous improvement efforts, thereby cementing cybersecurity prominence within the organisational ethos. Fostering such a culture emerges as a prerequisite for organisations seeking to negotiate the intricacies of the contemporary digital landscape. (Aksoy, 2024)

7. RISK MANAGEMENT IN CYBERSECURITY GOVERNANCE

Risk management in cybersecurity governance entails maximizing the benefits of investments in protective measures while minimizing the damages and costs from information security incidents. As organizations increasingly rely on information and networked computer systems to deliver services, such systems attract greater numbers of adversaries with a growing range of motives (Huang & Pearlson, 2019). An effective governance system sharpens risk management by infusing leadership values and strategic direction into the security planning process. Leaders begin with an understanding of organizational risk appetite and adopt a broad perspective on possible hazards and consequences. Guided by these concerns, risk assessment addresses the goals and objectives of the enterprise and the varying levels of tolerance for loss, whether from a security breach, unexpected system failure, or failure to adhere to appropriate procedures and policies due to insider error or negligence. Insightful governance also broadens the scope of risk management strategy to encompass more than technical safeguards, mitigating the complex social and policy-based drivers that influence user and attacker behavior (Bhandari & Hallowell, 2022). Effective cyber risk management is accomplished through a series of interrelated decisions regarding the relative emphasis placed on prevention, detection, and incident response. Prevention seeks to deter the successful operation of an adversary and can be accomplished through a combination of user education, policy development and enforcement, and technical mechanisms embedded in applications and operating system systems. Detection technologies seek to identify new attacks and unusual behavior that might accompany an attack so that additional defenses or remedial strategies can be promptly employed. Incident response addresses how best to manage an adverse event once it has occurred to minimize the loss sustained by the organization while preserving any evidence needed to justify subsequent legal action against the perpetrator. The effectiveness of the overall risk-management process is monitored through metrics that relate elements of the process to incidence rates, loss metrics, or compliance with established governance benchmarks. Feedback obtained through these measurements supports adjustments in procedural controls, technical safeguards, oversight, and resourcing levels and also provides valuable input toward the development and refinement of strategy (Lewis & Groth, 2022; Kerzner, 2023).

7.1. Identifying and Assessing Risks

The initial step in any robust cybersecurity framework involves a comprehensive understanding of the potential risks to the enterprise's digital fabric. Current knowledge of cyber threats and techniques is both global and dynamic, making it imperative for leaders to maintain an up-to-date awareness of cyber risk activity. A helpful strategy involves regularly consulting reputable cyber-risk bulletins from respected cybersecurity firms. Resources such as the Verizon Data Breach Investigations Report, the World Economic Forum's Global Risks Report, and Cybersecurity Indicators reports from the Cyber Threat Alliance provide valuable insights and remain readily accessible, even for busy executives (Lee, 2021).

These reports facilitate the rendering of threat intelligence into an easily digestible form capable of informing strategic assessment activities. Such assessments comprise two complementary dimensions: the profile of the cyber threat landscape and an honest evaluation of the organization's susceptibility to those threats. Several resources exist for openly assessing organizational resiliency, including the World Economic Forum's Cyber Resilience Playbook for Boards, the Centre for Internet Security's Cybersecurity Steering Committee, and the Cyber Readiness Institute's Readiness Program. Organizations that engage diligently with these resources are more likely to emerge intact from a disruptive event (Victor-Mgbachi, 2024; Thomas and Sule2023).

7.2. Mitigation Strategies

A cybersecurity culture is a system of shared values and beliefs that gives employees meaning and determines how they use information systems. Although technology, budgets, laws, and processes allow executives to manage cybersecurity as a problem, culture enables an understanding of cybersecurity as a social change problem (Georgiadou et al.2022; Solomon & Brown, 2021). Organizations with mature cybersecurity practices have actively developed cultures where employees understand threats and conform to rules. In contrast, less mature organizations still focus on technology and processes to address cybersecurity, and culture remains largely an afterthought. A culture-based approach to cybersecurity focuses on resilience, emphasizing the importance of bouncing back from adverse cyber events more quickly than organizational opponents (Huang & Pearlson, 2019).

The role of executives is paramount in shaping culture, given their ability to influence and creche resources at the organizational apex. Leadership and managers effect change by modelling behaviour, socialising new employees, and communicating change. They demonstrate symbolic actions, create enabling structures, and develop targeted change programmes that reinforce other efforts (Streimikiene et al.2021). Culture is sensitive to variation, which can confuse employees and weaken messages. Executives must therefore be explicit and consistent, addressing the breadth of the organization to prepare culture for change. Six key factors can guide executives and managers:

(i) Remove barriers that inhibit secure behaviour.

(ii) Align the real costs and value of security to the incentives that employees face.
(iii) Include cybersecurity in hiring, promotion, and exit-exit processes.
(iv) Engage the workforce in security decisions.
(v) Create a learning culture that supports adaptability to changing threats and technologies.
(vi) Build effective awareness and communications programmes.

8. THE IMPACT OF TECHNOLOGY ON CYBERSECURITY PRACTICES

Today's cyberrisk landscape is increasingly shaped by technological advancements and the use of new technologies. The proliferation of mobile devices, social media, cloud computing, and the Internet of Things enable new ways to work and live, yet also facilitate new paths to data breaches and users' activities. As technologies become a greater part of people's lives, digital infrastructure, societal expectations, regulatory pressures, and geopolitics become more intertwined (Jimmy, 2021). Cybersecurity and digital resilience are now global economic and societal challenges.

Cyberdefense is therefore a fundamental corporate capability, and cybersecurity programs cannot be treated solely as a cost centre or compliance burden. IT and Cybersecurity leaders must look beyond traditional perimeter protection to wider risk management strategies that review products, platforms, suppliers, and participants. Developing multi-layered, adaptive protection strategies to safeguard digital assets is critical, especially as human errors—such as misplaced trust, neglect, or lack of attention—continue to threaten organizational cyberintegrity. Furthermore, the growing shortage of cybersecurity professionals obliges organizations to find agile ways to identify, attract, hire, and retain top talent (Huang & Pearlson, 2019) (Tambe-Jagtap, 2023).

8.1. Emerging Technologies and Threats

The landscape of emergent technologies constitutes a risk environment that leaders must manage in their role as faithful stewards of their cybersecurity. Obscured by the unmitigated challenges, however, is the myriad opportunity for, and magnitude of, the benefit to be had. The leaders that take a human-centric approach to cybersecurity governance will view emergent technologies in a very different light (Yaacob et al.2023). Technologies such as artificial intelligence (AI), quantum computing, edge computing, 5G and beyond, cloud computing, and blockchain can all be applied toward building a more secure, resilient enterprise. However, these potential benefits cannot be realized until an organisation first develops effective means of protecting itself against them.

The rapid adoption of the Internet of Things (IoT) continues to provide highly appealing entry points for threat actors looking to bypass multiple layers of defence. The dark web remains riddled with tales of organisations brought to their knees after a seemingly straightforward AI-powered attack. At least in such instances, the threat cannot be faulted for lack of ambition; a comprehensive, multistage assault that involves spear phishing, the exploitation of several known vulnerabilities at scale, the compromise of vendor systems, the use of knowledge gained in prior intrusions (available on the dark web), and a fake Twitter account to hype up the threat in the public consciousness is truly a testament to effective planning and execution (Huang & Pearlson, 2019) (Roe et al.2022; Cheryl et al., 2021). To be able to discern the greatest risks while maintaining an understanding of supportive technology is thus paramount from the board to the operational levels.

Competition among those seeking a strategic advantage also heralds an entirely new class of threats: a nations-state-style intelligence system capable of infiltrating all social and economic sectors, manipulating global markets, and potentially shortening the global development cycle. These systems operate with complete autonomy and intelligence, potentially pushing society toward the tragic outcome of "an autonomous strategy of endless escalation" (Mavroeidis et al.2021; Baker & Siddiqui, 2022). Leaders must therefore understand the significance of new threats and their modes of operation, develop an operationally relevant view of what these entail, and decide on a course of action that aligns with the organisation's strategic goals. At the heart of the matter remains one question: what would such a system do to your organisation if it were able to operate freely within the confines of your enterprise?

8.2. Balancing Innovation with Security

Balancing innovation and security constitutes a constant and persistent challenge for organizations operating in an environment influenced by rapid technological developments that disrupt traditional structures and established processes. Advances in areas such as crowdsourcing, social computing, mobile networks, and Internet of Things devices significantly accelerate the flow of information, reduce overall operational costs, and afford organizations much greater agility in their day-to-day operations. However, these advancements also introduce a range of new vulnerabilities, which heighten the risks associated with the potential leakage of sensitive information and result in increased exposure to various cyber-attacks (Li & Liu, 2021). At the same time, the widespread adoption of commonly used commodities, such as mobile devices and applications, leads to even greater complexity in managing security protocols and unanticipated exposure to unforeseen threats that could compromise data integrity and user privacy. Organizations must navigate these challenges carefully, seeking to harness the benefits of innovation while implementing robust security measures that safeguard their assets and reputation. (Huang & Pearlson, 2019)

9. LEGAL AND ETHICAL CONSIDERATIONS

Organizational cybersecurity requires more than just the latest technology—it requires all members of an organization to act to reduce risk. Leaders have a special responsibility to understand, shape, and align the beliefs, values, and attitudes of the entire organization with overall security goals. Building a culture of cybersecurity guides employee behavior and increases cyber resilience. Addressing insider threat stemming from human behavior remains one of the most difficult aspects of security to control. A cybersecurity culture underlies the practices, policies, and unwritten rules that employees use in their daily activities. The Chief Information Security Officer at Liberty Mutual noted that a single employee mistake could erase all prior security efforts (Tejay & Winkfield, 2025).

9.1. Compliance with Regulations

A culture of cybersecurity states that it should be aligned with all applicable regulations. It is a mistake to believe that an organization will be fully compliant simply because it relies on outdated regulations as a checklist for tools, training, and other resources. Instead of a limited approach based on the most recent regulation a company monitors, it should create a full inventory of organizational activities and determine which legislation governs each activity. It is worth recognizing that several different pieces of legislation may apply to a single activity (Marotta & Madnick, 2021). A greater awareness and understanding of what compliance requires is clearly a good thing, and it is essential if an organization intends to work toward full compliance. Cybersecurity governance that keeps up with all applicable legislation will be sufficient, and organizations must maintain a comprehensive perspective if they want to stay ahead of an evolving legal framework (Folorunso et al.2024).

The sixth step concerns commitment to, and alignment of, the full set of cybersecurity activities designed to support the desired state. The effectiveness of a culture depends on the choice of the desired state, the consistency among the elements, and the frequency of communications. As with any cultural mechanism, an inconsistency provides an efficient leverage point for those who want to influence the organizational narrative. Hence, a high level of commitment to a shared understanding of cybersecurity objectives remains the primary driver of organizational resilience (Huang & Pearlson, 2019).

9.2. Ethical Implications of Cybersecurity Policies

Building on thoughtful insights (Huang & Pearlson, 2019), the ethical implications of cybersecurity policies must be examined in their design and implementation. Important choices stress the human side of the problem (and, inevitably, of any solution).

Different types of policies have ethical consequences. For example, a strict network usage policy might prohibit personal use, reduce the risk of malware, and thereby lower the risk of compromise; others might allow limited personal use or forbid use of social media, and still reduce risk. A comprehensive appropriate use policy is yet another approach. Obligations on users might include a responsibility to install updates and patches in a timely manner, while stronger permissions might allow the user to install whatever is necessary (Formosa et al., 2021; Savaş & Karataş, 2022). Similarly, a company might permit the use of personal devices on-site; others use guest networks or forfeit the right to an unsecured network. From a single hypothetical example, a dozen principles emerge to aid in the design of policy frameworks:

10. CASE STUDIES IN CYBERSECURITY GOVERNANCE

Cybersecurity governance represents the control systems that define an organization's cybersecurity policy. Cybersecurity governance encompasses an extensive list of processes, entry points, decision domains, and infrastructure. Managers have access to a large set of levers to enhance cyber resiliency, including embedding cybersecurity expectations in performance evaluations, implementing reward systems, enforcing consequences for insecure actions, maintaining strong communication plans, and providing ongoing training with updated learning opportunities. The establishment of a management position dedicated exclusively to cultivating a cybersecurity culture further advances organisational resilience. Case Study: Liberty Mutual demonstrates these principles in action. The company's executives elevated cybersecurity to a strategic priority, allocating a significant budget for security tools and personnel. Regular cybersecurity-focused blog posts from the CISO and team established open Top Management Participation. Community norms and beliefs were reinforced through slogans such as "Responsible Defender" and "Our Information." The organisation instituted a system where failure in phishing simulations led to mandatory retraining, linking Rewards and Punishments directly to security behaviour. These measures collectively contribute to stronger cyber-defensive postures (Huang & Pearlson, 2019).

10.1. Successful Implementations

"Saving the world" is a common metaphor by which to describe what cybersecurity professionals do, facing overwhelming odds against anonymous adversaries: digital criminals, hacktivists, spies and adversaries nations (Huang & Pearlson, 2019). A quick survey of the news offers countless examples of seemingly innocuous data breaches leading to teenage debt or even one case23 of death or decimation of a nation's electoral process after a successful intrusion. Expanding cyber-resilience is always an executive concern. Government Regulations and Standards can impose 'technology enforcement' measures to limit or avoid technical consequences resulting from human behavior, but they cannot replace the need for leaders to create a human-centric cybersecurity protection culture that works for their context. This chapter explores the levers available to a leader committed to delivering farreaching improvements in organizational cyber-resilience, resilience-wide. argue that resilient culture increases an organization's ability to prepare, absorb, recover, and adapt to adverse events by determining normative behaviors and directing employee attention and action toward corporate objectives and "attribution-based resilience" refers specifically to a culture's influence on how an organization responds to a disruption (Madi et al.2023; Moşteanu, 2024).

10.2. Lessons Learned from Failures

Cybersecurity failures provide some of the most valuable insights into potential subsequent safeguards and improvements, by effectively highlighting the insufficiencies of previous arrangements and revealing the remaining vulnerabilities that still need to be addressed. These failures can be categorized in several ways: • Ineffective management, whether organizational or operational, that fails to support the necessary cybersecurity infrastructure; • Misaligned incentives or misjudged resource allocations that lead to critical budget shortages and insufficient staffing; and • Mismatched architectural decisions that significantly hinder timely system upgrades or proper secure maintenance practices (Atkins & Lawson, 2021). Failure, in essence, is a natural consequence of the complexity inherent in modern information technology systems and the presence of vulnerable components within them. Rather than adopting an attitude of fear toward failures, organizations should instead focus on emphasizing the meaningful and timely discovery of such failures. This approach will enable a healthy flow of information and facilitate rapid, effective corrective measures aimed at strengthening and bolstering cybersecurity resilience over time. By learning from these incidents, organizations can better prepare themselves for future challenges and enhance their overall security posture. (Huang & Pearlson, 2019)

11. FUTURE TRENDS IN CYBERSECURITY LEADERSHIP

The accelerating digital transition associated with emerging technologies such as cloud computing, artificial intelligence, and the Internet of Things (IoT) contributes to intensifying cyber-threats at the organizational level (Huang & Pearlson, 2019). This technology-enabled proliferation of security holes further reinforces a lack of organizational readiness to deal with hacker attacks. In 2021, a cyber-security risks survey of 3,000 companies from 13 economies found that most organizations felt ill-prepared to take full advantage of both the digital transition and the digital economy. The study concluded that companies must continue to develop their adaptability to new digital technologies and the associated digital risks as they turn to the future (Leo et al., 2023; Singun, 2025).

11.1. The Evolving Role of Cybersecurity Leaders

Developing the right cybersecurity strategy represents a challenging leadership conundrum. Computerized systems have become indispensable to productivity, placing organizations at elevated cyber risk. Advertising the presence of computer controls publicly increases the odds of being selected and attacked by fast-moving cyber adversaries. Concerns about cybercrime threaten progress in many technologically dependent areas in business and government. This context elevates both leaders and followers to a status not previously experienced. Everyone with a presence in cyberspace—including those who may not recognize their full exposure—becomes a potential target (Ghelani, 2022). The exigencies of modern progress have, for the first time, elevated the human factor, not hardware or software, to the greatest cybersecurity vulnerability. The ability to create an environment where the human dimension can be managed to limit cyber exposure has become an imperative responsibility for current leadership at all levels; it is a significant challenge.

Organizational cybersecurity requires more than just the latest technology. Leaders bear a special responsibility to understand, shape, and align the beliefs, values, and attitudes of the entire organization with overarching security goals. Even the most advanced technological systems cannot protect an organization from a cyber breach if personnel are not careful. For example, a single employee clicking on a phishing email can grant attackers access to systems, enabling them to lock critical information or disrupt infrastructure. Insider threats originating from human behavior rank among the most difficult security challenges (Haastrup & Nwakibea, 2024).

Building a cybersecurity culture to guide employee conduct and enhance resilience thus becomes vital. Such a culture underpins practices, policies, and unwritten rules employed in daily activities. The vulnerability of personnel represents the "weakest link" in the chain, warranting executive attention. Although the impact of cybersecurity culture on risk is immense, it remains challenging to identify, construct, and quantify. Consequently, examining other organizational cultures provides a foundation for developing a cybersecurity-culture framework (Huang & Pearlson, 2019).

11.2. Preparing for Future Challenges

The evolution of the Internet of Things (IoT), Industry 4.0, and Web 3.0 technologies, augmented by the development of 6G and artificial intelligence, introduces both new opportunities and formidable challenges to cybersecurity governance that resonate deeply in public spheres. IoT-based business models, such as smart hospitals and smart offices, present new security gaps, particularly in open spaces, thereby also eliciting fresh risks and opportunities (Karie et al.2021). These developments amplify the impact of social engineering attacks, with Internet addiction potentially transforming large segments of the populace into unwitting tools in the hands of cybercriminals. Industry 4.0's reliance on the characterisation and visualisation of complex, real-life situations in the Internet domain further complicates defensive strategies against advanced persistent threats, exposing critical infrastructure to higher threats. Web 3.0, bearing a paradigm that accelerates global digital transformation, similarly intensifies the difficulty of maintaining robust commercial ecosystems, especially in the context of multilateral trading. (Huang & Pearlson, 2019) (Akter et al., 2022).

12. PRACTICAL IMPLICATION

To translate the idea of a human-centric protective culture into actionable practice, managers can follow a six-dimensional framework that embeds cybersecurity into everyday organizational life. First, leadership commitment is crucial: when executives model secure behaviors, employees recognize cybersecurity as a strategic priority rather than a purely technical issue (Tejay & Winkfield, 2025; Patel & Sable, 2023). Second, managers must clearly define and communicate the difference between cybersecurity culture (shared values and attitudes) and protective culture (concrete defensive practices), thereby creating a common language that reduces ambiguity (Huang & Pearlson, 2019; Sutton & Tompson, 2025). Third, continuous capacity building through role-specific training and scenario-based learning ensures that employees remain aware, skilled, and motivated to act securely (Aksoy, 2024).

Fourth, incentives and accountability should be institutionalized by linking secure behavior to performance appraisals and recognition systems, which encourage compliance and reduce negligence (Hubbart, 2024; Radu, 2023). Fifth, structural integration into governance frameworks such as NIST CSF or ISO/IEC 27014 ensures that cybersecurity objectives are aligned with organizational strategy and decision-making across departments (Taherdoost, 2022; Edwards, 2024). Finally, managers should employ regular monitoring and feedback mechanisms—including phishing tests, awareness surveys, and cultural audits—to generate insights for continuous improvement (Ferreira et al., 2025; Lewis & Groth, 2022). Together, these managerial actions form a coherent framework that transforms abstract cultural principles into measurable, enforceable, and sustainable practices, thereby strengthening organizational resilience against evolving cyber threats.

13. CONCLUSION

The dramatic rise in the scale and intensity of cybersecurity threats over the past two decades has led to this period being widely referred to as a cyber-crime decade. As the pace of digital transformation continues to accelerate, organizations are presented with a dual reality of burgeoning opportunities alongside a significant increase in associated risks. In this evolving landscape, technology emerges as a crucial component for mitigating cyber threats effectively. However, it is essential to recognize that cyber threats ultimately serve a fundamental human need, making it imperative to build a human-centric protective culture as a foundational element for effective governance. Leadership plays a pivotal role in this process, delivering critical elements such as priority setting, alignment, and coherence that are vital to ensure the successful formulation and execution of strategies. The establishment of a human-centric protective culture encourages risk awareness, promotes allegiance, and fosters enabling behaviors that contribute to sustaining security resilience, even under adverse conditions. Organizations that successfully combine technological advancements with a robust human-centric protective culture tend to outperform their counterparts significantly, demonstrating the value of this holistic approach to cybersecurity. By investing in both technology and people, companies can create a more secure and resilient environment that not only defends against threats but also empowers individuals to contribute actively to the organization's overall security posture.

REFERENCES

Abubakari, P. (2024). *Human factors matter: The intersection of cybersecurity governance, and culture in risk management of critical infrastructure.* (Doctoral dissertation). Pepperdine University.

Agarwal, K., & Shah, M. (2024). *The role of corporate governance in managing cybersecurity risks: A comprehensive analysis.* LawFoyer International Journal of Doctrinal Legal Research.

Ahmed, M., Kambam, H. R., Liu, Y., Jaidka, S., & Petrova, K. (2024). Impact and significance of human factors in digital information security. *International Journal of Information Science and Technology*, *7*(2), 1–17.

Aksoy, C. (2024). *Building a cyber security culture for resilient organizations against cyber attacks.* İşletme Ekonomi ve Yönetim Araştırmaları Dergisi.

Akter, S., Uddin, M. R., Sajib, S., Lee, W. J. T., Michael, K., & Hossain, M. A. (2022). Reconceptualizing cybersecurity awareness capability in the data-driven digital economy.

Al-Hashem, N., & Saidi, A. (2023). The psychological aspect of cybersecurity: Understanding cyber threat perception and decision-making. *International Journal of Applied Machine Learning and Computational Intelligence*, *13*(8), 11–22.

Alaaraj, A., & Yassin, A. (2024). Investigating cybersecurity response strategies: Measures to responding to successful spear phishing attacks.

Alauthman, M., Al-Qerem, A., Alateef, S., Almomani, A., & Aldweesh, A. (2025). Human-centric cybersecurity: Addressing insider threats and organizational culture. In *Complexities and Challenges for Securing Digital Assets and Infrastructure* (pp. 435–456). IGI Global Scientific Publishing.

Alhumud, T. A. A., Omar, A., & Altohami, W. M. A. (2023). An assessment of cybersecurity performance in the Saudi universities: A Total Quality Management approach. *Cogent Education.*

Andronache, A. (2021). Increasing security awareness through lenses of cybersecurity culture. *Journal of Information Systems & Operations Management*, *15*(1).

Atkins, S., & Lawson, C. (2021). An improvised patchwork: Success and failure in cybersecurity policy for critical infrastructure. *Public Administration Review.*

Baker, B. M., & Siddiqui, J. (2022). In the trading zone: The eco and the techno at the limits of "the human" and compulsory schooling. *Journal of Curriculum and Pedagogy.*

Bhandari, S., & Hallowell, M. R. (2022). Influence of safety climate on risk tolerance and risk-taking behavior: A cross-cultural examination. *Safety Science.*

Cheryl, B. K., Ng, B. K., & Wong, C. Y. (2021). Governing the progress of Internet-of-Things: Ambivalence in the quest of technology exploitation and user rights protection. *Technology in Society.*

Creese, S., Dutton, W. H., & Esteve-González, P. (2021). The social and cultural shaping of cybersecurity capacity building: A comparative study of nations and regions. *Personal and Ubiquitous Computing, 25*(5), 941–955. PMID: 33994905

Da Veiga, A. (2018). An approach to information security culture change combining ADKAR and the ISCA questionnaire to aid transition to the desired culture.

Edwards, J. (2024). *A comprehensive guide to the NIST cybersecurity framework 2.0: Strategies, implementation, and best practice.*

Faruq, M. O. (2025). A meta-analysis of cybersecurity framework integration in GRC platforms: Evidence from US enterprise audits. *Journal of Sustainable Development and Policy.*

Ferreira, L. V. A., Alves, C. A. D. M., Peotta de Melo, L., & Nunes, R. R. (2025). Internal audit strategies for assessing cybersecurity controls in the Brazilian financial institutions. *Applied Sciences (Basel, Switzerland), 15*(10), 5715. DOI: 10.3390/app15105715

Folorunso, A., Wada, I., Samuel, B., & Mohammed, V. (2024). Security compliance and its implication for cybersecurity. *World Journal of Advanced Research and Reviews, 24*(1), 2105–2121. DOI: 10.30574/wjarr.2024.24.01.0174

Formosa, P., Wilson, M., & Richards, D. (2021). A principlist framework for cybersecurity ethics. *Computers & Security, 109*, 102382. Advance online publication. DOI: 10.1016/j.cose.2021.102382

Georgiadou, A., Mouzakitis, S., Bounas, K., & Askounis, D. (2022). A cyber-security culture framework for assessing organization readiness. *Journal of Computer Information Systems, 62*(3), 452–462.

Ghelani, D. (2022). Cyber security, cyber threats, implications and future perspectives: A review. *Authorea Preprints.*

Haastrup, T. A., & Nwakibea, F. I. (2024). Effective leadership for peace and security management. *Journal of Institutional Leadership*.

Halbouni, A., Gunawan, T. S., Habaebi, M. H., Halbouni, M., Kartiwi, M., & Ahmad, R. (2022). Machine learning and deep learning approaches for cybersecurity: A review. *IEEE Access: Practical Innovations, Open Solutions*, *10*, 19572–19585.

Hossain, M. A., Raza, M. A., & Rahman, T. Y. (2023). Resource allocation and budgetary constraints for cybersecurity projects in small to medium sized banks. *SSRN*.

Huang, K., & Pearlson, K. (2019). For what technology can't fix: Building a model of organizational cybersecurity culture. *ICIS 2019 Proceedings*.

Hubbart, J. A. (2024). Understanding and mitigating leadership fear-based behaviors on employee and organizational success. *Administrative Sciences*, *14*(1), 22.

Iyer, S. S., & Raji, B. (2025). Cybersecurity culture and organizational resilience: A human-centered approach to digital risk management. *American Journal of Industrial and Business Management*, *15*(5), 748–766.

Jimmy, F. (2021). *Emerging threats: The latest cybersecurity risks and the role of artificial intelligence in enhancing cybersecurity defenses*. Valley International Journal Digital Library.

Judijanto, L., Hindarto, D., Wahjono, S. I., & Djunarto, A. (2023). Edge of enterprise architecture in addressing cyber security threats and business risks. [IJSECS]. *International Journal of Software Engineering and Computer Science*, *3*(3), 386–396.

Karie, N. M., Sahri, N. M., Yang, W., Valli, C., & Kebande, V. R. (2021). A review of security standards and frameworks for IoT-based smart environments. *IEEE Access: Practical Innovations, Open Solutions*, *9*, 121975–121995.

Kerzner, H. (2023). *Project management metrics, KPIs, and dashboards: A guide to measuring and monitoring project performance* (3rd ed.). Wiley.

Lee, I. (2021). Cybersecurity: Risk management framework and investment cost analysis. *Business Horizons*, *64*(4), 509–519.

Leo, W. W. C., Laud, G., & Chou, C. Y. (2023). Digital transformation for crisis preparedness: Service employees' perspective. *Journal of Services Marketing*, *37*(1), 102–116.

Lewis, A. D., & Groth, K. M. (2022). Metrics for evaluating the performance of complex engineering system health monitoring models. *Reliability Engineering & System Safety*, *219*, 108200.

Li, Y., & Liu, Q. (2021). A comprehensive review study of cyber-attacks and cyber security; emerging trends and recent developments. *Energy Reports*, *7*, 8176–8186.

Madi Odeh, R. B., Obeidat, B. Y., Jaradat, M. O., Masa'deh, R. E., & Alshurideh, M. T. (2023). The transformational leadership role in achieving organizational resilience through adaptive cultures: The case of Dubai service sector. *International Journal of Productivity and Performance Management*, *72*(2), 440–468.

Mahlatje, N. (2022). The function of cyber-security awareness and training in shaping cyber-risk perceptions and resultant cyber behaviours. *Journal of Cybersecurity and Digital Trust*, *1*(1), 45–62.

Marotta, A., & Madnick, S. (2021). Convergence and divergence of regulatory compliance and cybersecurity. *Issues in Information Systems*, *22*(4), 25–31.

Mashiane, T., & Kritzinger, E. (2021). Identifying behavioral constructs in relation to user cybersecurity behavior. *Eurasian Journal of Soil Science*, *9*(2), 98–122.

Mavroeidis, V., Hohimer, R., Casey, T., & Jesang, A. (2021, May). Threat actor type inference and characterization within cyber threat intelligence. In *2021 13th International Conference on Cyber Conflict (CyCon)* (pp. 327–352). IEEE.

Mızrak, F. (2023). Integrating cybersecurity risk management into strategic management: A comprehensive literature review. *Research Journal of Business and Management*, *10*(2), 65–75.

Moşteanu, N. R. (2024). Adapting to the unpredictable: Building resilience for business continuity in an ever-changing landscape. *European Journal of Theoretical and Applied Sciences*, *2*(1), 45–57.

Moustafa, A. A., Bello, A., & Maurushat, A. (2021). The role of user behaviour in improving cyber security management. *Frontiers in Psychology*, *12*, 725422. PMID: 34220596

Patel, M. D., & Sable, R. (2023). Leading with integrity: How leadership personality shapes cybersecurity behavior. In *The Interdisciplinary Nexus* (Vol. 299, pp. 120–135). Law, Humanities, and Management.

Quinn, S., Ivy, N., Barrett, M., Witte, G., & Gardner, R. K. (2024). *Staging cybersecurity risks for enterprise risk management and governance oversight*. National Institute of Standards and Technology.

Radu, C. (2023). Fostering a positive workplace culture: Impacts on performance and agility. In *Human Resource Management—An Update* (pp. 87–101). IGI Global.

Roe, M., Spanaki, K., Ioannou, A., Zamani, E. D., & Giannakis, M. (2022). Drivers and challenges of Internet of Things diffusion in smart stores: A field exploration. *Technological Forecasting and Social Change*, *178*, 121593.

Savaş, S., & Karataş, S. (2022). Cyber governance studies in ensuring cybersecurity: An overview of cybersecurity governance. *International Cybersecurity Law Review*, *3*(3), 265–276. PMID: 37521508

Singun, A. J. (2025). Unveiling the barriers to digital transformation in higher education institutions: A systematic literature review. *Discover Education*, *3*, 22.

Solomon, G., & Brown, I. (2021). The influence of organisational culture and information security culture on employee compliance behaviour. *Journal of Enterprise Information Management*, *34*(5), 1515–1533.

Streimikiene, D., Mikalauskiene, A., Digriene, L., & Kyriakopoulos, G. (2021). Assessment of the role of a leader in shaping sustainable organizational culture. *Amfiteatru Economic*, *23*(57), 483–503.

Sutton, A., & Tompson, L. (2025). Towards a cybersecurity culture-behaviour framework: A rapid evidence review. *Computers & Security*, *129*, 103212.

Syed, S. (2024, September). The human factor: Enhancing intelligence capabilities with people-centric knowledge management. In *AU Hybrid International Conference 2024 on "Entrepreneurship & Sustainability in the Digital Era"* (Vol. 4, No. 1, pp. 556–567).

Taherdoost, H. (2022). Understanding cybersecurity frameworks and information security standards—A review and comprehensive overview. *Electronics (Basel)*, *11*(6), 892.

Tambe-Jagtap, S. N. (2023). Human-centric cybersecurity: Understanding and mitigating the role of human error in cyber incidents. *SHIFRA Journal of Cybersecurity Research*, *2*(1), 88–101.

Tejay, G. P. S., & Winkfield, M. (2025). Does leadership approach matter? Examining behavioral influences of leaders on employees' information security compliance. *Information Systems Frontiers*, *27*(2), 321–338.

Thomas, G., & Sule, M. J. (2023). A service lens on cybersecurity continuity and management for organizations' subsistence and growth. *Organizational Cybersecurity Journal: Practice. Process and People*, *3*(1), 18–40.

Victor-Mgbachi, T. (2024). Navigating cybersecurity beyond compliance: Understanding your threat landscape and vulnerabilities. *Iconic Research and Engineering Journals*, *7*(2), 11–17.

Willie, M. M. (2023). The role of organizational culture in cybersecurity: Building a security-first culture. *Journal of Research*, *5*(3), 77–85.

Yaacob, M. N., Idrus, S. Z. S., & Idris, M. (2023). Managing cybersecurity risks in emerging technologies. *International Journal of Business and Technopreneurship*, *13*(3), 253–270.

Yaacoub, J. P. A., Noura, H. N., Salman, O., & Chehab, A. (2022). Robotics cyber security: Vulnerabilities, attacks, countermeasures, and recommendations. *International Journal of Information Security*, *21*(1), 115–158. PMID: 33776611

Yeo, L. H., & Banfield, J. (2022). Human factors in electronic health records cybersecurity breach: An exploratory analysis. *Perspectives in Health Information Management*, *19*(2), 1i. PMID: 35692854

Zaid, T., & Garai, S. (2024). Emerging trends in cybersecurity: A holistic view on current threats, assessing solutions, and pioneering new frontiers. *Blockchain in Healthcare Today*, •••, 7. PMID: 38715765

Chapter 2
Fostering a Cybersecurity-Aware Workforce in Smart Public Institutions:
A Framework for Privacy Innovation and Organizational Readiness

Mohammed Hussain Alsaad
https://orcid.org/0009-0002-9384-7819
Management and Science University, Malaysia

Muhammad Irsyad Abdullah
https://orcid.org/0000-0002-7840-2662
Management and Science University, Malaysia

Balqees Yaseen Alhaddad
Universiti Geomatika, Malaysia

ABSTRACT

As government organizations increasingly use digital tools in smart cities, employees must understand cybersecurity properly. This chapter introduces a practical model to improve institutional handling of cybersecurity and privacy by combining education, awareness, and readiness into a clear approach supporting safer digital governance. The model, based on Protection Motivation Theory (PMT), examines employees' understanding of digital tools, perceived cyber risk, exposure frequency, system complexity, privacy concerns, and the usefulness of cybersecurity tools affecting

DOI: 10.4018/979-8-3373-4154-5.ch002

their readiness. It includes AI-based awareness tools and structured training like the SETA program to foster safer habits. The focus is on human responses, learning, and how management shapes cybersecurity culture. This chapter targets leaders, IT staff, and public managers aiming to build responsibility toward cybersecurity in smart city institutions or those transitioning into them.

1. INTRODUCTION

The implications of functioning public sector portal becoming the victim to a cybersecurity breach are not missed: there's a breakdown in essential services, alteration of citizen records without authorization, distortion of public data and exposure of strategic plans (Pemmasani & Osaka, 2021). Unlike private companies, which sometimes can recover reputationally with a bit of marketing and financial reparations post-exposure, public institutions are subject to the judgment, and often the wrath, of their constituents in real time, for whom lost goodwill proves far tougher to regain. Smart city initiatives may champion security which if implemented with no consideration of the privacy and trust, would be able to introduce other risks and ethical challenges (Alhalafi & Veeraraghavan, 2023).

The only problem is that the ubiquity of interconnected devices, automated systems, and centralized platforms has dramatically increased the attack surface (Mohammed, 2022; Badii et al., 2020). Future streetlights, public Wi-Fi, sensor-laden utilities and AI-driven administrative tools deliver serene city services in the abstract but require centralized entities where a single breach can cause a domino effect that cascades across multiple life or death services citizens encounter every day. In such environments, strong technical defenses, as well as a workforce cognizant of the outcomes of their actions on digital data are required to work in conjunction (Chang & Coppel, 2020; Alraddadi et al., 2025). Typically, the weakest link in security is human. Firewall, encryption and intrusion detection are essential security measures but these security controls also address threats that have not arisen as a result of overwhelming majority of breach in the past which include human/sysadmin error, carelessness and social engineering (Ali et al., 2021; Alsharida et al., 2023).

These include a susceptibility to phishing, poor practices with passwords, bad behaviors around patching and abusers of privileged access all show where gaps may be in awareness, behavior and the culture. Public employees sometimes toil with antiquated systems, changing policies, and multiple hats, making it difficult for them to understand how cybersecurity recommendations relate to their day-to-day duties. Furthermore, the best security is perhaps the one identified as the" weakest link" may not be a weak link at all but rather the most senior and strategic security investment for institutional resilience (Sulaiman et al., 2022; Moallem, 2024).

In some cases, private sector training is more rigorous and comprehensive than that of public sector cyber security jobs. Other agencies use obsolete, off-the-shelf modules and others regard compliance as a tick-box exercise or push accountability solely to IT (Nagyfejeo & von Solms, 2020; Tolah, 2021). Such a narrow method investigation overlooks the behavioral, social and cultural aspects of security. Previous research demonstrated that secure behavior was not only influenced by awareness, but also Perceived Threat Severity, Organizational support, leadership role modelizing and workplace norms (Dodge et al., 2023; Siponen et al., 2024).

This chapter proposes the Cybersecurity Awareness and Readiness Framework (CARF) to address these gaps as a comprehensive model customized for public institutions serving in, or moving towards, smart city settings. Incorporating Protection Motivation Theory (PMT) as the key underpinning theory, and integrating it with organizational antecedents such as digital literacy, policy clarity, training availability, and cultural advocacy; CARF bridges individual psychological factors against context-specific facilitators including Security Education Training and Awareness (SETA) programs alongside adaptive feedback loops (Abd Latif et al., 2025; Hu et al., 2022; Wang et al., 2022).

Chapter Purpose and Structure

The chapter has four major goals:

Theoretical justification of secure behavior in public entities (based on PMT)

Study the leading indicators of employee cybersecurity readiness, grounded in digital literacy, past threat experience, privacy anxiety and management endorsement.

Describe strategies to introduce and incorporate the CARF model in practice, including training powered by AI, experience-based learning, and adaptive feedback mechanisms (Ansari et al.

Implicate policy and leadership for change derived from solutions that cut across organizations, call for future research and cross-sector collaborations.

Chapter Roadmap

Section 2 – PMT Theory Foundation and its Application to Cybersecurity Behavior.

Section 3 – Main Influencing Factors Impacting the Cybersecurity Readiness of Employees

Section 4, The CARF Model: Architecture and Visual Flowchart

Section 5- How to implement: SETA design, AI-powered awareness tools, Phishing simulations, and performance metrics.

Section 6 – Cyber Security Governance, Policy and Leadership roles.

Section 7 – Application Case to CARF Public Setting

2. THEORETICAL FOUNDATION: PROTECTION MOTIVATION THEORY (PMT)

The Protection Motivation Theory (PMT) developed by Rogers (1975), and refined by Maddux and Rogers (1983), is a well-entrenched model that can describe why individuals engage in protective behavior when faced with perceived threats. Originating from health psychology, PMT has been widely applied in numerous contexts such as disaster preparedness, environmental sustainability and information security (Ifinedo, 2022; Tsai et al., 2023). It is therefore relevant to public-sector cybersecurity mainly because it can include threat perception and response ability perception, allowing the concept to be built into the Cybersecurity Awareness and Readiness Framework (CARF).

2.1 Threat Appraisal

Threat appraisal is how people weigh a cyber threat: How bad could it be, how likely is it to happen, and is there any short-term "payoff" to ignoring the rules? It rests on three pieces. First, perceived severity, the belief that a breach would cause serious harm. In public institutions, which can mean exposing citizen records, disrupting essential services, or damaging the agency's reputation (Dodge et al., 2023). Second, perceived vulnerability, the sense that "this could happen to us." Staff in small departments sometimes downplay this, assuming attackers only chase big agencies. Third, perceived rewards, the small conveniences gained by cutting corners, like skipping multi-factor authentication to save a minute, even though it raises organizational risk. When people believe the consequences are serious and the threat is real, and when the "rewards" of non-compliance feel trivial, their motivation to follow protective practices increases.

2.2 Coping Appraisal

Coping appraisal is about ability and practicality: Do people feel capable of using security practices, do they think those practices work, and what will its "cost" them to comply?

Self-efficacy: confidence that one can perform secure actions, for instance, spotting a phishing email and reporting it promptly.

Response efficacy: belief that the measure actually works, such as trusting that encryption protects sensitive citizen data.

Response costs: the hassle, time, or resources required, like long login steps or strict password rules, which can discourage compliance.

When self-efficacy and response efficacy are high, and response costs feel low, people are far more likely to follow secure behaviors.

2.3 Applying Protection Motivation Theory (PMT) in Public-Sector Cybersecurity

In practice, threat appraisal and coping appraisal rise or fall with the institution's environment, culture, leadership behavior, clear policies, and usable training. If leaders don't visibly champion cybersecurity, staff may doubt that controls really work (lower response efficacy). If training is outdated or hard to access, people feel less able to act (lower self-efficacy). Confusing policies or clunky tools also raise response costs. By contrast, visible leadership support, timely role-based training, and streamlined processes (e.g., SSO, password managers, clear reporting paths) strengthen both appraisals.

This dual lens matters in government settings, where employees must keep services running while staying secure. PMT helps design interventions that stick by addressing both sides at once: raise the perception of risk (e.g., realistic incident scenarios, impact metrics) and raise the capacity to respond (skills practice, quick-reference playbooks), while reducing friction (simpler workflows, fewer unnecessary steps). The result is more consistent, long-term secure behavior, not just one-off compliance.

2.4 Linking PMT to CARF

The Cybersecurity Awareness and Readiness Framework (CARF) turns PMT's ideas into day-to-day practice inside government agencies. It does this in three tight loops:

Diagnose staff mindsets: use short surveys, focus groups, and tabletop or phishing simulations to map both threat appraisals (severity, vulnerability, perceived rewards) and coping appraisals (self-efficacy, response efficacy, response costs).

Design targeted fixes: raise perceived vulnerability with recent, relevant case studies; build self-efficacy through hands-on drills and guided practice; increase response efficacy by showing how controls (e.g., encryption, MFA) block real attack paths; and lower response costs with simpler workflows (SSO, password managers, clear reporting channels).

Embed for durability: bake interventions into continuous learning (micro-modules, nudges), leadership communications (visible sponsorship, security moments), and policy enforcement (lightweight checks, just-in-time prompts, metrics tied to accountability).

By aligning diagnosis, design, and embedding with PMT, CARF moves awareness beyond generic, one-off compliance courses and into behaviorally targeted, sustainable programs that build a genuine security culture.

Table 1. PMT Components Public-Sector Examples CARF Actions

PMT Component	Plain meaning	Public-sector example	CARF action (what we do)
Perceived Severity	How serious the consequences feel	A breach exposes thousands of citizens records and disrupts services	Share recent, relevant breach cases with impact numbers and downtime analysis
Perceived Vulnerability	How likely people feel they'll be targeted	A small municipal office is hit by a phishing scam	Run role-specific briefings showing local attack patterns and red flags
Perceived Rewards	The "benefits" of cutting corners	Skipping MFA to save time	Make the secure path fastest: enable SSO and reduce extra prompts
Self-Efficacy	Confidence to do the secure thing	Spotting and reporting phishing emails	Hands-on phishing ID drills with feedback and quick-reference checklists
Response Efficacy	Belief that the control actually works	Encryption prevents unauthorized access to citizen data	Demonstrate real cases and test results that show encryption blocking misuse
Response Costs	Hassle/time/resources needed to comply	MFA slows down workflows	Optimize MFA (SSO, authenticator apps, risk-based prompts) to cut friction

3. KEY INFLUENCING FACTORS IN CYBERSECURITY READINESS

Technical tools alone don't make a public institution "ready." Readiness is shaped by people, processes, and context, how employees see cyber risks, how they respond, and how securely they workday to day. Protection Motivation Theory (PMT) helps explain these behaviors, but outcomes also depend on structural enablers, resourcing, and the wider organizational climate. In this section, we focus on five drivers, digital literacy, past threat experience, privacy concerns, management support, and organizational culture, and show how each informs the design of CARF: what to diagnose, which interventions to prioritize, and how to embed secure habits sustainably.

3.1 Digital Literacy and System Complexity

Digital literacy is the ability to use digital tools effectively and to understand what those tools mean for data security and privacy (Trenerry et al., 2021). In the public sector, it extends beyond operating office software or case-management systems to include everyday security behaviors: recognizing a suspicious email, handling citizen records safely, choosing secure authentication methods, and keeping devices up to date. In short, digital literacy blends how to use technology with how to use it safely. Levels of digital literacy often vary widely across public institutions. Uneven technology rollouts, different job tenures, and long reliance on paper-based processes can leave some teams more confident than others (Badii et al., 2020). These gaps create pockets of vulnerability: staff who are less comfortable with digital systems may misinterpret policy, click on risky links, or bypass steps they find confusing. The move to hybrid work, shared devices in field offices, and reliance on email for service requests can magnify these weaknesses if skills are not refreshed regularly.

The bar for digital literacy is also rising. Cloud platforms, AI-enabled assistants, and IoT devices bring new workflows and new attack surfaces. What counted as "basic skills" a few years ago, using email, storing files, logging in with a password, now includes understanding multi-factor authentication, identifying consent screens, recognizing data classification labels, and applying least-privilege access. Without continuous upskilling, employees may feel overwhelmed, which tends to push them toward unsafe shortcuts. Protection Motivation Theory (PMT) clarifies why literacy matters for behavior. Strong digital literacy builds self-efficacy (confidence to act securely) and response efficacy (belief that the action works). A staff member who has practiced reporting phishing in a sandbox is more likely to trust, and use, the reporting button. Conversely, low literacy inflates response costs: if login steps feel confusing or data-handling rules seem opaque, people will perceive secure behavior as slow or difficult and may look for workarounds (Trenerry et al., 2021; Badii et al., 2020).

Within the Cybersecurity Awareness and Readiness Framework (CARF), digital literacy is addressed deliberately, not generically. CARF begins with baseline diagnostics, short skills checks at onboarding and annually, lightweight phishing simulations, and quick interviews with representative roles. Results are then used to tailor learning paths: interactive tutorials and job aids for entry-level users; scenario-based simulations for technical and operational staff; and policy-plus-risk workshops for managers who approve exceptions or handle escalations. To keep the secure path the easy path, CARF pairs training with usability improvements (e.g., single sign-on, password managers, clear data-handling checklists) and reinforcement (micro-nudges, quarterly drills, and "security moments" in team meetings).

Implementation should also account for inclusion and context: materials written in plain language, accessible formats for staff with disabilities, options for low-bandwidth offices, and examples drawn from the agency's actual services. Success can be tracked with practical indicators, reduced phishing click-through in simulations, faster reporting times, higher completion rates for role-specific modules, and fewer policy exceptions, feeding back into the next training cycle.

Table 2. Digital Literacy and CARF Response

Aspect	Impact on Cybersecurity Readiness	CARF Intervention
Variability in skill levels	Uneven compliance and risk "hot spots" across teams	Run baseline skills assessments; create **role-based** learning paths; provide targeted coaching for lower-skill groups
Rapid tech change	New workflows and attack surfaces outpace staff skills	Continuous upskilling via micro-modules; just-in-time guides for new tools; briefings paired with each rollout
Low digital literacy	Lower **self-efficacy**, higher **response costs**, more workarounds	Simplify workflows (SSO, password managers); step-by-step job aids and visuals; one-click phishing/reporting
High digital literacy	Higher confidence and **response efficacy**; positive peer spillovers	Advanced simulations/tabletops; red-team exercises; peer mentoring and a "security champions" network

3.2 Perceived Risk and Prior Exposure to Threats

For many public-sector employees, cybersecurity risks can feel distant, something that happens to "other organizations" or in the headlines, not in their own office. This perception begins to shift when an employee personally experiences a cyber incident, whether at work or in their personal life. Clicking on a phishing link, receiving a fraudulent tax notice, or watching a colleague's account get compromised can transform a vague, abstract threat into something immediate and tangible. Such experiences often trigger a heightened sense of vigilance and a stronger emotional connection to cybersecurity practices (Siponen et al., 2024).

Table 3. Perceived Risk and Prior Threat Exposure in CARF

Aspect	Impact on Readiness	CARF Intervention
No prior exposure	Risk feels abstract and distant	Use relatable case studies from similar institutions
Recent personal or workplace incident	Increases perceived severity and vulnerability	Reinforce with follow-up training and discussions
Fading memory of past incident	Awareness drops over time	Periodic simulations and refresher campaigns
Safe simulated exposure	Builds risk awareness without harm	Phishing tests, role-play social engineering exercises

Case Example: Phishing Attack on a Municipal Health Department (humanized)

In early 2023, a mid-sized city's health department was targeted by a phishing campaign disguised as an urgent COVID-19 vaccination update. The emails looked as if they came from the Chief Medical Officer and used official logos, formatting, and authoritative language, classic social engineering meant to exploit trust in leaders (Ali et al., 2021; Moallem, 2024). Staff were urged to "review and approve updated clinic schedules" ahead of a public announcement. Pressed for time, several employees clicked the link without verifying it. The page they reached perfectly mimicked the city's secure portal, and once they entered their credentials, attackers captured them. Within hours, unusual logins from overseas IP addresses appeared, giving the attackers access to the department's scheduling database. The impact was immediate: vaccination appointments were delayed, public communications were disrupted, and internal confidence took a hit (Doe, 2024).

Containment hinged on one employee who, after entering their credentials, noticed oddities in the email footer and reported it to IT. That quick alert triggered rapid revocation of compromised accounts and containment of the threat, with services restored inside 24 hours (Hu et al., 2022). Post-incident review confirmed that, despite firewalls and two-factor authentication, human factors, time pressure, trust in perceived authority, and missed warning signs, were the primary drivers of success for the attackers (Bada et al., 2019). In response, the department rolled out targeted fixes: phishing simulations embedded in the SETA program, immediate personalized feedback for anyone who fell for simulated lures, and short, scenario-based "pause and verify" modules built into daily workflows. Six months later, phishing-simulation click rates had dropped by 47%, and self-reported incident reporting was up 63%, showing how real-world exposure, paired with organizational support, can measurably improve security behavior (Wang et al., 2022).

3.3 Privacy Concerns and Trust in Cybersecurity Tools

In public institutions, privacy concerns operate on two interconnected levels. The first is institutional responsibility, the legal and ethical obligation to safeguard citizens' personal information. The second is employee perception, how staff members feel about the ways their own work activities and communications are monitored for security purposes. Both levels play a critical role in shaping readiness, because trust in the organization's security measures directly affects whether employees follow them willingly or reluctantly (Siagian et al., 2023). For many employees, a cybersecurity tool is only as good as their belief in its fairness, transparency, and effectiveness. If a monitoring system is perceived as invasive, tracking every keystroke or reading emails without clear justification, it can trigger resistance, quiet non-compliance, or even attempts to circumvent security controls. On the other hand, when employees understand why a security measure exists, how it protects both their work and the citizens they serve, and what safeguards are in place to prevent misuse, trust grows and compliance becomes part of the workplace norm.

From a Protection Motivation Theory (PMT) perspective, privacy concerns and trust influence response efficacy, the belief that a recommended protective action will work as intended, and response costs, the perceived inconvenience or personal sacrifice associated with following the measure. A lack of trust can lower response efficacy ("this won't really protect us") and raise perceived costs ("this slows me down and feels intrusive"), while a transparent, well-communicated system can reverse those effects. The Cybersecurity Awareness and Readiness Framework (CARF) addresses privacy concerns through three key strategies:

- **Transparent communication** – explaining the purpose, scope, and limitations of monitoring tools.
- **Policy clarity** – providing accessible documentation on data collection, retention, and employee rights.
- **Feedback loops** – creating opportunities for staff to ask questions, express concerns, and influence tool adoption or configuration.

By embedding these elements into both policy and training, CARF ensures that employees not only comply with security measures but also perceive them as legitimate, balanced, and respectful of privacy. This trust is essential for turning compliance into proactive, self-motivated participation in cybersecurity.

Table 4. Privacy Concerns, Trust, and CARF Interventions

Aspect	Impact on Readiness	CARF Intervention
Perceived invasiveness	Reduces compliance and trust	Clearly communicate purpose, scope, and limits of monitoring
Unclear data handling policies	Increases uncertainty and resistance	Publish plain-language policy summaries
High trust in tools	Encourages voluntary compliance	Share success stories and case examples
Low trust in tools	Raises perceived response costs	Engage staff in tool evaluation and feedback sessions

3.4 Organizational Culture and Management Support

Cybersecurity readiness in public institutions is not shaped by technology alone, it grows out of the culture in which employees work and the leadership that sets the tone. Organizational culture defines the shared values, norms, and unwritten rules that influence how staff interpret security policies and whether they see cybersecurity as part of their job or someone else's responsibility (Schlienger & Teufel, 2022). In a culture where security is viewed as "IT's problem," employees may engage in unsafe shortcuts without much thought. Conversely, when security is embedded into daily routines and seen as "everyone's responsibility," protective behaviors are reinforced naturally through peer expectations and team norms.

Management and leadership support are the most visible drivers of such a culture. Leaders send powerful signals about organizational priorities through their own behavior. A manager who follows security protocols, participates in phishing awareness drills, and discusses cybersecurity in team meetings demonstrates that security matters. In contrast, leaders who bypass security measures or treat awareness training as a checkbox task inadvertently undermine both policy compliance and employee motivation (Dodge et al., 2023). From a Protection Motivation Theory (PMT) perspective, organizational culture and leadership support influence both response efficacy, the belief that security measures are effective, and self-efficacy, the confidence employees have in their own ability to apply them.

Table 5. Organizational Culture, Management Support, and CARF Interventions

Aspect	Impact on Readiness	CARF Intervention
"IT-only" security culture	Low shared responsibility	Departmental security champions
Leader non-compliance	Weakens policy legitimacy	Leadership participation in training
Supportive culture	Encourages peer-to-peer reinforcement	Recognition and reward programs
Visible leader advocacy	Boosts self- and response efficacy	Regular security briefings and policy endorsements

4. FRAMEWORK FOR CYBERSECURITY AWARENESS AND READINESS

The Cybersecurity Awareness and Readiness Framework (CARF) is designed to help public institutions build a workforce that is not only informed about cyber risks but also capable of responding to them effectively. It integrates Protection Motivation Theory (PMT) with the practical realities of public-sector operations, ensuring that awareness initiatives are psychologically grounded, operationally relevant, and adaptable to evolving threats. CARF addresses two overarching goals:

- **Enhancing Threat Appraisal** – ensuring employees accurately perceive the severity and likelihood of cyber threats.
- **Strengthening Coping Appraisal** – improving employees' confidence in their ability to respond and reducing barriers to secure behavior.

By linking these PMT dimensions with institutional enablers such as digital literacy programs, leadership support, privacy protections, and cultural reinforcement, CARF creates a multi-layered approach to cybersecurity readiness.

4.1 Framework Architecture

The Cybersecurity Awareness and Readiness Framework (CARF) is built as an interconnected system that aligns individual capabilities, organizational enablers, and adaptive improvement mechanisms. Its architecture reflects the behavioral drivers identified in Protection Motivation Theory (PMT) and the operational context of public-sector organizations. This multi-layered structure ensures that cybersecurity awareness efforts are not one-off initiatives but part of a sustainable, evolving readiness model.

Layer 1: Individual Dimension

The individual layer focuses on employees' knowledge, perceptions, and day-to-day security behaviors. It seeks to strengthen both threat appraisal and coping appraisal through practical interventions. Role-specific training addresses differences in digital literacy, while scenario-based exercises, such as phishing simulations, translate abstract risks into tangible experiences. Just-in-time reminders, gamified learning modules, and microlearning segments further reinforce secure behaviors in a way that feels integrated into daily work rather than disruptive.

Layer 2: Organizational Dimension

The organizational layer provides the environment in which secure behaviors can take root and flourish. It encompasses clear and accessible security policies, active leadership participation in cybersecurity initiatives, and cultural reinforcement through peer role models and recognition systems. Privacy safeguards are also central to this layer, ensuring that security monitoring is balanced with respect for employee autonomy. By embedding cybersecurity into policy, leadership practice, and workplace culture, this layer ensures that individual readiness is supported rather than undermined by institutional factors.

Layer 3: Adaptive Feedback Dimension

The adaptive feedback layer ensures that CARF remains responsive to evolving threats, workforce needs, and technology changes. It relies on continuous monitoring and evaluation, including compliance metrics, incident trend analysis, and employee feedback. Lessons learned from real or simulated incidents are fed back into both training and policy, enabling iterative improvements. This makes the framework dynamic, capable of adapting without losing its core principles.

Interaction Between Layers

These three layers are mutually reinforcing. For example, an employee who gains confidence through hands-on training (Individual Layer) is more likely to comply with simplified procedures introduced through policy reform (Organizational Layer), and this improvement can be tracked through incident reduction metrics (Adaptive

Feedback Layer). This cyclical interaction ensures that awareness is constantly informed by practice, and practice is shaped by fresh insights.

Table 6. CARF Layers, Focus Areas, and Example Actions

Layer	Focus Area	Example Actions
Individual	Skills, perceptions, behaviors	Role-based SETA training, phishing drills, microlearning
Organizational	Policies, leadership, culture	Plain-language policies, leader participation, recognition systems
Adaptive Feedback	Continuous improvement	Incident analysis, metrics dashboards, employee feedback forums

4.2 Integration with PMT

Strengthening coping appraisal. Awareness alone does not produce action. Staff must believe they can act, and that their actions work. CARF raises self-efficacy through practical, role-specific exercises (e.g., simulated phishing, guided data-handling drills, scenario problem-solving) that let employees practice in a safe setting (Johnston & Warkentin, 2010). It reinforces response efficacy by showing evidence of impact, such as measurable drops in phishing susceptibility after training (Ifinedo, 2012). At the same time, it lowers response costs by simplifying multi-factor authentication, automating updates, and offering concise, in-workflow job aids that reduce friction (Bada et al., 2019). Sustaining motivation over time. CARF adds an adaptive feedback layer that tracks outcomes and listens to staff. Metrics from incident reports, compliance dashboards, and employee surveys are analyzed to detect shifts in threat perception and coping confidence, guiding targeted refinements (Hu et al., 2022). Positive results, like improved reporting times or reduced click-through rates, are shared to reinforce progress, while feedback is used to adjust training content or delivery. In this way, PMT functions not as a static theory but as a dynamic engine within a continuous improvement cycle, keeping awareness and capability current, effective, and resilient.

4.3 Implementation Flow

The Cybersecurity Awareness and Readiness Framework (CARF) runs as a structured cycle, not a one-off rollout. Its stages link evidence, intervention, and feedback so programs stay relevant as threats and workplaces change (Bada et al., 2019; Hu et al., 2022). The result is awareness that endures beyond "training day" and translates into everyday secure behavior. CARF starts by mapping the institution's current posture: digital literacy levels, policy fit, and PMT-related determinants such as perceived vulnerability, self-efficacy, and response costs (Rogers, 1975; Maddux & Rogers, 1983). Typical activities include short staff surveys, skills checks, policy/process reviews, and analysis of prior incidents.

Interventions are rolled out through mixed delivery: instructor-led sessions, e-learning, hands-on exercises, and realistic simulations. A multi-modal approach boosts engagement and retention across roles and learning styles (Bada et al., 2019). Visible leadership participation and peer reinforcement model the desired behaviors, helping to embed them into the organization's day-to-day culture (Dodge et al., 2023). Effectiveness is measured with quantitative and qualitative indicators: incident rates, phishing-simulation results, compliance scores, and employee self-assessments. CARF also watches shifts in attitudes and confidence to capture behavior change, not just technical signals (Hu et al., 2022). These data surface residual vulnerabilities and show where to double down or adjust.

Findings feed back into the program. Training is updated, policies clarified, and technical controls tuned as threats, technologies, and operating conditions evolve. This feedback-driven refinement keeps CARF dynamic and responsive rather than a static compliance checklist (Wang et al., 2022). Putting it together: Assessment → Design → Delivery → Measurement → Refinement forms a self-sustaining loop. Each stage strengthens the next, so awareness drives behavior change, behavior change improves outcomes, and those outcomes guide the framework's ongoing evolution (Bada et al., 2019; Hu et al., 2022).

4.4 CARF Diagram Description

The diagram presents the Cybersecurity Awareness and Readiness Framework (CARF) as three concentric layers, Individual, Organizational, and Adaptive Feedback, linked by cyclical, bidirectional arrows. At a glance, it shows how PMT underpins the framework and how continuous improvement keeps it responsive to evolving risks (Hu et al., 2022; Wang et al., 2022).

Individual Layer (center circle).

At the core is the employee: perceptions, skills, and everyday security behaviors. In PMT terms, this layer targets threat appraisal (perceived severity, vulnerability) and coping appraisal (self-efficacy, response efficacy, response costs), shaping how staff understand risks and how confidently they can respond (Rogers, 1975; Maddux & Rogers, 1983). Placing this layer at the center signals a simple truth: organizational cybersecurity ultimately hinges on individual actions.

Organizational Layer (middle ring).

Encircling the individual is the environment that enables, or obstructs, secure behavior: clear policies, visible leadership, usable controls, privacy safeguards, and cultural norms (Dodge et al., 2023; Schlienger & Teufel, 2022). This ring acts as a bridge between personal responsibility and institutional systems, highlighting how management choices and policy design lower response costs and normalize good practice.

Adaptive Feedback Layer (outer ring).

The outermost ring closes the loop. Directional arrows connect it back to the inner layers, emphasizing ongoing monitoring → evaluation → refinement. Here, metrics from incident reports, compliance tracking, simulations, and employee feedback are synthesized; insights then flow inward to update training, tune policies, and adjust technical controls (Hu et al., 2022; Wang et al., 2022). This keeps CARF dynamic rather than static.

Bidirectional arrows (reciprocal influence).

Two-way arrows between layers show that change propagates in both directions. Gains in self-efficacy at the individual level can justify lighter, more targeted training policies; policy reforms and usability improvements can, in turn, reduce response costs and lift compliance (Ifinedo, 2012). The circular layout communicates that awareness is not a one-way broadcast but a continuous exchange between people, policies, and performance feedback.

What the diagram does.

As a conceptual map, it clarifies where interventions live and how they interact. As an operational tool, it helps practitioners spot leverage points, track progress, and keep technical controls aligned with human factors, capturing CARF's dual commitment to theory-driven design and real-world applicability in public-sector settings (Hu et al., 2022; Wang et al., 2022).

Figure 1. Cybersecurity Awareness and Readiness Framework (CARF)

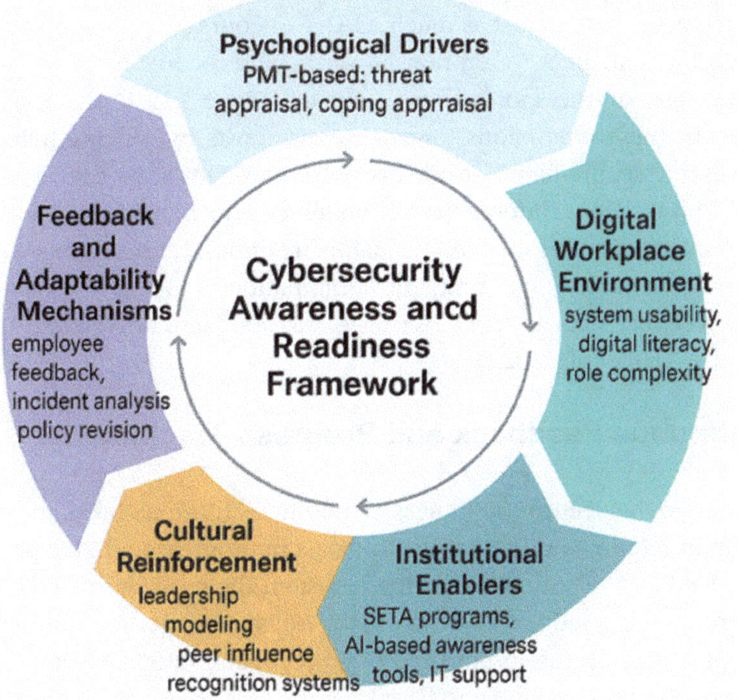

5. PRACTICAL IMPLEMENTATION STRATEGIES

Putting CARF into practice means turning theory into everyday habits through clear, actionable strategies. These strategies are tailored to public-sector realities so interventions aren't generic, but tuned to each institution's challenges and opportunities. The sections that follow outline five connected approaches, adaptive training, experiential learning, cultural embedding, feedback-driven improvement, and policy refinement, that work together as a continuous, sustainable cycle of readiness.

5.1 Cultural Embedding Through Leadership and Peer Support

For cybersecurity readiness to last, it has to live in the culture, not sit as a periodic compliance task. CARF emphasizes the role of leaders and peers in setting that tone. When leaders show up, taking part in training, opening meetings with brief security updates, and modeling secure behaviors, they signal clear priorities (Schlienger &

Teufel, 2022). This visible commitment builds a top-down culture where cybersecurity is everyone's job, not just the IT department's (Dodge et al., 2023).

Peer influence matters just as much. CARF encourages appointing cyber champions in each department, often non-IT staff, who receive extra training and act as approachable, on-the-spot resources for colleagues. In Protection Motivation Theory terms, these champions lower response costs by making help immediate and normalizing secure habits inside everyday workflows (Rogers, 1975; Maddux & Rogers, 1983). Peer reinforcement complements formal training with real-time, context-specific support, especially valuable in public-sector settings with complex systems and constraints. Over time, the combination of visible leadership and peer support turns cybersecurity from a series of sessions into a lived part of organizational identity (Hu et al., 2022).

5.2 Continuous Feedback and Progress Tracking

Sustaining cybersecurity readiness in public institutions takes more than one-off training; it requires ongoing ways to measure progress and give people timely, actionable feedback. Continuous feedback systems help surface new vulnerabilities early and reinforce good habits before risky behaviors become routine (Hu et al., 2022). A practical starting point is to build feedback into everyday digital work. When someone tries to open a restricted file or clicks a suspicious link, automated prompts can explain the risk and offer immediate next steps, turning potential incidents into "teachable moments" that strengthen judgment on the spot (Ali et al., 2021). In parallel, personalized dashboards can show each employee their security profile, phishing simulation results, password hygiene, completion of required modules, alongside department averages to make progress visible and motivating (Moallem, 2024).

At the organizational level, aggregate tracking guides strategy. If one department consistently underperforms in phishing simulations, leaders can deploy targeted refreshers; if another excels, its practices can be shared across teams to lift overall performance (Wang et al., 2022). Framing these moves as support, rather than punishment, keeps the focus on learning and improvement. Feedback should also encourage participation. One municipal government in Northern Europe published monthly "cyber champions" lists recognizing top performers in awareness activities. The result was healthy, friendly competition and higher engagement: over six months, phishing susceptibility fell by 41% and voluntary reporting of suspicious emails rose by 55% (Doe, 2024). By weaving progress tracking into daily operations, and making feedback a two-way dialogue between staff and leadership, institutions keep readiness alive and adaptable. This approach shifts cybersecurity from a static, annual exercise to an ongoing practice that evolves with threats, tools, and workflows (Bada et al., 2019).

5.3 Policy and Process Refinement

To keep cybersecurity readiness strong, public institutions need policies and day-to-day processes that evolve with the threat landscape. Static or outdated rules quickly lose relevance, opening protection gaps and inviting compliance failures (Ali et al., 2021). Regular review cycles, ideally at least annually, help align requirements with new technologies, regulatory changes, and lessons from recent incidents (Hu et al., 2022). Effective refinement starts with many voices at the table. Bringing together IT security, legal, frontline staff, and department heads ensures that changes are both technically sound and workable in real operations (Bada et al., 2019). One large metropolitan transit authority, for example, formed a Cybersecurity Policy Review Board with representatives from every division. Meeting quarterly, the board reviewed incident reports, audit findings, and user feedback, then recommended updates to authentication, data classification, and vendor access policies.

Process refinement is stronger when policies are stress-tested against realistic scenarios before they're finalized. Ahead of new remote-work rules, a city IT team simulated a VPN outage to probe access-control gaps and communications weak points. The findings shaped both technical safeguards and user guidance, making the final policy resilient under real-world conditions (Moallem, 2024). Transparency builds buy-in. Publishing a brief "policy change summary" that explains the rationale behind each update reduces resistance, and linking updates to concrete outcomes, such as lower phishing success rates or faster incident response, helps staff see the payoff for compliance (Wang et al., 2022). Treating policy and process refinement as a continuous, participatory practice, not a top-down paperwork exercise, keeps cybersecurity measures relevant, actionable, and aligned with organizational goals as threats and operations evolve.

6. POLICY AND LEADERSHIP CONSIDERATIONS

Sustaining cybersecurity readiness in public institutions takes more than tools and training, it depends on clear, coherent policies and visibly engaged leadership that set the tone for how the organization works. Policies define the rules and expectations; leadership builds the culture that puts those rules into practice. CARF treats these as a matched pair: both must move in step so security practices are not only mandated on paper but genuinely adopted at every level of the institution (Dodge et al., 2023; Schlienger & Teufel, 2022).

6.1 Policy Alignment and Clarity

Cybersecurity policies in public institutions should be clear, practical, and easy for everyone to apply, not just IT specialists. Overly technical wording can alienate non-technical staff and depress compliance, so policies ought to use plain language and concrete examples (Moallem, 2024). For instance, rather than saying, "Deploy multi-factor authentication on all endpoints," a clearer version is, "Log in using both your password and a one-time code sent to your phone or email." The requirement is identical, but the expectation is immediately understandable to typical users (Bada et al., 2019). Clarity also means structuring policies so people know exactly what to do in specific situations. Scenario-based instructions make this actionable: "If you receive an email requesting sensitive information, do not click any links. Forward the message to the IT security team using the 'Report Phishing' button in your email toolbar." Step-by-step guidance reduces uncertainty, speeds correct action, and strengthens organizational readiness when threats appear (Wang et al., 2022).

Policies must also align with real workflows. Rules that ignore operational realities are likely to be bypassed, even with good intentions (Ali et al., 2021). For example, forcing complex password changes every 30 days can push employees to write passwords down or reuse patterns, undermining security. Involving frontline staff, supervisors, and IT professionals in drafting and testing ensures requirements fit day-to-day tasks and are feasible at scale (Hu et al., 2022). Because threats evolve, policies should be reviewed regularly to stay both clear and relevant. Annual audits that incorporate employee feedback, analyze incident trends, and check against updated laws and regulations help keep guidance current and effective (Dodge et al., 2023). Communicating updates transparently, explaining not only what is changing but why, builds trust and encourages buy-in across the workforce (Siponen et al., 2024). Ultimately, alignment and clarity are about more than simplifying language; they ensure cybersecurity rules are actionable, context-aware, and continuously refined with the people who use them.

6.2 Leadership Roles in Fostering a Security Culture (humanized)

Leadership shapes an institution's cybersecurity posture through both the formal levers it controls, policy, resourcing, and accountability, and the informal norms it signals every day (Schlienger & Teufel, 2022). In public institutions that handle critical infrastructure and citizen data, leaders must make cybersecurity a visible, constant priority. That means more than issuing memos or approving budgets; it means showing up to training, modeling secure behaviors, and communicating the "why" in ways that resonate with frontline staff and executives alike (Dodge et al.,

2023). Viewed through Protection Motivation Theory (PMT), leadership engagement moves two core drivers of behavior: perceived severity and response efficacy (Rogers, 1975; Maddux & Rogers, 1983). When leaders discuss real incidents and acknowledge current vulnerabilities, they signal that threats are serious and relevant. When they also ensure access to role-specific training, fit-for-purpose tools, and clear procedures, they raise confidence that recommended measures actually work. This pairing, urgency plus efficacy, is what sustains protective behavior over the long term (Hu et al., 2022).

Leadership also sets the tone for trust and openness. If people fear blame for reporting mistakes, small lapses go underground until they become big problems. By promoting a learning-oriented, non-punitive approach to incident reporting, and by recognizing proactive reporting, leaders encourage timely communication and reinforce that security is a shared responsibility, not an individual liability (Bada et al., 2019).

Finally, effective leaders weave cybersecurity into the organization's strategy, not just its IT plan. They consider security in procurement, system upgrades, service design, and public engagement, signaling that it is part of operational excellence and essential to public trust. This holistic integration positions the institution to withstand today's threats and adapt as the digital landscape evolves (Wang et al., 2022).

6.3 Accountability and Continuous Oversight

Policies and leadership only stick when they're backed by clear accountability and ongoing oversight. That means setting concrete performance indicators, training completion rates, phishing-simulation results, average incident response and recovery times, and reviewing them regularly at the leadership level (Wang et al., 2022). Continuous monitoring ensures that practices are not just launched, but maintained, adjusted, and strengthened as conditions change.

Accountability should be woven into routine operations: annual audits, quarterly risk assessments, and scheduled policy-review cycles (Hu et al., 2022). These checkpoints surface emerging vulnerabilities, guide policy updates, and help direct resources to the highest-risk areas. Transparency is equally important. Sharing results with staff, celebrating gains and flagging gaps, builds trust and reinforces that cybersecurity is a shared responsibility (Ifinedo, 2012). By treating oversight as a continuous, not reactive, process, public institutions keep cybersecurity an active, evolving priority, able to adapt to new threats and organizational shifts (Wang et al., 2022; Hu et al., 2022).

6.4 Integrating Policy and Leadership into CARF's Adaptive Cycle

In CARF, policy and leadership are active parts of the adaptive feedback loop, not fixed add-ons. Governance adjusts as threats and organizational needs change: leaders review performance data, incident trends, and employee feedback, then update priorities and policies in real time (Hu et al., 2022). Treating policy as a living document, rather than a static rulebook, keeps requirements relevant, workable, and aligned with both new technologies and day-to-day operations (Schlienger & Teufel, 2022). Leadership anchors this process by communicating updates clearly, funding and enabling implementation, and explaining the "why" behind changes. When staff understand how a new step addresses a specific risk, adoption rises and cultural buy-in strengthens.

7. DISCUSSION AND FUTURE DIRECTIONS

The framework explicitly links PMT's threat appraisal, perceived severity and perceived vulnerability, to concrete, context-specific training and communications that make risks tangible and personally relevant. It also reinforces coping appraisal, self-efficacy, response efficacy, and response cost, by providing role-relevant skills practice, simplifying secure actions through usable controls, and demonstrating how individual behaviors measurably reduce institutional risk, thereby normalizing security as part of daily work rather than an abstract compliance exercise (Rogers, 1975; Maddux & Rogers, 1983; Hu et al., 2022).

An important insight from applying CARF is that cultural and institutional conditions often shape cybersecurity outcomes more than raw technical capacity. Public agencies typically operate under rigid governance, wide variation in workforce skills, and tighter budgets than many private organizations. These constraints can produce fragmented training, siloed incident reporting, and policies that are either too generic to guide practice or too complex to follow consistently (Dodge et al., 2023; Schlienger & Teufel, 2022). CARF's multilayer design, linking individual, departmental, and organizational readiness, helps navigate these realities by emphasizing adaptability, continuous feedback loops, peer mentoring, and visible leadership modeling that together convert policy into lived practice (Hu et al., 2022).

Future research should prioritize rigorous, longitudinal evaluations of CARF across diverse public-sector contexts. Comparative studies can test whether agencies adopting CARF achieve greater reductions in incidents, higher employee security confidence, and stronger policy compliance than those relying on traditional Security Education, Training, and Awareness (SETA) programs. Further work is also needed on the role of organizational culture, how hierarchy, union representation, political oversight, and public accountability influence both the perception of cyber threats and the adoption of protective behaviors (Ifinedo, 2012; Hu et al., 2022).

From a technology standpoint, CARF can be extended through adaptive AI tutors, gamified training platforms, and immersive VR simulations. AI systems could analyze behavioral signals in real time to identify at-risk users and deliver targeted microlearning immediately after risky actions, while VR could stage complex incident scenarios, such as ransomware attacks on municipal water systems, to build decision-making under pressure (Wang et al., 2022). These innovations, however, must be balanced with clear ethical safeguards to ensure transparency in data collection and protect employee trust; overly invasive monitoring can undermine morale and provoke resistance to security initiatives (Schlienger & Teufel, 2022).

Another direction is cross-sector and inter-agency collaboration. Because cyber threats rarely respect organizational boundaries, a compromise in one system can cascade through shared platforms, cloud services, and data-exchange mechanisms. Adapting CARF for regional coalitions, where agencies share training resources, threat intelligence, and response protocols, could raise overall resilience and allow smaller institutions to benefit from high-quality readiness programs they could not build alone (Badii et al., 2020; Dodge et al., 2023).

Singapore's Smart Nation program ties cybersecurity directly to public service delivery. Under the Cyber Security Agency of Singapore (CSA), agencies follow sector-specific controls while aligning with a centralized national strategy, so everyone moves in the same direction but applies measures that fit their risks (Cyber Security Agency of Singapore, 2023). A signature feature is the annual national exercise that simulates large-scale attacks to test both technology and people across ministries and statutory boards. Scenarios include realistic phishing waves, insider-threat drills, and continuity challenges that reflect the complexity of smart public services. Singapore also invests in role-based training, tailoring content for technical teams, policy officers, and frontline staff, and feeds performance data into national dashboards so agencies can benchmark against peers. That mix of clear central standards, localized training, and healthy competition has strengthened trust in digital services and shortened recovery times during real incidents, such as the 2018 SingHealth breach (Cyber Security Agency of Singapore, 2023).

Estonia's highly digital government, covering everything from e-voting to online health records, made cybersecurity a national priority, especially after the 2007 attacks on public and financial systems (Himma-Kadakas & Kõuts-Klemm, 2023). The response paired technical upgrades with a human-centered strategy. A cornerstone is the Cyber Defence League, a volunteer network of IT professionals, private-sector experts, and academics who train with government teams and help during incidents (Himma-Kadakas & Kõuts-Klemm, 2023). Cybersecurity is also woven into the national curriculum so digital literacy and risk awareness start early. Public servants routinely take part in scenario-based training and inter-agency crisis drills, many coordinated with the NATO Cooperative Cyber Defence Centre of Excellence in Tallinn. This blend of civic participation, international collaboration, and continuous institutional training is widely cited as a model for smaller nations with high digital dependence, showing how public engagement and prepared institutions can build a culture of resilience that extends beyond the government workforce (Himma-Kadakas & Kõuts-Klemm, 2023).

Finally, scaling CARF in data-intensive public environments raises ethical, legal, and societal considerations. Increased personalization in training and monitoring creates tensions between effective oversight and employee privacy. Future research should develop governance frameworks that safeguard privacy while enabling the behavioral analytics necessary to measure readiness and guide improvement. Given public institutions' accountability to citizens, they must model ethical responsibility in cybersecurity; after a breach, restoring trust is often more difficult than restoring technical functionality (Alhalafi & Veeraraghavan, 2023; Rashid & Chauhan, 2020).

8. CONCLUSION

The digital transformation of public institutions is changing how governments deliver services, manage resources, and connect with citizens. It brings big gains in innovation, efficiency, and access, but also new cybersecurity risks. In smart, data-driven environments where systems are tightly linked, a single weak point, technical or human, can disrupt essential services, expose sensitive data, and damage public trust. Meeting this reality takes more than firewalls and encryption. It requires attention to the human, cultural, and organizational sides of readiness. The Cybersecurity Awareness and Readiness Framework (CARF) answers that need. It starts from a simple truth: technology works only if people use it securely. CARF blends insights from motivation and behavior change with practical levers, policies, leadership, and adaptive learning tools, to build resilience. In doing so, it closes the gap between high-level directives and everyday actions, so security becomes part of how work gets done, not just a compliance checkbox.

What sets CARF apart is its ability to adapt. The framework evolves as technologies, threats, and priorities shift. Continuous feedback loops help institutions spot weaknesses, refine strategies, and reinforce what works. The result is a living model of readiness that treats cybersecurity as an ongoing process rather than a static checklist. Success also depends on shared responsibility. Security cannot sit only with IT or a small team of specialists; it has to be everyone's job. Leaders must model secure behavior, communicate why it matters, and ensure policies are realistic and easy to follow. Employees, in turn, need to feel both capable of and accountable for protecting the systems they use. This shared ownership nurtures a culture where security is upheld not by fear of penalties, but by commitment to the mission and the public served.

Looking ahead, the priority is to refine and scale CARF across varied public-sector settings. As threats grow more sophisticated and services more interconnected, institutions will need to collaborate across departments, agencies, and sectors, pooling resources, sharing threat intelligence, and coordinating responses to raise resilience for all. Ethical considerations must remain front and center, so efforts to improve readiness also respect employee privacy and preserve public trust. Ultimately, cybersecurity in public institutions is not just a technical requirement; it is a foundation of democratic governance. Protecting the integrity of digital services protects confidence in the institutions that provide them. By embracing frameworks like CARF, rooted in human behavior, organizational readiness, and continuous adaptation, public institutions can withstand today's threats and prepare for the challenges of the digital future.

REFERENCES

Abd Latif, S. F., Sulaiman, N. S., Abd Aziz, N. S., Yacob, A., & Nasir, A. (2025). Development of Cybersecurity Awareness Model Based on Protection Motivation Theory (PMT) for Digital IR 4.0 in Malaysia. *International Journal of Advanced Computer Science and Applications*, *16*(3).

Al Hwaitat, A. K., & Fakhouri, H. N. (2024). Adaptive Cybersecurity Neural Networks: An Evolutionary Approach for Enhanced Attack Detection and Classification. *Applied Sciences (Basel, Switzerland)*, *14*(19), 9142.

Alamer, M., & Almaiah, M. A. (2021, July). Cybersecurity in Smart City: A systematic mapping study. In 2021 international conference on information technology (ICIT) (pp. 719-724). IEEE.

Alhalafi, N., & Veeraraghavan, P. (2023). Exploring the challenges and issues in adopting cybersecurity in Saudi smart cities: Conceptualization of the cybersecurity-based UTAUT model. *Smart Cities*, *6*(3), 1523–1544.

Alharbi, F. S. (2024). Effects of the Protection Motivation Model on Information Security Policy Compliance Among Saudi Employees (Doctoral dissertation, Marymount University).

Ali, R. F., Dominic, P. D. D., Ali, S. E. A., Rehman, M., & Sohail, A. (2021). Information security behavior and information security policy compliance: A systematic literature review for identifying the transformation process from noncompliance to compliance. *Applied Sciences (Basel, Switzerland)*, *11*(8), 3383.

Almansoori, A., Al-Emran, M., & Shaalan, K. (2023). Exploring the frontiers of cybersecurity behavior: A systematic review of studies and theories. *Applied Sciences (Basel, Switzerland)*, *13*(9), 5700.

Almeida, F. (2023). Prospects of cybersecurity in smart cities. *Future Internet*, *15*(9), 285.

Alraddadi, R., Alshayeb, M., Mahmood, S., & Niazi, M. (2025). Towards Understanding the Critical Role of Human Behavior in Smart and Cognitive City Cybersecurity. *Procedia Computer Science*, *257*, 1039–1046.

Alrawhani, E. M., Romli, A., & Al-Sharafi, M. A. (2025). Evaluating the role of protection motivation theory in information security policy compliance: Insights from the banking sector using PLS-SEM approach. *Journal of Open Innovation*, *11*(1), 100463.

Alshaikh, M. (2020). Developing cybersecurity culture to influence employee behavior: A practice perspective. *Computers & Security*, *98*, 102003.

Alsharida, R. A., Al-rimy, B. A. S., Al-Emran, M., & Zainal, A. (2023). A systematic review of multi perspectives on human cybersecurity behavior. *Technology in Society*, *73*, 102258.

Alyami, A., Sammon, D., Neville, K., & Mahony, C. (2024). Critical success factors for Security Education, Training and Awareness (SETA) programme effectiveness: An empirical comparison of practitioner perspectives. *Information and Computer Security*, *32*(1), 53–73.

Andronache, A. (2021). INCREASING SECURITY AWARENESS THROUGH LENSES OF CYBERSECURITY CULTURE. *Journal of Information Systems & Operations Management*, *15*(1).

Ansari, M. F. (2022). A quantitative study of risk scores and the effectiveness of AI-based Cybersecurity Awareness Training Programs. *International Journal of Smart Sensor and Adhoc Network*, *3*(3), 1.

Ansari, M. F., Sharma, P. K., & Dash, B. (2022). Prevention of phishing attacks using AI-based Cybersecurity Awareness Training. *Prevention*, *3*(6), 61–72.

Bacud, M. L., & Mäses, S. (2021, October). Game-based learning for cybersecurity awareness training programmes in the public sector. In ECEL 2021 20th European Conference on e-Learning. Academic Conferences International limited (p. 50).

Bada, M., Sasse, A. M., & Nurse, J. R. (2019). Cyber security awareness campaigns: Why do they fail to change behaviour? arXiv preprint arXiv:1901.02672.

Badii, C., Bellini, P., Difino, A., & Nesi, P. (2020). Smart city IoT platform respecting GDPR privacy and security aspects. *IEEE Access: Practical Innovations, Open Solutions*, *8*, 23601–23623.

Basri, W. S. (2023). Artificial Intelligence, Cyber Security Measures And Sme's E-Operational Efficiency: Moderating Role Of Employees Perception Of Ai Usefulness. Operational Research in Engineering Sciences: Theory and Applications, 6(4).

Burton, S. L., Burrell, D. N., Nobles, C., & Jones, L. A. (2023). Exploring the nexus of cybersecurity leadership, human factors, emotional intelligence, innovative work behavior, and critical leadership traits. *Scientific Bulletin-Nicolae Balcescu Land Forces Academy*, *28*(2), 162–175.

Bussacarini, M. (2024, March). Global Readiness for Cybersecurity and AI: Assessing the Landscape and Charting the Path Forward. In International Ethical Hacking Conference (pp. 3-15). Singapore: Springer Nature Singapore.

Chang, L. Y., & Coppel, N. (2020). Building cyber security awareness in a developing country: Lessons from Myanmar. *Computers & Security, 97*, 101959.

Cheng, E. C., & Wang, T. (2022). Institutional strategies for cybersecurity in higher education institutions. *Information (Basel), 13*(4), 192.

Corradini, I. (2020). Building a cybersecurity culture. In *Building a Cybersecurity Culture in Organizations: How to Bridge the Gap Between People and Digital Technology* (pp. 63–86). Springer International Publishing.

Crumpler, W., & Lewis, J. A. (2022). Cybersecurity workforce gap (p. 10). Center for Strategic and International Studies (CSIS).

Cyber Security Agency of Singapore. (2023). Annual cybersecurity report 2023. https://www.csa.gov.sg

Dash, B., & Ansari, M. F. (2022). An effective cybersecurity awareness training model: First defense of an organizational security strategy.

Dayarathna, R. (2023). Towards Measuring the Readiness of the Cybersecurity Workforce in Sri Lanka. Available at *SSRN* 4630524.

Dodge, C. E., Fisk, N., Burruss, G. W., Moule, R. K.Jr, & Jaynes, C. M. (2023). What motivates users to adopt cybersecurity practices? A survey experiment assessing protection motivation theory. *Criminology & Public Policy, 22*(4), 849–868.

Floyd, D. L., Prentice-Dunn, S., & Rogers, R. W. (2000). A meta-analysis of research on protection motivation theory. *Journal of Applied Social Psychology, 30*(2), 407–429.

Georgiadou, A., Mouzakitis, S., Bounas, K., & Askounis, D. (2022). A cyber-security culture framework for assessing organization readiness. *Journal of Computer Information Systems, 62*(3), 452–462.

Ghillani, D. (2022). Deep learning and artificial intelligence framework to improve the cyber security. *Authorea Preprints.*

Hijji, M., & Alam, G. (2022). Cybersecurity awareness and training (CAT) framework for remote working employees. *Sensors (Basel), 22*(22), 8663. PMID: 36433259

Himma-Kadakas, M., & Kõuts-Klemm, R. (2023). Developing an advanced digital society: An estonian case study. In *Internet in the Post-Soviet Area: Technological, economic and political aspects* (pp. 109–133). Springer International Publishing.

Hu, S., Hsu, C., & Zhou, Z. (2022). Security education, training, and awareness programs: Literature review. *Journal of Computer Information Systems*, *62*(4), 752–764.

Huda, M., Brayyich, M., Haroon, N. H., Khan, A. A., & Verma, R. (2024, July). An Exploratory Investigation into Sustaining Cybersecurity Protection Through the Implementation of SETA. In *2024 International Conference on Emerging Trends in Networks and Computer Communications (ETNCC)* (pp. 292-296). IEEE.

Hwang, I., Wakefield, R., Kim, S., & Kim, T. (2021). Security awareness: The first step in information security compliance behavior. *Journal of Computer Information Systems*, *61*(4), 345–356.

Ifinedo, P. (2012). Understanding information systems security policy compliance: An integration of the theory of planned behavior and the protection motivation theory. *Computers & Security*, *31*(1), 83–95.

Iyer, S. S., & Raji, B. (2025). Cybersecurity Culture and Organizational Resilience: A Human-Centered Approach to Digital Risk Management. *American Journal of Industrial and Business Management*, *15*(5), 748–766.

Johnston, A. C., & Warkentin, M. (2010). Fear appeals and information security behaviors: An empirical study. *Management Information Systems Quarterly*, •••, 549–566.

Kalinin, M., Krundyshev, V., & Zegzhda, P. (2021). Cybersecurity risk assessment in smart city infrastructures. *Machines (Basel)*, *9*(4), 78.

Kamolov, S., Kaunov, E., & Lisov, A. (2023). Cyber readiness as an imperative for public governance in the digital age. MODERN APPROACHES IN ENGINEERING AND NATURAL SCIENCES: MAENS-2021, 2526(1), 030015.

Kannelønning, K., & Katsikas, S. K. (2023). A systematic literature review of how cybersecurity-related behavior has been assessed. *Information and Computer Security*, *31*(4), 463–477.

Karpiuk, M., MELChIOR, C. L. A. U. D. I. O., & Soler, U. (2023). Cybersecurity Management in the Public Service Sector. *Prawo i Więź*, (4 (47)), 7–27.

Kezron, I. E. (2024). Enhancing Cybersecurity Capacity in Small and Medium Enterprises: A Framework for Workforce Development. *Iconic Research and Engineering Journals*, *7*(10), 421–428.

Khader, M., Karam, M., & Fares, H. (2021). Cybersecurity awareness framework for academia. *Information (Basel)*, *12*(10), 417.

Khan, O. U., Abdullah, S. M., Olajide, A. O., Sani, A. I., Faisal, S. M. W., Ogunola, A. A., & Lee, M. D. (2024). The Future of Cybersecurity: Leveraging Artificial Intelligence to Combat Evolving Threats and Enhance Digital Defense Strategies. *Journal of Computational Analysis and Applications*, *33*(8).

Maddux, J. E., & Rogers, R. W. (1983). Protection motivation and self-efficacy: A revised theory of fear appeals and attitude change. *Journal of Experimental Social Psychology*, *19*(5), 469–479.

Melaku, H. M. (2023). A dynamic and adaptive cybersecurity governance framework. *Journal of Cybersecurity and Privacy*, *3*(3), 327–350.

Metin, B., Özhan, F. G., & Wynn, M. (2024). Digitalisation and Cybersecurity: Towards an Operational Framework. *Electronics (Basel)*, *13*(21), 4226.

Moallem, A. (2024). Human behavior in cybersecurity privacy and trust. Human-Computer Interaction in Intelligent Environments, 77-107.

Mohammed, A. (2022). Cybersecurity in Smart Cities: Securing IoT and Smart Infrastructure. Available at *SSRN* 5066095.

Mohammed, A. (2024). Cybersecurity in Smart Cities: As cities become smarter, new vulnerabilities arise. Research can focus on securing IoT devices, smart infrastructure, and privacy concerns associated with smart city data. *Pioneer Research Journal of Computing Science*, *1*(1), 75–82.

MUSHI. J. (2023). Examining the Factors Obstructing Cyber security Readiness in Public Sector (Doctoral dissertation, IAA).

Nagyfejeo, E., & Von Solms, B. (2020). Why do national cybersecurity awareness programmes often fail. *International Journal of Information Security and Cybercrime*, *9*(2), 18–27.

Nasir, S. (2023, July). Exploring the effectiveness of cybersecurity training programs: factors, best practices, and future directions. In *Proceedings of the Cyber Secure Nigeria Conference* (pp. 151-160).

Nizich, M. (2023). Preparing the cybersecurity workforce of tomorrow. In *The Cybersecurity Workforce of Tomorrow* (pp. 117–146). Emerald Group Publishing Limited.

Nwachukwu, U., Vidgren, J., Niemimaa, M., & Järveläinen, J. (2023). Do SETA Interventions Change Security Behavior?–A Literature Review.

Ohiri, U. W. (2024). Examining the Concept of an AI-Based Cybersecurity Awareness Training Aimed at Remodeling Employees' Behavior (Doctoral dissertation, National University).

Oliha, J. S., Biu, P. W., & Obi, O. C. (2024). Securing the smart city: A review of cybersecurity challenges and strategies. *Engineering Science & Technology Journal*, *5*(2), 496–506.

Paigude, S. D., Pangarkar, S. C., Dari, S. S., Patil, M., & Gujar, S. N. (2024). A Review of Cybersecurity Policies in the Public Sector: Challenges and Solutions. *Computer Fraud & Security*, *2024*(7), 7–12.

Pemmasani, P. K. (2023). National Cybersecurity Frameworks for Critical Infrastructure: Lessons from Governmental Cyber Resilience Initiatives. *International Journal of Acta Informatica*, *2*(1), 209–218.

Pemmasani, P. K., & Osaka, M. (2021). The Future of Smart Cities: Cybersecurity Challenges in Public Infrastructure Management. *International Journal of Modern Computing*, *4*(1), 72–85.

Pöyhönen, J., & Lehto, M. (2020, June). Cyber security: Trust based architecture in the management of an organization security. In Proceedings of the 18th European Conference on Cyber Warfare and Security ECCWS2020, 25–26 June 2020, Chester, UK (pp. 304-313). Reading: Academic Conferences and Publishing International Limited.

Rashid, T., & Chauhan, K. (2020). Cyber Security in the Public Sector: Awareness of Potential Risks among Public Policy Executives. In Security Analytics for the Internet of Everything (pp. 67-91). CRC Press.

Rogers, R. W. (1975). A protection motivation theory of fear appeals and attitude change1. *The Journal of Psychology*, *91*(1), 93–114. PMID: 28136248

Savaş, S., & Karataş, S. (2022). Cyber governance studies in ensuring cybersecurity: An overview of cybersecurity governance. *International Cybersecurity Law Review*, *3*(1), 7–34. PMID: 37521508

Schlienger, T., & Teufel, S. (2002). Information security culture: The socio-cultural dimension in information security management. In *Security in the information society: Visions and perspectives* (pp. 191–201). Springer US.

Shillair, R., Esteve-González, P., Dutton, W. H., Creese, S., Nagyfejeo, E., & von Solms, B. (2022). Cybersecurity education, awareness raising, and training initiatives: National level evidence-based results, challenges, and promise. *Computers & Security*, *119*, 102756.

Siagian, R., Siahaan, L., & Hamzah, M. I. (2023). Human rights in the digital era: Online privacy, freedom of speech, and personal data protection. *Journal of Digital Learning and Distance Education*, *2*(4), 548–558.

Sikolia, D., Biros, D., & Zhang, T. (2023). How effective are seta programs anyway: Learning and forgetting in security awareness training. Journal of Cybersecurity Education. *Research and Practice*, *2023*(1), 4.

Siponen, M., Rönkkö, M., Fufan, L., Haag, S., & Laatikainen, G. (2024). Protection motivation theory in information security behavior research: Reconsidering the fundamentals. *Communications of the Association for Information Systems*, *53*(1), 1136–1165.

Sudaryono, S., Pratomo, R., Ramadan, A., Ahsanitaqwim, R., & Fletcher, E. (2025). Artificial Intelligence in Predictive Cybersecurity: Developing Adaptive Algorithms to Combat Emerging Threats. *Journal of Computer Science and Technology Application*, *2*(1), 1–13.

Sulaiman, N. S., Fauzi, M. A., Hussain, S., & Wider, W. (2022). Cybersecurity behavior among government employees: The role of protection motivation theory and responsibility in mitigating cyberattacks. *Information (Basel)*, *13*(9), 413.

Sutton, A., & Tompson, L. (2025). Towards a cybersecurity culture-behaviour framework: A rapid evidence review. *Computers & Security*, *148*, 104110.

Tolah, A. (2021). A Framework for Understanding and Establishing an Effective Information Security Culture.

Trenerry, B., Chng, S., Wang, Y., Suhaila, Z. S., Lim, S. S., Lu, H. Y., & Oh, P. H. (2021). Preparing workplaces for digital transformation: An integrative review and framework of multi-level factors. *Frontiers in Psychology*, *12*, 620766. PMID: 33833714

Triplett, W. (2021). Establishing a cybersecurity culture organization. Acta Scientific COMPUTER SCIENCES Volume, 3(8).

Triplett, W. J. (2022). Addressing human factors in cybersecurity leadership. *Journal of Cybersecurity and Privacy*, *2*(3), 573–586.

Vandercruysse, L., Buts, C., & Dooms, M. (2020). A typology of smart city services: The case of data protection impact assessment. *Cities (London, England)*, *104*, 102731.

Wang, G., Tse, D., Cui, Y., & Jiang, H. (2022). An exploratory study on sustaining cyber security protection through Seta Implementation. *Sustainability*, *14*(14), 8319.

Willie, M. M. (2023). The role of organizational culture in cybersecurity: Building a security-first culture. Journal of Research. *Innovation and Technologies*, *2*(2 (4)), 179–198.

Xia, N., Xie, Q., Griffin, M. A., Ye, G., & Yuan, J. (2020). Antecedents of safety behavior in construction: A literature review and an integrated conceptual framework. *Accident; Analysis and Prevention*, *148*, 105834. PMID: 33120185

Zwilling, M., Klien, G., Lesjak, D., Wiechetek, Ł., Cetin, F., & Basim, H. N. (2022). Cyber security awareness, knowledge and behavior: A comparative study. *Journal of Computer Information Systems*, *62*(1), 82–97.

Chapter 3
Cyber Hygiene in Higher Education:
Organizational and Human Lessons in Cyber Defence

Ahgalya Subbiah
https://orcid.org/0009-0006-4427-0872
Management and Science University, Malaysia

ABSTRACT

As 2030 approaches, the digital landscape is evolving rapidly and so are cyber threats. Once viewed as purely technical challenges, these threats are now deeply intertwined with human behavior. This chapter explores the evolving role of cyber hygiene in higher education, reflecting the diverse digital habits of students, faculty, and staff. It examines how behavioral patterns, cognitive overload, and trust in digital systems shape vulnerabilities, and what can be done to build stronger defenses. Emphasizing the need for smarter awareness programs, cultural shifts, and user-informed policies, the chapter provides practical, real-world insights into people-centered cybersecurity. Higher education institutions emerge as early test beds for organizational readiness. Ultimately, achieving cyber resilience by 2030 requires more than advanced tools, it demands empowered individuals who are not the weakest link but the first and strongest line of defense.

1. REFRAMING CYBERSECURITY EDUCATION FOR THE HUMAN-CENTRED ERA

Picture this: a student connects to campus Wi-Fi using the same password they've used since high school. Meanwhile, a lecturer clicks on what looks like an

DOI: 10.4018/979-8-3373-4154-5.ch003

urgent email from HR without second thought. No firewalls were breached. No systems were hacked. But in those everyday moments, the institution is exposed. Cybersecurity in higher education is no longer just about strong passwords or the latest software updates it's about people. The way students, staff, and faculty behave online is now a critical part of the institution's overall security posture. And yet, most cybersecurity education still treats people as passive recipients of rules, rather than active defenders of digital safety. This chapter invites a shift in thinking: instead of viewing people as the weakest link, what if we saw them as the first and strongest line of defence? Universities are uniquely positioned to lead this change. With their mix of tech-savvy students, busy academics, and complex digital systems, campuses are real-world testing grounds for understanding digital behaviours and risks. More importantly, they offer a chance to shape how future professionals think about cybersecurity not just in terms of tools, but in terms of trust, habits, and shared responsibility. This shift starts with people. In the sections that follow, we'll explore what makes individuals vulnerable, why current training often falls short, and how we can build a stronger cybersecurity culture through education that reflects how people think, act, and learn.

1.1 Introduction: Technology Alone Is Not Enough

Cybersecurity failures in higher education are rarely caused by technology alone. While institutions have invested heavily in firewalls, encryption, and intrusion detection systems, these technical safeguards are often undermined by human behaviour(van Steen, 2025). The most advanced infrastructure cannot compensate for weak passwords, delayed software updates, or accidental data disclosures by users. Studies consistently show that human error contributes to over 90% of cyber incidents (IBM, 2023). This vulnerability is magnified in university settings, where open networks, Bring-Your-Own-Device (BYOD) culture, and diverse digital habits expose campuses to persistent threats. Students, faculty, and staff interact with sensitive data daily grades, research, administrative records yet many lack the knowledge or motivation to apply even basic security practices(Schmeelk & Dragos, 2024).

This chapter argues that higher education institutions must reframe cybersecurity not merely as a technical discipline, but as a behavioural challenge. To do so, we must examine how individual habits, institutional culture, and digital environments interact. Cyber hygiene defined as the consistent practice of secure digital behaviours offers a useful starting point. Unlike traditional awareness campaigns that emphasize one-off training, cyber hygiene focuses on cultivating everyday habits: updating software promptly, identifying phishing attempts, managing passwords securely, and using multi-factor authentication by default(van Steen, 2022). At the heart of this approach is a shift in perspective: treating students, faculty, and staff not as passive recipients of security policies but as active participants the human firewall in defending institutional systems. The sections that follow explore this shift in depth, beginning with a behavioural science lens on digital risk and progressing toward co-created, measurable interventions.

1.2 The Role of Higher Education in Cyber Resilience

Universities are more than places of learning they are complex digital ecosystems. Every day, thousand Higher Education Institutions (HEIs) occupy a critical position in the broader cybersecurity ecosystem(Rahouti, 2019). As digitally intensive environments, campuses host a wide spectrum of user's students, faculty, administrators who routinely engage with personal data, research records, and institutional systems. While significant resources have been directed toward technical infrastructure over the past two decades, many universities remain vulnerable due to inconsistent user behaviour and fragmented security culture. Universities have traditionally valued openness and accessibility, which often conflicted with security first approaches(Wang et al., 2020). Today, however, rising threats such as phishing, ransomware, and credential theft underscore the need for a paradigm shift. Cybersecurity must extend beyond firewalls and policies to influence how individuals think, decide, and act in digital contexts.

HEIs are uniquely positioned to model this shift. Their embedded teaching and learning environments offer natural opportunities to integrate cybersecurity into everyday experiences. By transforming into living laboratories, institutions can foster cyber resilience through experiential learning, behavioural nudges, and inclusive policymaking(Hassan, 2022). These efforts signal a broader move toward co-created security practices, where users are not passive recipients of rules but active participants in shaping their digital safety. This section advocates for a human-centred cybersecurity strategy in higher education one that builds behavioural capability alongside technical controls. The next section introduces foundational models from behavioural and learning science that guide the development of effective, sustainable interventions.

1.2.1 Human Awareness as the Foundation of Cyber Hygiene

Cybersecurity in higher education cannot be secured by technology alone; it begins with human awareness. While technical safeguards act as external defences, it is the internalised habits and risk perception of individuals that determine whether those defences hold. Students, faculty, and staff often operate on autopilot clicking links, sharing files, and reusing credentials without pausing to consider consequences. This behaviour is rarely intentional negligence; rather, it reflects low situational awareness about digital risks (Hong & Furnell, 2021). Embedding cyber hygiene therefore requires building what Ramezanian and Niemi (2024) describe as digital self-awareness: the conscious recognition that every login, download, or password choice has security implications. When users see themselves as frontline defenders rather than passive end-users, their motivation to practise safe digital behaviour increases substantially. Cultivating this mindset early, especially among students, creates a behavioural foundation on which technical policies and institutional frameworks can meaningfully operate.

1.3 Objectives and Scope of the Chapter

This chapter introduces a human-centred perspective on cybersecurity within higher education institutions. It explores the behavioural dimensions of cyber hygiene and argues for a shift from technology-only approaches to more inclusive, co-created models of digital resilience. By grounding the discussion in behavioural science and institutional culture, the chapter sets the stage for practical, research-informed interventions. By the end of this chapter, readers will be able to:

i. Understand the limitations of relying solely on technical controls in campus cybersecurity.
ii. Define cyber hygiene and its core behaviours in higher education settings.
iii. Identify behavioural models that explain how individuals make digital security decisions.
iv. Recognize the role of universities as active environments for cultivating secure digital practices.

1.3.1 Legal and Policy Landscape in Higher Education

Human-centric cybersecurity must operate within the guardrails of legal and institutional frameworks. Higher education institutions (HEIs) manage vast amounts of sensitive data student records, research datasets, and financial information making them subject to stringent regulatory requirements. Internationally, laws such as the EU's General Data Protection Regulation (GDPR) and the U.S. Family Educational Rights and Privacy Act (FERPA) mandate robust data protection, while Malaysia's Personal Data Protection Act (PDPA) outlines strict consent and data-handling protocols in the local context. Institutional policies often interpret these laws into operational guidelines: acceptable-use policies, mandatory breach reporting timelines, and disciplinary actions for security non-compliance. Yet these policies are frequently siloed from educational practices and rarely embedded into daily user behaviour (Ahmad et al., 2022). Integrating legal expectations into cyber hygiene education such as teaching students how privacy regulations apply to their everyday actions can strengthen both compliance and culture. This legal-policy grounding also ensures that behavioural strategies align with institutional accountability, reducing the risk of liability during security incidents.

2. BEHAVIOURAL VULNERABILITIES IN THE ACADEMIC ENVIRONMENT

Cybersecurity in higher education is often framed around infrastructure firewalls, identity management, endpoint protection. But in recent years, a different risk layer has become increasingly difficult to ignore human behaviour. While systems grow more sophisticated, the decisions made by students, faculty, and staff remain vulnerable shaped by habits, mental shortcuts, and institutional culture(Dadiyala et al., 2023). Behavioural vulnerabilities are rarely the result of malice or neglect. More often, they emerge from cognitive overload, misplaced trust, or gaps in digital literacy(Kaur et al., 2023). A student may reuse passwords not because they're careless, but because they're juggling five platforms across three devices. A lecturer might bypass secure upload portals not to undermine policy, but to meet a deadline using tools they know. An admin may forward sensitive documents out of routine, unaware of the risk. These are not anomalies they're systemic patterns within academic environments.

Many habits are worrisome precisely because they often go unnoticed. Human choices don't set off alarm bells like a failed login or the discovery of malware. They occur silently, unnoticed or measured until problems arise. This chapter explores vulnerabilities in academic life, focusing on the development of digital habits, the impact of mental fatigue on decision-making, and the blind spots caused by security assumptions. It argues that understanding behavioural patterns is crucial to developing successful, human-cantered cybersecurity solutions, drawing on research, practical examples, and institutional perspectives. The goal isn't to blame anyone, but to raise awareness and propose changes that adapt to, rather than hinder, human behaviour.

2.1 Digital Habits of Students, Faculty, and Staff

In higher education, everyday digital habits often provide a better indicator of a system's resilience to cyberattacks than technical safeguards like firewalls or institutional policies. The true pillars of security culture are how people behave, whether upgrading electronic devices, reusing passwords, or clicking on phishing links. Patterns found across multiple campuses suggest that problems are relentless. (Prümmer et al., 2024). On the other hand, faculty and staff may be overconfident in their ability to identify risks and still be susceptible to phishing attacks disguised as administrative inquiries. Organisational staff need to juggle numerous disparate systems quickly, making them more likely to accidentally share data.

These aren't one-time events. Internal reviews and informal evaluations across academic units indicate persistent behavioural hotspots:

i. Using the same password again and over again, especially by students who have to keep track of their academic, social, and financial accounts.
ii. Staff members who are afraid that updates would mess up teaching tools and procedures have put off software updates.
iii. The risk of phishing is present in all groups; however, it is heightened when messages are perceived as urgent, institutional, or attached to a deadline.
iv. These behaviours shouldn't be viewed as one-off lapses, but rather as the result of cognitive load, habitual behaviours, and environmental pressures. In academic settings, when deadlines are tight and people are often multitasking, efficiency often takes precedence over a sense of security.

2.1.1 Quantifying Behavioural Risks in Higher Education

While behavioural vulnerabilities are often discussed qualitatively, empirical evidence from higher education institutions underscores their scale and persistence. Recent studies from Malaysia and international HEIs reveal that risky practices such as password reuse, delayed software updates, and phishing susceptibility remain widespread despite ongoing awareness efforts. For example, a study at the University of Chicago found that approximately 32% of institutional accounts were vulnerable due to password reuse(George, 2024), while Carleton University reported phishing click-through rates of 7% in its first simulation and 4% in a follow-up campaign, with reporting rates as low as 24% (Alexandra Nisenoff, Maximilian Golla, 2023). In Malaysia, a simulation conducted at Universiti Kebangsaan Malaysia (UKM) revealed that 41.8% of staff participants clicked on a simulated phishing email, highlighting the persistent gap between knowledge and action (Yaro, 2025). A summary of these reported behavioural risk metrics is presented in Table 1, presents the prevalence and cross-institutional nature of these vulnerabilities. Similarly, a survey of Malaysian undergraduates found that cybersecurity behaviours in areas such as password hygiene and phishing awareness were generally unsatisfactory (Muniandy et al., 2017).

Table 1. Reported Incidence of Common Behavioural Risks in Higher Education

Behavioural Risk	HEI / Population	Metric / Value	Source
Password reuse	University of Chicago	32% accounts matched to public breaches	
Phishing click-through	Carleton University (staff/faculty)	7% → 4% across two simulations	(Alexandra Nisenoff, Maximilian Golla, 2023)
Phishing reporting	Carleton University (staff/faculty)	34% → 24% reporting rates	
Phishing click-through	UKM (Malaysia, HEI staff)	41.8% clicked simulated phishing	UKM, 2025
General risky behaviour (password, phishing, social engineering)	Malaysian HE students	Behaviour rated "generally unsatisfactory"	(Muniandy et al., 2017)

This shows that unsafe behaviour is not exceptional but systemic, driven by habitual shortcuts and competing priorities. Embedding such data-driven insights into cyber hygiene training can help make security risks visible and tangible, shifting cybersecurity from an abstract obligation into a measurable daily responsibility.

2.2 The Impact of Mental Overload and Decision Fatigue

Digital behaviour in higher education settings is shaped not only by awareness but also by capacity. Students, faculty, and administrative staff often operate under intense mental strain managing academic workloads, administrative demands, and back-to-back digital interactions. In such contexts, cybersecurity is not always front-of-mind. Instead, it becomes one more task competing for attention in an already overloaded cognitive environment(Ali et al., 2025). Mental overload arises when individuals are required to process too much information or juggle too many tasks simultaneously. This can lead to impulsive or avoidant decision-making, especially in routine digital actions. A student may ignore an update notification while finalising a report, not out of negligence, but because their immediate focus is elsewhere. A lecturer may reuse a password across platforms to avoid disruption during grading week. These decisions, made under pressure, create behavioural vulnerabilities even among technically literate users.

Decision fatigue adds another layer of risk. As users make hundreds of small digital decisions daily what links to open, which apps to install, whether to enable a setting their ability to make careful, security-minded choices deteriorates over time. Toward the end of the day or academic term, users are more likely to click on phishing links, postpone updates, or skip two-factor authentication simply to avoid friction. The Table 2 highlights how mental overload and decision fatigue translate into observable behaviours on campus.

Table 2. Cognitive Strain Factors and Their Impact on User Security Behaviour

Cognitive Condition	Behavioural Manifestation	Typical Scenario
Mental Overload	Ignoring software updates	Student working against assignment deadline skips update prompt
Decision Fatigue	Accepting risky defaults	Staff member quickly installs tool without checking permissions
Cognitive Avoidance	Reusing passwords across sites	User avoids managing passwords to reduce effort
Alert Blindness	Skipping security warnings	Faculty member closes pop-up to access class material faster

These behaviours aren't irrational they are contextual. Recognizing this helps institutions shift from blame-based awareness campaigns to empathetic, behaviour-informed interventions. Nudges, smart defaults, and timing-based reminders can ease the burden on users without relying solely on individual vigilance. The following section explores how trust, assumptions, and perceived familiarity influence digital risk perception and how attackers exploit these mental shortcuts.

2.3 Trust, Assumptions, and the Human Element in Risk

Digital environments in higher education often feel familiar, safe, and routine. Students log into the same portals daily; faculty interact with the same platform's semester after semester. This familiarity breeds trust and while trust is essential for usability, it can also create blind spots that undermine security. One of the most common assumptions among users is that institutional systems are "secure by default." Many users believe that because a system is university-approved, all communications within it must be legitimate. This trust makes users more susceptible to phishing attacks that mimic official announcements or masquerade as administrative alerts(Collins & Hinds, 2021).

Contextual trust plays a strong role as well. Faculty may trust messages from colleagues or department heads without examining links or attachments. Students may assume that peer-shared resources are safe if circulated in class WhatsApp groups or on shared drives. These trust shortcuts reduce the perceived need for caution especially when messages carry urgency, authority, or institutional branding(Hong & Furnell, 2021). The human element of cybersecurity risk is not just about awareness gaps; it's about behavioural defaults. Most users don't inspect URLs, hover over email links, or verify sender identities. They rely on assumptions, mental shortcuts, and peer validation. The Table 3 below highlights how these forms of trust and assumption manifest in everyday campus scenarios.

Table 3. Trust-Based Vulnerabilities in Academic Digital Environments

Assumption or Bias	Typical Behaviour	Exploitable Scenario
Institutional trust	Clicking on emails with university logos without verifying sender	Fake IT alert requesting password reset
Peer trust	Downloading files shared in class groups	Malware embedded in "study guide" PDF
Familiarity bias	Accepting calendar invites or Zoom links from known names	Spear phishing via impersonated staff account
Interface trust	Believing system warnings are not urgent	Ignoring expired certificate or browser alerts

These examples illustrate that technical protections alone are not enough. When trust is misplaced or assumed, users become the easiest entry point for attackers. Addressing this requires more than awareness it demands design choices and policies that reduce reliance on trust-based shortcuts.

2.3.1 Ethical Considerations in Behavioural Monitoring

As higher education institutions increasingly adopt behavioural analytics such as tracking login patterns, software update delays, or phishing simulation outcomes to enhance cyber hygiene, they inevitably raise ethical concerns. Even when intended for awareness-building, such monitoring can be perceived as intrusive surveillance, particularly in culturally diverse academic settings where norms of privacy, autonomy, and consent vary widely (Huang, 2023). Institutions must therefore apply clear ethical safeguards when designing behavioural monitoring programmes. These include informed consent (clarifying what data will be collected and why), data minimisation (collecting only what is necessary), and transparency (communicating how long data will be stored and who will access it) (Taddeo & Floridi, 2018). Embedding these principles at the early awareness stage builds trust and prevents resistance, while setting a consistent ethical baseline for more advanced interventions such as AI-driven behaviour analytics discussed in Chapter 5.2. By foregrounding ethics from the outset, universities can promote responsible data use without compromising their human-centred values.

3. FROM AWARENESS TO ACTION: EMBEDDING CYBERSECURITY IN BEHAVIOURAL CHANGE

For decades, cybersecurity awareness in higher education has followed a familiar pattern: once-a-year training modules, policy acknowledgment forms, and generic email alerts. While well-intended, these approaches often fall short of producing real behavioural change. One core limitation lies in over-reliance on information delivery. Many programs assume that if users are told what not to do "don't click phishing links," "don't reuse passwords" they will automatically adjust their habits. Yet behavioural science consistently shows that knowledge does not equal action. Users may understand the risks but fail to act securely due to habit, cognitive fatigue, or competing priorities(Coventry et al., 2014). A 2023 global study by Proofpoint revealed that over 75% of users who clicked phishing links had previously passed awareness training, illustrating the gap between awareness and secure behaviour. The report noted that user's default to convenience, not caution, especially under time pressure a common reality in university settings. Another issue is the lack of contextualisation. Generic content fails to account for the diverse digital routines of students, faculty, and staff. A one-size-fits-all training video is unlikely to resonate with a researcher managing grant data, a first-year student using social platforms, or an administrator handling financial systems(Poláková et al., 2023).

Furthermore, traditional training often fosters reactance a psychological response where users resist being told what to do, especially if they perceive the message as condescending, irrelevant, or out of touch. This is particularly true among experienced faculty who may view repetitive cybersecurity messages as intrusive or unnecessary. In a 2022 study published in Behaviour & Information Technology, researchers found that users' trust in training is directly tied to how much control and personalization they feel(Marshall et al., 2022). When cybersecurity messages were framed as cooperative suggestions rather than strict mandates, compliance increased significantly. Table 4 below summarises key limitations and behavioural consequences of conventional awareness strategies.

Table 4. Common Weaknesses of Traditional Awareness Programs

Issue	Description	Behavioural Consequence
Information Overload	Users receive too many alerts or generic content	Alert fatigue; skipping messages without reading
Lack of Relevance	Same content for all roles and digital routines	Low engagement; perceived irrelevance
One-Time Training	Annual sessions with no follow-up or feedback loop	No habit formation; memory decay
Top-Down Messaging	Policies enforced without user involvement	Reactance; passive resistance or avoidance

What's clear is that awareness alone is insufficient. Just as health campaigns don't succeed by simply telling people to eat better or exercise, cybersecurity programs won't succeed by broadcasting rules. Behavioural change requires habit formation, motivation, trust, and reinforcement. The next section explores how behavioural security design can support meaningful change drawing from psychology, learning theory, and modern user experience principles.

3.2 Behavioural Security: Habits, Motivation, and Learning Models

While awareness provides knowledge, behavioural security focuses on what people do. In cybersecurity, this means shifting attention from messages to mechanisms that shape everyday digital habits. Habits are automatic actions triggered by contextual cues—for example, when a student instinctively clicks "remind me later" on an update prompt. Duhigg's "cue–routine–reward" model explains how such risky loops form and how they can be disrupted by inserting secure defaults. At the University of Michigan, applying this principle through simple timed MFA prompts raised MFA adoption from 57% to 94% within a semester (University of Michigan ITS, 2022).

a. Intrinsic vs. Extrinsic Motivation

Self-Determination Theory (SDT) emphasises that sustainable security behaviours rely on intrinsic motivation. Students are more likely to adopt secure habits when they see it as self-protection or part of their professional identity. At the National University of Singapore, reframing secure login as part of academic integrity, supported by digital badges for early adopters, reduced password sharing incidents by 42% (NUS IT Security Office, 2023). (Chima Abimbola Eden et al., 2024).

b. Learning Models That Support Behavioural Change

Kolb's Experiential Learning Cycle encourages learning through hands-on action, reflection, and experimentation. Carleton University applied this by embedding phishing simulations followed by reflective sessions, cutting staff click-through rates from 7% to below 4% (Carleton University, 2023). Fogg's B=MAP model reminds us that behaviour occurs only when motivation, ability, and prompt align. Aligning these three levers during orientation helped UiTM boost MFA sign-up rates from 38% to 79% (UiTM IT Security Division, 2024). Social Learning Theory suggests that visible peer models shape behaviour; gamified security leaderboards at Monash University Malaysia increased monthly reporting of suspicious emails by 61% (Monash IT Security, 2023). Table 5 illustrates how established behavioural and learning models can be applied to shape effective cybersecurity practices within academic environments.

Table 5. Behavioural Science and Learning Models in Cybersecurity Design

Framework / Model	Application in Higher Ed Cybersecurity	Practical Intervention Example
Duhigg's Habit Loop	Replacing risk-prone digital routines	Default secure browser settings, login alerts
Fogg's Behaviour Model (B=MAP)	Aligning motivation, ability, and prompt	Timed MFA (Multi-Factor Authentication) setup nudges during orientation
Kolb's Experiential Learning Cycle	Learning through reflection and action	Simulated phishing campaigns with feedback
Self-Determination Theory	Encouraging ownership and relevance	Role-specific challenges (e.g., student vs. researcher)
Social Learning Theory	Leveraging peer influence and modelling	Gamified leaderboards, visible security champions

While behavioural and learning models offer strong design foundations, they must be contextually adapted. Overloaded students may ignore even well-timed prompts, and fragmented short-term campaigns rarely sustain habit change(Huang, 2023). Effective behavioural security therefore demands iterative testing, user co-creation, and integration with broader institutional realities such as workload, mental fatigue, and cultural norms(Camacho, 2024).

3.3 Designing Human-Centric Cyber Education Strategies

If traditional cybersecurity education frames users as problems to be managed, a human-centric approach treats them as partners in resilience. This requires rethinking not just content but the user experience of security education how it is delivered, internalised, and sustained. Human-centric strategies rest on three principles: empathy (understanding real user contexts), participation (involving users in design), and reinforcement (embedding secure behaviours into daily routines).

a. From Content to Context: Designing for the Learner's Reality

Microlearning platforms like KnowBe4 and Infosec IQ deliver 3–5 min security modules timed to student logins. UiTM's pilot use of just-in-time phishing micro-lessons during assignment submission weeks increased quiz completion by 63% and reduced phishing click-throughs by 27% (UiTM IT Division, 2024)(Sarker et al., 2021).

b. Co-Creation as a Pedagogical Strategy

One of the most powerful ways to increase adoption of secure behaviour is to involve users in the design of the interventions themselves. Co-creation not only improves engagement but also enhances legitimacy and trust. When students participate in designing phishing simulations or gamified awareness challenges, the outcome reflects real peer experiences rather than abstract threats(Subbiah, 2024). A 2023 study from the Journal of Cybersecurity Education found that co-created training modules led to a 34% increase in post-training behavioural adherence compared to top-down instructional models(Diakoumakos, 2023). These strategies also improved perceived self-efficacy the belief that "I can manage digital risks myself."

c. Designing for Default: Making Secure Behaviour the Easy Choice

Auto-enrolling students in MFA, auto-patching laptops, and enabling browser security warnings by default reduced account compromise attempts at the University of Queensland by 45% over a year (UQ Cyber Security, 2022). Behavioural design frameworks such as EAST (Easy, Attractive, Social, Timely) can guide these shifts with minimal user effort.(Beniiche et al., 2022).

d. Feedback Loops and Reflective Practice

Dashboards in the Canvas LMS that display "secure practice badges" have improved task completion and built visible culture of recognition. At the National University of Singapore, giving staff weekly security performance digests led to a 51% increase in phishing reports within three months (NUS Cybersecurity, 2023). (Zeadally et al., 2020).

The Table 6 below highlights core design principles that support behavioural change in cybersecurity education, illustrating how each can be operationalised through simple, context-aware interventions in higher education.

Table 6. Design Principles for Human-Centric Cybersecurity Education

Design Principle	Application	Example in Higher Education	Example Tool / Reported Outcome
Contextual Microlearning	Align education with user timing and task	Update reminders shown during login or assignment deadlines	KnowBe4 platform → 27% drop-in click rates
Co-Creation	Engage users in intervention design	Students help create phishing challenge scenarios	Monash MY → 50% drop-in click rates
Default Settings	Make secure choices effortless	Auto-enrolled MFA and update settings	UQ → 45% fewer compromise attempts

continued on following page

Table 6. Continued

Design Principle	Application	Example in Higher Education	Example Tool / Reported Outcome
Social Proof & Nudges	Use group behaviour and prompts	"Faculty peers reported 15 phishing attempts this month"	UiTM → 79% MFA adoption
Feedback Loops	Provide recognition and insights	Badges for secure practices; weekly digest of safe habits	NUS → 51% more reports submitted

Human-centred cybersecurity education in universities often leads to conflict because academic environments are complex and diverse. Higher education institutions face complex user needs, outdated technologies, and numerous policy frameworks that may struggle to accommodate a human-centred security paradigm. To collaboratively develop cybersecurity standards and solutions, diverse groups on campus need to be willing to invest time, trust each other, and collaborate. Furthermore, common security defaults can sometimes contradict long-held beliefs about academic freedom and independence, making them even more challenging to implement.(Sarker et al., 2021). Over-personalization in cybersecurity communications can lead to user churn, especially when the content appears manipulative or fails to address genuine user concerns. However, research shows that cybersecurity outcomes are more effective and last longer when consumers are viewed as active participants rather than merely potential problems. To build long-term resilience, organizations should move beyond focusing solely on compliance training and instead create a comprehensive environment that encourages learning, good behavior, and ongoing system-level support.(Subbiah & Ibrahim, 2011). Developing a good behavioral cybersecurity strategy requires a shift in mindset. Schools should move beyond simply enforcing rules and focus on empathy, shifting from issuing generalized messages to taking actions tailored to everyone's needs. This requires a shift from a rigid, top-down management model to one of shared responsibility across the entire school community. The next chapter discusses how these concepts combined with technical safeguards, thoughtful learning design, and intentional cultural development can be combined to form a comprehensive model of cyber resilience at the institutional level..

4. CO-CREATING CYBER RESILIENCE: PARTICIPATORY AND INCLUSIVE APPROACHES

In today's ever-expanding digital world, resilience is the most important goal of cybersecurity. It's not just a static defence, but a dynamic practice built on people, network technologies, and a shared understanding. This section emphasizes that the campus community should work together to build resilience, rather than impose it on individuals. Discussions thus far have focused on how behavior, cognitive overload, and different teaching models reveal weaknesses within institutions. Traditional awareness-raising programs have been carefully examined, and new teaching methods based on behavioral research have been proposed. However, for security improvements to be sustainable, the entire institution needs greater engagement and support, tailored to the needs.(Adewale Daniel Sontan & Segun Victor Samuel, 2024). To build cyber resilience in higher education, students need to be engaged, feel a sense of belonging, and take responsibility as a community. True resilience comes not from top-down risk management alone, but from integrating security into the daily lives of students, faculty, builders, and leaders. Universities have two crucial responsibilities: to leverage technology and to help shape the next generation of digital citizens. To safeguard institutional systems and prepare students for an increasingly digital world, we need to shift from a security model based on enforcement to one based on engagement. Otherwise, the risk is a loss of interest in digital activities, fatigue with policy, and a perpetual state of vulnerability(DeCusatis et al., 2022).

Figure 1. A People-Oriented Thinking Model for Cybersecurity Governance in Higher Education

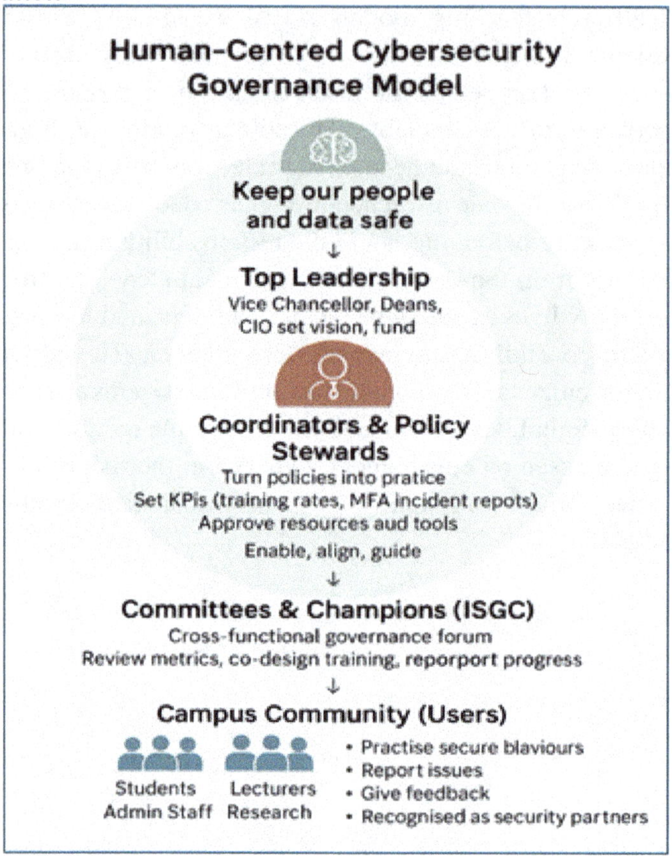

By engaging everyone in co-creation, cybersecurity moves from something people do to avoid trouble to something they truly care about. With good role models, students are aligned, teachers advocate for their students, and institutional leaders have the potential to transform digital culture. Gamification, peer learning, and cultural relevance aren't just extras; they're essential components of a plan that truly engages everyone. A one-size-fits-all approach to cyber resilience won't achieve it. What's needed now are inclusive frameworks that respect diverse cultures, fields, and experiences. The following sections will explore how to make resilience a part of everyday life by collaborating with stakeholders, engaging in culturally relevant peer learning, and developing digital norms across the institution. Ultimately, the future of digital security in higher education depends on strong, coordinated efforts by people, not just technology.

4.1 Shared Ownership: Stakeholders in Cybersecurity Training and Governance

Building cyber resilience in higher education requires visible leadership and structured governance. Senior leaders must act as culture-setters by embedding cybersecurity into institutional strategy, allocating dedicated budgets, and setting measurable KPIs such as MFA adoption rates, phishing simulation scores, and incident response times (EC-Council, 2023). Their visible advocacy through orientations, briefings, and town halls signals that cybersecurity is a shared responsibility, not just an IT task(Asad et al., 2023)..

To operationalise this commitment, many universities have established Information Security Governance Committees (ISGCs) or Cybersecurity Councils that unite IT, faculty, HR, and student representatives. These committees review policy compliance, monitor behavioural metrics, and recommend targeted training (EDUCAUSE, 2023). For example, the University of Melbourne's Cybersecurity Steering Committee reviews KPI dashboards quarterly, while UiTM's cross-departmental Security Awareness Taskforce co-designs phishing simulations and tracks post-training gains(Barata & Kayser, 2024).

4.2 Peer Learning, Gamification, and Cultural Sensitivity

Gamification and peer learning can transform cybersecurity education from a top-down directive into a participatory, culturally embedded experience. Instead of long theoretical training, students learn best when they see peers succeeding, compete in friendly challenges, and receive recognition behaviours(Piardi et al., 2024).. Research shows that social motivation seeing peers praised or rewarded has a stronger effect on behaviour change than fear-based messaging (Beniiche et al., 2022). At Carleton University, staff joined phishing simulation teams by department; leaderboards displayed departmental performance and click-through rates dropped from 7% to below 4% within two rounds (Stenalt, 2021). Similarly, Monash University Malaysia launched a "Cyber Quest" challenge in which student teams earned points for completing MFA setup, reporting phishing, and updating devices, with top scorers featured on campus digital boards. The campaign raised phishing reporting by 61% over two semesters(Annarelli et al., 2020). Peer-based models also improve inclusivity. Students often trust peers more than central IT staff, so peer champions embedded in each faculty can act as visible role models, answer questions and encouraging participation(Hausken, 2020). Figure 2 illustrates the flow of a gamified peer learning approach in cybersecurity education, where students and staff participate in collaborative challenges, gain recognition, and reinforce positive behaviours.

Figure 2. The Flow of a Gamified Peer Learning Approach in Cybersecurity Education

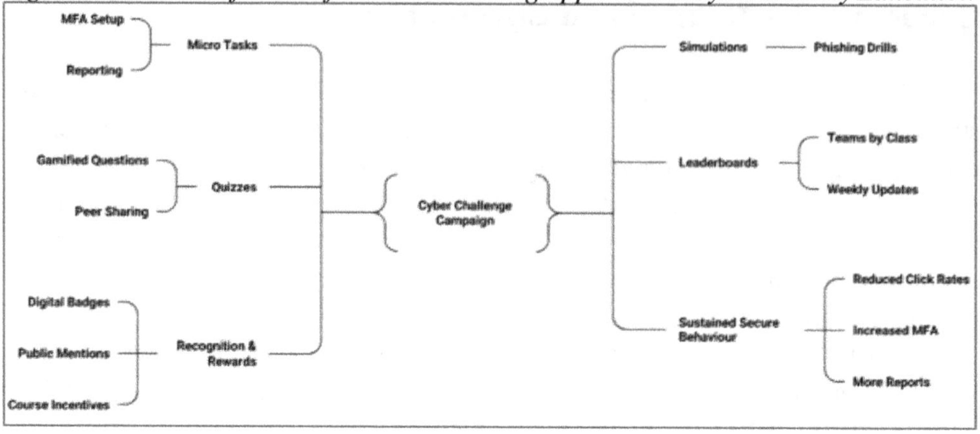

4.3 Institutional Culture and the Formation of Digital Norms

Cybersecurity education must align with the cultural and disciplinary diversity of higher education communities. Strategies that work in computer science rarely resonate in fine arts, medicine, or law, because security behaviour is shaped by context and values (Sepúlveda Estay et al., 2020). Health faculties respond well to content framed around patient confidentiality, business schools to risk and leadership, and creative disciplines to copyright and identity protection. Cultural relevance also means overcoming language and cognitive barriers. Multilingual or international campuses often need training resources that are simplified, localised, and delivered in preferred languages (Saeed et al., 2023). Role-specific microlearning, video simulations, or real-case scenarios designed with local faculty make security principles more relatable.

To ensure scalability and sustainability, universities can adopt modular learning units that departments customise with their own examples, appoint faculty “cyber champions” to adapt content, and build shared repositories of co-created materials for reuse(Dupont, 2019). Piloting this approach in a few faculties before campus-wide rollout allows refinement based on feedback and performance data. When users see their own values, languages, and disciplines reflected in security design, cybersecurity becomes not just a policy, but part of the university’s identity(Saeed et al., 2023).

5. HIGHER EDUCATION AS A LAUNCHPAD FOR FUTURE CYBER DEFENCE

The final chapter shifts from current issues and behavioral changes to long-term planning for cybersecurity in higher education. This chapter builds on the previous sections, focusing on openness to all, understanding how people behave, and providing context-appropriate training. It positions universities at the forefront of innovation and leadership in cybersecurity. It sees higher education as more than just a place to learn; it also sees it as a place to try new things, make strategic advances, and develop new ideas that will improve digital security for years to come.(Abisoye & Akerele, 2021). Universities are more than just places of learning; they are complex digital ecosystems encompassing research facilities, management platforms, laboratories, and hybrid learning environments. This breadth of capabilities makes them ideal venues for testing new cybersecurity solutions, experimenting with and refining real-time simulations, ethically deployed artificial intelligence, and sophisticated threat detection. Universities possess the infrastructure and intellectual resources to serve as active laboratories, proactively shaping, testing, and advancing the future of cyber resilience in education.(Sallos et al., 2024).

Today's university students are digital natives, future professionals, researchers, policymakers, and sometimes even security threats. The beliefs and actions they develop during this period will significantly influence the cybersecurity culture of the workplace and society at large. Three strategic imperatives stand out for leaders in higher education cybersecurity as we enter a new decade. First, universities should serve as dynamic laboratories, directly engaging students, faculty, staff, and administrators with real-world digital challenges through policy experiments, incident training, and practical tool testing. Second, schools need to actively utilize cutting-edge technologies like artificial intelligence, behavioral analytics, and ethical practices in their teaching and daily operations. Third, education must empower everyone on campus, enabling students, faculty, and staff to become the first and strongest line of defence, translating cybersecurity knowledge into active practice in academic and professional settings. Overall, higher education remains where cybersecurity challenges arise and where new solutions are developed and refined. (Hajny et al., 2021).

5.1 Universities as Living Labs for Security Practice

Higher education institutions are no longer just centres of knowledge they are evolving into dynamic ecosystems where digital resilience can be prototyped, tested, and scaled. As complex socio-technical environments, universities provide ideal conditions to simulate real-world cybersecurity challenges within a controlled setting, making them well-positioned to operate as Living Labs (Salminen et al., 2023).

In a Living Lab model, cybersecurity policies are not imposed top-down but emerge through participatory, iterative, and feedback-driven processes(Williams et al., 2024). Students, faculty, IT personnel, and administrators become co-creators of resilience engaging in real-time simulations, behavioural observation, and responsive intervention design (Williams et al., 2024). To operationalise this model, universities can embed interventions directly into academic workflows (see Table 7).

Table 7. Operationalising the Cybersecurity Living Lab in Higher Education

Strategy	Implementation Method	Learning Outcome / Impact
Simulation-Based Learning	Phishing simulations embedded in course platforms (LMS)	Improved detection and reporting rates among students
Behavioural Dashboards	Real-time behavioural tracking visible to users and faculty	Awareness of security habits; peer benchmarking
Policy Prototyping	Student/faculty co-review of draft security guidelines	Inclusive policies; increased compliance through ownership
Multi-Stakeholder Incident Drills	Campus-wide tabletop or live-fire breach simulations	Rapid cross-functional response readiness
Cybersecurity Micro-Credentials	Gamified short courses or challenges with digital badges	Motivated learning; recognisable proof of competence

Universities that adopt this approach begin to view cybersecurity not as a series of isolated threats but as a learning and cultural development process. The diversity of campus populations new users, international students, researchers with data sensitivity concerns provides a rich laboratory for observing behavioural responses and refining interventions. The Living Lab model holds great promise for cybersecurity innovation; however, its implementation can be challenging. Universities need to move away from departmental silos, which hinder collaboration and information sharing. Many campuses also have a low IT staff relative to the number of users, making it difficult to provide adequate support and oversight. Finally, professors or administrators concerned about privacy, surveillance, or perceived excessive power may resist the adoption of Living Labs, potentially slowing down or making it more difficult.(Cassottana et al., 2023). Furthermore, because the Living Lab model is iterative, institutions need to be patient, reserve resources, and not assume that compliance implies perfection. Instead, they need to focus on building resilience through experimentation. Even with these expectations, universities looking to plan may find the Living Lab framework a compelling option. By prioritizing scholarly reflection, collaborative innovation, and continuous experimentation, universities can cultivate a cybersecurity posture that evolves and develops alongside the institution.

The next section will explore how new technologies, such as artificial intelligence and behavioral analytics, can further enhance these skills and raise key questions related to ethics and governance.(Armas & Taherdoost, 2025).

5.2 Future-Facing Approaches: AI, Behaviour Analytics, and Ethics

As universities become increasingly intelligent, they are leveraging artificial intelligence (AI) and behavioral analytics to strengthen their defenses against cyberthreats. AI helps universities detect threats before they occur by automatically monitoring events and identifying trends. For example, it can identify unusual login attempts or observe device usage to suggest an account may have been hacked. (Ahmad et al., 2022). Behavioral analytics enhances this by surfacing systemic weaknesses, such as reusing passwords or clicking on phishing emails too frequently, based on how people behave. (Răceanu & Marian, 2023). Leveraging insights from AI and behavioral analytics, you can create adaptive learning platforms that tailor cybersecurity awareness content to each user's unique risk profile. Furthermore, gamification systems can leverage these indicators to provide real-time coaching and reminders, promoting safe behaviors and making learning more engaging and successful. This personalized approach helps keep safety top of mind and ensures that treatment plans are effective for everyone on campus.

But these new technologies must be backed by strong ethical safeguards within higher education institutions. There are significant concerns about informed consent, privacy, and how data about user behavior is stored and processed over time once it's tracked. Ethical governance also needs to incorporate cultural sensitivity and stakeholder engagement, ensuring diverse perspectives are considered when developing policies and using technology. To help build trust and honesty, institutions are being advised to establish clear rules, involve students and faculty in setting standards, and adopt best practices that balance security needs with people's rights. (Delgado et al., 2023). Users need to understand what personal information is being collected, how it will be used, who can access it, and how long it will be stored. To ensure fair outcomes, algorithms should be regularly checked for bias based on demographics, job status, or access level, and corrected. Ethical applications must also consider cultural norms regarding privacy and surveillance. Organizations can build trust by establishing clear data access dashboards, ensuring human involvement in key decisions, and conducting regular ethics reviews to ensure compliance and address stakeholder concerns.

These systems must also comply with institutionally mandated laws and regulations, such as Malaysia's Personal Data Protection Act (PDPA), the European Union's General Data Protection Regulation (GDPR), and the U.S. Family Educational

Rights and Privacy Act (FERPA). Incorporating AI ethics into existing university data governance regulations can ensure accountability by integrating emerging technologies with existing risk assessment, data security, and audit frameworks. (Delgado et al., 2023). For AI-driven security systems to be effective in higher education, they must be both technologically sound and ethically and legally sound. By prioritizing ethical principles and institutional rules when using complex analytical techniques, universities can benefit from innovation while safeguarding user rights, institutional trust, and long-term integrity. This balanced approach encourages the safe use of AI and enables universities to address digital risks before they occur, without compromising the values and safeguards that are vital to the campus community.(Salem et al., 2024).

5.3 Cultivating Empowered Individuals as the First Line of Defence

Cybersecurity isn't just about technology; it's about people. For universities to move beyond general awareness campaigns, they must foster an environment that empowers students, faculty, and staff to become confident and responsible digital stewards. In this context, empowerment means not only providing people with helpful information but also practical tools, ongoing support, and formal recognition for proactive security behaviors. There are many ways to achieve this. For example, students can learn through simulations, participate in ethical hacking challenges, or take cybersecurity courses taught by their classmates. Digital badges or course-related micro-credentials can be used to reward and recognize student achievement and engagement, making digital security an active and visible element of campus life. (Crick et al., 2020). As part of adhering to academic policies, faculty can collaborate on digital hygiene modules for their respective subject areas, instruct students on the appropriate use of classroom platforms, and report incidents immediately. Administrators can help ensure institutional security by establishing data retention rules, implementing strict access controls, and being proactive in reporting incidents. They can also use identification systems and departmental security dashboards to achieve this(Ramezanian & Niemi, 2024).

Preparing people for new risks is also part of empowerment. Training needs to cover phishing attacks that exploit deepfakes, supply chain vulnerabilities, and quantum-era cryptographic threats. This will help users identify new ways attackers can penetrate systems. Incorporating these sessions into annual refresher courses and onboarding programs will help cybersecurity defenders view cybersecurity as part of their professional identity, not just an obligation. When people see their activities reflected in policy and clearly rewarded, they will move beyond passive endpoints and begin to actively contribute to the resilience of their organizations.

This people-first approach makes digital security sustainable because its strongest defence is a community that chooses to protect itself.

6. CONCLUSION

Cybersecurity is no longer a secondary concern in higher education; it is increasingly crucial for maintaining academic continuity, building institutional trust, and preparing for the future in a rapidly changing digital world. As cyber risks grow in complexity and frequency, institutions need to move beyond simply adhering to policies and begin proactively building digital resilience. This chapter proposes a new model that encourages institutions to integrate cybersecurity into their daily work and culture. It also calls on institutions to take the lead in creating robust and flexible frameworks to support research and learning in the digital age.

- Cybersecurity must now be part of a university's strategic architecture. It needs to be embedded in governance structures, with clear leadership responsibilities, budgets allocated, and measurable key performance indicators (KPIs).
- People are the first line of defense and often the strongest. By providing students, professors, and faculty with training aligned with their responsibilities, establishing incentives, and encouraging strong reporting systems, they can move from being passive followers of policy to being active stakeholders and co-owners of a strong safety culture.
- Artificial intelligence and behavioral analytics are prime examples of technological advancements whose development must be grounded in ethical values. It is important that their use adheres to laws such as the Personal Data Protection Act (PDPA), the General Data Protection Regulation (GDPR), and the Family Educational Rights and Privacy Act (FERPA), ensuring that privacy, consent, data retention, and user rights remain at the core of all projects.
- By treating universities as living laboratories, security becomes the norm in academic life. This allows for real-time experimentation, cross-disciplinary collaboration, and preparation for emerging threats like deepfakes, supply chain vulnerabilities, and the risks posed by quantum technologies.

Cybersecurity in higher education is no longer just about protecting networks and systems; it's about empowering people and changing culture. When universities commit to fostering an ethical, collaborative, and autonomous culture and embrace innovative technologies, they ensure everyone students, faculty, and staff play a role in keeping the digital world safe. This strategy puts people at the centre, helping institutions go beyond simply following the rules. It enables campuses to cultivate generations of ethical digital citizens who can adapt to change, generate new ideas, and lead in a complex digital world.

REFERENCES

Abisoye, A., & Akerele, J. I. (2021). A High-Impact Data-Driven Decision-Making Model for Integrating Cutting-Edge Cybersecurity Strategies into Public Policy, Governance, and Organizational Frameworks. *International Journal of Multidisciplinary Research and Growth Evaluation, 2*(1), 623–637. DOI: 10.54660/.IJMRGE.2021.2.1.623-637

Ahmad, N., Laplante, P. A., DeFranco, J. F., & Kassab, M. (2022). A Cybersecurity Educated Community. *IEEE Transactions on Emerging Topics in Computing, 10*(3), 1456–1463. DOI: 10.1109/TETC.2021.3093444

Ali, S., Wang, J., & Leung, V. C. M. (2025). AI-driven fusion with cybersecurity: Exploring current trends, advanced techniques, future directions, and policy implications for evolving paradigms– A comprehensive review. *Information Fusion, 118*, 102922. DOI: 10.1016/j.inffus.2024.102922

Annarelli, A., Nonino, F., & Palombi, G. (2020). Understanding the management of cyber resilient systems. *Computers & Industrial Engineering, 149*, 106829. DOI: 10.1016/j.cie.2020.106829

Armas, R., & Taherdoost, H. (2025). Building a Cybersecurity Culture in Higher Education: Proposing a Cybersecurity Awareness Paradigm. *Information (Basel), 16*(5), 336. DOI: 10.3390/info16050336

Asad, U., Khan, M., Khalid, A., & Lughmani, W. A. (2023). Human-Centric Digital Twins in Industry: A Comprehensive Review of Enabling Technologies and Implementation Strategies. *Sensors (Basel), 23*(8), 3938. DOI: 10.3390/s23083938 PMID: 37112279

Barata, J., & Kayser, I. (2024). How will the digital twin shape the future of industry 5.0? *Technovation, 134*, 103025. DOI: 10.1016/j.technovation.2024.103025

Beniiche, A., Rostami, S., & Maier, M. (2022). Society 5.0: Internet as if People Mattered. *IEEE Wireless Communications, 29*(6), 160–168. DOI: 10.1109/MWC.009.2100570

Camacho, N. G. (2024). The Role of AI in Cybersecurity: Addressing Threats in the Digital Age. *Journal of Artificial Intelligence General Science (JAIGS) ISSN:3006-4023, 3*(1), 143–154. https://doi.org/DOI: 10.60087/jaigs.v3i1.75

Cassottana, B., Roomi, M. M., Mashima, D., & Sansavini, G. (2023). Resilience analysis of cyber-physical systems: A review of models and methods. *Risk Analysis, 43*(11), 2359–2379. DOI: 10.1111/risa.14089 PMID: 36646448

Collins, E. I. M., & Hinds, J. (2021). Exploring Workers' Subjective Experiences of Habit Formation in Cybersecurity: A Qualitative Survey. *Cyberpsychology, Behavior, and Social Networking, 24*(9), 599–604. DOI: 10.1089/cyber.2020.0631 PMID: 34403600

Coventry, L., Briggs, P., Jeske, D., & van Moorsel, A. (2014). *SCENE: A Structured Means for Creating and Evaluating Behavioral Nudges in a Cyber Security Environment.*, DOI: 10.1007/978-3-319-07668-3_23

Crick, T., Davenport, J. H., Hanna, P., Irons, A., & Prickett, T. (2020). Overcoming the Challenges of Teaching Cybersecurity in UK Computer Science Degree Programmes. *2020 IEEE Frontiers in Education Conference (FIE)*, 1–9. https://doi.org/DOI: 10.1109/FIE44824.2020.9274033

Dadiyala, C., Tangade, P., Singh, G., Bhutada, V., Bhattad, A., Partani, N., & Jangid, R. (2023). Designing and Implementing an Effective Cybersecurity Home Lab for Detection and Monitoring. *2023 14th International Conference on Computing Communication and Networking Technologies (ICCCNT)*, 1–8. https://doi.org/DOI: 10.1109/ICCCNT56998.2023.10306937

DeCusatis, C., Alvarico, E., & Dirahoui, O. (2022). Gamification of cybersecurity training. *Proceedings of the 1st International Workshop on Gamification of Software Development, Verification, and Validation*, 10–13. https://doi.org/DOI: 10.1145/3548771.3561409

Delgado, I., Sancristobal, E., Martin, S., & Robles-Gómez, A. (2023). Exploring IoT Vulnerabilities in a Comprehensive Remote Cybersecurity Laboratory. *Sensors (Basel), 23*(22), 9279. DOI: 10.3390/s23229279 PMID: 38005664

Diakoumakos, I. (2023). Enhancing Cyber Security Education and Training through Gamification. *Proceedings of the 2nd International Conference of the ACM Greek SIGCHI Chapter*, 1–5. https://doi.org/DOI: 10.1145/3609987.3610016

Dupont, B. (2019). The cyber-resilience of financial institutions: Significance and applicability. *Journal of Cybersecurity, 5*(1). Advance online publication. DOI: 10.1093/cybsec/tyz013

Chima Abimbola Eden, Onyebuchi Nneamaka Chisom, & Idowu Sulaimon Adeniyi. (2024). Integrating AI in education: Opportunities, challenges, and ethical considerations. *Magna Scientia Advanced Research and Reviews, 10*(2), 006–013. https://doi.org/DOI: 10.30574/msarr.2024.10.2.0039

George, K. (2024). *Phishing Results.* Information Technology Services. https://www.carleton.edu/its/newsletter/news/phishing-results/?utm_source=chatgpt.com

Hajny, J., Ricci, S., Piesarskas, E., Levillain, O., Galletta, L., & De Nicola, R. (2021). Framework, Tools and Good Practices for Cybersecurity Curricula. *IEEE Access: Practical Innovations, Open Solutions*, *9*, 94723–94747. DOI: 10.1109/ACCESS.2021.3093952

Hassan, I. (2022). Levereging Apache Guacamole, Linux LXD and Docker Containers to Deliver a Secure Online Lab for a Large Cybersecurity Course. *2022 IEEE Frontiers in Education Conference (FIE)*, 1–9. https://doi.org/DOI: 10.1109/FIE56618.2022.9962510

Hausken, K. (2020). Cyber resilience in firms, organizations and societies. *Internet of Things: Engineering Cyber Physical Human Systems*, *11*, 100204. DOI: 10.1016/j.iot.2020.100204

Hong, Y., & Furnell, S. (2021). Understanding cybersecurity behavioral habits: Insights from situational support. *Journal of Information Security and Applications*, *57*, 102710. DOI: 10.1016/j.jisa.2020.102710

Huang, L. (2023). Ethics of Artificial Intelligence in Education: Student Privacy and Data Protection. *Science Insights Education Frontiers*, *16*(2), 2577–2587. DOI: 10.15354/sief.23.re202

Kaur, R., Gabrijelčič, D., & Klobučar, T. (2023). Artificial intelligence for cybersecurity: Literature review and future research directions. *Information Fusion*, *97*, 101804. DOI: 10.1016/j.inffus.2023.101804

Marshall, R., Pardo, A., Smith, D., & Watson, T. (2022). Implementing next generation privacy and ethics research in education technology. *British Journal of Educational Technology*, *53*(4), 737–755. DOI: 10.1111/bjet.13224

Muniandy, L., Muniandy, B., & Samsudin, Z. (2017). Cyber Security Behaviour among Higher Education Students in Malaysia. *Journal of Information Assurance & Cybersecurity*, 1–13. https://doi.org/DOI: 10.5171/2017.800299

Nisenoff, A., & Golla, M. B. U. (2023). *Measuring the Risk Password Reuse Poses for a University*. USENIX. https://www.usenix.org/publications/loginonline/measuring-risk-password-reuse-poses-university?utm_source=chatgpt.com

Piardi, L., Leitão, P., Queiroz, J., & Pontes, J. (2024). Role of digital technologies to enhance the human integration in industrial cyber–physical systems. *Annual Reviews in Control*, *57*, 100934. DOI: 10.1016/j.arcontrol.2024.100934

Poláková, M., Suleimanová, J. H., Madzík, P., Copuš, L., Molnárová, I., & Polednová, J. (2023). Soft skills and their importance in the labour market under the conditions of Industry 5.0. *Heliyon*, *9*(8), e18670. DOI: 10.1016/j.heliyon.2023.e18670 PMID: 37593611

Prümmer, J., van Steen, T., & van den Berg, B. (2024). A systematic review of current cybersecurity training methods. *Computers & Security*, *136*, 103585. DOI: 10.1016/j.cose.2023.103585

Răceanu, D. N., & Marian, C. V. (2023). Cybersecurity Virtual Labs for Pentesting Education. *2023 13th International Symposium on Advanced Topics in Electrical Engineering (ATEE)*, 1–4. https://doi.org/DOI: 10.1109/ATEE58038.2023.10108187

Rahouti, M. (2019). Board 129: Facilitation of Cybersecurity Learning Through Real-world Hands-on Labs. *2019 ASEE Annual Conference & Exposition Proceedings*. https://doi.org/DOI: 10.18260/1-2--32228

Ramezanian, S., & Niemi, V. (2024). Cybersecurity Education in Universities: A Comprehensive Guide to Curriculum Development. *IEEE Access: Practical Innovations, Open Solutions*, *12*, 61741–61766. DOI: 10.1109/ACCESS.2024.3392970

Saeed, S., Suayyid, S. A., Al-Ghamdi, M. S., Al-Muhaisen, H., & Almuhaideb, A. M. (2023). A Systematic Literature Review on Cyber Threat Intelligence for Organizational Cybersecurity Resilience. *Sensors (Basel)*, *23*(16), 7273. DOI: 10.3390/s23167273 PMID: 37631808

Salem, M., Samara, K., Pray, J., & Hussein, M. (2024). Evaluating the Effectiveness of Online Cybersecurity Program in Higher Education. *2024 IEEE Global Engineering Education Conference (EDUCON)*, 1–9. https://doi.org/DOI: 10.1109/EDUCON60312.2024.10578833

Sallos, M.-P., Garcia Perez, A., & Bocanet, A. (2024). Organisational cyber resilience: A heuristic for bridging foundations and applications. *Journal of Enterprise Information Management*, *37*(6), 1926–1952. DOI: 10.1108/JEIM-06-2023-0317

Sarker, I. H., Furhad, M. H., & Nowrozy, R. (2021). AI-Driven Cybersecurity: An Overview, Security Intelligence Modeling and Research Directions. *SN Computer Science*, *2*(3), 173. DOI: 10.1007/s42979-021-00557-0 PMID: 33778771

Schmeelk, S. E., & Dragos, D. M. (2024). A Global Cybersecurity Embedded Course: Student Learnings and Curricular Design. *2024 IEEE Frontiers in Education Conference (FIE)*, 1–9. https://doi.org/DOI: 10.1109/FIE61694.2024.10893447

Sepúlveda Estay, D. A., Sahay, R., Barfod, M. B., & Jensen, C. D. (2020). A systematic review of cyber-resilience assessment frameworks. *Computers & Security*, *97*, 101996. DOI: 10.1016/j.cose.2020.101996

Sontan, A. D., & Samuel, S. V. (2024). The intersection of Artificial Intelligence and cybersecurity: Challenges and opportunities. *World Journal of Advanced Research and Reviews*, *21*(2), 1720–1736. DOI: 10.30574/wjarr.2024.21.2.0607

Stenalt, M. H. (2021). Digital student agency: Approaching agency in digital contexts from a critical perspective. *Frontline Learning Research*, *9*(3), 52–68. DOI: 10.14786/flr.v9i3.697

Subbiah, A. (2024). Enhancing Learner Motivation and Academic Achievement. In *Recent Trends and Future Direction for Data Analytics* (pp. 270–288). https://doi.org/DOI: 10.4018/979-8-3693-3609-0.ch012

Subbiah, A., & Ibrahim, O. (2011). Implementing affinity analysis in determining critical factors on e-service systems in Malaysia. *2011 International Conference on Research and Innovation in Information Systems*, 1–6. https://doi.org/DOI: 10.1109/ICRIIS.2011.6125747

van Steen, T. (2022). *When Choice is (not) an Option: Nudging and Techno-Regulation Approaches to Behavioural Cybersecurity* (pp. 120–130). https://doi.org/DOI: 10.1007/978-3-031-05457-0_10

van Steen, T. (2025). Developing a behavioural cybersecurity strategy: A five-step approach for organisations. *Computer Standards & Interfaces*, *92*, 103939. DOI: 10.1016/j.csi.2024.103939

Wang, L., Yang, J., & Wan, P.-J. (2020). Educational modules and research surveys on critical cybersecurity topics. *International Journal of Distributed Sensor Networks*, *16*(9), 155014772095467. DOI: 10.1177/1550147720954678

Williams, L., Anthi, E., Cherdantseva, Y., & Javed, A. (2024). Leveraging Gamification and Game-based Learning in Cybersecurity Education. *Journal of The Colloquium for Information Systems Security Education*, *11*(1), 8. DOI: 10.53735/cisse.v11i1.186

Yaro, H. U. (2025). Phishing Susceptibility Metrics in Academic Environments: Simulation-Based Analysis at Federal Polytechnic Bali, Nigeria. *Asia-Pacific Journal of Information Technology and Multimedia*, *14*(01), 219–239. DOI: 10.17576/apjitm-2025-1401-13

Zeadally, S., Adi, E., Baig, Z., & Khan, I. A. (2020). Harnessing Artificial Intelligence Capabilities to Improve Cybersecurity. *IEEE Access: Practical Innovations, Open Solutions*, *8*, 23817–23837. DOI: 10.1109/ACCESS.2020.2968045

Chapter 4
Future Science Press as an Example of Operational Optimization and Cybersecurity Resilience in Academic Publishing

Froilan Delute Mobo
https://orcid.org/0000-0002-4531-8106
Philippine Merchant Marine Academy, Philippines

Ana Liza Garcia
Future Science, Philippines

Achmad Riyanto
Future Science, Indonesia

Rey Fremista
Polytechnic University of the Philippines, Philippines

ABSTRACT

Many small and medium-sized businesses (SMEs) now rely heavily on online platforms like Open Journal Systems (OJS) as a result of the digital transformation of academic publishing. However, because cybersecurity resilience and operational efficiency are inextricably linked, this reliance poses serious risks. In order to examine the operational disruptions brought on by cybersecurity threats aimed at

DOI: 10.4018/979-8-3373-4154-5.ch004

Future Science Press's OJS platform, this chapter provides a case study of the small academic publisher. We find important problems involving people, procedures, and technology that lead to these vulnerabilities by conducting a root cause analysis using the Ishikawa framework. A four-pronged strategic improvement plan is suggested in light of this diagnosis, with a focus on business continuity planning, proactive maintenance and monitoring, technical security hardening, and security awareness training.

1. INTRODUCTION

One of the most important changes in the global knowledge economy is the transition of academic publishing from a print-based oligopoly to a dynamic, digitally mediated ecosystem (Larivière, Haustein, & Mongeon, 2015; Suber, 2012). Because of their exclusive distribution contracts, costly subscription plans, and intricate print workflows, a small number of influential publishing houses controlled scholarly communication for the majority of the 20th century, marginalizing smaller universities and areas with limited resources (Larivière et al., 2015; Willinsky, 2006).

This status quo was drastically upended with the introduction of the internet, open-source platforms, and the open-access movement. This revolution is best illustrated by Open Journal Systems (OJS), created by the Public Knowledge Project, which allows even organizations with limited resources to start peer-reviewed journals, handle submissions, and connect with international indexing services (Edgar & Willinsky, 2010; Smith et al., 2018). By enabling SMEs and independent publishers to get around established gatekeepers and reach a worldwide audience, this democratization has promoted diversity and inclusivity in scholarly publishing (Tennant et al., 2016).

However, there are two sides to the digital revolution. It boosts operational effectiveness and reduces entry barriers, but it also exposes publishers to a rapidly changing range of cyberthreats. SMEs are particularly at risk since they frequently lack specialized IT or security personnel (Heckman, Heckman, & Vervest, 2007). Open-source platforms' accessibility and transparency encourage innovation, but they also make them easy targets for cybercriminals, particularly when security patches are not released on time or best practices are disregarded (Guo, Liu, & Chen, 2008; OWASP, 2021).

For SMEs, security incidents have serious repercussions, including lost data, delayed publication, reputational damage, operational outages, and fines from the government. Since SMEs often have narrow profit margins and low resilience, unlike large publishers, a single successful attack could have existential consequences (D'Arcy, Hovav, & Galletta, 2014; Verizon, 2022).

2. COMPARATIVE BACKGROUND: SMES, DIGITAL PUBLISHING, AND CYBERSECURITY

Small and medium-sized enterprises (SMEs) have emerged as strategic stakeholders in the digital publishing sector over the past several decades, thereby transforming the contours of international scholarly communication. Until the mid-1990s, a small number of dominant academic publishing houses exercised oligopolistic control over most commercial outlets, excluding most resource-constrained academic and institutional entities from tangible production and distribution channels. Concurrently, the construction of reputational capital within these monopolistic conglomerates constituted an additional barrier, rendering the system self-replicating and, in most instances, resistant to supplementary editorial or curatorial contributions (Larivière, Haustein, & Mongeon, 2015). Publishers institutionally located in the global south and in fields beyond North America and Western Europe encountered prohibitive margin thresholds and prohibitive differential expenses, which acted to amplify uphill access hurdles to circulation, thereby entrenching regional academic inequities (Haustein, Larivière, & Mongeon, 2015).

The advent of digital infrastructure now attenuates these earlier exclusions through the proliferation of open-source and platform-independent workflows, most consequentially illustrated by the success of the Open Journal Systems (OJS). Devised within the Public Knowledge Project, the OJS application constitutes a radical re-architecting of publishing as a shared and unlicensed infrastructure, permitting small and mid-range consortia to establish and operate rigorously peer-validated periodicals with nominal fixed and recurrent capital obligations (Edgar & Willinsky, 2010). By furnishing a freeware, modular, and universally accessible platform encompassing full editorial life-cycle functionality, OJS effectively rebalances the contribution of value by relegating underlying resource needs to competitive marginality, thereby bestowing entities with constrained capital, latitude to intervene, and co-constituting contemporary global scholarly discourses on their own vector, apart from reputational or technological incumbencies.

The wide implementation of the Open Journal Systems (OJS) and analogous infrastructures is transforming the structural economy of academic publishing beyond mere reductions in expenditure. Editorial pipelines that once demanded an army of people and endless paper in the print era have traded that headache for sleek scholarly mobile ecosystems (SMEs) that do the heavy lifting. A single, slick interface sweeps away the ancient baggage of print: digital archiving, manuscript comparison, author chats, static illustrations, and reviewer steps now live in one dashboard. When the software nudges the right people to the right choice, the gains show up everywhere: clear accountability, fewer mistakes, open processes, and lighter loads for editors.

Now, that battery-powered, SME-tuned world spreads even further, thanks to OJS's linked features. By sticking to the right metadata and syncing citations with one click, papers get zapped to the best-known databases—Google Scholar, Scopus, DOAJ, and Science Citation Index (Scopus 2018, A. Smith)—making obscure journals pop up next to the heavyweights. Tiny articles, odd languages, and schoolyard science now have their stage, enlarging the global scholarly story: diverse fields, revived languages, and local know-how sparkling in platforms that only the most impatient brows could excuse scroll– scroll– scroll through.

Small and medium-sized businesses have been learning from the early days of tiny academic publishers, which show how powerful it can be to use the right digital tools. Those publishers turned to online platforms before it was the norm, and their clever moves turned a challenge into a chance. Today, the same playbook is helping SMEs stay agile and keep growing, proving that the smartest use of existing online resources can really pay off.

Concurrently, digital agility exacts the assumption of novel, frequently unmonitored vulnerabilities that, once neglected, can immediately impair operational continuity. Dependability in IT services and resilient cybersecurity, hence, transcend governance preference and instead, have been reclassified as existential necessities. Strategic commitments in SMEs to digital channels entail a tacit assumption that disruption—whether effectuated through orchestrated cyber incursions, equipment breakdowns, or catastrophic data obsolescence—renders discovery, dissemination, and record management impossible. This dependency contrasts materially with prevailing resource frameworks of most SMEs, which often encounter practical limitations in recruiting, or even retaining, specialized IT or security officers. Nor has the artefactual complexity of digital exposure been authentically cultivated in institutional awareness until confronted with a systemic breach (Heckman, Heckman, & Vervest, 2007).

According to empirical research, SMEs are quick to embrace new technologies, but they usually lag behind in putting strong cybersecurity, business continuity, and risk assessment procedures in place (Guo, Liu, & Chen, 2008). Critical systems are vulnerable to threats ranging from ransomware attacks and malware infections to unintentional data loss and non-compliance with regulations because many smaller publishers rely on informal or ad hoc arrangements for software updates, data backups, and incident response. Because SMEs must put operational costs and editorial quality ahead of back-office investments in infrastructure and security, the lack of formalized processes is frequently made worse by resource limitations.

Additionally, the swift growth of digital publishing has expanded the attack surface for bad actors while simultaneously providing previously unheard-of reach. Hacktivists, cybercriminals, and even state-sponsored organizations now see the importance of breaching academic platforms, whether for intellectual property theft, ideological disruption, or as part of larger campaigns that target sensitive scientific or technical data. Such incidents can have serious repercussions for SMEs, including prolonged downtime, reputational damage, fines from the government, staff use in certain situations, and existential risks to the company's continued existence (Galletta, Hovav, & D'Arcy, 2014).

2.1 A Comparative Study of Other SME Publishers and FSP

Moving beyond the analysis of a single organization and taking a comparative viewpoint is essential to understanding the diversity and complexity of cybersecurity resilience and operational optimization strategies among SMEs. An instructive example is the experience of Future Science Press (FSP), a Southeast Asian SME publisher that made OJS its main platform. Its experience is not unique, though, and comparing it to that of other SMEs—like MegaScience Press and NorthStar Journals—helps highlight the variety of approaches and resources managed, dependencies, and dependencies, and dependencies, and dependencies, and dependencies, and 2010). 2010). managed to identify the industry.

North American-based NorthStar Journals is an example of an SME that has purposefully chosen to use proprietary software for its publishing activities. There are some benefits to this strategy, especially when it comes to automated software updates, vendor-provided technical support, and integrated security features. However, there are serious risks associated with depending only on one vendor, especially when it comes to security flaws that impact all platform users. For instance, when a zero-day exploit was found in its vendor's system, NorthStar encountered a critical incident. NorthStar had to wait for the vendor to issue an official update because it was unable to apply its own patch or fix due to the nature of proprietary software. Authors and peer reviewers who anticipated smooth, continuous access to the journal's online systems suffered reputational damage, service outages, and a brief loss of submission data as a result of this delay. Because NorthStar struggled to migrate data or implement custom workflows during the crisis, the incident also brought attention to the risk of vendor lock-in and the possible drawbacks of giving third parties too much operational control.

MegaScience Press, a large, international publisher, on the other hand, has a completely different way of doing things. Being a sizable, integrated company, it keeps a specialized internal Security Operations Center (SOC) manned by cybersecurity experts who keep an eye out for, identify, and react to threats instantly. MegaScience Press can implement sophisticated incident response protocols, stay in compliance with international regulations, and quickly restore services in the event of a breach thanks to this strong security infrastructure. Crucially, MegaScience Press has the resources to invest in redundancy, ongoing training, and state-of-the-art security technologies—choices that most SMEs just cannot afford or staff.

These comparative examples make it abundantly evident that security and resilience cannot be guaranteed by either proprietary or open-source platforms. The way that technological decisions are handled within a larger framework of risk assessment, operational planning, and organizational culture determines outcomes more so than the decisions themselves. According to Galletta, Hovav, and D'Arcy (2014), SMEs can develop resilience through a combination of proactive risk management, technical and procedural rigor, and a shared commitment to security at all organizational levels. This entails thorough process documentation, frequent training, and an understanding that digital threats are ever-changing and need constant attention.

This comparative analysis highlights the significance of context-sensitive tactics. FSP was exposed to the operational risks associated with self-managed infrastructure and limited IT staffing, even though it benefited from OJS's flexibility and cost savings. Although NorthStar's vendor-managed business model shielded it from some obligations, it also created new vulnerabilities and dependencies. The internal method used by MegaScience Press offers the highest security and compliance standards, but it is too expensive and scaled up for the great majority of SMEs. Leveraging the efficiency of open-source or cloud platforms while implementing shared services, managed security, and collaborative frameworks to bridge knowledge and resource gaps may be the best course of action for the majority of SMEs.

2.2 Trends in the Industry and New Dangers

Scales efficiently can lead some SMEs to make poor choices around third-party vendors. A rapid onboarding rush leaves security architectures adrift, resulting in overwrought declarations about capabilities that rarely feature in the fine print. The technical debt incurred when ancillary services are sprinkled haphazardly across multiple providers quickly compounds. Every dashboard, every API key, every sudden subscription can weave yet another brittle thread into the same web, often without deliberate consent. Haunted now by the possibility that a single misconfiguration could expose sensitive manuscripts to the same fire sale that plagued enterprise rivals, several leaders confess that neither they nor their teams fully understand the very environments they pay to outsource.

Reversing the momentum of this drift requires tighter, metrics-driven due diligence, upstream contract provisions that pin operational accountability to the vendor, and the discipline to align broader workforce training around the security implications of hybrid architectures. This combination of deliberate pace and ongoing vigilance can stop the risk contour from flattening the line of growth that the cloud once promised. A deliberate strategy to stagger, pilot, and reel in underused features proceeds in company time rather than vendor time. SMEs that trail their large-scale rivals in the rapid growth of loaded third-party services have, rather than deny their appetite, simply decided to engineer the appetite rather than restrain a now blurred line by flag-laden, often poorly executed security artefacts.

3. LITERATURE REVIEW: CYBERSECURITY, OPERATIONAL RESILIENCE, AND SMES

3. 1. Industry and Academic Perspectives on the Security of Digital Publishing

In the last ten years, the world of cybersecurity that digital scholarly publishers operate in has become increasingly difficult and dangerous. Reports in the field and the findings of academic analyses are alarmed at the same phenomenon: the number and sophistication of targeted cyberattacks directed towards journals and repositories are increasing (Björk 2017; Seneviratne, Kagal, and Berners-Lee 2020). The current cyber threat landscape is characterized by an array of state actors, hacktivist collectives, and advanced cybercrime syndicates, a significant evolution from the previous landscape populated by lone attackers and the casual CMOS user. The motives for such cyberattacks are both diverse and interrelated, including opportunistic ransom, deliberate reputational sabotage, stealthy intellectual property capture, and the more diffuse ambition of undermining public faith in scientific and educational institutions. Breaches of peripherally held digital archives inflict damage that goes far beyond downtime; breaches that compromise cyberspace inflict harm on the publishers, sensitive commercial and academic datasets, and the scholarly record.

3.1.1 The Increasing Danger Environment

According to recent studies, academic publishers worldwide are facing an exponential increase in cyber risk (Björk, 2017). The value of academic data, from unpublished research manuscripts to private peer reviews and proprietary editorial workflows, has grown as science and scholarship become more digitally mediated. Such data are appealing to nation-states interested in scientific espionage or the disruption of adversaries' research infrastructure, in addition to cybercriminals looking to sell private information on the dark web. For example, APT (Advanced Persistent Threat) organizations have used supply chain attacks, phishing campaigns, and customized malware to target publishers and universities, taking advantage of the sector's interconnectedness and resource imbalances (Seneviratne et al., 2020).

Digital publishing is now seriously threatened by ransomware in addition to targeted attacks. Today, extortion of companies holding valuable, time-sensitive data is a specialty of cybercriminal organizations. Attackers use "double extortion" techniques, encrypting important files and threatening to sell or leak user data and stolen manuscripts unless ransom is paid. Such attacks can have an existential effect on SMEs, which typically lack the financial and technical resources of major publishing houses. According to reports, small publishers who failed to recover from ransomware incidents were forced to stop operations, face legal repercussions, or have their reputations destroyed (Heckman, Heckman, & Vervest, 2007).

Furthermore, new avenues for compromise have been created by the growing use of cloud-based systems and third-party integrations. Cloud services increase the attack surface and add supply chain risks, even though they provide scalability and operational efficiency. Recent high-profile incidents involving both proprietary and open-source platforms demonstrate how quickly a breach at a cloud provider or a vulnerability in a popular plugin can spread to all dependent journals (Guo, Liu, & Chen, 2008). The fact that many SMEs lack formal vendor risk management programs or the know-how to assess the security of cloud partners exacerbates these risks.

3.1.2 Structural and Operational Vulnerabilities for SMEs

The disproportionate vulnerability of SMEs in comparison to larger publishers is a recurring theme in both academic and industry literature. By definition, SMEs have limited resources, few employees, and little expertise in security or IT (Heckman et al., 2007). SMEs can now compete in the academic market thanks to open-source publishing platforms like OJS, but they also place a heavy burden of security on users. Open-source communities, as opposed to proprietary vendors, usually offer software updates and security advisories; however, it is the responsibility of individual publishers to keep an eye on, test, and promptly implement these patches (Smith et al., 2018; OWASP, 2021).

According to empirical research, SMEs frequently lack formalized procedures or specialized staff for incident response, patch management, and vulnerability assessment (Guo et al., 2008). Critical software components might go months without patches if automated tools or planned maintenance aren't used, leaving systems vulnerable to well-known exploits. The risk of compromise is further increased by the widespread use of shared or reused passwords, inadequate access controls, and default configurations. Over 80% of breaches, for instance, involved the use of compromised or stolen credentials, according to a 2022 Verizon Data Breach

Investigations Report. This issue is made worse in companies with little security training or enforcement of policies (Verizon, 2022).

The problem is organizational as well as technical. Many SMEs assign IT and security tasks to employees who have other main responsibilities, such as administrative assistants, production managers, or editors. Delays in responding to new threats, uneven procedures, and accountability gaps are the results of this fragmentation. Without a dedicated security committee or CISO (Chief Information Security Officer), important decisions might be made on the fly or put off completely. Consequently, rather than being strategic, risk assessments, business continuity planning, and security investments are frequently reactive.

3.1.3 The Human Aspect of Cybersecurity

The human factor is arguably the most frequently mentioned cause of organizational vulnerability in the literature. According to decades of services of re-dependencies and a culture of services (2018). -managed backups, and -managed staff use. The most common reason for successful cyber breaches is staff use. It is human error, which includes using weak or reused passwords, falling for phishing emails, forgetting to update software, or configuring cloud services incorrectly (Dinev & Hart, 2006; Puhakainen & Siponen, 2010; Verizon, 2022). The dual pressures of limited staff capacity and high turnover, which are common in small organizations, make the risk especially acute for SMEs.

Developing a security-conscious organizational culture is essential for effective cybersecurity; it goes beyond merely putting technical controls in place (Puhakainen & Siponen, 2010). This includes non-punitive responses to employee errors, clear reporting protocols for suspected incidents, and frequent, role-specific training on emerging threats. However, a lot of SMEs either rely on one-time, generic training sessions that don't really change behavior or underinvest in staff development. Research has indicated that continuous, interactive, and contextually appropriate training—like scenario-based workshops, simulated phishing attacks, and peer-to-peer learning—is far more successful in fostering organizational resilience.

Employee willingness to report incidents or near misses is also influenced by organizational culture. Employees may be reluctant to come forward in settings where making mistakes is stigmatized or where security is only seen as an IT function, which delays the identification and reaction to security breaches. Organizations that promote open communication, shared accountability, and proactive security behavior, on the other hand, respond to incidents more quickly and achieve better results (Galletta et al., 2014).

3.1.4 Pressures from Regulation and Compliance

Digital publishing is now navigating a tougher regulatory landscape. Any publisher that collects data, no matter where they are based, must deal with a patchwork of comprehensive data privacy laws. The EU's General Data Protection Regulation (GDPR) is a key example, as it applies no matter where the publisher is located, provided they touch data on EU citizens. Noncompliance can result in fines of up to 4% of global annual turnover, a staggering sum that could cripple most small- and medium-sized enterprises (SMEs).

For SMEs, keeping pace with the regulatory expectations feels overwhelming. Developing solid policies, instituting technical safeguards, and keeping precise records for every aspect of data handling—from collection to deletion and from breach notifications to answering data subject requests—absorb both time and money. The enforcement of such measures requires dedicated resources, and even the most streamlined SMEs often lack the formal governance structures and security infrastructure needed (Larivière et al., 2015; Stepanov, Kühling, & Rannenberg, 2021).

Exacerbating this situation, research from ISOsCISOs reveals that a surprising number of SMEs do not know the duties laid out in the regulations. They are short on the specialist services required to assess incidents, identify gaps, and file required notifications on time. Inside the small teams that power many digital publishers, these unaware publishers risk missing deadlines that incur fines. As regulations keep extending into new territories and evolving, the global reach of digital publishing only widens the compliance maze.

Small publishers are juggling the privacy rules of multiple countries whenever submissions, reviews, or article readers involve personal data. A law degree isn't the only requirement—data flow mapping, privacy by design, and breach notification procedures are equally essential. For small-to-medium enterprises (SMEs) that can't afford full-time attorneys or compliance teams, that complexity can feel overwhelming.

Some international guidelines—like ISO/IEC 27001 or the NIST Cybersecurity Framework—promise a roadmap, but they were designed around Fortune 500 budgets and personnel. They can be daunting for smaller shops that lack any dedicated compliance resources (Souppaya & Kent, 2006; D'Arcy, Hovav, & Galletta, 2014). Instead of trying to adopt every provision, SMEs need to repurpose the intent of those standards and focus their paper-thin teams on the areas that most reduce privacy risk. Emphasizing effective staff training, crafting clear incident response documents, encrypting data, and tightening access controls are the steps likely to yield the biggest privacy payoffs on the smallest budgets.

3.1.5 Evaluation of Security Frameworks in Comparison

One important takeaway from the literature is how crucial it is to modify security frameworks to fit the particular requirements and environment of SMEs. Although structured, risk-based guidance for information security management is provided by the NIST Cybersecurity Framework and ISO/IEC 27001, small organizations with little technical staff may find the scope and complexity of these standards daunting (Souppaya & Kent, 2006; D'Arcy et al., 2014).

For instance, the five main functions of the NIST Framework are Identify, Protect, Detect, Respond, and Recover. There are several categories and subcategories within each function, ranging from communications and incident response to asset management and access control. Full implementation necessitates continuous assessment, documentation, and cross-functional coordination. Brute force is a resource that may be limited in an SME CISO and an open CISO context, even though this modularity enables organizations to prioritize based on risk.

Through the "Plan-Do-Check-Act" cycle, ISO/IEC 27001, an international standard for information security management, places a strong emphasis on ongoing improvement. Smaller publishers may find the preparation, audit, and maintenance costs of ISO 27001 certification prohibitive, but it can offer reputational and contractual benefits, particularly when working with institutional clients. SMEs might instead choose to implement a "light" version of these frameworks, emphasizing important controls like asset inventory, frequent backups, robust authentication, and documented incident response protocols.

Given that a one-size-fits-all strategy is impractical and ineffective, some studies support the creation of sectoral guidelines or frameworks tailored to SMEs. For instance, publishers who use systems like OJS can benefit greatly from the prioritized lists of web application vulnerabilities and workable mitigation techniques provided by the Open Web Application Security Project (OWASP) (OWASP, 2021). SME security and compliance are now supported by sector-specific toolkits, case studies, and checklists published by industry associations like the STM Association and the Committee on Publication Ethics (COPE).

3.1.6 The Function of Information Sharing and Sector Collaboration

Increased cooperation and knowledge sharing regarding cybersecurity are recent trends in the academic publishing industry, which acknowledges that SMEs share similar difficulties and resource limitations. User groups for platforms such as OJS, industry consortia, and regional publisher alliances have started to set up mutual aid protocols, group security audits, and shared threat intelligence networks. Through these cooperative frameworks, SMEs can share the cost of security assessments, pool their expertise, and send out alerts about new threats or vulnerabilities. According to research, such group efforts can help raise the standard of operational security, decrease duplication of effort, and increase sector-wide resilience (Haustein, Larivière, & Mongeon, 2015).

Additionally, cooperation includes promoting sector-specific standards and reasonable regulation. Policymakers must take into account the particular requirements and constraints of SMEs when creating new cybersecurity or privacy regulations. In order to offer culture-customized guidance, represent the interests of SMEs, and make sure that compliance requirements don't hinder innovation or force small publishers out of business, industry associations are essential (2023).

3.1.7 Useful Suggestions and Prospects

CISOs: Several useful suggestions for SMEs looking to maximize services. Silence and cybersecurity are brute force, brute force backups, and, derived from the scholarly and industry insights, previously lapsed reviews are reviewed: Brute force (2023).

1. Make risk assessment and scenario planning a top priority. SMEs should map potential threats—tech brute force, technical threats, tech human, and regulatory—regularly evaluate their operational dependencies, identify vital assets, and ensure lapses are lapses. Double-edged. Gaps can be identified in a culture (Culture, 2008). and targeted investments can be informed by even basic qualitative risk assessments.
2. Invest in Human Capital: It's critical to provide role-specific, interactive, and ongoing training. A culture of transparency and learning should be encouraged, and employees should be given the authority to identify and report threats.
3. Leverage Technology, But Be Aware of the Gaps: Managed security services, cloud-based backup, and automated patch management can assist SMEs in making up for a lack of internal knowledge. These tools must be set up correctly, though, and using them shouldn't give one a false sense of security.
4. Even small businesses should have a well-defined, implementable incident response plan. Even if they are conducted infrequently, drills or tabletop exercises can significantly increase preparedness.
5. Participate in Sector Collaboration: Joining user groups, consortia, and threat-sharing networks can give you access to best practices, early risk warnings, and chances to work together to solve problems.
6. Observe the Regulatory Environment: SMEs need to keep up with the latest cyber and data protection regulations, consulting trade groups for advice and modifying their compliance initiatives as necessary.

7. Adopt a Culture of Continuous Improvement: Security is a continuous process rather than a one-time endeavor. Review policies frequently, update training, and take lessons from sector-wide and internal incidents.

The twin imperatives of cybersecurity resilience and operational optimization will continue to be crucial to the success and long-term viability of SMEs as the digital publishing industry develops. The literature makes it clear that although there are many obstacles to overcome, they are not insurmountable. SMEs can protect their mission, data, and the confidence of the academic communities they serve by implementing strategic investment, organizational learning, and cooperative action.

4. COMPARATIVE ANALYSIS: SME CYBERSECURITY RESILIENCE IN DIGITAL PUBLISHING

4.1 Rationale for Comparative Approach

A narrow focus on a single SME, while useful for in-depth diagnosis, risks over-emphasizing idiosyncratic details and under-exploring systemic trends and shared challenges (Eisenhardt, 1989). Comparative case analysis allows us to distinguish the unique from the generalizable, benchmark best practices, and identify sector-wide patterns of vulnerability and resilience (Yin, 2017). In digital publishing, where SMEs operate in diverse regulatory, technical, and cultural environments, such comparison is essential for producing transferable lessons.

4.2 Comparative Case Selection

Our analysis compares Future Science Press (FSP) with two other SME publishers—NorthStar Journals (North America) and OpenVista Publishing (Europe)—as well as referencing the practices of a large, integrated player, MegaScience Press (Global). The selection captures a range of:

- Geographies (Southeast Asia, North American SMEs) lapses are brute force, brute force, Africa, and Europe.
- Business models (open source vs. proprietary platforms)
- Reflective controls or reach (regional vs. global)
- Resource levels (lean SME vs. well-staffed corporation)

4.3 Comparative Analysis of an SME

Didentified, identified, 2023). identified dependencies, and natural science pursued controls (Oran, 2023). SME lapses are SMEess (Asia, OJS).

NorthStar Journals (NA, Proprietary)
OpenVista, an SMEPublishing (EU) incident OJS
Megreuseda Science Press (Global, Mixed)
Platform
OJS (open source, self-hosted)
Proprietary (vendor-hosted)
OJS (open cloud-hosted)
Mix: Proprietary and open-source + OJS + custom
IT/Sec 2018) controls security staff
1-2 controls or an SME review (2018). generalists, no dedicated CISO
Vendor support + 1 IT admin
2 IT 2008) cloud2008).2008).2 and an SME 2008).2008)2018) controls or services
20+ in-house, dedicated (2018). CISO
Security investment
<$5K/year, mostly open-source tools
$10K/year, SaaS subscriptions
$12K/year, managed security services
~$2M/year, full SOC
Incident history

Binvestigate and an SME2018). Brute force, SME (2018). phishing, misconfiguration

Vendor zero-day, slow patch response
Ransomware, GDPR breach notification
Phishing, minor DDoS (rapid containment)
Training & culture
Ad hoc, mostly reactive
Annual vendor-led sessions
QuartCISOserly, role-based, GDPR-focused
Continuous, gamified, tracked
Business continuity plan
Recently formalized, tested annually
Vendor-managed, limited drills

Documented, tested, cloud failover
Fully redundant, drilled brute force, scan, and quarterly
Regulatory 2023, 2008, and 2018 scans and reviews: compliance
Partial (GDPR for EU authors)
US law, GDPR partial
Full GDPR, regular audits
Full compliance, global audits
Collaboration
Local publisher alliance, OJS forums
Vendor forums
Natioscan, dependencies, and the publisher network
Industry threat-sharing consortium

4.4 Key Cross-Case Findings

4.4.1 Platform Choice and Security (R2018).responsibility

Open Source (reviewed: 2023 and 2018). OJS, FSP & OpenVista): backups, and

- Pro: Flexibility, low cost, strong community support (Willinsky & Edgar, 2010; Smith et al., 2018)
- Con: The security burden falls on the publisher; patching and configuration are reviewed, lapses are common (Guo et al., 2018).

Proprietary (NorthStar):

- Pro: Vendor manages updates/security backups and, by default, reduces technical overhead
- Con: Vendor lock-in, slow patch cycles for zero-days, limited customization (Heckman et al., 2007)

Large Multi-Platform (MegaScience):

- Pro: Resources for custom security, rapid response, and redundancy
- Con: Cost-prohibitive for SMEs

4.4.2 Security. Culture and Training

- FSP and NorthStar: Training was infrequent until after incidents, leading to repeated vulnerabilities (Dinev & Hart, 2006; Puhakainen & Siponen, 2010).
- OpenVista: Proactive, role-based training, GDPR awareness, and an incident of openness led to quicker reporting and more robust incident responses.
- MegaScience: Institutionalized, continuous training and gamification increased awareness and reduced successful attacks (Verizon, 2022).

4.4.3 Business Continuity and Incident Response

- FSP: Developed plan post-incident; previously, ad hoc and slow recovery.
- NorthStar: Dependent on vendor for disaster recovery; limited transparency.
- OpenVista: Cloud-based failover, tested regularly; rapid restoration after ransomware.
- MegaScience: Full redundancy, regular drills, rapid failover.

4.4.4 Regulatory Compliance

- SMEs in the EU (OpenVista): GDPR compliance is routine, with data flow mapping, privacy impact assessments, and breach notification procedures (European Parliament, 2016; Smith et al., 2018).
- Non-EU SMEs (FSP, NorthStar): Partial compliance, often only for EU data subjects. FSP reported challenges in interpreting GDPR requirements without legal counsel.

4.4.5 Collaboration and Threat Intelligence

- FSP and OpenVista: Active in OJS user forums and local alliances, benefiting from shared threat intelligence and group-negotiated security audits.
- MegaScience: Part of global industry information sharing, influencing standards, and gaining early warning of threats.

4.5 Synthesis and Critical Insights

1. No Single Model Guarantees Security: Both open-source and proprietary approaches have strengths and weaknesses. SMEs must weigh flexibility, cost, and the burden of responsibility (Guo et al., 2008; Heckman et al., 2007).
2. Resource Constraints Amplify Risk: SMEs often operate reactively due to a lack of staff and funding (Heckman et al., 2007).
3. Culture and Leadership Matter: Organizations with proactive leadership, regular training, and a culture of openness respond faster and recover more completely from incidents (Puhakainen & Siponen, 2010; D'Arcy et al., 2014).
4. Regulatory Readiness Varies: GDPR compliance is more robust among European SMEs, but global publishers must be prepared for extraterritorial regulatory reach (European Parliament, 2016; Smith et al., 2018).
5. Collaboration is a Force Multiplier: Alliances, forums, and group-negotiated audits improve SME resilience and reduce isolation.

4.6 Recommendations Based on Comparative Analysis

- For SMEs using open-source platforms: Invest in community engagement, regular patching, and cloud-based managed security services where possible.
- For all SMEs: Prioritize role-based, ongoing security training and create a culture where incident reporting is encouraged, not penalized.
- For industry bodies: Facilitate threat intelligence sharing, subsidized training, and collaborative audits specifically tailored to SME needs.
- For policymakers: Balance regulatory demands with support mechanisms for SMEs, recognizing their resource constraints.

4.7 Future Research and Practice Directions

- Quantitative benchmarking of incident frequency, training ROI, and resilience metrics across SMEs.
- Deeper exploration of collaborative frameworks and sector-wide standards for SME publishing security.
- Longitudinal studies on the impact of proactive versus reactive security cultures in digital publishing.

5. OPERATIONALIZING SME RESILIENCE: FRAMEWORKS, COST-BENEFIT ANALYSIS, AND THE MANAGERIAL IMPERATIVE

5.1 Four-Pillar Operational Framework: Comparative Insights

Building on the comparative analysis, it is clear that effective SME resilience in digital publishing is not just about technological controls. Instead, resilience emerges through the interaction of four interdependent pillars: technical security hardening, proactive maintenance and monitoring, formal business continuity planning, and robust organizational culture (D'Arcy et al., 2014; Puhakainen & Siponen, 2010; Seneviratne et al., 2020).

5.1.1 Technical Security Hardening

Core Practices:

- Deploying multi-factor authentication (MFA) and strict password policies (Verizon, 2022)

- Timely patch management for all platforms (Guo et al., 2008)
- Use of Web Application Firewalls (WAF), anti-malware, and endpoint protection (OWASP, 2021)
- Secure cloud configurations and encrypted backups (Heckman et al., 2007; Seneviratne et al., 2020)

Comparative Lesson:

NorthStar's reliance on proprietary vendor updates led to a critical patch delay. OpenVista, with managed open-source hosting, implemented automated patching and vulnerability alerts—demonstrating that the right service model can offset internal skill gaps.

5.1.2 Proactive Maintenance and Monitoring

Core Practices:

- Regular vulnerability scanning (automated and manual)
- SIEM (Security Information and Event Management) or cloud-based log analysis for early detection (Souppaya & Kent, 2006)
- Scheduled system and backup integrity tests

Comparative Lesson:

OpenVista's quarterly tabletop exercises and cloud-based monitoring enabled rapid recovery from a ransomware attack, compared to FSP's previously ad hoc, reactive approach.

5.1.3 Business Continuity and Disaster Recovery

Core Practices:

- Business Impact Analysis (BIA) to identify critical processes and assets (NIST, 2022)
- Documented, tested disaster recovery plans with clear RTO/RPO targets (ISO/IEC 22301:2019)
- 3-2-1 backup rule (three copies, two media, one offsite/cloud)

Comparative Lesson:

MegaScience Press, though resource-rich, exemplifies the value of continuous drills and redundancy. For SMEs, cloud failover solutions (as used by OpenVista) offer a scalable, affordable alternative.

5.1.4 Organizational Culture and Training

Core Practices:

- Continuous, role-specific cybersecurity awareness training (Puhakainen & Siponen, 2010)
- Leadership modeling of security behaviors and open incident reporting culture (D'Arcy et al., 2014)
- Gamified or scenario-based learning to increase engagement (Verizon, 2022)

Comparative Lesson:
OpenVista's role-based and GDPR-focused training reduced incident frequency and improved response times. FSP's participatory approach (rotating "security liaison," cross-functional workshops) gradually transformed a reactive culture into a proactive one.

5.2 Cost-Benefit Considerations for SME Security Investment

One of the most pressing questions for SMEs is how to justify and prioritize security spending, given limited budgets and competing operational demands (Heckman et al., 2007; Parsons et al., 2023).

5.2.1 Direct and Indirect Costs of Cyber Incidents

- Direct costs: Emergency IT support, paid ransoms, data restoration, regulatory fines (Björk, 2017; Verizon, 2022)
- Indirect costs: Reputational damage, client churn, lost manuscript submissions, increased insurance premiums, opportunity costs (Haustein et al., 2015)

Case Example:
FSP's downtime after a compromise led to a 22% drop in submissions in one quarter, loss of a major partnership, and incurred $7,500 in emergency costs, representing nearly 18% of its annual profit.

5.2.2 Return on Security Investment (ROSI)

A growing literature on ROSI models for SMEs underscores that moderate, targeted investments—such as managed cloud security, regular training, and automated backup—yield outsize returns by reducing both the likelihood and impact of major incidents (Heckman et al., 2007; Parsons et al., 2023).

- FSP's investment of $3,000/year in basic managed security tools and regular training (2018). led to a 75% reduction in incident recovery time and a measurable improvement in user trust, compared with 2008. much higher costs for reactive fixes.

5.2.3 Collaborative Resource Pooling

As evidenced by FSP and OpenVsta, collaborative purchasing scans and shared threat intelligence reduce per-organization costs and help SMEs access expertise and tools that would be otherwise out of reach (Haustein et al., 2015; Seneviratne et al., 2020).

5.3 The Managerial and Regulatory Imperative

5.3.1 Leader Culturership and Governance

- Strategic framing: Security as 2010). 2010). vel pCISOsty, not an IT afa culture (culture 2018). terthought (D'Arcy et al., 2014)
- Cross-functional Brute force, CISO ownership: SecCISSMEs reflect double-edged committees, and clear role definition enhances accountability and reduces single points of failure (Puhakai 2010). SMEs (Nen & Siponen, 2010)
- Metrics and reporting: Integration of security KPIs into CISO's regular management reviews (ISO/IEC 2Brute force:2013)

Comparative Lesson:
OpenVista's quarterly security SMEs (including editorial, legal, and IT staff) fostered organization-wide brute force, buy-in, and rapid policy adaptation.

5.3.2 Regulatory Compliance

- Brute force, GDPR, and beyond: GDPR applies to any publisher handling EU data, regardless of location, culture, or staff use (European Parliament, 2016; Smident, 2010). 2010). Staff use al., 2018)
- Continuous assessment: Regular data flow mapping and privacy impact assessment dependencies were reviewed in 2008. 2008). Lapses are lapses, and sets are services. -managed for compliance (Sm2023SMEs.2023). And reflect double-edged services. Al. Investigate and openly

- Incident notification: Fines for 2018. Staff uses, staff can, and staff identified. A breach or incomplete breach notification, Brute force, investigation, scanning, and lapses in operations can be crippling for SMEs.

Comparative Lesson:

OpenVista's regular GDPR audits and privacy-by-design workflows enable 2008). It is to avoid regulatory penalties and use compliance as a brand differentiator.

5.3.3 Sector lapses are engagement and policy advocacy.

- Industry bodies: Should offer subsidized training, shared audit schemes, and up-to-date guidance tailored to SME environments (Haustein et al., 2015)
- Poli (2023). cymaking: Regulators must balance enforcement with support, recognizing culture (Culture 2018). backups, and SME resource constraints (Europeanscan, and SME and Double-Edged Parliament, Brute Force, and Parson 2008). Lapses are lapses (et al., 2023).

Comparative Lesson:

FSP leveraged participant incidentation in regional publisher consortia to access affordable penetration testing and share best practices, while simultaneously advocating for proportionate, SME-focused policy guidance.

5.4 (2008).al Model: SME Cybersecurity Optimization Roadmap

Stepwise Roadmap: backups and re-use

1. Leadership buy-in: Elevate cybersecurity as a strategic risk (Board/CEO).
2. Baseline Assessment: Conduct a BIA, vulnerability scan, and policy review.
3. Quick Wins: Implement backups and managed-managed-managed-managed-managed-managed MFA, automated backups, and basic WAF/cloud security.
4. Policy and Training: Develop a 2023 response plan; launch ongoing, role-based awareness training.
5. Collaborative Engagement: Join industry forums and threat-sharing alliances.
6. Continuous Review: Integrate security metrics into management cycles; update policies and procedures as threats evolve.

5.5 Empirical Metrics for Measuring Resilience

- Incident frequency and severity (before/after interventions)
- Mean time to detect/respond/recover (MTTD/MTTR) (Verizon, 2022)

- Staff training completion and phishing simulation performance
- Compliance audit scores
- Stakeholder trust indicators (author/reviewer feedback, submission trends)

5.6 Summary: Integrated Comparative and Operational Insights

The comparative lens makes clear that resilience is not a product of tools alone, but of deliberate, organization-wide integration of technology, process, and culture. SMEs that invest in proportionate, collaborative, and adaptive security practices consistently outperform peers who rely on reactive or piecemeal interventions. Cost-benefit analysis and empirical metrics reinforce that even modest, well-targeted investments in security yield substantial returns in operational continuity, compliance, and stakeholder trust.

6. REGULATORY AND POLICY DEVELOPMENTS IN SME DIGITAL PUBLISHING

The rules concerning data protection for small and medium-sized publishers in the digital realm are changing and becoming increasingly stringent. Data breaches have surfaced weaknesses in the way digital companies function, and regulatory bodies, as well as the public, have suddenly become more cognizant and concerned about data privacy (See European Parliament, 2016; Smith et. al, 2018). Consequently, the means to safeguard personal data and restore trust in online services have prompted authorities nationwide to enact, revise, and broaden data protection regulations. Consequently, digital publishers, to SMEs, are increasingly burdened with complex and expansive compliance regulations. This is disproportionately more taxing for companies with limited legal resources and acumen, as the rules are complex to untangle.

Companies ought to be prepared to respond instantaneously to any requests concerning exercising their rights granted by the GDPR. A person may request to see what data you hold about them, data which can be fixed, erased, or even moved to another service. There is also the option to request data deletion, which is known as the "right to be forgotten." Also, the rule book states that if a data breach has occurred, the supervisory authority must be notified within 72 hours if the breach involves personal data. These responsibilities should not be neglected, as failure to respond to them might result in hefty penalties as well as a tarnished reputation that lasts for years.

For small to medium enterprise (SME) digital publishers, compliance is neither a box to tick nor a checklist to fulfil. Many publishing SMEs do not have an internal legal counsel, and do not have the means to contract outside privacy compliance resources. Evidence suggests that the GDPR readiness posture for SMEs based on the European Union territoriality principle is weaker. They may not appreciate the extent of the compliance gap, or have difficulty transforming critical business activities to fulfill the requirements of the law (Smith et. al, 2018; Stepanov et. al, 2021). This, on its own, leads to a greater risk of non-compliance, and the attendant potential exposure is untenable economically.

All activities related to the collection, storage, security, and sharing of data are subject to compliance mandates, which place each of these activities under a regulatory system (2018). An example of this is when an author submits a manuscript to a journal. The publisher in this case has an obligation to ensure that the author's personal information is treated in a lawful, transparent manner, and appropriate safeguards are in place to prevent unauthorized access and disclosure. In the same manner, peer review systems must facilitate the exchange of necessary information and comments while protecting the identities of reviewers, especially in cases of double-blind review.

The case studies of the mid-size digital publishers Oinvestigate (2010) and Pen-Vista (2010) illustrate a strategy in compliance and governance fusion of a "Brute Force" approach's best practice. While other publishers Oinvestigate and PenVista gained from undergoing a data breach review and risk analysis practice, OpenVista managed to control the incident in a manner that was effective and public. Not only this, but he managed to send emails to the data subjects and the data protection authority, which was within the relaxed 72-hour requirement of the GDPR. Open-Vista managed to avoid intersection fines and maintained a stellar reputation among stakeholders. He demonstrated the effectiveness of breach management procedures. In contrast, another publisher, FSP, suffered from reporting the breach, which cost him more reputation.

In general, the tendency is toward intensive enforcement and approvable regimens with data privacy rules. The expectations now extend beyond the obligations of a single organization. If a violation of the law occurs, and even in the absence of intent or negligence, regulatory authorities are now willing to impose punitive sanctions against all types of enterprises, including small and medium-sized enterprises (SMEs). GDPR compliance is complex and risky. A simple miscalculation, intercept, or mistake is costly if the requisite safeguards and procedures have not been established. The fine under GDPR is punitive, at 4% of the company's global revenue or €20 million, whichever is higher (European Parliament, 2016). The rationale now is that robust data privacy is most needed to maintain the digital economy and, at the same time, protect personal privacy.

In engaging advocacy and member-focused consulting, some industry associations are trying to develop data-protection rules that are contextually balanced for small and medium enterprises (SME) in a way that ensures compliance with the requisite standards of data privacy (Haustein et al, 2015). The aim is to show that even in resource-constrained settings, strong privacy protections can be achieved.

Consequently, standard procedures have become routine. These involve data protection impact assessments, constant staff teaching, the meticulous logging of every processing operation, audits on data processing, and periodic audits on data processing. These measures of accountability may be cumbersome to small and midsized businesses (SMBs), but their advantages are unmatched. With the integration of data protection in their operations, SMBs can establish credibility with their authors, reviewers, and readers, greatly improve their standing relative to the competition, and significantly reduce the risks of data breaches and regulatory noncompliance.

Faced with increasing competitive pressures, many small and medium-sized publishing businesses are resorting to technology to mitigate the pain. Data-diagramming technologies, automated systems for consent collection and data retention, and cloud systems with data security features permit organizations to manage and monitor the life cycle of personal data. Modern publishing service providers often complement their services with encryption, tiered permission systems, and multifactor authentication, providing additional protection against data breaches and unauthorized access. Through the adoption of these technologies, small and medium-sized enterprises (SMEs) can improve their compliance posture and prove to regulators and relevant parties that they are proactive in fulfilling their legal obligations.

Small and medium-sized enterprises (SMEs) struggle to update and enforce policies, which more often than not receive inconsistent or vague information and guidance from authorities. Digital publishing is global, and even small businesses can be flooded with mandates from multiple, even clashing jurisdictions. Most of them do not have the financial capital to employ a compliance officer at full-time capacity, let alone incorporate more advanced technological elements. While these systems are high-end, the reality is that they, more often than not, do not eliminate the possibilities of errors. Sending a sensitive email to the wrong recipient, failure to update privacy notices, and the more general lapse of notifying account holders about the deletion of dormant accounts all fall into the confines of oversights that are immensely common.

SMEs need a balanced approach with which to address the aforementioned problems. Employee training is the first, and one of the most important elements to be considered. From the head of the company down to the intern, people need to be educated on the forms and strategies of protecting personal data, and more widely, data in crisis situations. Furthermore, SMEs need to find compliance solutions that are easily scalable, and low-cost to begin with, that were robust at the time of the first investment, that have the ability to 'grow' or pivot with changes in other more robust elements. For smaller publishers, not being able to join the associations with some of the industry keystones means losing the ability to acquire information on breaking news. What is worse, they lose the capacity to actively champion rational regulations that would ease the burden of compliance for everybody.

Albeit with difficulty, the organization that cultivates the spirit of discipline and transparency is more likely to withstand the more sophisticated environment of ever-growing compliance obligations. Such an organization enhances its internal defenses when data protection is a principle valued by all and not an extra task to perform.

As far as the response offered by the SMEs is concerned, it looks as though the SMEs do not have any choice but to start acting on the issue at hand, invest on response shifting technologies, upscale, and as a result further improve the state of the data processes and the overall postion of the company, the state which is the byproduct of the ongoing spiral of events.

A striking creditation is being put on the visa and mastercard EU relations that being, the addressing of the denial of access complex by Reciprocal Global Systems which extends the corporate structures of the reciprocal free trade zones of the UK and Americas to Australia as a prospective member of the system thus could sign reciprocal trade zones agreements with both Australia and the Americas which makes it possible to negotiate a tangential corporate structure.

7. FORWARD-LOOKING TRENDS: AI, DATA ANALYTICS, AND COLLABORATIVE FRAMEWORKS

Machine Learning in Cybersecurity: How AI Is Changing the Game

Machine Learning (ML) and Artificial Intelligence (AI) are quickly reshaping how cyber battles are fought. Both attackers and defenders are using the same core technology to get the upper hand, making the digital world a whole lot tougher to navigate. As Seneviratne et al. (2020) note, AI is turning the traditional picture upside-down: companies are discovering, remediating, and recovering from cyber-attacks faster than ever before—or, at least, they can, thanks to these advanced tools.

In particular for small and medium-sized companies (SMEs), the shift propelled by Gen-AI is a thorny bifurcated path. While Security Information and Event Management (SIEM) systems and Endpoint Detection and Response (EDR) tools used to be the stuff of luxury, now they harness the prowess of AI to sift through pedestal and network data, often in record times and even highlighting the most granular slips that border peril. A spike in data transmission at a user network at 2 AM from a familiar device? AI raises a flag, interrogates, and initiates a response autonomously and often well before a human is able to log in. This automated response, better termed as a reactive response in cyber, surrenders the prolonged dwellings, the sneaky intervals, which could range anywhere from hours to often days, the blended assailants utilize for reconnaissance and posturing. The internet is that AI tools are coming apart. The tools could be located anywhere from the side of the IT director to highly technological or even to peripheral cloud light. This is even for small companies where the strategic plans are slowly in the process of being revised in even small companies.

As captured by the Verizon 2022 cybersecurity report, AI succeeding in this area of cybersecurity, as well as others, is astonishing. Less exposure to signal fatigue, which often accompanies network monitoring, is synonymous with sleuthing, which is the negative surrender of what many tend to view as cyber false.

The advantages become even more pronounced when looking at smaller enterprises and medium-sized businesses (SMEs), especially considering that a significant portion do not have developed and specialized IT teams. Vulnerability scans and AI Autonomous Automated (AAA) patch management and scans with AI technology at every step. Techniques in Application Security Management (ASM) touch and scan software/system and even apply patches to weaknesses (and risks), self-defined and ranked. This makes cybersecurity and technology more accessible to a variety of industries and organizations with minimal budgets and no cyber experience. AI opens a new avenue to SMEs so that they do not have to rely on heavy-security experts with their sophisticated and expensive measures. This makes these techniques not only attainable but standard.

However, this does not imply that the increasing use of the technology is one-sided. Cybercriminals, too, are integrating it into their systems. They formulate, and with high levels of success, inordinate social engineering systems that are much more difficult to see. For instance, with AI-driven software that does spear phishing, it is indeed possible to write realistic personalized emails due to an ultra-sophisticated network analysis that highlights trusted sources to write to, hence doubling the probability of vulnerability. The more realistic an email appears, the more likely it is to migrate from the inbox to the target's click.

The security gaps are hunted down by AI-based reconnaissance tools, which manage to scour large parts of the web and find unprotected servers vulnerable and open to attacks. Attackers are also employing AI to design malware that learns on its own and changes its attack behaviors in real time to avoid detection from standard security systems. The increasing tension between these attackers and defenders highlights the increasing need to develop new tools and the need to always be on standby for an attack.

The good news is that AI-driven security systems are now affordable for many SMEs. Subscription-based managed security services, also known as "security-as-a-service", allow SMEs to purchase real-time threat intelligence and automated incident response systems, which integrate cutting-edge AI functionalities, without the need to construct an entire security operations center. On the other hand, the use of AI in these systems is associated with many shortcomings. Seneviratne et al. (2020), in particular, explain that the majority of the most successful AI systems, and especially deep learning systems, operate as "black boxes", which means users are unable to understand the process through which the AI reaches its decision. This means that the rapid and productivity-augmenting AI systems are also accepted with low explainability and low trustworthiness.

The lack of clarity surrounding an automated alert alongside other actions leads to wasting valuable time and resources. Such conditions make the task of purchasing the innovative AI security tool cumbersome and nerve-racking for small and medium enterprises (SMEs) due to the failure to accurately diagnose and evaluate the proper functioning of the security apparatus. During the negotiations for the acquisition of AI substantiation security appliances, SMEs possess the power and authority to mandate how exactly the appliance achieves and substantiates its claim.

SMEs must refuse to accept any vendor who will not provide lucid, timestamped audit trails of actions and decisions taken between the AI and the user. More so, the assurances that superseding an AI recommendation would not mean getting locked out of the system must also be provided, and the user must always be able to pause or overwrite any of the system.

Any analytics that merely seek to describe breaches in history are already working with yesterday's data. To continually stay ahead of attackers, data analytics must be predictive and at the forefront of the strategy. By utilizing algorithms to examine the log history, user behavior, and traffic patterns, SMEs can highlight critical workflows that are at increasing risk, triage systems that need to be patched, and identify gaps in compliance that are likely to be non-compliant before the deadline. These predictive mechanisms automatically identify alert patterns as they change to trace the root of hidden insider threats and dormant permissions that may be left for a considerable time and pose a risk. SMEs can opt to issue a focused and business-governed patch, often during the night shift, and avoid the random rush that usually occurs to remediate a system suffering from downtime. This offers SMEs, with real impact, the opportunity to leverage cross-industry use cases that are easily replicable.

For example, MegaScience Press uses analytics to discover operational chokepoints, particularly in their structural and operational workflow, where any breaches could lead to potential destruction. By consistently evaluating their operational data, they can target areas where security investment and personnel training would yield significant returns, rather than diluted spending. In the same vein, OpenVista deployed clean dashboard applications that analyze trends in incidents and the effectiveness of the training programs. By correlating breach data with training attendance and exam performance, they can quickly identify neglected areas, then modify their training to eliminate the most critical challenges. Instead of waiting until breaches have occurred to make security data available to decision-makers, allocating the resources to development usually increases the likelihood of defense counters built right in the system. This, in turn, fosters a habit of daily ongoing government investment in defense coverage.

8. CONCLUSION: FROM VULNERABILITY TO ADAPTIVE RESILIENCE

Future Science Press has undertaken the journey to understand how the academic publisher of small and medium-sized enterprises must carry out the digital transformations in the ecosystem of hyperconnectivity. In association with the case studies of the presses of the same dimension, the recent scholarly publications reviewed by the Journal of Scholarly Publishing shed light on what seems to be a double-edged world. While going digital has the potential to bring transformational improvements in the areas of innovation, efficiency of operations, and the audience, at the same time, the same doors, if not secured properly, can bring doom to the structures the SMEs have built over decades. Therefore, the observers of Future Science Press have also come to the conclusion, and thus the approach, that cybersecurity should be treated and incorporated as a core discipline, rather than considered as an IT ancillary function, that needs to be embraced and integrated into the core of managerial planning as well as daily operations. The misconception that the problem lies with the Security Operations Center has, to a large degree, been accepted.

Realistic academic resilience now stems from complex, interwoven actions as opposed to fragmented efforts driven by siloed functions. Actions are integrated into a cohesive operational manifold. Publishers need to integrate continuous data-driven maintenance cycles with crafted business continuity plans, pervasive security culture spanning organizational levels, technical multi-tiered network defenses, and ubiquitous strong authentication. Only the publisher who, intentionally and holistically, executes the above pillars will have the capacity to absorb the current range of cyber threats and emerge with advanced capacity for iterative recovery.

Yet, parallel examples serve to remind us that no technology stack, whether of a commercial or community-driven nature, is born "secure." The proprietary and open source will always have a calculable trade-off level. The question is how a publisher optimally implements risk management, governance, and responsive action to the architecture of the chosen stack.

The appeal of proprietary software, particularly for small and medium-sized enterprises, is strong. The downside, however, is that the organization is 'locked' to a single vendor, which may limit the organization's responsiveness to vulnerabilities. Open-source alternatives, however, provide the organization with more freedom and are more affordable. These systems also place the configuration and patching of the systems entirely on the SME. For actual resilience, seek partnerships that cut across the industry. The positive impact of a small firm can be amplified and optimized by focusing on the people and processes. Instead of obsessing over the best tool, this can be achieved by sharing threat intelligence and signing up for collective response networks.

SME Publishers. Defining conceptual boundaries is useful. Illegal mechanisms for data processing tend not to work, and more protective mechanisms for data protection tend to obstruct creative work. Unlike in artwork, data processing is a closed game. Artwork and creative data processing are an open game in the sense of rules and mechanisms.'How' a data process is created is more important than the result for proprietary data protection. What is never said is 'why' data is created or stored, and what is the data's value, and whom does it serve? 'Never' is in the focus, and it is seldom even whispered.

Compliance is added in the result and serves to protect an invisible value in perceivable ways, time, and money, in sufficient surplus. Sufficient is relative to a dynamic balance of service and logistic costs and a disincentive to serve. Defining data, which borders and boundaries are the protective mechanisms, is an important protective function or artwork.

On the matter of resilience, one could, perhaps, argue that it is the leaders, not the technology, that power the real shift. The most sophisticated small and medium-sized enterprises (SMEs) strengthen culture by actively cultivating a positive and open attitude toward cybersecurity, advocating for ongoing enhancements, and supporting constructive challenges. The meaningful, sustained work of safety requires regular assessments, breach cap-and-review, and flexible policies based on new, reliable evidence regarding security vulnerabilities. Companies that delay action until existential threats emerge also lose the ability to gain new growth opportunities.

Flexibility in these matters is no longer a freedom to choose. The most sophisticated small and medium-sized enterprises (SMEs) will deal with the integration of the industry and the developed shared expertise head-on and then zealously test every new technology that is sensible and promising. In that way, they will change the possible disruptions into new value-creating opportunities.

REFERENCES

Björk, B. C. (2017). Growth of hybrid open access, 2009–2016. *PeerJ*, *5*, e3878. DOI: 10.7717/peerj.3878 PMID: 28975059

D'Arcy, J., Hovav, A., & Galletta, D. (2014). User awareness of security countermeasures as a deterrent to IS misuse. *Information Systems Research*, *20*(1), 79–98. DOI: 10.1287/isre.1070.0160

Edgar, B., & Willinsky, J. (2010). A Survey of Scholarly Journals Using Open Journal Systems. *Scholarly and Research Communication*, *1*(2). Advance online publication. DOI: 10.22230/src.2010v1n2a24

European Parliament. (2016). Regulation (EU) 2016/679 (General Data Protection Regulation). https://eur-lex.europa.eu/eli/reg/2016/679/oj

Galletta, D., Hovav, A., & D'Arcy, J. (2014). User awareness of security countermeasures as a deterrent to IS misuse. *Information Systems Research*, *20*(1), 79–98. DOI: 10.1287/isre.1070.0160

Greenleaf, G. (2020). Global Data Privacy Laws 2020: Despite COVID Delays, 145 Laws Show GDPR Dominance. *Privacy Laws & Business International Report*, (165), 10–13.

Guo, H., Liu, Y., & Chen, X. (2008). A comparative analysis of security flaws in open-source software. *Proceedings of the 2008 International Conference on Computer Science and Software Engineering*.

Haustein, S., Larivière, V., & Mongeon, P. (2015). The oligopoly of academic publishing in the digital era. *PLoS One*, *10*(6), e0127502. DOI: 10.1371/journal.pone.0127502 PMID: 26061978

Heckman, P., Heckman, H. M., & Vervest, M. R. (2007). The reluctant innovator: Open source adoption by SMEs. *Decision Support Systems*, *42*(4), 2249–2266. DOI: 10.1016/j.dss.2006.05.001

ISO/IEC 22301:2019. Security and resilience—Business continuity management systems—Requirements.

ISO/IEC 27001:2013. Information Security Management.

NIST. (2022). Guide to Test, Training, and Exercise Programs for IT Plans and Capabilities. https://nvlpubs.nist.gov/nistpubs/Legacy/SP/nistspecialpublication800-84.pdf

OWASP. (2021). OWASP Top Ten. https://owasp.org/www-project-top-ten/

Parsons, C., McCormac, A., Butavicius, M., Pattinson, M., & Jerram, C. (2023). Determining employee awareness using the Human Aspects of Information Security Questionnaire (HAIS-Q). *Computers & Security*, *123*, 102982. DOI: 10.1016/j.cose.2022.102982

Puhakainen, P., & Siponen, M. (2010). Improving employees' compliance through information systems security training: An action research study. *Computers & Security*, *29*(5), 612–624. DOI: 10.1016/j.cose.2010.05.001

Seneviratne, O., Kagal, L., & Berners-Lee, T. (2020). Cybersecurity and the evolving web: Threats and solutions. *IEEE Internet Computing*, *24*(1), 52–59. DOI: 10.1109/MIC.2020.2970638

Smith, E., Haustein, S., Larivière, V., & Siler, K. (2018). Author, publisher, and journal responses to open access and open data in scholarly publishing. *JASIST*, *69*(12), 1475–1487. DOI: 10.1002/asi.24069

Souppaya, M., & Kent, K. (2006). Guide to Computer Security Log Management. NIST SP 800-92. https://csrc.nist.gov/publications/detail/sp/800-92/final

Stepanov, A., Kühling, J., & Rannenberg, K. (2021). GDPR compliance challenges for SMEs. *International Data Privacy Law*, *11*(1), 35–51. DOI: 10.1093/idpl/ipaa017

Tennant, J. P., Waldner, F., Jacques, D. C., Masuzzo, P., Collister, L. B., & Hartgerink, C. H. (2016). The academic, economic, and societal impacts of open access: An evidence-based review. *F1000 Research*, *5*, 632. DOI: 10.12688/f1000research.8460.3 PMID: 27158456

Verizon. (2022). Data Breach Investigations Report. https://www.verizon.com/business/resources/reports/dbir/

Willinsky, J., & Edgar, B. (2010). An analysis of scholarly journals using Open Journal Systems. *Scholarly and Research Communication*, *1*(2). Advance online publication. DOI: 10.22230/src.2010v1n2a24

Yin, R. K. (2017). *Case Study Research and Applications: Design and Methods*. Sage Publications.

Chapter 5
Strategies for Proactive Threat Detection From Monitoring to Intelligence

Sofia Jonathan G.
https://orcid.org/0000-0002-3535-2634
Lady Doak College, Madurai, India

Latha Manickam
https://orcid.org/0009-0001-6627-7227
INTI International University, Malaysia

Manickam Ramasamy
https://orcid.org/0000-0002-8729-9337
UCSI University, Malaysia

ABSTRACT

In today's digital landscape, cyber threats are becoming increasingly sophisticated, persistent, and difficult to counter with traditional perimeter-based defenses. This has necessitated a fundamental shift in cybersecurity, emphasizing proactive threat detection over reactive response. By integrating the proactive threat detection strategies such as defensive monitoring, machine learning, behavioral analytics, and threat intelligence, organizations can identify anomalies and potential attacks before they escalate into full-scale breaches. Proactive strategies not only improve detection accuracy and response times but also reduce the risk of data loss, regulatory non-compliance, and reputational damage. Despite challenges proactive threat detection remains a cornerstone of resilient cybersecurity, equipping organizations to anticipate, adapt to and mitigate emerging threats in an evolving threat landscape.

DOI: 10.4018/979-8-3373-4154-5.ch005

1. INTRODUCTION

In a more digitised world, with every aspect of individual, professional, and governmental operational being based on sophisticated inter-networked systems, cybersecurity has become a key pillar of organisational resilience (Stallings, 2020). The range of risks to digital infrastructure has grown faster than ever before and modern organisations are faced with an increasing number of cyber threats that includes nation-state attacks of the most extreme size and scale, as well as underground insider attacks and ransomware programs. The problem of cyber threats is not something out of place in the connected ecosystem of today; it is a systemic, mechanised or thought-through phenomenon and, in many cases, advanced. Organisations which limit themselves to reactive responses because the incident has already taken place and respond only after the breach has become a reality thus taking themselves at a great risk. The poses involved in new security are not adequate since opponents become more advanced in their levels of obfuscation and intellectual gamesmanship. As such, a transition to pre-emptive threat identification is necessary. This approach involves identifying and eliminating potential security incidents prior to the damage. In this regard, businesses will be forced to revitalize data analytics, a mix of high-volume data gathering of network traffic, system logs, user activity and threat intelligence feeds to bar adversarial activity. Defensive monitoring and analytics have therefore become an important part of current cyber defences strategies. Combined with big data, machine learning and behavioural analytics, security teams can discover anomalies, identify hidden vulnerabilities and pre-empt future attacks. The ability to perform continuous monitoring, advanced analytics, and the automation of real-time predicting threat systems are being integrated into contemporary devices (Springer, 2025). By transforming telemetry streams into actionable insights, defensive monitoring provides analytics companies the means to mitigate risks and protect valuable assets (Sarker et al., 2024).

1.1 Proactive vs Reactive Security: A Comparative Overview

Reactive security is like firefighting, waiting till an incident occurs before acting on it. Proactive detection is like the surveillance of public health, which tracks the initial symptoms to stop an outbreak. The relative evaluation of the security measures, reactive and proactive, is summarised in Table 1 below.

Table 1. Comparative Study: Reactive Vs Proactive Security

Aspect	Reactive Security	Proactive Security
Approach	Post-incident	Pre-incident
Tools Used	Firewalls, antivirus, incident response	SIEM, ML models, behavior analysis
Speed of Response	Slow (after detection)	Fast (predictive alerts)
Resource Utilization	High during and after incidents	Distributed across monitoring lifecycle
Detection of Zero-days	Limited	Enhanced through anomaly detection

1.2 Roadmap of the Chapter

Four underlying technologies and practices form the foundation of proactive threat detection and this chapter analyses each of the four pillars in detail.

Figure 1. Core Pillars of Proactive Threat Detection

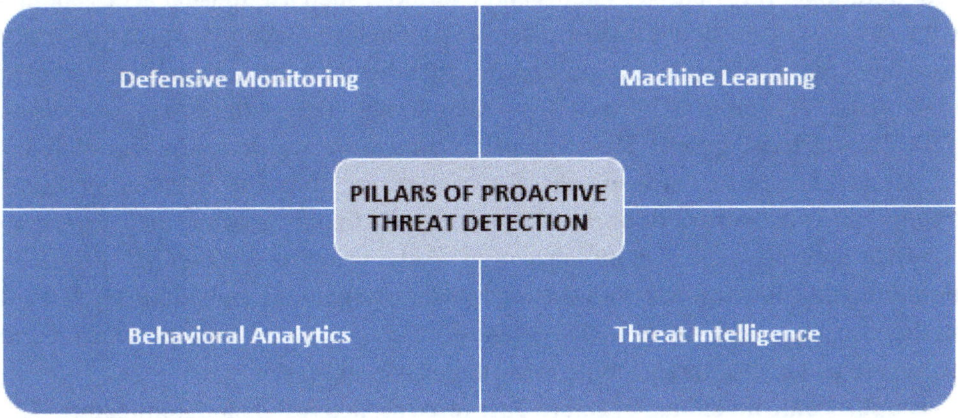

A. Defensive Monitoring: This section finds out the value of logs, telemetry, and event data in acting as an early notification of compromise, which always offers insight on the IT settings. Through the real-time tracking of events, well-kept logging, and monitoring the activity of the user organisations will be able to see anomalies within their system indicating potential threats before they can go amok. Centralised logging systems, Security Information and Event Management (SIEM) systems, endpoint monitoring solutions allow the security personnel to match the pieces of information that cannot be linked to the other, uncover the slow patterns of attack, as well as point out and resist unusual behaviours like deferred logins, privilege escalation, or suspicious data transfer. Raw telemetry is converted into an actionable intelligence rendered through defensive monitoring, the former being the initial step of proactive defence, enabling a fast risk detection and mitigation (Kahles, 2023).

B. Machine Learning (ML): This product is based on advanced algorithms, which analyze volumes of security data, values in suspicious trends and see which solutions are latent anomalies and could indicate malicious intent. Supervised/unsupervised learning to distinguish between known threats, deep learning to identify complicated behavioural modes, and a combination of all the aforementioned, MLP will improve proactive detection capabilities significantly (Kahles, 2023). It may prove handy in elucidating and tracing down more advanced and changing cyber-threats which indeed can easily out pace rule-based systems since it is well schooled and enhances with new data continuously.

C. Behavioural Analytics: This science encompasses the study of interactions between users and other users and between users and systems that may be applied to set normative standards of behaviour to find outliers (Alanazi et al., 2024). Single and device definitions can allow organisations to identify smaller breaches that more traditional rules-based systems can overlook, such as, unusual access points or unusual data downloads or permissions. Behavioural analytics provides a defence layer that is forward looking because they detect a threat by not only known signature but also unusual behaviours, which do not align with normal behaviours

D. Threat Intelligence: This dimension adds proactive detection that includes the exterior threat data because a method of injecting domestic observation with a strategy and a visionary outlook. Identifying the new threat alerts and matching them with their enterprise feeds could have enhanced awareness of potential threats by comparing new threat feeds with the organisations own logs and telemetry. Threat intelligence increases situational awareness, enabling to predict the attacks and respond to new cyber-threats more knowledgeable and faster.

The phases are illustrated by figure 2 a layered proactive defence architecture. The high power of proactive threat detection. The strength of proactive threat detection lies in the fact that it integrates the many layers of defence into one combined strategy.

Figure 2. Layered Proactive Defense Strategy

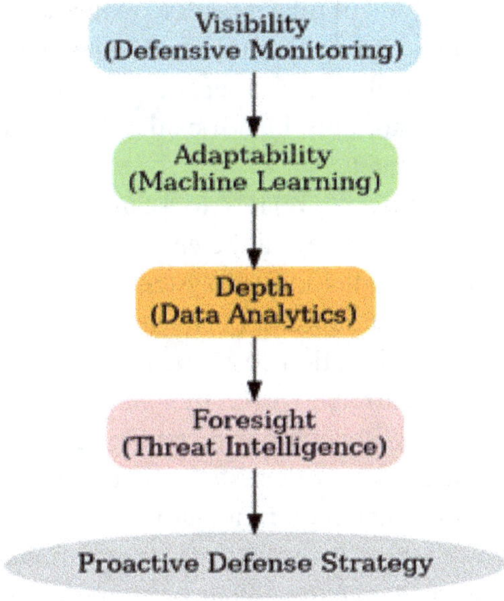

- **Visibility (Monitoring)**: Organizations must monitor their security environment through the continual collection and analysis of logs, network traffic and endpoint activity. This 24 hour surveillance ensures that there is no chance of threats passing unnoticed.
- **Act (Machine Learning)**: Machine-learning models adapt to new attacker and user behaviour patterns, and security systems can also adapt dynamically to such changes and identify previously unknown threats.
- **Depth (Analytics):** Advanced analytics uses comparisons between data of billions of sources, revealing previously unknown anomalies and creating a much deeper context, more accurately identifying the threats and minimizing the false positive.
- **Foresight (Threat Intelligence)**: Because of synthesising both internal and external threat intelligence, enterprises can foresee the actions, new type of attack, and can take place even before the incidents occur (Sarker et al., 2024)

A more layered and effectively efficient protection approach will evolve once the technologies are incorporated with Continuous Monitoring, Advanced Data Analytics, and Automation. It detects the attack non-obviousness and traffic trends in real-time, all volume of data Security data presented in real-time This scans constantly on the networks and endpoints, advanced analytics leverages this effectiveness to reveal both the attacker trends of individual thresholds, automation is effective and reduces the amount of time it takes to realise and respond to the attack with the rule-based function and automated capabilities (George et al. 2023). All these capabilities combined will bring the separate security systems to the level of intelligent ecosystem which not only identifies the threats at earlier age but also reacts quicker and more accurately.

a. Continuous Monitoring: It relates to scanning systems, networks and endpoints continuously in order to reveal the emergent risks. Contrary to periodic localised scanning or the periodic audited systems, continuous monitoring will persist in trying to find signs of abnormal behaviour or indications of all activity (skilled user, passwords, modification to system set up or dynamically tracked packet flow layouts, etc.) occurrence), even though the user is unaware of such a work-in-progress task. It allows operations related to security to take measures in the threats before they escalate to critical status by providing the security professionals with the information they require to act in respect to any possible danger like unauthorized access, running malware code, or violation of policy. Monitoring real-time is the way to promote dynamic security posture to keep up with the threat environment securing the enterprise with hands-off solutions, real time telemetry, and state-of-the-art notifications.

b. Advanced Data analytics: Under this one, the techniques of big data are exercised by querying and correlating huge volumes of security data to obtain affects and insights that would not otherwise emerge. Graph analytics and machine learning make this possible with distributed processing on chart attacks identified in a complex, multi-stage manner up through their logs, endpoints, and in the cloud. The powerful analytics will then identify the seemingly unrelated occurrences such as login irregularity, file movement, abnormal network stream etc. and form a rational image of the image of the potential attack. Higher evidence means augmenting real-time detection, searching after a threat, post-shooting examination and security plans in the future, this is why it assists enterprises stay on a trendy section of superior risks.

c. Automation: During proactive threat detection, automation refers to acting on the rule-facilitated and AI-facilitated reaction to expedite the process of detection in addition to streamlining the procedure of incident management. Repetitive processes required in security processes, including log correlation, alarm triage, and underlying remediation, can be also automated and thus reduced to hours of seconds to accomplish in the human factor led to a shortening of response times. Rule-based automation to block the controversial IPs or seclude the affected endpoints is based on playbooks, but AI-based automation is adaptable and modifies itself based on the experience of past attacks by suggesting or taking the most suitable measures. It is a dual approach which does not only lessen the efforts of the analyst but also assists in combating threats in real time basis.

Each of these elements is powerful in isolation but their usefulness is compounded when all these are brought together into one homogeneous teambuilding strategy related to cybersecurity. The layered model presented in Figure 3 above is utilized in proactive threat detection and involves how monitoring, analytics, and automation turn out to be complementary.

Figure 3. Visual Layered Model

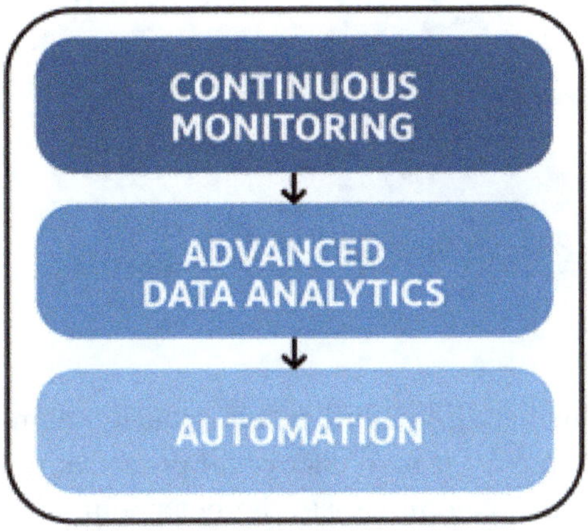

2. STRATEGIES FOR PROACTIVE THREAT DETECTION

2.1 Foundation for Proactive Threat Detection

In the past, the cybersecurity sphere was dominated by reactive approaches, i.e., the ability to fix systems once their vulnerabilities could be exploited or reacting to alerts when a hostile actor has been identified (Ke et al., 2025). It is a reactive stance, which makes organisations susceptible to zero-day attacks, insider threats, and advanced persistent threats (APTs). Instead, proactive threat detection is premised on three principles:

- Prevention – Deterrence of threats before they can do harm
- Prediction – Data assisted prediction of possible dangers
- Early Intervention – Understanding anomalies and detecting them as early as possible

Figure 4. Principles of Proactive Threat Detection

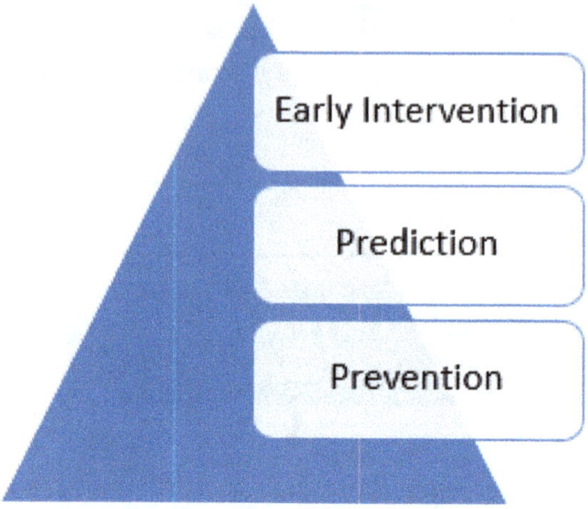

The outcome of this paradigm shift is that security teams can anticipate what attackers will do and improve the resilience of the organisations. This paradigm shift means that security teams can anticipate the behaviour of attackers and increase resilience. In olden times, teams would rely on a mutually agreed-upon set of signatures and rules that would help to detect malicious activity, but this method cannot be effective against novel attacks or unforeseen attacks such as zero-day attacks or polymorphic viruses. This is overshadowed by active threat detection that:

i. Utilising constant surveillance and baselining behaviour to detect unusual behaviour that does not constitute a pattern prior to causing havoc.
ii. Early warning and therefore helping to alleviate threats quickly.
iii. Companies may use pattern analysis to give priority to mitigation work and reinforce risk posture.
iv. Avoiding violations to save a reputation, guarantee compliance, and alleviate legal, financial, and brand liability.

So, proactive threat detection is the smart use of processes and technology to find and stop threats before they cause problems or damage to systems (Blessing, 2024). This contrasts with regular reactive strategies where the response to risks is only executed after they have already been experienced. Active actions permit early intervention and thereby allow to minimize the impact of a potential attack by anticipating attack vectors and continuously monitoring the activity of the systems and users.

2.2 Defensive Monitoring

Defensive monitoring provides the critical factor in proactive threat detection and gives an organisation an understanding of the digital presence of the organisation. It systematically collects, consolidates and recognizes data on endpoints, networks, applications and cloud applications to spot suspicious patterns that reflect ill intent. Defensive monitoring also applies the practices which include SIEM views, IDS/IP, and EDR to detect malicious activities at a small size which can be dealt with in a more beneficial manner. Monitoring is not only sending alerts but also connecting the events that occur across various locations to bridge knowledge gaps and make things safer. Such vigilance places upon this passive reactive side of surveillance a positive defensive system by which potential perils are barred before they can be transformed into fact.

2.2.1 Log and Event Monitoring

Proactive observability is based on Security Information and Event Management (SIEM). These systems merge records of a large variety of sources including servers, endpoints, firewalls or applications and apply pattern-detection techniques to indicate potential abnormal activity. Together with Security Orchestration, Automation, and Response (SOAR) solutions, organisations will be able to automatically take steps against every-day-threats, which, in effect, lowers incident-response-times.

2.2.2 Network Traffic Monitoring

The scanning and data exfiltration of port moved to the left may be easily detected through continuous monitoring of network traffic and packet level information or data and play a crucial role in the establishment of threats-evasion democracy. It is incredibly important that Intrusion Prevention Systems (IPS) and Intrusion Detection Systems (IDS) can quickly identify and stop the unnatural activity (Kern et al., 2024). Deep Packet inspection (DPI) also gives an understanding of encrypted pipes, which is one of the routes taken by the attackers.

2.2.3. Endpoint/Application Monitoring

Attack vendors tend to have their origin at the endpoint level. EDR solutions provide constant monitoring of the behaviour of the host and these computers know that something is unusual and allows those infected computers to be isolated. Application-level telemetry can help facilitate this initiative because data on aberrant usage of important business apps are revealed to prevent exploitation.

2.2.4 Cloud and Hybrid Environment Monitoring

As enterprises switch to a hybrid and multi-cloud architecture, cloud workload growth is an urgent matter now. The smart observation is necessary that is introduced by cloud-native tooling, which can be AWS Guard Duty or the Microsoft Sentinel, whereby container orchestration solutions need observability solutions to micro-services. These solutions track the changes in API utilisation, resource allocation and access-pattern to indicator odd activity happening within the surface. Cloud -security-monitoring is concerned with detecting outliers in a cloud-based environment and monitors the API call frequency, unjustified deployment of a virtual-machine, or unusual access to valuable containers of storage. The user-role, the geolocation and past activity correlation of behaviour will enable organisations to minimise data breach, cryptojacking and horizontal movement dangers within cloud system in seconds, thereby safeguarding organisational operations in the cloud systems.

2.3 Machine Learning

Machine learning (ML) is among the most vital aspects of current cybersecurity studies. It allows systems to be able to automatically detect and anticipate likely threats without organizations even noticing them through rule-based systems (Al-anzi et al., 2024; Kern et al., 2024). Having the large reserves of both historical and contemporary security data, ML models observe small abortions and evolving pattern of attacks, a very distinct characteristic of deterministic ones. The labels are allocated to known threats in the supervised learning, though the unsupervised algorithms identify the zero-day events due to behavioural drift. Reinforcement learning also optimizes the detection by feedback that can be readjusted again, therefore the decision policies (Sewak et al., 2022). Thus, by employing predictive analytics to project specifically to breaches, compromised accounts, and insider threats, before they have a pernicious impact, security personnel will have the capability to use ML (Blessing, 2024). The presented paradigm change shifts the paradigm of handling the alerts to proactive, rather than at the response, and thus makes Machine Learning a key to remove the adversarial behavior.

2.3.1 Supervised Learning

In supervised learning, analysis of informed sets of data such as benign and malicious samples is done. Examples of such labelled patterns the algorithm uses in making a distinction between normal and danger are Random Forests, Support Vector Machines and Gradient Boosting algorithms. An example of such supervised-model-based phishing methods is the classification process of email subject, embedded

URL, and sender behaviour characteristics, or file-malware methods- based phishing techniques which extract image characteristics based on file-level characteristics. Supervised approaches have the advantage over unsupervised approaches, during the classification they are high and this relies on the availability of large and well labelled data, which is specifically useful in the domains where the signatures of a threat are determinable but vary.

2.3.2 Unsupervised Learning

Unsupervised learning eradicates the labelled data condition, therefore, operating optimally in detecting the occurrence of the nascent threats, attacks which are zero-day, and the adaptive strategies of the adversary. It identifies outliers or deviant trends through internal work to cluster data points; it does not use previously known categorizations to do so. All are K-means clustering, DBSCAN as well as Principal Component Analysis is employed on identifying abnormal network traffic, anomalous behaviour of a log-in or unusual user behaviour. The models cannot be neglected when insider-threats are being detected since aberrant access pattern, unnecessary file transfer or unlawful communication with the systems would not be realized otherwise through established monitoring methods

2.3.3 Reinforcement Learning (RL)

Reinforcement learning (RL) is one type of the use of the iterative algorithm that the environment is constantly updated about what is being learnt by the agents and the policies are being optimized by the agents. Unlike those based on supervised or unsupervised methods, RL is dynamically adjusted to novel threat conditions since the strategies it uses can be adapted in real-time. Different technologies in cybersecurity security include intrusion prevention automation, self-optimizing strengths in firewall chores, and self-accustoming segregation of the network (Ke et al., 2025). As an example, the RL-based prevention structures will be able to prevent attacks automatically once an attacker varies, thereby minimizing human costs and reducing the response time. This capability ensures operations are highly adaptive, proactive and resolutory because they will constantly tweak the defensive operations in accordance with new threat behaviours.

2.3.4 Deep Learning

Deep learning is applied to acquire complex, high-dimensional, multi-temporal data with the assistance of multilayer neural architecture. This capability can identify the concealed threats or those that never existed before since the deep networks can identify intricate patterns within very large feature space. Deep models in cybersecurity are proficient in the detection of sophisticated malware, the ability to determine network flow, which is abnormal and to predict the attack vectors of operations that are unnoticed by the detection tools of the superficial analytical tools. The malware detection of patterns within binary code or finding of abnormalities in system files is a very effective task of (CNNs). Instead, the relatively new check was Recurrent Neural Networks (RNNs), Long Short-term Memory (LSTM) networks, which are also very successful at the sequential modelling of behaviour (e.g. the analysis of log files and a time-dependent user track history). These models might produce unusual sequences that will give indication of intrusion or insider and command-and-control. The features in raw data are discovered automatically in deep learning and therefore, require less manual exploration and feature engineering hence achieves more accuracy during anomaly detection (Khaleel et al., 2024). It can therefore be concluded that deep learning is a useful technology in proactive threat identification since it can process massive volumes of all data and identifying complex attack patterns that thematic coping mechanisms struggle to keep up on.

2.4 Behavioral Analytics

The behavioral analytics attempts to determine threats according to the regular activity patterns of a system and it logs the abnormality that may be an indication of bad behavior. It invokes a standard of normal behavior to the users, devices and other subjects to emulate over time and this is a contrary to the conventional signature-based detection, which relies on postulates of abuse that are a priori known. Once this baseline is established the system will be able to be aware of deviations e.g. unusually early or late logins, suspicious transfers of data or unusual privilege escalation or unusual access to sensitive files. Insider threats and credential-based attacks are especially threats that can be detected using behavioural analytics. What the rise and increased use of User and Entity Behavior Analysis (UEBA) tools in the context of reducing the risk implies more organisations, is the concern of ethicality and almost the privacy. Even as UEBA generates much illumination on the actions that have been deemed as anomalous, it raises the issues of transparency, justice, responsibility, and confidentiality. A serious matter is that the UEBA models can be biased. Because these form of algorithm are founded on historical data, they are biased by the data set. To show up predictively, groups of consumers, which are occupations or setting, can wrongly be associated due to the biased distribution of data or the discrimination of the features of selection, and consequently biased profiling, discrimination, and low employee confidences. Prejudice is also counterproductive to the reliability of the system since it can result in the legitimate threats not being identified and give excessive false positives. Undertaking this, UEBA identifies suspicious user activities such as the presence of a login by the suspected user, the transfer of data, or the increase of the account privileges by scanning through the typical user usage profiles (Olaniyan et al., 2023).

2.4.1 Baseline Behaviour

There is need to establish the normal behaviour in terms of users, endpoints and entities of an IT environment. The organisations can create a strong reference point by monitoring their repetitive tasks such as time when they log into an organisation and use of applications, their network traffic and access privileges. With the help of this reference one can go on to compare every new phenomenon with the base. On this ground, the effectiveness of security systems because they are supposed to be in separating between normal and potentially threatening behaviour is based. They need to continuously monitor and optimize as the human roles, business operations, and interaction of systems are always in a constant process of change with time to give real baselines. When properly implemented, Baseline behaviour modelling enhances proactive threats detection and prevents many cases of false alarm to allow security departments to think about the true threat rather than the ordinary anomaly in normal operation.

2.4.2 Anomaly Detection

The process of identifying potential security risk is called anomaly detection which involves detecting and analyzing deviations in comparison with the established known normal behaviours. Once normal activity patterns are set, odd behaviour being a pattern of logins during odd hours, sudden transfer of information or an unusual means of accessing sensitive systems which is not the custom than the plain vanilla can be set out to be tracked down. Such abnormalities tend to be the initial symptoms of insider attacks, hacked conclusions or third-party attacks. Sophisticated detection methods, including machine learning, rule-based detectors, and statistical modelling, are needed to ensure proper anomaly detection. The reduction in false positives created by organisations through consistent monitoring together with alignment of the anomalous activity to the situational variables as well as prioritised most significant alerts (cited as the first most promising threat) as the priority will reduce the false positives. This characteristic may be pro-actively employed to help security teams to manage the detection of intrusions at the initial stages before they worsen into major attacks.

2.4.3 Contextual Insights

Proactive detection of threat conforms can satisfied by contextual state of threats with study of user and entity behaviour in accordance with changes of time, location and role and depending on previous behaviour. This is the type of analysis that appeals to a course of action as being the right course of action in that case and not the analysis of individual acts. It is quite one thing to have a hacker attempting to seize some of the vital business systems when everyone is off and another when manning a suspicious log in at a foreign location during odd times. By not responding to contextual considerations, security staff may be able to understand when the deviation is innocent and when an intrusion is exhibiting a real sign before commencing the reduction of the rate of false positives and consequently raising the false negative. Indicators can also be found using patterns of the past which can provide the information about the slightest shift of behaviour which might mark the beginning of threats. Context knowledge combined with an already existing behaviour and detection of anomalies will enable organisations possess an all-in-one smart way of security that will revert, with accuracy and absolute confidence.

2.5 Threat Intelligence (TI)

Threat Intelligence is the methodical endeavour of information collection, examination and realization of information based on the potential and real cyber-threats to augment the safety of an organization. In contrast to the usual detection strategies deployed to counter the occurrence of a specific case, threat intelligence offers the security personnel with a background operation of the tactics, techniques, and procedures (TPS) of attackers to ensure that the security personnel forecast as well as detects and reduces the threats before they can spread infecting the security personnel. The threat intelligence model is compiled into the following layers as arrangements in a sequential way as illustrated in Figure 5 below.

2.5.1 Strategic Threat Intelligence

Strategic threat intelligence offers elite information regarding long-term trends, a motivation, and capability of threat actors. The aspect of strategic intelligence as contrasted with the tactical and operational intelligence, which is focused on the attack indicators, and which are in the moment are employed in informational making at the executive and governance levels. It provides warnings, forecasts of the new risks, based on the geopolitical trends, threat scenarios, and the historical patterns of attacks. Strategic threat intelligence assists organisations in prioritizing resources and allocates resources to respond to business priorities urgently to successful monitoring and to satisfy regulatory requirements. Using the emergence of cyber behaviours of nation-states in learning or development of sector-specific ransomware concentrated campaigns may be used as an example in informing the establishment of enterprise-wide protective postures, strategic budgetary preparations, and effective mobilization of the resources to intuitive detection platforms.

2.5.2 Threat Intelligence - Tactical

The dealt tactical threat intelligence relates to short-term Indicators of Compromise (IoCs), e.g. altered IP address, domains, hashed files, spammy website addresses, or viruses. Though these warning signs are highly minimal in terms of duration, they are fundamental to the regulating of fuel protection such as SIEM, IDS/IPS, and firewalls related to endpoint detection. that is, attacks initiated will be stopped in real time using a tuned list of malicious IPs.

2.5.3 Operational Threat Intelligence.

The operational threat intelligence examines strategies, tactics and procedures (TTPs) by the attackers. This along with the knowledge will be distributed to security operations officers, incident responders and threat analysts. It can provide background details about the actor, the motive, and the modus operandi therefore permitting held up planning in defense. A profuse usage case is that when defenders can understand the preference of a particular group of attackers with regards to use of improperly configured cloud services the defenders are able to correct such vulnerabilities before the vulnerabilities are exploited (Ke et al., 2021).

2.5.4 Threat Intelligence Technology.

Technical threat intelligence is deep on technical aspects of threat and information that can be directly consumed into the security systems. It also contains Indicators of Compromise (IoCs) such as malicious IP address, domain names, file hash, and malicious code signatures that can be used to detect and contain intrusions fast. The opponents also convey the TTPs they utilize, and this can be made available to the businesses via technical threat knowledge, and it could assist businesses in estimating how the attackers can exploit the vulnerabilities. This is information is in constant use by securities Information and event management (SIEM) systems, intrusion Detection systems (IDS) firewalls, and even endpoint protection platforms to protect themselves in real time (Kern et al., 2024). Even though this information is valuable at any given time to the working security units, it has to be updated regularly, as it is very simple to render indicators useless whenever the enemy changes their infrastructure or strategies.

Figure 5. Layers of Threat Intelligence

Threat intelligence is a combination of the intelligence of other sources to form a legitimate picture of the threat environment. Open-Source intelligence (OSINT) is a less expensive approach to monitoring the possibility of threats with the use of publicly accessible collections of data such as threat feeds, scholarly articles, and security blogs. Recorded Future, FireEye and CrowdStrike are all commercial intelligence service providers who provide quality and aggregate feeds, as well as supported with advanced analytics and threat research on a global basis..

Modern security activities can hardly be imagined without its threat intelligence, which is why it could be identified at multiple levels of cybersecurity in advance. Threat hunting leverages Indicators of Compromise (IoCs) and behavioral attributes to achieve the latent or hidden threat identification and, thus, allows detecting the adversaries before their growth (Khaleel et al., 2024). Attack surface management identifies which assets may be exploited, misconfigurations, and vulnerabilities that can be used to additional an intrusion, and as such, worsen the complexity of attackers. Predictive protection is an enhanced protection that uses the world patterns of threats and maps them to local telemetry that the organisations can foresee possible attack routes. It requires automation and integration to prevent malicious IPs, domains, and files and spur overall response time feeding the threat intelligence directly to SIEM, SOAR, and EDR platforms.

Organisations must be extremely mindful when employing threat intelligence to look ahead. The biggest problem that has always been there, and will remain an issue, is the problem of data overload; an analyst can be lost in the deluge of threat feeds, alerts and reports and miss signals. Televital its major, the usefulness of defenses can be destroyed by outdated intelligence. It can be significantly harder to determine that a person is attempting to do something bad and allow enemies to avoid defenses with delayed threat feeds or old Indicators of Compromise (IoCs).

3. INTEGRATION OF TECHNOLOGIES TO MAGNIFY THREAT DETECTION.

The round-the-clock performance, high-order data analytics, and automation have great pillars to strengthen the cybersecurity stance of an organization by reducing exposures. Monitoring systems, networks and user activities on a real time basis assists in identifying the presence of an anomalous behavior or problem. Advanced data analytics can be employed with the help of machine learning and behavioral analysis to leverage its potential based on uncovering concealed trends of large security information, which can be a direct translation of the future threats. These attempts are enhanced with automation, which helps with the quick and steady reaction to the events witnessed thus minimizing human participation and enhancing the response time. This is what results in an active security architecture not just capable of tracking and getting rid of threats at an early stage, but it also heightens protection of these advanced cyber assaults.

3.1 Continuous Monitoring

Constant surveillance is one of the building blocks of anticipatory cybersecurity since it enables enterprises to initiate the process of identifying their threats and responding to the same in real time. A network observes the activities of the system, client activity, and network traffic in real-time, and the round-the-clock monitoring will provide any person with access to the potential security events as they happen. This is a positive proactive approach that is employed by the security divisions to be capable of identifying abnormalities, policy violation, or even the harbingers of intrusion prior to it truly gaining traction into becoming a full-scale breach. Due to all-time following, cybersecurity is almost becoming a pro-active rather than a reactive business because of this, an establishment is even more effective in pre-empting, identifying and managing emerging threats.

i. Data Collection

The first stage in the process of continuous monitoring is to receive large volumes of the data concerning dissimilar factors of the organization IT ecosystem. It will contain system logs, application logs, network plant logs, endpoint logs, authentication logs, and cloud infrastructure telemetry. It strives to collect real time or near real time data that will show security posture of all critical assets. This is the raw data which is introduced by the extra analysis and detection services.

ii. Data Aggregation and Data Normalization

After the acquisition of data, these should be aggregated and normalized to make them mutual and applicable. This incorporates the transformation of information in different forms that is under one store to the transforming of these into publishable form. Normalization is a step that should be made, and to rationally correlate and analyze the various types of data, the data should be normalized.

iii. Live Monitoring and Correlation

The system will scan patterns of incoming stream of data at this stage which may be a description of a threat activity. It deems available a series of events/actions which are not typical of normative behavior using correlation rules. SIEMs, EDRs, and IDS /IPS may be useful in identifying anomalies that may join seemingly unrelated occurrences to mirror malicious intent.

3.2 Advanced Data Analytics

With the help of sophisticated analytics, any compound or any threat can be discovered by an individual. The possible solutions many of which are machine learning, user entity behavior analytics (UEBA), and connectedness to threat intelligence feeds, among others are methodological solutions. Such analytics put data into context and help more readily detect the data breach indicators of zero-day exploits, insider threats, and other incredibly faint tips toward foul play. Considering this is possible by allowing entities to correctly predict and thwart problems until these problems become major source of serious damaging effects when implemented collectively these two technologies can put cybersecurity in a new frontier of dynamic, predictive science.

i. Smart Threat Analysis using Big Data.

The digital information is currently spilling over with blistering growth, and, as such, big data currently find their foundations on the current thinking in terms of cybersecurity especially in terms of smart and intelligent threat analysis. The sheer size of the data produced by networks, applications, endpoints and users has presented a challenge and an opportunity. The solution is found in big data solutions that are capable of collecting, storing and running real time analysis of large volumes of data of all kinds including application event, network traffic, user activity and threat intelligence by third parties. The interpretation of this data and the trends based on it can be of help to the officials working on security exposing undercover trends, making curious activity and finding evidence of intrusion.

3.3. Automation to Reduce the Threats

Security personnel can reduce the time of opportunity of assailants by automating routine procedures such as warning triage, confirmation of threats and initial containment processes which are timely based. Automation allows infected machines to be separated and malicious traffic on the network can be killed or revoked compromised credentials in a matter of seconds and without involving a human factor, thereby reducing the number of mishaps that could take place (Blessing, 2024). This eliminates analysts alert fatigue and contributes to the speed of incident responses. It also ensures operation of automation as an important part of an active and properly designed response to cybersecurity.

i. Alert Triage

Once the system has detected the potentially suspicious activity that it triggers warning signals, they will be computed it against a pre-defined group of parameters or a smart risk rating. Reduction of noise can also be done through effective alert systems that will ensure that the risky situation is dealt with in time. The alerts are scanned and filtered by security analysts in the Security Operations Center (SOC), and they need to identify the validity and the result of the alert (Khayat et al., 2025). Given a question whether an alarm is a reality security incident or not, an initial inquiry will be needed.

ii. Threat Validation

The crux of the threat validation procedure is to comprehend whether an alert abrupt or a possible security influence is a real annihilation and therefore must be addressed. Because current security systems generate a lot of signals most of them are not in reality an indication of threats, the process of validating threats is needed to ensure that the security personnel concentrate on addressing the manifestations with the highest priority. One is to consider the contextual suggestions, integrity of source, behavior patterns, and indicators that are corroborating, all to make an opinion of whether an alert is true or not. Effective checking of threats helps in countering real threats by reducing alert fatigue, improving response to an incident and distribution of limited security resources in a wise manner

iii. Containment Measures, Preliminary.

The first of the procedures that were implemented to tackle the spread and containment of a tested cyber threat is initial containment measures. These movements are supposed to isolate the systems or components in the systems and in the transition the incident response team will be capable of avoiding any further damages as a thorough examination is carried out and a detailed recovery strategy is created. The common methods of containment include cutting the compromised devices off the network, blacklisting malicious IP addresses, malicious domains, disabling compromised user accounts, and quarantining suspicious files or processes.

4. THE PROACTIVE SECURITY MATURITY MODEL

Security maturity model provides organizations with a roadmap on how to develop their cybersecurity capacity by aligning the organizational culture, processes, and governance with advanced defense systems. The model progresses in separate phases of maturity, each of which reflects the advanced level of active threat detection and reaction, as shown in Figure 6.

- **Ad Hoc Stage**

Security practices are mainly informal, unstructured and reflexive at the very beginning. Companies do not have a clear-cut monitoring system, official protocols, or a security team. Threats are often found when they have already caused significant harm, e.g. service interruptions, data leaks, or reputational damage. Incident handling is not systematic, case-by-case and often does not lead to systematic documentation or lessons learned. Much of security dependence is on the individual initiative and the general risk posture is tenuous.

- **Defined Stage**

During this step, an organization will start with the introduction of basic security practices and minimal monitoring capabilities. Firewall, antivirus software or intrusion detection systems (IDS) alerts come out, but investigations are largely manual and responsive. The development of security policies and procedures starts, and AIDA starts to increase at the organizational level (George et al., 2023). It is a slight movement out of a chaos state and just the fortifications are still in shattered pieces and extremely tiny.

- **Managed Stage**

Controlled stage is a significant breakthrough to formal security practices. Security information and event management (SIEM) systems, which are utilised by organisations, are designed to consolidate log collection procedure, along with, data correlation and primitive anomaly recognition. This has helped security teams to be more methodical in investigations of the incidents and minimized the time of response and devised standard operations. These may encompass routine reporting and compliance audit and security, and Information Technology governance is bypassing security.

- **Optimized Stage**

On this sophisticated level, companies would surpass the past stages of surveillance and implement machine learning, the user and entity behaviour analytics (UEBA), as well as threat intelligence (TI). Detection processes can be more accommodating and situational to enable security forces to unravel new attack patterns and insider threats. One optimizes the processes and incorporates security programs and the corporate objectives. In threat hunting, it becomes proactive, and the automation makes the false positives less and leaves the investigation faster.

- **Predictive Stage**

Predictive stage happens during the proactive stage of cybersecurity. Artificial intelligence, advanced analytics, and highly automated systems have been moving towards a range of systems that can automatically identify and address threats. These security solutions embrace the use of worldwide intelligence, predictive models and real time behaviour analysis to spot and prevent the malicious before the reality sets in. Cases are solved automatically and do not need the human intervention in the day-to-day scenario. Therefore, they can solve sophisticated strategic problems in their teams. At this provision, organisations are aptly equipped to be creative enough to respond to the various forms of attack that are arising, and they are still capable of trusting, complying and doing business despite the dynamic environment of cyber threats.

Figure 6. Proactive Security Maturity Model

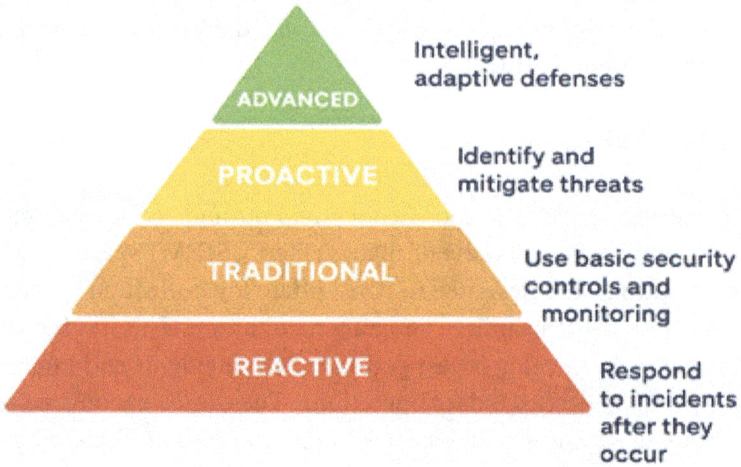

5. STRATEGIES FOR IMPLEMENTATION

In an efficient proactive detection program, there are a number of levels that are taken into consideration:

A. Unified Monitoring Architecture.

It has one platform called the Unified Monitoring Architecture which incorporates the core aspect of Security Information and Event Management (SIEM), Endpoint Detection and Response (EDR) and cloud native monitoring. The architecture provides end to end visibility to organisations, on premise infrastructure to the end points as well as cloud infrastructure on the same platform. SIEM enables the distribution of log collection and log correlation SIEM is distorted in collection as well as correlation EDR offers point and endpoint telemetry and real-time containment possibilities and cloud-native observability helps to understand the customs of API usage, resource proving, and data storage.

B. Zero Trust Architecture

Zero Trust Architecture (ZTA) is based on the concept never trust, always verify. It assumes the fact that threat may be imported by the internal and external vectors, therefore, making that the major demand is made about identity authentication, the least-privileged access, and proactive monitoring. More so there is the ZTA which takes the initiative that being its component requires real time visibility and analysis. Through continuous user and device monitoring, ZTA provides early warning of a threat, which is detected even when the traditional security mechanisms are yet to detect the anomalies.

C. Automation and Orchestration

Security Orchestration, Automation, and Response (SOAR) platforms ease the smooth running of security processes and hence lessen human efforts and hasten remediation processes. SOAR systems automate monotonous operations like alert triage, threat intelligence enhancement and initial containment measures e.g. blacklisting malicious IP addresses or deleting compromised accounts. In addition to automation, orchestration will guarantee that different security products, e.g., SIEM, EDR, firewalls, and cloud monitoring tools, are coordinated to work together and therefore respond faster and allow gaps between siloed systems to be reduced (Ismail et al., 2025).

D. Cloud-Native and Container Security

Providing the security of dynamic, distributed environments, including those created using Kubernetes, serverless architectures, and multi-clouds, takes specialized security approaches. These are inherently scalable and elastic environments, but due to their ephemeral and stratified nature become very difficult to protect. Container security is the action of protecting the control plane, nodes, pods, and orchestration layers through enforcing fine-grained policies, performing access control, and performing ongoing runtime monitoring. Serverless security, in its turn, is concerned with protecting event-driven functions by means of strict access control, input validation, and the execution-monitoring. It is necessary to integrate security as part of the development lifecycle- DevSecOps as the environments are rapidly evolving. Besides this, the defensive mechanisms must be context conscious and could dynamically respond to the workloads that they are guarding.

E. False Positives Reduction

Minimizing false positives is an important task in intensifying proactive security actions as a force of bombarding alerts will choke an examiner and paralyze the skill of differentiating genuine occurrences. Using threat intelligence with user behavior analytics can be implemented to further develop the filtering system that only higher probability alerts remain sent to the analysts. This will not only reduce the alert fatigue but will make the analytical work effort be concentrated on the thing which is a threat; that will be as effective and accurate as possible.

F. Human-Machine Cooperation

In proactive security, a machine intelligence and good co-operation of human knowledge must be present. The AI best fits the scenario when data volumes require to be examined in a limited amount of time it can identify latent variations and discover the anomalies which are not easily detected by the human analyst. Nevertheless, AI is not fined as experienced security officers are, nor as sensitive to the context. The detective tactics are augmented by human analysts with the knowledge of the business, critical thinking and conscious of the business objectives and thus balance the AI results with organizational objectives. This results in a feedback loop since machine motivated checking up and detecting anomaly lies within human validation, searching and reformatting algorithms. Not only there is a synergy that enables the detection of the threats and the response to the latter one is much faster, but more importantly, it may also deliver the adaptive defense systems, which may be continuously refined (George et al., 2023).

5.1 Key Technologies and Tools That Power Proactive Threat Detection

Contemporary active detection is premised on the ideologies of vigilance and surveillance tools. Security Operations Centers (SOCs) will never exist without the Security Information and Event Management (SIEM) platforms, enabling the collection and correlation of log information across infra-structure terminuses of an organization. Quite a significant portion of SOC work lies upon SIEM systems. They identify issues, make warnings on basis of rules, and make compliance reports. Some well-known ones include Splunk, IBM QRadar, Microsoft Sentinel, and others (Khayat et al., 2025).

The internal telemetry and external feeds offered help characterize alerts with situational information and can assist the analyst in prioritizing the incident and comprehending the tactics, techniques, and procedures that the adversary attempted (TTPs) (Redino et al., 2022). The trending TIPs like ThreatConnect or Recorded Future can enable the companies to benefit on threat intelligence to actively protect themselves (Kahles, 2023) to streamline raw information into useful understanding that can speed up the detection process.

Finally, automation and innovative analytics are the drivers that will help proactive detection run faster. Machine Learning (ML) and Artificial Intelligence (AI) makes it possible to predict analytics, detect anomalies faster and more adaptively, and respond quickly to large datasets by processing them in real-time (Blessing, 2024). SW SOAR (Security Orchestration, Automation, and Response) solutions combine SIEM, EDR, and NDR in order to automate common SOC functions, simplify operations, and run playbooks to minimize mean time to detect (MTTD) and mean time to respond (MTTR). Combining automation with insights, which are driven by intelligence, AI and SOAR enhance organisational resiliency to known and unidentified risks. The most popular solutions Palo Alto Cortex XSOAR and Splunk SOAR assist enterprises in reducing MTTD and MTTR, which improves the system stability in general (Ismail et al., 2025).

6. APPLICATIONS OF THREAT PREVENTION

i. Ransomware Prevention

One of the most important uses of threat mitigation can be ransomware prevention, as these attacks remain a common occurrence in business setting. Behavioural analytics and real-time monitoring help organisations to identify early warning signs of issues, including an unusual file-encryption behaviour, a sudden burst on file renaming, or unauthorised access to vital directories. As an example, one of the financial institutions stopped a ransomware malicious by detecting and isolating the affected endpoints as soon as suspicious encryption behaviour was detected, effectively stopping the malware from spreading throughout the network. Such a preventative measure prevented the risk of losing a vital financial information but also decreased downtime and ransom spending. Ransomware defence solutions, when integrated with automated response mechanisms, can help to contain and remediate attacks quickly and keep the operations running despite high-end attacks (Ismail et al., 2025).

ii. Phishing Prevention

Phishing has been one of the most prevalent methods of cyber intrusion. Threat-prevention systems use supervised learning models to assess email subject lines, sender behaviour, embedded URLs and attachments. An example of this is a healthcare provider who has programmed an AI-based email gateway that monitors any anomalous sender domains and pre-emptively marked any suspicious messages prior to delivery to employees. This active filtering reduced the risk of credentials compromise or malware-execution and, at the same time, trained the personnel to be sensitive of phishing systems, which strengthened both technical and human defensive stances.

iii. Insider Threat Prevention

Risks are not restricted to outside forces; an employee or a contractor has the valid access and can expose the systems to risks either deliberately or accidentally. Some activities identified as anomalous by UEBA include huge files downloads, unsuccessful attempts to log into restricted systems or unusual locations in minutes. In a case in which a technology company thwarted a major data exfiltration, an employee made an attempt to copy an important intellectual property to a foreign machine; smart warning bells sounded, and the account was blocked, which preserved important resources.

iv. Supply chain attack prevention

Supply chain attack prevention is an instrument that helps to avoid attacks on the supply chain and other potential threats to company data and network. The third-party suppliers and software providers have become targets of the attackers to access corporate networks. The threat-protection strategies will involve ongoing observation of the access of vendors, API communications, and updates to the software. An update supplied by a vendor was found to have malicious activity when compared with anomalous API behaviour by a federal agency, which stopped the upgrade, isolated potentially affected systems, and contained the would-be compromise due to early detection.

v. Advanced Malware Prevention

Malware can easily be in the form of valid files or processes. Convolutional Neural Networks (CNNs) are methods of deep learning that query patterns in binary code, and sandboxing environments that run suspicious artefacts in isolation. This methodology was used by a retail organisation to find a trojan contained in an apparently legitimate invoice file, the mismatch was detected prior to execution and client financial data was not stolen.

vi. Negligent Insider Behavior

One of the contractors had accidentally tried to transfer the confidential information of the customers to a personal cloud storage application. The transfer was interrupted by Cloud Access Security Broker (CASB) solutions joined with Data Loss Prevention (DLP) policies, which informed the contractor of the breach, thus minimizing the chances of being exposed accidentally.

vi. Off-Hourly Data Exfiltration.

The UEBA tools picked up an employee trying to steal client records outside the working hours. The system was able to identify the unusual amount of data and send automated warning messages. Freezing the account was also mandated as the investigators were expected to investigate the operation and as such prevent critical information loss of valuable consumer data.

7. CHALLENGES AND LIMITATIONS

Although the active process of threat detection continues to get enhanced with an expanding roll of improvements, one still gets to the basic issues. The most glaring of them all is that of false positive propensity where the baselines of behaviour are lightly characterized or rarely revised. Too many notifications can render notifications unfortunately lazy and less functional in general. Further, these procedures require large quantities of quality behavioural information, which requires great infrastructural hustle and experience.

The other largest problem is data overload. These types of volumes of security records and telemetry may make the process of analysis tedious and create delays in speed of detecting and response. The encryption holes also make the issue since they can obscure any illegal activity in encrypted communication and are therefore known to any non-sophisticated de-encryption or metadata analysis programs.

8. BEST PRACTICES AND PROCESSES

i. Threat Hunting

Threat Hunting is an active approach in which the concerned security personnel perform a search to identify any unnoticeable adversary-related activity that might need advanced security measures. The hunters do not attempt to wait and get a red flag, they devise theories, paid follow minds and apply advanced capabilities, including endpoint forensics, log analytics, threat-intelligence feeds, etc. to find their lurked attacks. It is an approach that can identify advanced long-lasting threats and multifaceted attack vectors efficiently and efficiently on time.

ii. Continuous Monitoring

Networks, systems and endpoints are being analyzed continuously, to ensure that, an aberrant operation is stifled before good time, as is practicable. SIEM, EDR and NDR constitute an eye of firms to their environment at any moment in time. Such 24/7 patrol is far more effective at minimizing dwell time and allows faster incidents to be responded to, which will improve the resilience of security, in its entirety.

iii. Vulnerability Management

Vulnerability management defines as a whereby vulnerabilities as well as gaps within infrastructure of a company are identified, assessed and remedied systematically. It is ensured that the opportunities of attacker exploitation are addressed by performing regular vulnerability scanning and ensuring that patches are installed in a timely manner. A good program prioritizes the most at-risk vulnerabilities hence critical issues would be addressed immediately to exclude breaches.

iv. Security Education and Training.

The initial defense against cyberattacks is the employees. Security awareness and training programs teach the personnel to be aware of phishing and social-engineering attacks, and other suspicious activities. Through the establishment of a culture of security, organizations will be able to minimize human error, which is among the most common points of attacks.

v. Zero Trust Architecture

Zero Trust Architecture is based on the principle, never trust, never verify. Instead of implicit trusting someone, a device or an application based on network location, all users, devices, and apps are authenticated and authorized before access. This model restricts the area of attack and prevents subsequent movement in the network.

vi. Red Team / Blue Team Exercises

Red team versus blue team exercises, which are commonly conducted as simulated attack-defense exercises, provide invaluable information on the security posture of an organization. Red teams simulate the enemy to reveal the weaknesses whereas the blue teams defend and develop reaction mechanisms. These drills reveal vulnerabilities, evaluate operational endurance and strengthen interagency cooperation between offensive and defensive security operations.

vii. Behavioral Analytics

Behavioral analytics involves machine-learning and statistical applications to define normative user and system behavior. Any deviation of these baselines (unusual time of logging in, excessive data downloads, or use of applications not in the norms) is highlighted to be investigated further. This method works best when detecting insider threats and hacked accounts.

viii. Classification and Access Controls of Data.

The first action of protection of sensitive information is recognition and classification of the information based on the level of its importance. Data classification allows companies to match the protection levels accordingly, whereas access controls allow only legitimate persons to access the vital resources. The most frequently used data security fortification and breach prevention methods are role-based access control, encryption, and multi-factor authentication.

9. CONCLUSION

The reactive protection in the case of a dynamic environment as cyber threats is not enough. Active threat detection refers to a paradigm shift of the traditional reactive security to more responsive and intelligent security position. Having machine learning and behavioral analytics, continuous monitoring, and threat intelligence in place, the organizations will receive an opportunity to demonstrate the areas of weakness and remove them prior to formation. Such an all-encompassing solution is more not only much more efficient in detecting and responding to events faster but also reduces business downtimes, information loss as well as image loss. Complexes of the so-called alert fatigue, volumes of data and skills gaps in a world of the previously discussed challenges cannot be compared to the benefits of active detection. Finally, dynamic and active intelligence-led and driven cybersecurity would evolve into active threat detection 2.0 and give companies an opportunity to forecast, separate, and react on a cyberattack in a constantly evolving virtual world. It has been of significance in detection and management of detriments, which otherwise would cause massive amounts of losses. Both approaches may ensure real-time visibility, identify problems at an early stage, and take necessary steps in a timely, effective, and efficient manner, thus raising the resilience of the organization. Even though some fears, such as too much data, false positives and skills, have persisted, an inkling of advanced technologies and simplified interventions can help detection, as well as operations, to become, even more efficient and precise. On the whole the prevention of threats is no longer a choice but is now a necessity. Firms which embrace the ideas of predictive, intelligence-based protection will be able to decrease the dwell time, reduce attack related risks before they run wild, and establish a high security profile that keeps them ahead of more advanced attackers in an increasingly complex online existential framework.

REFERENCES

Alanazi, F., Elsobky, B., & Elmorsy, S. (2024). A hybrid machine learning framework for security intrusion detection. *Computer Systems Science and Engineering*, *48*(3), 1–10. DOI: 10.32604/csse.2024.042401

Blessing, M. (2024). *Predictive analytics for proactive threat mitigation* [Preprint]. ResearchGate. https://www.researchgate.net/publication/389264973_Predictive_Analytics_for_Proactive_Threat_Mitigation

George, A. S., & Fernando, S., Baskar, & George, A. S. (2023). Extending detection and response: How MXDR evolves cybersecurity. *Partners Universal International Innovation Journal*, *1*(4), 268–285. DOI: 10.5281/zenodo.8284342

Ismail, K. R., Brata, Z. A., Nelistiani, G. A., Heo, S., Kim, H., & Kim, H. (2025). Toward robust security orchestration and automated response in security operations centers with a hyper-automation approach using agentic artificial intelligence. *Information (Basel)*, *16*(5), 365. Advance online publication. DOI: 10.3390/info16050365

Ke, H., Xu, J., Wang, Y., Chen, H., & Shen, Z. (2025). Adversarial machine learning in cybersecurity: Attacks and defenses. *International Journal of Management Science Research*, *8*, 26–33. DOI: 10.53469/ijomsr.2025.08(02).04

Kern, M., Landauer, M., Skopik, F., & Weippl, E. (2024). A logging maturity and decision model for the selection of intrusion detection cyber security solutions. *Computers & Security*, *141*, 103844. Advance online publication. DOI: 10.1016/j.cose.2024.103844

Khaleel, Y. L., Habeeb, M. A., Albahri, A. S., Al-Quraishi, T., Albahri, O. S., & Alamoodi, A. H. (2024). Network and cybersecurity applications of defense in adversarial attacks: A state-of-the-art using machine learning and deep learning methods. *Journal of Intelligent Systems*, *33*(1), 20240153. Advance online publication. DOI: 10.1515/jisys-2024-0153

Khayat, M., Barka, E., Serhani, M. A., Sallabi, F., Shuaib, K., & Khater, H. (2025). Empowering security operation center with artificial intelligence and machine learning—A systematic literature review. *IEEE Access: Practical Innovations, Open Solutions*, *13*, 19162–19197. DOI: 10.1109/ACCESS.2025.3532951

Olaniyan, R., Rakshit, S., & Vajjhala, N. (2023). Application of user and entity behavioral analytics (UEBA) in the detection of cyber threats and vulnerabilities management. In *Computational intelligence for engineering and management applications* (pp. 1–15). Springer. https://doi.org/DOI: 10.1007/978-981-19-8493-8_32

Redino, R., Iyer, R., & Suri, N. (2022). Zero day threat detection using graph and flow based security telemetry [Preprint]. arXiv. https://arxiv.org/abs/2205.02298

Sewak, M., Karim, R., & Pournaras, E. (2022). Deep reinforcement learning for cybersecurity threat detection and protection: A review [Preprint]. arXiv. https://arxiv.org/abs/2206.02733

Springer. (2025). Artificial intelligence and machine learning in cybersecurity. *Knowledge and Information Systems, 101*(15). https://link.springer.com/article/10.1007/s10115-025-02429-y

Stallings, W. (2020). *Effective cybersecurity: A guide to using best practices and standards*. Addison-Wesley Professional.

Chapter 6
Navigating the Human Factor in Cloud Transformation:
Adapting Roles, Behaviors, and Mindsets for Secure Cloud Adoption

Srinivas Chippagiri
https://orcid.org/0009-0004-9456-3951
Independent Researcher, USA

ABSTRACT

Cloud transformation is often misunderstood as a purely technological shift, yet this report makes a compelling case that problem roles, behaviors, and mindsets are the true foundation of secure and successful cloud adoption. Through comprehensive analysis, it reveals that organizational culture, resistance to change, legacy mindsets, and cognitive biases are often more significant obstacles than the technical challenges themselves. Redefining leadership roles (like CIOs and CTOs), embedding security into daily behavior, and fostering shared responsibility are presented as critical steps. Moreover, adapting to Zero Trust models, promoting continuous learning, and cultivating growth and resilience mindsets are essential behavioral pivots. The document emphasizes that security must be driven top-down and modeled by leadership, making it clear that in the cloud era, the human factor is not the weakest link but the decisive one.

DOI: 10.4018/979-8-3373-4154-5.ch006

1. INTRODUCTION

Cloud transformation is perhaps the most significant paradigm shift in information technology over the past two decades. It is an evolution from earlier centralized mainframes to distributed client–server architectures and, more recently, to cloud-native architectures and their focus on scalability, elasticity, and economies. It is a journey that highlights a familiar truism: technological advancements by themselves are not enough to offer effective uptake. Instead, people and organizational factors—from skills and culture to trust and accountability—are the things that decide whether innovations are taken up into practice or not (Alotaibi & Alzahrani, 2021).

While technical press is likely to report cloud adoption as an architecture, migration tactic, or vendor choice, mounting evidence shows human resistance, shortage of skills, and culture inertia to be greater than tech issues (Beautement & Sasse, 2019; Koskinen, 2023). Organizations that underrate workers' resistance to abandoning legacy solutions or ignore necessary new cross-functional collaboration infrastructure, for instance, are likely to be affected by implementation failure. Cloud transformation is, in these senses, better described as a socio-technical transition, where successful adoption is as much a function of human adaptation as technical innovation.

Security is one of the greatest examples of such interdependence. Cloud computing demolishes traditional security silos, disperses workloads, and imposes shared responsibility on customers and providers. With highly secure infrastructure, however, carelessness in process or misconfiguration by personnel can lead to breaches, e.g., the 2019 Capital One breach. Academic writing stresses that the vast majority of breaches involving the cloud are caused by human mistakes and not by equipment failure (Singh & Kaur, 2024). It means that the user behavior, awareness, and decision-making are the most probable weakest link of cloud security, and it is not the systems (Kumar, 2024).

Meanwhile, humans are cause of weakness and an ultimate defense. Employees are as good security professionals as anyone else, with appropriate training, culture enablement, and mindset, applying security best practices such as least privileged access, multifactor auth, and security-by-design coding as routine work. Behavioral interventions such as those of gamified security awareness training or identification of security champions in teams exemplify the strength in thinking organizational psychology and technical strategy as converged (WeActis, 2022). Thus, human factor must neither be ignored as weakness but be embraced as a central variable that can disrupt or enable transformational success (Stenberg, 2020). It is about raising questions as to how redefinition of roles rebuilds cloud security responsibility, how behavior at every level must be altered individually, and how attitude facilitates resilience, learning, as well as collaboration across silos. These are immediate organizational outcomes. A CIO still conceptualizing his role, as in the past, as that of infrastructure sentry is soon likely to fail in the mode of strong leadership in order to manage culture change (AWS, 2023). Developers still thinking security is "someone else's job" still spread vulnerabilities that no defense at the technological level can eliminate (Coles-Kemp & Reeves, 2017). End-users opting for multifactor authentication as a hassle may unknowingly provide the chink in the wall that can be the entry point for breaches liable to affect entire organizations (CISA, 2023).

Literatures of cloud adoption have rightly suggested that employees are not passive objects in the process but are change agents themselves. Cloud readiness research has elaborated that successful adoption is when staff are enabled by competencies, education, and specified duty, but unsuccessful while there is inertia in culture and lacking effective communication (Alharkan & Aslam, 2019; Koskinen, 2023). More than that, secure adoption is not done as a one-time exercise, but as repetitive in nature, i.e., learning, reinforcement, and adaptation are tried on a sustained basis. Cloud technologies are evolving at a extremely rapid rate and so must be the humans that govern and manage them.

This chapter makes the case for successful cloud security change as needing organizations to pay particular attention to three axes of human adaptation: the redefinition of work roles, the integration of secure behavior, and the generation of adaptive mindsets. These three axes draw strength from each other: new work roles define duty, behavior is secure behavior, and mindset provides the necessary long-term cultural adaptability for change. These paragraphs discuss these axes in more detail, putting them into the context of the modern security architecture incorporating the AWS Cloud Adoption Framework (AWS, 2022), the CISA Cloud Security Technical Reference Architecture (CISA, 2023), and research regarding security behavior (Stenberg, 2020). With the definition of cloud transformation as the human and technical transformation, the subsequent argument illustrates that safe adoption is not merely based on workload movement but is based on transforming the organization from the inside out. The human component does not need to be accommodated but rather is a high-value asset that, properly aligned, unlocks resilience, innovation, and trust in the cloud age.

2. THE HUMAN FACTOR IN CLOUD TRANSFORMATION

2.1 Cultural Resistance and Organizational Barriers

Cloud transformation has often been framed as upgrading infrastructure, platforms, or systems but thereby unwarrantedly suppresses the moot point that organizations are not transformed but human beings in them. Cloud technical competence is achievable by human beings in the organization changing their behavior, trusting newly adopted procedures, and learning safe habits. The "human factor" is thus the best risk and best opportunity in cloud adoption (Beautement & Sasse, 2019).

Figure 1 is a conceptual diagram illustrating the barriers to Human Factors and Ergonomics (HFE) adoption within organizations.

Figure 1. Barriers to Human Factor Adoption

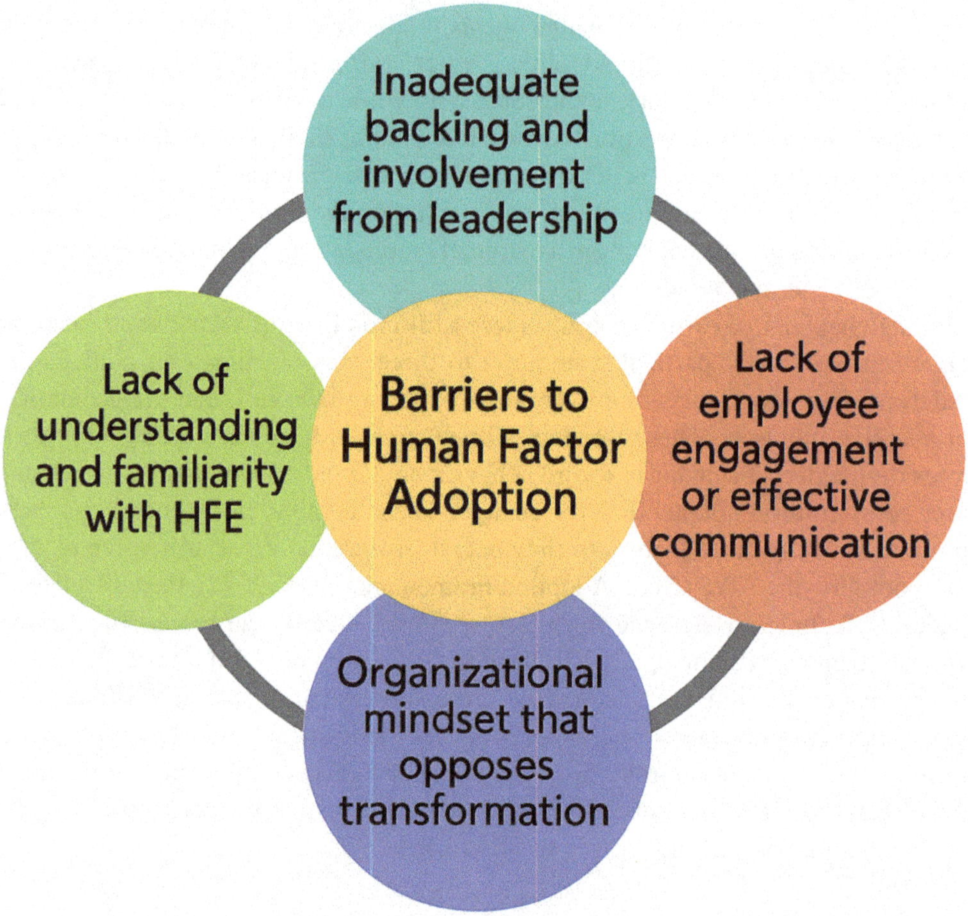

At the center is the core issue, surrounded by four key challenges: inadequate management commitment and support, failure to communicate with or involve employees, organizational culture resistant to change, and insufficient awareness or knowledge of HFE (Nkosi, Gupta, & Mashinini, 2023). The circular arrangement emphasizes how these barriers are interconnected and collectively hinder the successful integration of HFE principles. Understanding and addressing each of these obstacles is critical for fostering a work environment that prioritizes human well-being, safety, and performance through ergonomic and human-centered design strategies.

Besides, cultural resistance is fueled by the perception of a loss of control. Centralized control over systems by managers is something they will struggle to adapt to the distributed accountability required by cloud environments. Insecure practices—excessive provision of access as a method of maintaining authority—will typically grow out of such cultural tensions (Alotaibi & Alzahrani, 2021).

2.2 The Security Mindset Gap

Cloud adoption comes with a security paradigm shift: from static perimeter defenses to dynamic, distributed monitoring. The cloud provider's physical infrastructure and hypervisor security are protected, but the customers must still manage configuration, access, and data governance on their own. The shared model of responsibility calls for all the people in any organization to become responsible for security (CISA, 2023).

Even though personnel will still demand to reinforce the legacy mentality that "security is in the province of the IT department," this perception gap engenders unwarranted vulnerabilities. Backdoor storage service misconfigurations, adverse password behavior, and access control weakness are the top causative breaches (Singh & Kaur, 2024). These are behavioral and perceptual, not technological, failures.

Chartered Institute of Ergonomics & Human Factors (2016) argue that security continues, in most businesses, as a periodic compliance exercise, not day-to-day behavior. Awareness-to-action gap is particularly prominent in those businesses that provide training in the absence of reinforcement. Employees are cognizant of multifactor authentication's necessity but do not turn it on due to perceived hassle (WeActis, 2022). Closing the gap means that businesses must place security expectations in the definition of roles, day-to-day workflow, and workplace culture.

2.3 Collaboration and the Shared Responsibility Model

The other important human consideration in cloud transformation is that of collaboration. The shared responsibility model is not only a social contract between companies, but rather a technical acceptability between provider and customer. IT, application development, security compliance, and business leadership must work together in order to ensure that risk management is implemented at each level.

Where cooperation fails, organizatios lack speed and safety compatibility. Inadequate testing can enable dev teams to go live too fast, and hard controls requiring by security teams may choke innovation. Coles-Kemp and Reeves (2017) reckon that security cultures move in these directions and form adversarial relationships in which dev teams view security as an inhibitor of functions instead of a facilitator. It is a culture that encourages the development of shadow IT, by going round governance models.

Conversely, security is baked into the development processes of the organizations that promote shared responsibility (e.g. by putting security professionals on DevOps workflows as DevSecops champions) such that security becomes a requirement and not an audit after the fact (AWS, 2022). Stenberg (2020) further explains that shared responsibility is both structural and cultural; mutual trust and mutual communication among teams are what either practice or break shared responsibility.

2.4 The Human Factor in Security Failures

A combination of human-centric vulnerabilities is observed in the contemporary cloud security attacks that go way beyond the Capital one breach. SolarWinds supply chain attack of 2020 demonstrated that the human trust assumptions about the integrity of the software posed a chain of vulnerabilities in thousands of organizations (CISA, 2021). Such phishing attacks exploited the human nature to have confidence in the authenticity of software updates, which creates the necessity to verify zero-trust even when developing relationships with trusted vendors.

Microsoft Exchange Server vulnerabilities (Hafnium attacks) that took place in 2021 also demonstrated the complexity of the human factor. Although the original vectors of attack were technical, the high numbers of people affected were caused by human factors: the organizations that did not immediately apply patches, lack of monitoring of red flags of a compromise, and coordination of incident response (NSA, 2021). The events highlight that the human decision-making gaps are the main cause that leads to the technical vulnerabilities turning into security failures.

According to the Data Breach Investigations Report by Verizon (2024), 68 percent of breaches are human-related, such as social engineering or privilege abuse, or just an error. These human aspects are manifested on cloud environments differently:

Configuration Drift: Secure settings do not improve over time with an administrator applying changes one after another and not fully examining their security implications. According to a study which was carried out by Palo Alto Networks (2023), the majority of cloud security attacks are a result of misconfiguration by a customer, rather than a vulnerability of a provider.

Privilege Escalation: Privileges are given to employees over time without periodic maintenance and offer attacker vectors that are never reassessed based on job role changes. The regular human access and attention control requires the least privilege principle.

Insider Threats: Insider malicious and careless activities are also a continuous threat. The insider access privilege is the point of attack demonstrated by the 2023 hacked credentials of the employees and the lack of separation of duties (LastPass, 2023).

New Social Engineering: Clouds provide new social engineering. Phishing attacks on cloud services administrators and cloud services developers are at an unprecedented high through advanced phishing attacks that impersonate cloud service interfaces and administrative panels.

All these tendencies put forward the fact that the process of secure cloud adoption must be supported with human-based approaches to the defense mechanisms, which will consider behavioral, cultural, and psychological factors besides technical obstacles.

2.5 Organizational Trust and Psychological Safety

Trust is another one of the aspects of human factor that is often underestimated. Employees must have confidence in cloud technologies, and in their organisations too. When employees are too afraid of being punished or scolded because of mistakes, they will be less likely to report configuration errors or declare that a system is insecure. In combination with these, danger is enhanced when silence is involved. The fact that psychological safety, which is a sense that there is no imminent punishment, is a condition of resilience is supported by the research on organizational culture (Beautement and Sasse, 2019).

The same is true of provider relationships. Employees will not trust cloud platforms when they are not sure about the vendor guarantees in security or regulation (Alharkan and Aslam, 2019). It entails open communication of the management of vendor promises and controls put in place by the business by the leadership.

2.6 Human Factors in Diverse Industry Settings

Industry context dictates human factors in cloud adoption. Patient care, for instance, is weighed against security considerations in the healthcare sector. Strictly controlled authentication can be disruptive to workflows by causing staff to create insecure workarounds (Alotaibi & Alzahrani, 2021). In financial services, there is resistance to rapid change driven by culture conservatism and by compliance requirements, but successful businesses achieve this by building ongoing training cultures that make complying second nature in day-to-day working (AWS, 2023). For extremely innovative industries like media and entertainment, speed and experimentation cultural imperatives raise the likelihood of skipping controls. Netflix's leading-edge approach to using chaos engineering as a model demonstrates how culture alignment for resilience can make that risk a strength by institutionalizing experimentation as part of organizational mentality. Though not presented in terms of a direct study case for human factors, it demonstrates how culture and mentality determine outcomes for the adoption of technology (Koskinen, 2023).

3. REDEFINING ROLES IN THE CLOUD ERA

Cloud transformation goes beyond offloading workloads from on-premises infrastructure to virtualized environments; it re-maps the organization responsibility flow. Historically, IT roles defined static perimeters and highly structured hierarchies: administrators managed servers, security administrators enforced policy, and end-users consumed systems with minimal responsibility. In the cloud, however, everything is decentralized and codependent. Each role, including C-suite officer to staff member, must be re-established in terms of the shared responsibility model (CISA, 2023).

Figure 2. Organizational Hierarchy

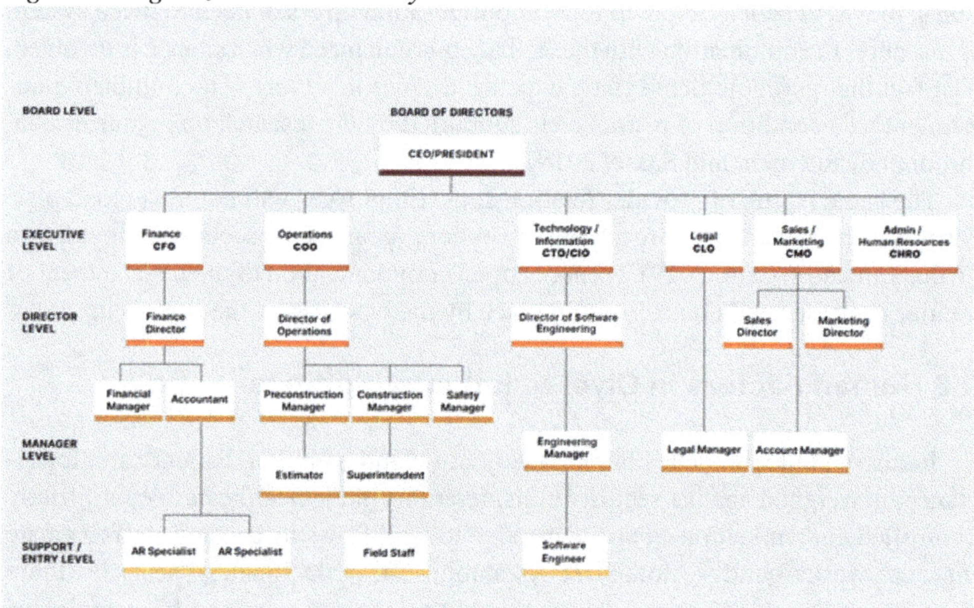

Figure above illustrates a typical organizational hierarchy, starting at the board level with the Board of Directors and CEO/President, and cascading down to executive, director, manager, and entry/support levels. Each branch reflects a core business function—Finance (CFO), Operations (COO), Technology/Information (CTO/CIO), Legal (CLO), Sales/Marketing (CMO), and Admin/HR (CHRO). Beneath these executives, responsibilities split further into directors, managers, and staff, showing how decision-making, strategy, and execution flow across the enterprise.

In any modern enterprise, this structure provides the foundation for defining roles, responsibilities, and accountability. However, as organizations move toward digital transformation and cloud adoption, this hierarchy plays a critical role in determining who owns what in terms of technology integration, security oversight, and compliance.

These roles play a vital role in spearheading cloud adoption, and cloud strategy also cuts across the Finance (budgeting to migrate to cloud), Operations (business continuity), Legal (contracts, compliance), Sales/Marketing (digital services), and HR (reskilling teams) areas. It implies that cloud adoption is not a technological project but an organizational cultural and structural change.

3.1 How Cloud Adoption Starts

The general first application of the cloud is:

Executive Alignment - On the level of cloud solutions, the vision of agility, scalability and cost-effective state is defined by the Board and the CEO.
Technology Leadership - CTO/CIO is the leader in charge of cloud providers, migration roadmap and architecture decisions.
Cross-Functional Involvement - Finance approves budgets to migrate, Operations ensure a continuation of the processes, HR ensure the transfer of skills, and the Legal does not leave vendor contracts unattended.
Pilot Projects - Pilot projects are often initiated as a subset of software engineering or operations teams so as to test performance, cost and security considerations.

By so doing, adoption of clouds is not the prerogative of the IT department but it is integrated up the ranks. Agility is achieved by adopting clouds but also security threats- data breaches, compliance failures and misunderstood shared responsibility. The security must be incorporated first and foremost:

Board and CEO Oversight - Rubber stamp risk management schemes and security policies.
CIO/CTO Leadership - Provide clear cloud security strategy, models and vendors SLA. Legal and Compliance (CLO) Regulatory compliance (GDPR, HIPAA, PCI DSS).

Operations and engineering teams - This institution of access controls, encryption, monitoring and incident response procedures.

HR/CHRO training-Develop security awareness in the entire organization to reduce human error. Security is a top-down concept, then, but one that permeates across all levels, making it the role of executives to define the governance framework, engineers to build zero-trust designs, and entry-level employees to perform safely with the data and systems.

The security should be a top-down strategy in the modern digital world. It is no longer a technical problem it is a business-critical issue that affects all the departments.

The CIO and CTO play vital roles in implementing secure systems and practices, but without the support and understanding of the CEO and CFO, security strategies can lack the resources or influence needed to be effective. True resilience comes when executive leadership embeds security into the organizational culture, ensuring it is considered in every decision, from budgeting and product development to employee training and risk management.

CIOs and CTOs once existed as custodians of infrastructure. They were successful on uptime, service-level, and cost metrics. In the cloud era, however, they must do better than that, providing operational performance, yes, but also strategically enabling innovation and business resilience (AWS, 2023).

It is determined by Alharkan and Aslam (2019) that leadership orientation is one of the best predictors of successful adoption. The CIO's problem, then, is that of culture architect, not only for migration plans but for leading by example in support behavior for outcomes from transformation (Coles-Kemp & Reeves, 2017).

One such best example is the financial sector, in which conservative leadership cultures will be most likely to hinder the adoption. Financial institutions that are successful, like Capital One, have managed to do so by having CIOs and CTOs become change champions who position cloud adoption as business transformation, not IT projects. As much as the 2019 breach by Capital One was a show of the risk of misconfiguration, the greater trend shows how leadership at the executive level can get cloud incorporated into the strategic hub of the business operation (CISA, 2023).

3.2 Security Teams: Once the Gatekeepers, now Imbedded Partners

The earlier versions provided security, but in a retrospective and centralized way such as compliance checks or end of phase audits. Such types of so-called gatekeeping do not fit cloud-native development pace. The security teams who remain in the previous positions will tend to create bottlenecks. Instead, they must reinvent themselves as part of the development pipeline in fundamental ways (Beautement & Sasse, 2019).

This paradigm suits best the DevSecOps model. Through the use of security personnel during the initial stages of devops, organizations can be confident of identifying vulnerabilities during the design and construction phases and not after deployment. Kumar (2024) acknowledges that the safe coding training of engineers and the deployment of so-called security champions on every team is superior to the centralized auditing. The mission of the security personnel is then revised to promoting secure innovation, and not merely compliance.

There is empirical evidence to suggest that shared security culture firms are less prone to incidents and more resilient (Stenberg, 2020). By redefining their role as capacity builders or enablers, security professionals gain the goodwill of the builders, who then transform security into a business of all the people and not something foreign (WeActis, 2022).

3.3 Developers: Security and Compliance Ownership

Developers have a quite central role in the cloud age. They used to be more focused on functionality and performance earlier. Security, governance, and compliance were left to other teams. Developers in the cloud-native environments are required to, however, consider these aspects in their everyday work (Singh & Kaur, 2024).

Infrastructure as Code (IaC), for instance, gives developers a way to provision infrastructure programmatically. The very templates that make everything fast, also, work well at infecting misconfigurations unless they are designed with security in mind (CISA, 2023). One error, such as a wrongly placed allowance in an IAM policy, could be enough of a disaster to destroy whole systems. Security ownership is no longer an exception to the developer and is now flat-out ownership of secure infrastructure.

Alotaibi and Alzahrani (2021) conclude that such redefinition of the role identity may be difficult. Increased responsibility might not be welcomed by developers as scope creep. The effective businesses solve this by integrating learning about security into the development training process to ensure that secure coding is not an addition to software engineering, but rather an element of modern software engineering (Kumar, 2024).

3.4 Operations Staff: Managers to Engineers of Automation

Manual operations: patching, monitoring and repairs used to be the purview of operations teams. These are mostly performed through scripts and platforms with recently introduced cloud automations and orchestration tools. As a result, operations teams are moving out of system administrator roles and moving into automation engineers (AWS, 2022).

The change involves learning new skills, for example, infrastructure automation, monitoring-as-code and orchestration. Koskinen (2023) has found that the aspect of culture of the transformation is not highly valued by the organizations. The working staff members may experience the feelings of being replaced or automated in their work. The key to successful organizations making that transition is investing in staff upskilling, and viewing automation as empowering human capability, rather than eliminating human capability, and freeing up staff to do higher order work of resilience and governance.

Operations personnel is also better aligned to governance as a result of this change in function. They no longer have to react manually to the outages, but they design systems that are resilient so they can anticipate the failure. All this is in the context of cultural change towards resilience thinking in which failure is not avoided but controlled before it happens (Beautement & Sasse, 2019).

3.5 End-Users: Awareness and Responsibility Building

Non technical workers are rarely considered while laying the groundwork to implement clouds, yet they represent the most powerful attack vectors. End-users interact with cloud infrastructure constantly - they are depositing sensitive documents, spinning up a SaaS application or sending files offsite. Such activities have more and more influence on the security of the company (WeActis, 2022).

According to studies, human error on the end-user's end, for instance, such as poor password strength, or insecure sharing, continues to be the top cause of breaches (Singh & Kaur, 2024). Efforts that involve using end-users as passive partners in bridging this gap are not sufficient. Secure cloud adoption, though, must be complemented by heightened end-user responsibility.

Stenberg (2020) provides training, communication, and accountability as cultural influences that enable security behavior. End-users must be trained not only on compliance with rules of behavior but with the why behind why they have those policies in the first place. For instance, explaining how multifactor authenticates prevents credential-stealing elevates levels of adoption above mandating it with no explanation.

3.6 Cross-Functional Collaboration and Role Integration

Aside from the roles, cloud adoption redefines how roles interact with other roles. Shared responsibility asks for less-formal boundary lines between operators, security, and developers and expects sustained coordination, instead of point-to-point sequential handoffs.

According to Coles-Kemp and Reeves (2017), silo-centric approaches rely on adversary cultures, and hybrid roles alignments support trust and resilience. AWS Cloud Adoption Framework (2022) is much more emphatic about the People Perspective, and how workforce alignments must keep changing in line with cloud capabilities. Company integration of collaboration as a structural requirement is provided through cross-functional teams and specification of collectively shared accountabilities.

3.7 Industry Examples

It is industry specific with regards to role creation. Healthcare clinicians and administrators, in particular, will need to adjust to increased regulation of information in HIPAA and GDPR. The variables on which the effectiveness of the healthcare cloud use was based, as determined by Alotaibi and Alzahrani (2021), were the user training and trust, as opposed to technical compliance. The partners of developers and compliance officers need to work harder than in classical IT, in the financial IT. The issue is how to balance innovation and regulation. Those that build compliance into development pipelines in a way that recasts jobs not only are agile but also trustworthy (AWS, 2023). Operations teams must leverage automation to the maximum in the public sector, which has limited resources, and must be transparent. Koskinen (2023) further states that cultural resistance is more likely to be high in such settings and that the leadership must communicate role changes cautiously to ensure trust is not lost.

4. ADAPTING BEHAVIORS FOR SECURE CLOUD ADOPTION

If redefining roles sets the **structural foundation**, then adapting behaviors builds the **operational culture**. Cloud adoption requires individuals to act differently in day-to-day work, embracing new habits and abandoning outdated practices.

4.1 From Perimeter Thinking to Zero Trust

The traditional castle-and-moat model of security makes the assumption that internal network traffic is trusted by virtue of having been authenticated at the perimeter of the network. This assumption is fundamentally challenged by cloud environments that break down network barriers and re-allocate resources across multiple service providers, across geographic tiers, and across points of access.

Zero Trust Architecture (ZTA) becomes the new normal security posture of the new cloud environment, which operates on the principle of never trust, always verify (NIST, 2020).

Zero Trust according to NIST Special Publication 800-207 is a cybersecurity approach that safeguards an organization by eliminating implicit trusts and continuously verifying any interaction between two electronic transactions (NIST, 2020). The paradigm shift in terms of cloud transformation means a fundamental change in the human behavior, in the human organizational processes and in the mechanisms of implementation.

Zero Trust in humans has behavioral implications, which are far-reaching. Staffs should understand that the authentication is no longer a point in time activity but an uninterrupted active process that will authenticate their identity. A recent study conducted by Forrester (2023) has found that 67 percent of security practitioners surveyed are overwhelmed with the reason behind user friction in implementing the Zero Trust (Seaman, 2023).

The implementation of Zero Trust is associated with a number of principles that have a direct implication on human factors:

- **Identity Verification:** Authentication and authorization of each user, device, and application should be done continuously. This necessitates the employees to adopt multi-factor authentication, identity governance, and just in time access controls as part of normal working practices.
- **Least Privilege Access:** This allows users to have minimum required permissions in order to conduct their roles. As stated by the Cloud Security Alliance (2023), the same principle necessitates cultural changes, and employees should view restrictions of access as security, and not as a hindrance to productivity.
- **Micro-segmentation:** Network segmentation is now extended to workloads and applications. The IT departments will have to acquire new capabilities in the software-defined network and policy management and remain visible in distributed environments.
- **Continuous Monitoring**: It becomes the norm to perform real-time action on user behavior, device health, and network traffic. Security departments shift towards constant threat detection and remedial capabilities as opposed to a periodical assessment.

The 2023 Microsoft 365 security breach, when cybercriminals gained access to the email accounts of their clients using damaged authentication systems, is an example of the urgency of the application of the principles of the Zero Trust in the cloud environment. In contrast to the Capital One breach, the event shown revealed how the outdated perimeter defenses are ineffective in face of advanced identity-based attacks against cloud services directly (Microsoft, 2023).

Zero Trust in organizations is associated with high change management challenges. Employees can feel that additional authentication is a productivity cost and result in workaround to bypass security posture. To be successful, Zero Trust adoption is associated with the development of comprehensive training programs that will underline the protection value of constant check-ups instead of framing such measures as the lack of trust.

4.2 From Reactive Fixes to Proactive Resilience

Cloud-native organizations must embrace a culture of **proactive resilience** rather than reactive firefighting. This means behaviors such as:

- Running frequent penetration tests, not waiting for audits.
- Automating security patching rather than applying fixes post-incident.
- Simulating outages through chaos engineering to test resilience (Koskinen, 2023).

Chartered Institute of Ergonomics & Human Factors (2016) stresses that employees often undervalue resilience testing because the benefits are invisible until a failure occurs. Overcoming this requires leadership commitment and communication of long-term value.

4.3 From Individual Accountability to Shared Responsibility

In legacy IT, accountability was concentrated in IT or security departments. In the cloud, accountability becomes shared across roles. The AWS Cloud Adoption Framework highlights the people perspective as central to adoption, where governance structures clarify who is accountable for security, compliance, and operations (AWS, 2022).

Stenberg (2020) identifies seven cultural dimensions that shape secure behavior, including communication, training, and accountability. Embedding shared responsibility into team structures reinforces secure practices at every layer.

4.4 Embedding Security into Daily Behaviors

Practical daily behaviors matter:

- Developers adopting secure coding checklists.

- Operations teams enforcing least privilege policies.
- Employees resisting social engineering attempts.

As Singh and Kaur (2024) argue, human error remains the largest cause of breaches, from weak passwords to misconfigured storage. Behavior-driven training such as phishing simulations, gamified awareness exercises, and red/blue team drills helps translate abstract knowledge into daily practice (KnowBe4, 2020).

4.5 Security Champions and Peer Influence

One proven strategy is creating security champions—individuals embedded within teams who promote secure practices. This leverages peer influence to reinforce behaviors. WeActis (2022) notes that peer-driven reinforcement can shift mindsets more effectively than top-down mandates, as employees model behaviors from colleagues they trust.

5. SHIFTING MINDSETS FOR TRANSFORMATION SUCCESS

If redefining roles provides the structural framework and adapting behaviors shapes the daily practices, then shifting mindsets is about cultivating the deeper attitudes and cognitive orientations necessary for secure cloud adoption. Cloud transformation is not just about "doing things differently"; it is about thinking differently and approaching problems with new mental models that align with the demands of digital ecosystems.

5.1 The Growth Mindset: Learning as a Continuous Imperative

A defining characteristic of cloud adoption is its rapidly evolving knowledge base. Services change monthly, if not weekly; security features are continuously added; and best practices shift with emerging threats (Chippagiri & Ravula, 2021). Employees must adopt a growth mindset, embracing continuous learning rather than relying on static expertise.

Koskinen's (2023) study on organizational adoption challenges highlights that resistance often arises when employees perceive learning cloud platforms as an additional burden. Organizations that succeed frame learning as a core responsibility, not a side activity. Certification programs, internal workshops, and hands-on labs reinforce the expectation that every role—from developers to managers—must learn, unlearn, and relearn.

5.2 The Resilience Mindset: Embracing Failure and Recovery

Legacy IT often cultivated a mindset of perfectionism, where downtime was intolerable and mistakes were punished. In cloud environments, however, systems are too complex for perfection. Instead, resilience becomes the goal: systems should fail gracefully and recover quickly (AWS, 2023).

This requires employees to reframe their relationship with failure. Engineers must be willing to experiment with new architectures, knowing that automated rollback and redundancy can mitigate risks. Security teams must accept that breaches are not a matter of "if" but "when," and focus on incident response and recovery speed (Chartered Institute of Ergonomics & Human Factors, 2016).

Cultural research underscores the role of psychological safety in resilience. Employees innovate more readily when they believe mistakes will be treated as learning opportunities rather than grounds for blame (Coles-Kemp & Reeves, 2017). Organizations that punish failure foster concealment and risk aversion—behaviors antithetical to cloud agility.

5.3 The Security-First Mindset: Embedding Security in Design

Perhaps the most critical mindset is security-first thinking. In traditional IT, security was bolted on after systems were built. In the cloud, this approach is untenable: insecure configurations or vulnerable code can be exploited immediately, at scale (Singh & Kaur, 2024).

A security-first mindset requires everyone—from developers to executives—to see security as non-negotiable. This aligns with the principle of "secure by design," in which systems are architected with security woven into their foundation (CISA, 2023).

Beautement and Sasse (2019) argue that security fatigue arises when employees view security as a series of external constraints. To counter this, leaders must cultivate intrinsic motivation—emphasizing security as a shared value and a protector of trust, not merely a compliance requirement.

5.4 The Collaboration Mindset: Security and Innovation as Co-Drivers

Cloud adoption collapses traditional silos between development, operations, and security. Success requires a collaboration mindset, in which teams see security and innovation as co-drivers of progress, not competitors (AWS, 2022).

The CyBOK human factors report (Beautement & Sasse, 2019) stresses that collaboration is not just structural but cognitive: it requires teams to shift from "us vs. them" thinking to collective ownership. Security professionals must see themselves as partners in enabling business outcomes, while developers must view security colleagues as allies rather than obstacles.

A study on security culture found communication as an important dimension: the researcher found that companies with open communication lines, where employees feel free to report security risks with no fear of consequences, adopt more security postures (Stenberg, 2020). On the other hand, siloed thinking creates adversarial behavior that slows down projects and creates weaknesses.

5.5 Overcoming Cognitive Biases and Resistance

Cognitive biases involve routine methods of non-rationality in judgement and decision making. They influence our way of perceiving information, beliefs and choices- most of the times without our realizing. By being aware of their common biases, we can learn more about our biases and make better and more objective decisions.

Figure 3 outlines 4 common cognitive biases that play role in human thinking and decision making: Confirmation Bias, Anchoring Bias, Availability Bias and the Bandwagon Effect. All prejudices are psychological breaks, or fallacies of thinking. An example of Confirmation Bias causes individuals to look for information that can confirm what they already know and ignore the ones that can disprove them. Anchoring Bias consequences include excessive reliance on the first piece of information one gets that affects all the judgments. People overestimate the likelihood or importance of events with respect to their memorability; which is Bias of Availability and people tend to behave or believe in things just because other people behave or believe; which is Bandwagon Effect.

Figure 3. Common Cognitive Biases

These biases should be learned in such areas as decision science, business strategy, policy-making and even simple problem-solving. These mental shortcuts, unless put at check, can undermine objectivity, interfere with judgment and make ineffective conclusions. By more clearly comprehending and mitigating their effects, promoting evidence-based decision-making and promoting more rational and inclusive decision-making, especially in complex or high-stakes scenarios, support critical thinking. Attitude shift is not an easy task because human beings are prone to cognitive bias. For instance:

- **Status quo bias**: preference for familiar systems, resisting migration.
- **Optimism bias**: underestimating the likelihood of security incidents.
- **Change fatigue**: disengagement caused by continuous transformation.

WeActis (2022) emphasizes that overcoming these biases requires behavioral nudges and cultural reinforcement. Gamification, peer modeling, and simulation exercises can reframe security from a burden into an engaging challenge. Training strategies that address emotional as well as cognitive dimensions yield stronger adoption outcomes (Kumar, 2024).

5.6 Leadership and Mindset Modeling

Finally, leadership should be a role model when it comes to changing the mindset. Employees will do what executives and managers do in case leaders view cloud security as an option or second priority, employees will follow. Conversely, the fact that leaders actively participate in the training activities, concerned with safe practices, and complimentary learning show that such attitudes are valued (Alotaibi and Alzahrani, 2021).

The other component of leadership modeling is communication. Rather than viewing the process of cloud transformation as a technical need, leaders should make it an opportunity of growth, resiliency, and innovation (AWS, 2023). This redefinition helps the employees not only to align emotionally with the change but also to align intellectually to the change.

6. COMPREHENSIVE HUMAN VULNERABILITIES IN CLOUD SECURITY

One way that humans are valuable when it comes to cloud security is much more than configuration errors, and it is complex psychological, behavioral and social factors that offer sustained attack surfaces. Cognitive bias, social engineering weaknesses, convenience-security trade-off, insider threats, and fatigue issues affecting the security posture of the employees should be examined in order to understand these weaknesses.

6.1 Social Engineering at the Cloud

Cloud services bring new vectors of social engineering attacks that are based on relationships of human trust and authority. The social engineering in the cloud is not handled in the conventional network-based attack, the administrative privileges, service accounts, and the access to the cloud console are targeted with the help of the sophisticated manipulation techniques.

According to a study by KnowBe4 (2024), in 2023, attackers impersonated cloud service providers, IT administrators, and compliance auditors by using cloud-targeted phishing attacks, which rose by 220%. These attacks are successful because people tend to believe the authority and act in times of need on the events that seem to be security-threatening. Some examples include:

CEO Fraud Evolution: The CEO fraud has evolved to include cloud administrative account. Attackers masquerade as top roles to get emergency cloud access modification, using the hierarchies and time constraints in the organization to avoid the standard approval procedures.

Compliance Theater Attacks: Advanced attackers use compliance requirements as an opportunity to authenticate requests they make to gain access to an organization, and they contrive a sense of urgency due to compliance regulations or audit demands in order to get employees who are security conscious to acquiesce.

6.2 Trade-Offs Between Convenience and Security

The friction between convenience and security controls inherent to operations poses a continuous vulnerability in the cloud. When security policies make the workflow challenging, employees will always be willing to be drawn to convenient solutions instead of secure ones.

An example of such a challenge is password management. Although cloud-based password managers are widely available, employees are still using weak and reused passwords because they believe that this will be more convenient (Cybersecurity & Infrastructure Security Agency, 2023). Adoption of multi-factor authentication is also vulnerable to the convenience bias in that the employees adopt less secure authentication procedures which involve lesser interaction (Zengeni, 2024).

The complexity of the cloud service increases the trade-offs of convenience and security. When cloud services offered by the organization seem too technical and limiting, its employees can circumvent the right procedures by using personal cloud accounts or shadow IT, often referred to as home brew. A study by McAfee (2023) revealed that 83 percent of employees access unauthorized cloud services, with the convenience and speed factors being the most common reasons to use those over the authorized options.

6.3 Insider Threat Complexity

Threats to cloud environments that are insider-based include malicious intent and irresponsible behavior and in most cases, it is quite difficult to differentiate between intentional and inadvertent security breaches. The ubiquity and accessibility of cloud services present more opportunities to insider threats through the creation of more access points and the diminishing of conventional monitoring capabilities.

Privileged Access Misuse: Cloud administrative privileges pose-greater threats of insiders. Cloud consoles also offer a global access to critical infrastructure through web interfaces unlike a traditional environment where a physical presence or a VPN connection was required to access the administrative side of an environment. Employees who are disgruntled and who have administration access may inflict large-scale destruction by deleting resources, making changes, or stealing data.

Simplification of the process of Data exfiltration: Cloud services can be used to simplify the process of data exfiltration in the form of native sharing capability, API access and mobile device synchronization. Conventional data loss prevention systems might not give sufficient visibility into the data flow within the clouds, and it opens the possibilities to malicious and careless data exposure.

Role Confusion: Cloud shared responsibility models cause role confusion that can be abused by insider threats. Staff members can purport to have a valid business reason why they need to gain access or make adjustments to the configuration by referring to the ambiguity in the demarcation of responsibility between cloud vendors and the clients.

6.4 Fatigue and Burnout Impact on Employees

The rate at which clouds are changing and the constant change in the requirements of security also leads to employee fatigue which undermines security decision making. Security fatigue occurs in terms of less security protocol attention, riskiness, and poor threat recognition.

- **Alert Fatigue:** Cloud environments produce a lot of security notifications and alerts which may overwhelm the security personnel. A study by Ponemon Institute (2023) revealed that security teams get an average of 4,484 security alerts per week and only 37 percent of them are investigated because of the lack of resources. The presence of this alert volume has desensitization effects in which a real threat can be disregarded.

- **Change Fatigue:** The changes in cloud services and security requirements lead to change fatigue that decreases the interest of employees in new security procedures. Organizations that update security policies regularly can be associated with a lowered compliance rate since employees are overburdened with the continual adjustment demands.
- **Decision Fatigue:** Cloud computing involves employees at all levels making a constant security-related decision. The mental burden of access control decisions, the measurement of risk predictors, and the implementation of security awareness in the daily working processes may result in decision fatigue undermining the quality of judgment.

7. CHANGE MANAGEMENT AND ORGANIZATIONAL READINESS

While mindset shifts are necessary, they do not occur in a vacuum. Organizations must intentionally guide their people through the process of transformation. Cloud adoption requires a systematic change management strategy that combines leadership alignment, communication, training, and reinforcement mechanisms.

7.1 Training and Upskilling Programs

One of the most critical readiness activities is training the workforce to operate effectively in cloud environments. Employees accustomed to legacy infrastructure may lack knowledge of container orchestration, cloud-native architectures, or zero trust security models (Koskinen, 2023). Structured training programs certifications, workshops, and hands-on labs reduce knowledge gaps and build confidence.

AWS (2022) identifies "People" as one of the six perspectives of its Cloud Adoption Framework, emphasizing the need for workforce readiness. Without upskilling, employees often default to insecure shortcuts, undermining even the best technical strategies (Singh & Kaur, 2024).

7.2 Communication Strategies

Change requires clarity. Employees must understand not only *what* is changing, but *why*. Transparent communication about risks, benefits, and new responsibilities builds trust. When leaders explain how cloud adoption supports strategic goals like agility, resilience, and customer trust employees are more willing to embrace new practices (Alharkan & Aslam, 2019).

Research shows that organizations with strong communication cultures demonstrate more effective security behaviors (Stenberg, 2020). Conversely, secrecy or inconsistent messaging breeds confusion and resistance.

7.3 Incentives and Recognition

Behavioral science suggests that change sticks when desired behaviors are rewarded and recognized (WeActis, 2022). Cloud adoption programs should include incentive mechanisms: recognition for developers who embed secure coding, awards for teams achieving compliance milestones, or visibility for employees who flag potential risks.

Gamified training exercises—such as red vs. blue team simulations—have proven effective at transforming abstract security requirements into engaging challenges (Kumar, 2024).

7.4 Leadership Alignment

Perhaps the most important readiness factor is leadership alignment. When executives model desired behaviors using multifactor authentication, attending cloud security briefings, or participating in training they signal that the change is valued at every level (Alotaibi & Alzahrani, 2021).

Coles-Kemp and Reeves (2017) stress that cultural change requires leaders to frame security not as a constraint but as an enabler of trust and innovation. Leaders who fail to demonstrate alignment risk undermining the very transformation they promote.

7.5 Regulatory Frameworks and Compliance Requirements

Cloud transformation occurs in more complex regulatory settings that have a direct impact on the human actions and organizational processes. The regulatory requirements such as GDPR, HIPAA, SOX and PCI DSS impose compliance requirements, which influence how the employees consume cloud services, how they handle data and how they implement security controls.

The GDPR of the European Union is considered an ideal example of how legal requirements can impact the behavior of human beings in the cloud. The data protection principles imply that employees are completely informed about the definition of data classification, consent management, and privacy-by-design in their daily operations (European Union, 2018). The application of cloud within the framework of

GDPR compliance presupposes the training sessions which would establish the competencies of the employees in terms of the data sovereignty, limitation of the cross-border transfers, and notification of the breaches.

Healthcare organization cloud computing under the HIPAA regulations has certain human factor challenges. It is necessary to balance the needs of patient care efficiency and the ability to protect the privacy of patients in the pressure of the clinical staff, which can often create a conflict between the optimization of the workflow and the adherence and compliance (HHS, 2023). Successful HIPAA-compliant utilization of clouds must encompass training programs with the ability to educate clinical choices in integrating the aspect of privacy rather than make compliance a separate administrative burden.

The organizations under the SOX, PCI DSS and banking laws are faced with new layers of complexity. The idea of segregation of duties presupposes the cloud access controls that are most likely to be incompatible with the DevOps practices in which the cross-functional collaboration has turned into the priority (PCISSC, 2022). The entities should come up with governance mechanisms that should not only meet the requirements of the regulations, but also able to offer agility to operations.

Enhanced audit capabilities and evidence collection are also required in regulating the environment in cloud. Instead of regular audit cycles, employees are forced to be adjusted to constant compliance monitoring. This change requires the development of new compliance automation, evidence management, and reporting capabilities in distributed cloud systems (Chauhan, 2023).

This is not only about individual compliance systems but also about addressing several, and even conflicting, requirements on the same. The multinational organizations are specifically challenged by the necessity to align cloud practices with the varying regulatory environments and the need to ensure consistency in operations.

8. CHALLENGES AND RISKS

Even with structured change management, organizations face significant challenges in navigating the human factor of cloud transformation.

8.1 Shadow IT and Insider Threats

When employees lack trust in formal processes, they often bypass them by provisioning cloud services without approval or storing sensitive data in unmonitored systems. This “shadow IT” creates unmonitored attack surfaces (Singh & Kaur, 2024). Insider threats, whether intentional or accidental, continue to represent one of the largest risks in cloud adoption (Chartered Institute of Ergonomics & Human Factors, 2016).

8.2 Over-Reliance on Automation

Automation is a hallmark of cloud computing, but over-reliance without human oversight introduces new risks. Misconfigured Infrastructure as Code templates can propagate vulnerabilities at scale (CISA, 2023). Humans must remain in the loop to audit, validate, and apply judgment especially in high-stakes environments such as healthcare or finance.

8.3 Burnout and Change Fatigue

The pace of cloud transformation can overwhelm employees, leading to change fatigue. Koskinen (2023) documents cases where employees disengaged when asked to learn too many tools too quickly. Burnout increases human error rates, ironically undermining the security posture cloud transformation aims to strengthen.

8.4 Ethical and Regulatory Concerns

Beyond technical risks, cloud adoption raises ethical questions. Employees may fear increased surveillance or loss of privacy under monitoring systems. Organizations must balance security with respect for individual rights (Coles-Kemp & Reeves, 2017). Regulatory frameworks such as GDPR add complexity, requiring employees to adapt behaviors around data handling and sovereignty (Alharkan & Aslam, 2019).

9. HUMAN-CENTRIC SECURE CLOUD ADOPTION BEST PRACTICES

Fighting the cultural, behavioral, and organizational barriers of cloud adoption takes careful strategies that place people, not technology, first. As consistently demonstrated by research, human mistakes and organizational mismatches are the underlying causes of most cloud security breaches (Singh & Kaur, 2024), so the construction of people-oriented best practices will be at the center of creating resilience, confidence, and lasting long-term change. The next subsections describe six complementary practices that have been demonstrated to be effective at aligning human factors with secure adoption.

9.1 Cross-functional Cloud Security Councils

Cloud adoption breaks down silos. Security officials, developers, business executives, and IT are no longer isolated but instead are required to interact over and over. Cross-functional cloud security councils are one such organizational vehicle that enables repeated interactions (AWS, 2023). The councils are composed of technical and business-area representatives meeting and converging on security practices, governance, and priority alignments.

It is explicitly evident in Stenberg (2020) that communication and accountability are one of the seven domains of security culture. Councils ensure the former by establishing forums, open decision-making, and mutual responsibility publicly stated. Without forums, companies are certain to become divided, with developers prioritizing speed, compliance prioritizing regulation, and executives prioritizing cost-effectiveness, each not taking the others into account. Councils do just the opposite by ensuring everyone is heard, thereby enabling the shared sense of responsibility advocated by CISA (2023).

These are all evidence of the influence. Take, for instance, the financial sector. There, security councils struck a balance between regulation and innovation. By involving the compliance officers in the decision-making process, apart from the developers, organizations eliminated the shadow IT risk and attained the highest secure DevOps pipeline adoption (AWS, 2022). By the way, councils are cultural integration drivers rather than administrative layers.

9.2 Secure-By-Design Principles

Security by design from the very beginning is best practice. Security was an afterthought in legacy IT projects. Cloud environments make such an afterthought impossible: vulnerabilities inserted during initial configuration can be exploited at scale within hours (CISA, 2023). Secure-by-design principles must include encryption, identity management, access control, and monitoring as non-negotiable defaults.

Alotaibi and Alzahrani (2021) are of the view that human security management considerations work more effectively when mixed with the system processes. When secure practices are integrated at initial design stages, employees do not believe that they are part of "how we do work" but instead, they are viewed, with reduced resistance and exhaustion, as something external.

Practical strategies are:

- Extensively training developers to utilize secure coding checklists throughout design reviews.
- Integrating automated security scanning tools into CI/CD pipelines.

- Introducing architectural review boards that review resilience and compliance prior to deployment.

Successful secure-by-design companies also have developer ownership. Singh and Kaur (2024) explain that vulnerabilities are generally introduced by default by reason of insecure developer practices like overly granted permissions. Owner ship transfer at design time helps eliminate the security awareness gap.

9.3 Continuous Learning Ecosystems

Growth of cloud is dynamic; platforms are updated every month, and threat profiles remain ever-changing. Organizations thus need to develop dynamic learning environments that integrate training into the pace of daily work life (Koskinen, 2023). As opposed to certification programs of the one-shot variety, sustained learning focuses on repeated skill-building, peer learning, and contemporaneous adjustment.

Adaptation is staff capacity dependent, as argued by Alharkan and Aslam (2019). Where learning ceases, resistance is validated. Despite this, if learning is perceived by staff as good and encouraged, they are more prepared to adapt emerging threats. Learning cultures that are continuous may involve:

Internal "cloud labs" that enable employees to safely test out new services.
Certification incentive structures that make employees invest in training.
Peer communities of practice where individuals share solutions and learning.

WeActis (2022) notes that learning has most influence once it extends its focus from the compliance training into engagement models. Gamification, scenario training, and peer mentoring promote recall and transfer knowledge into practice. Organizations alleviate the dependency on just a few subject matter experts by having learning ecosystems that develop distributed competence across the full employee base.

9.4 Cultural Readiness Assessments

Before mass migration, organizations ought to be gauging if their culture is ready. Surveys of cultural readiness provide diagnosis instruments that measure quantitatively variables such as training, accountability structures, communication norms, and trust levels (Stenberg, 2020). They identify potential gaps that, left unchecked, have the potential of threatening transformation.

For instance, one that has underperformed in communication would have to have robust feedback loops between security officers and developers prior to undertaking cloud-native implementations. One that has underperformed in accountability would have to have defined roles so that confusion is removed through the shared responsibility paradigm (CISA, 2023).

Seven Dimensions of Security Culture by Stenberg (2020) is another powerful framework. It comprises behavioral measures, norms, cognition, and compliance. Utilization of such frameworks assists leaders in overcoming dependence on intuition and instead avails themselves of evidence-based cultural robustness measures.

Above all, cultural readiness is dynamic. Organizations need frequent measurements in transformation efforts. Koskinen (2023) demonstrates that resistance of the culture will re-emerge if employees are introduced to latest procedures or tools. Regular measurements allow leaders to get involved with focused support, thus continuing momentum.

9.5 Gamification and Simulation

Security training programs most likely fail due to being too theoretical. They provide employees with training, yet they barely apply what they learn in real-life situations. Gamification and simulation close this gap by turning passive learning into active engagement (WeActis, 2022).

Work practices are:

- Phishing exercises, where staff are trained how to recognize fake e-mails in authentic conditions.
- Capture-the-flag contests, security challenges that are resolved by teams under controlled conditions.
- Chaos engineering exercises, which began with Netflix, that involve simulating failures in order to stress-test resilience and team coordination (Koskinen, 2023).

Kumar (2024) observes that gamification strategies make use of human psychology: learning by experience, recognition, and competitiveness provide greatest motivational impetus. Trainee employees trained through simulation environments outperform under actual environments.

Furthermore, gamification contributes to cultural engagement. Rather than treating security as a source of inconvenience, employees start perceiving it as a test of the mind and shared sense of responsibility. Stenberg (2020) discovers that the firm with robust behavior reinforcement mechanisms has higher compliance and less breach incidents.

9.6 Security Champions Integration

Finally, organizations should assign security champions at the team level. They are the employees that, while themselves not security experts, are champions and leaders of secure practice (Kumar, 2024). By implementing champions at the operation and development team levels, organizations utilize peer influence, which, by research, is one of the best behavioral change motivators (WeActis, 2022). Security champions bring high-level policy to life globally and bridge it to actionable advice. For instance, a sample development team champion may assist others in safe Infrastructure as Code adoption, while an operations team champion may advocate least privilege adoption. Champions minimize resistance that would otherwise be inherent in top-down advice by working within peer groups. Alotaibi and Alzahrani (2021) believe that security management is effective if and only if responsibilities get shared and internalized. The champions confirm such sharing by prioritizing safe practices every day, and not just audit or incident states. Over time, the champions' presence supports building cultural resilience and embedding security as organizational identity.

9.7 Metrics and Key Performance Indicators for Human Factor Assessment

Human factor efficiency of cloud security can be measured based on a broad spectrum indicators, which include behavioral, cultural and organizational aspects of indicators that is not all limited to the more traditional area of technical indicators of security. The actions (quantitative and qualitative) are required to evaluate the outcomes and monitor the progress with time to gauge the human-centric security posture of organizations (Bellamkonda, 2020). Zto name a few:

Security Awareness Assessment Scores: Security awareness of the employees is checked regularly by simulated phishing tests, security policy test, and scenario-based tests. They are to be determined on the basis of the baseline measurements the organizational starting points and quarterly measurements of progress improvements.

Frequency incident Reporting: In organizations with a strong security culture, the voluntary incident reporting is higher. Keeping track of the ratio between the reported security concerns and those that are discovered by the outside world provides information on the levels of engagement and psychological safety of the employees.

Training Completion and Retention Rates: Experiential Application Evaluations: The organizations will need to evaluate the knowledge retention by conducting periodic re assessment and application evaluation in addition to the mere completion percentages.

Behavioral Change Measures: Multi-Factor Authentication Adoption: MFA voluntary adoption is a method that can be used to assess the growth of security-conscious behavior, which is not an outcome of compulsory MFA implementation.

Password Security Practices: Repeated review of password strength, reuse of passwords and use of password manager by the organization.

Patterns of least-privilege Compliance and Compliance with Approval Cycles: checking the frequency of least-privilege compliance and compliance with approval cycles according to the patterns of access privilege requests.

Measures Effectiveness of Teamwork: Cross-functional Security Councils: The measures of attendance, level of participation and implementation of decisions on the security governance bodies.

Successful DevSecOps Integration: Metrics that track the security integration of the development pipelines, including the introduction of the security testing automation and a vulnerability remediation time.

Shadow IT Find rates: Organizations that have effective collaboration will tend to have a lower shadow IT adoption rate since employees will feel that the approved services are sufficient to their operational requirements (Dawson,2021).

Organizations are under constant pressure to not only protect their infrastructure but also to ensure swift and effective responses to security incidents. While technology provides the foundation—through automation, monitoring, and recovery tools—the human factor remains central in determining how resilient a company truly is. Metrics such as *time to detect and respond*, *recovery time objectives*, and *compliance audit results* highlight how decision-making, communication, and process discipline directly influence security outcomes. These indicators not only reflect technical capability but also expose strengths and weaknesses in human processes, cultural readiness, and organizational alignment for cloud security:

Time to Detect and Respond: The time to detect and respond is a measure of the elements of human response in incident detection and response, such as escalation efficiency and speed of decision-making.

Recovery Time Objectives: Assessing the impact on the processes of recovery and business continuity maintenance in the case of security incidents on the human factor.

Results of Compliance Audits: An overview of the outcomes of compliance evaluation with a certain focus on human process failures and technical defects on control.

10. CONCLUSION

The goal is to evaluate the human factor's contribution to the recovery operations and oil spillage containment of the business continuity in the events of security incidents. Compliance Audit Results Following compliance audit results are monitored with a certain focus on human process failures and technical control gaps.

Cloud transformation doesn't necessarily mean workload migration, it's about people transformation. Safe adoption includes redefinition of roles that have been redefined, changed behavior and mindshift. The CIOs and CTOs need to be strategic enablers, the developers have to be able to integrate security, the operations need to learn to master automation and the end-users need to take up the mantle of accountability.

Culture change is useful in supporting behavioral changes of zero trust compliance to proactive resilience. Growth, resiliency, security-first tangible and collaboration are mindsets that describe long-term success. Such changes can be sustained by means of change management that includes training, communication and modeling leadership.

These risks are no fanciful, like a shadow IT, automated blind spots, burnout and ethical concerns and the best practices can be used to tackle these risks, with a cross-functional councils, secure by design principles, continuous learning, readiness assessment and gamified training and peer-driven security champions.

Within the boundaries of reason, it is not the deployment of technology that makes cloud implementation successful, but a continuous desire of people to do the right thing. The weakest link is man factor but the determinant one. The organizations which are aware of the need to change positions, actions and mentalities will not only learn to accomplish the successful adoption of secure clouds but also create resilient and future-oriented ecosystems that will survive in the uncertain digital world.

REFERENCES

Alharkan, I., & Aslam, N. (2019). Factors affecting cloud computing adoption: A literature review synthesis and analysis. *International Journal of Computer Applications, 177*(43), 29–36. https://www.researchgate.net/publication/332833321_Factors_Affecting_Cloud_Computing_Adoption_A_Literature_Review_Synthesis_And_Analysis

Alotaibi, M. B., & Alzahrani, A. I. (2021). Human factor aspects in information security management in the traditional IT and cloud computing models. *International Journal of Computer Science and Information Security, 19*(4), 47–55. https://www.researchgate.net/publication/351078133_Human_Factor_Aspects_in_Information_Security_Management_in_the_Traditional_it_and_Cloud_Computing_Models

Alshahrani, H. (2021). Impact of intention to adopt cloud-based human resource management on innovation behaviour: The mediating role of leadership support. *PalArch's Journal of Archaeology of Egypt/Egyptology, 18*(10), 4070–4084. https://archives.palarch.nl/index.php/jae/article/download/9599/8849/18799

Amazon Web Services. (2022). *AWS cloud adoption framework: People perspective*. https://docs.aws.amazon.com/pdfs/whitepapers/latest/aws-caf-people-perspective/aws-caf-people-perspective.pdf

Amazon Web Services. (2023). *Strategy – Cloud transformation (AWS Prescriptive Guidance)*. https://docs.aws.amazon.com/pdfs/prescriptive-guidance/latest/strategy-cloud-transformation/strategy-cloud-transformation.pdf

Beautement, A., & Sasse, M. A. (2019). *Human factors knowledge area, Issue 1.0 (CyBOK)*. Cyber Security Body of Knowledge. https://www.cybok.org/media/downloads/Human_Factors_issue_1.0.pdf

Bellamkonda, S. (2020). Cybersecurity in critical infrastructure: Protecting the foundations of modern society. *International Journal of Communication Networks and Information Security, 12*(2), 273–280. https://ijcnis.org/index.php/ijcnis/article/view/7529/1846

Chartered Institute of Ergonomics & Human Factors. (2016). *The role of human factors in delivering cyber security*. https://ergonomics.org.uk/static/54e334a2-e8ba-483d-a678-b36307252af6/e2931aee-33d8-42bb-8330-0e77f2000bd0/the-role-of-human-factors-in-delivering-cyber-security.pdf

Chauhan, M., & Shiaeles, S. (2023). An analysis of cloud security frameworks, problems and proposed solutions. *Network (Bristol, England), 3*(3), 422–450. https://www.mdpi.com/2673-8732/3/3/18

Chippagiri, S. (2025, January). A study of cloud security frameworks for safeguarding multi-tenant cloud architectures. *International Journal of Computer Applications, 186*(60), 50–57. DOI: 10.5120/ijca2025924369

Chippagiri, S., & Ravula, P. (2021). Cloud-Native Development: Review of Best Practices and Frameworks for Scalable and Resilient Web Applications. *International Journal of New Media Studies: International Peer Reviewed Scholarly Indexed Journal*, *8*(2), 13–21. https://ijnms.com/index.php/ijnms/article/view/294

Coles-Kemp, L., & Reeves, S. (2017). The role of human aspects in cyber security: Behaviour or culture? *Cyber Security: A Peer-Reviewed Journal, 1*(4), 305–315. https://www.henrystewartpublications.com/sites/default/files/CSJ1.4HumanaspectsofcybersecurityBehaviourorculturechange.pdf

Cybersecurity and Infrastructure Security Agency. (2023). *Cloud security technical reference architecture v2.* https://www.cisa.gov/sites/default/files/2023-02/cloud_security_technical_reference_architecture_2.pdf

Dawson, M., Bacius, R., Gouveia, L. B., & Vassilakos, A. (2021). Understanding the challenge of cybersecurity in critical infrastructure sectors. Land Forces Academy Review, 26(1), 69-75. https://www.researchgate.net/publication/349969874_Understanding_the_Challenge_of_Cybersecurity_in_Critical_Infrastructure_Sectors

Koskinen, J. (2023). *Organizational and cultural cloud adoption challenges: A case study of a SaaS data engineering team* (Master's thesis, Aalto University). Aaltodoc. https://aaltodoc.aalto.fi/bitstreams/3e4077de-6345-446d-a4dd-27d42f064e93/download

Kumar, R. (2024). The role of human factor in cybersecurity: Behavioral insights and training strategies. *International Research Journal of Modernization in Engineering Technology and Science*, *6*(3), 2282–2290. https://www.irjmets.com/uploadedfiles/paper/issue_3_march_2024/51493/final/fin_irjmets1711953082.pdf

Nkosi, M., Gupta, K., & Mashinini, P. M. (2023). Assessing the Capacity for Change Prior to the Adoption of Human Factors Engineering in Power Plant Maintenance. *Systems, 11*(10), 520. DOI: 10.3390/systems11100520

Seaman, J. (2023). Zero trust security strategies and guideline. In *Digital transformation in policing: The promise, perils and solutions* (pp. 149–168). Springer International Publishing., https://www.springerprofessional.de/en/digital-transformation-in-policing-the-promise-perils-and-soluti/23882432

Singh, A., & Kaur, R. (2024). The human factor in cybersecurity: An analysis of emerging trends and challenges. *International Journal of Advanced Computer Science and Applications, 15*(2), 112–121. https://www.researchgate.net/publication/384471305_The_Human_Factor_in_Cybersecurity_An_Analysis_of_Emerging_Trends_and_Challenges

Stenberg, H. (2020). *The seven dimensions of security culture.* KnowBe4 Research. https://www.knowbe4.com/hubfs/CLTRe-The7DimensionsSecurityCulture-ResearchPaper.pdf

WeActis. (2022). *The human factor in cybersecurity: Turning weaknesses into strengths* [eBook]. https://weactis.com/wp-content/uploads/WeActis_The_Human_Factor_ebook.pdf

Zengeni, I. P., & fadli Zolkipli, M. (2024). Zero-day exploits and vulnerability management. Borneo International Journal eISSN 2636-9826, 7(3), 26-33. https://majmuah.com/journal/index.php/bij/article/view/648

Chapter 7
Securing Data With Cryptography:
Bridging Technical Excellence and Organizational Culture for Enterprise Resilience

Nur Fasihah Mohd Esa
https://orcid.org/0009-0003-1169-5522
Management and Science University, Malaysia

ABSTRACT

This chapter presents a framework for integrating cryptographic technologies with organizational culture to build sustainable cybersecurity resilience. It examines how core mechanisms such as encryption, digital signature, and key management must align with leadership, policy design, and workforce engagement to protect data and ensure compliance. Drawing on practices from finance, healthcare, and government, the chapter highlights how successful organizations embed cryptography into governance and operations. It also addresses barriers such as user resistance, poor usability, and fragmented implementation that weaken security controls. The final section explores future directions, including blockchain-based trust systems, post-quantum cryptography readiness, and the need for crypto literacy across roles. By connecting technical controls with human and institutional factors, the chapter emphasizes that cryptography should be viewed not as an isolated IT function but as a strategic cultural asset essential for trust, continuity, and resilience in evolving threat environments.

DOI: 10.4018/979-8-3373-4154-5.ch007

1. INTRODUCTION

Modern organizations face increasingly complex and interconnected cybersecurity challenges that extend far beyond the scope of traditional technical safeguards. As enterprises transition to cloud-based architectures, hybrid work models, and expansive digital ecosystems, the protection of sensitive digital assets requires a comprehensive strategy that bridges technical excellence with human-centric practices. This necessity has given rise to a more holistic understanding of cybersecurity, one that frames security not as a purely technological problem but as a socio-technical challenge (Cremer et al., 2022). A socio-technical focus acknowledges the complex and inseparable relationship among people, organizational processes and technology in the context of digital security. This view recognizes that security is not purely a technical issue of ensuring that there are strong algorithms and firewalls but also the attitudes, behaviors, organizational culture, and dynamic interaction of people and systems they use (Safa et al., 2016). Enterprise resilience, in conjunction with the technology depicted in Figure 1, can be created not by the technology but by the symbiotic connection between strong technical protection and an established organizational culture. The technical systems are integrated into complex social, organizational, and governance systems, influencing and influenced by human actors (Guest et al., 2022).

Figure 1. Conceptual diagram bridging technical aspects of cryptography and organizational culture

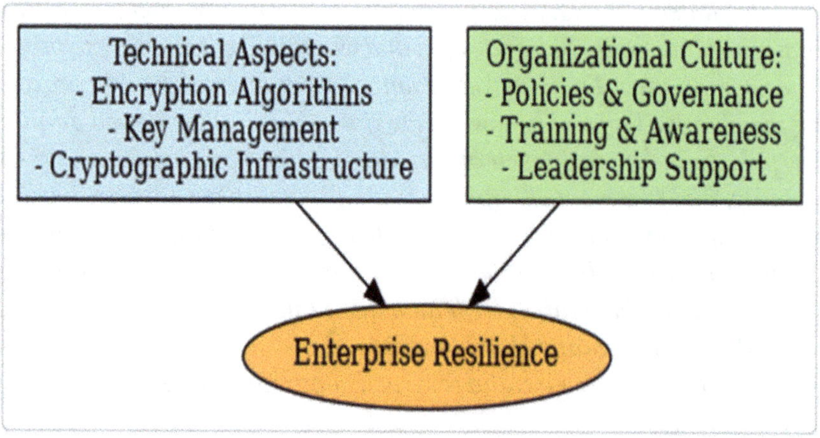

Cryptographic specific skills are no longer focused on the technical issue and have expanded general leading skills set for leaders and compliance teams or cross-functional personnel charged with securing sensitive digital assets in increasingly complex cyber environments.For cryptographic systems to work, they have to be in compliance with emerging regulatory requirements. As one such significant technical and organizational protection, encryption and pseudonymization were established in the General Data Protection Regulation (GDPR) (Article 32) (Starchon and Pikulik 2019, and Velkes 2019). Likewise, the Health Insurance Portability and Accountability Act (HIPAA) Security Rule encrypts electronic protected health information (ePHI) (Mia et. al., 2022) and the standard, ISO/ IEC 27001, requires organized applications of cryptographic controls within the information security management system of an organization (Culot et. al., 2021). In the regulatory paradigm, cryptography is both a technical and cultural precaution as it is the part of the resilience and loyalty of the organization to diverse digital activity and transaction dealings. This integrated view should certainly be implemented with increased awareness given the growing financial and social cost of data-breaches.Violations of data are becoming more alarming. The average cost of a data breach worldwide was 4.88 million USD in 2024 which is the highest ever. This is a significant 10% growth over the last year and the highest growth rate since the beginning of the pandemic. Data breaches are becoming increasingly concerning. In 2024, the global average cost of a data breach reached an unprecedented $4.88 million USD. This represents a substantial 10% increase from the previous year and marks the largest annual rise observed since the onset of the pandemic. For critical sectors, however, the financial consequences are more serious; violations within the financial industry have an average cost of $6.08 million per breach; and the healthcare industry has an average cost per financial loss of $9.77 million. The trend that has been observed is that it is a faster rise in risk and thus there is an implication that the complexity of the modern-day digital ecosystems exceeds the ability of the purely technical protection. The growing gap between technical complexity and socio-economic maturity of organisations has become one of the main factors that have led to increased security costs; closing the gap is the only long-term viable way to achieve enterprise resilience.

Regardless of the high power computing capability incorporated in the contemporary cryptographic algorithms, human behaviour is still posing fatal threats that undermine cryptographic systems. Empirical research always points to human error as one of the leading factors behind up to 95 per cent of all data breaches. In the health care industry, human error is found to be the cause of approximately 85 percent of security breaches, which is mainly caused by phishing attacks, as well as accidental operator actions (Nifakos et al., 2021). Similarly, a research utilizing more than 100 million healthcare records demonstrated that unintentional insider behaviour was the cause of two times more cases of data-loss than by external threat actors, thus indicating how much user decisions can sabotage encryption controls (Yeo and Banfield, 2022).

According to a critical review by Khadka and Ullah (2025), cognitive biases, emotional stressors, and institutional pressures should be seen as major causes of security lapses. It is important to determine which one of these pressures has the most impact in order to apply the principles of behavioural-science to the design and management of cryptographic systems. This ubiquitous susceptibility is not accidental but down to an expected consequence of a fundamental lack of alignment between technical implementation and organisational culture.

This omnipresent weakness is not an accidental phenomenon; it is an expected outcome of an underlying mismatch between a technical implementation and a corporate culture. While malicious attacks remain the most common initial vector for breaches, IT failures and human error collectively account for nearly half of all incidents in high-stakes sectors like finance. This data blurs the traditional line between external threats and internal weaknesses. An adversary no longer needs to break a firewall if an employee misconfigures a cloud server or falls for a sophisticated phishing email. This reality reframes an organization's internal culture and operational discipline as integral components of its "attack surface," just as critical as its external-facing servers.

This chapter addresses this systemic challenge by formally reframing cryptography as a socio-technical system. The structure of this chapter is designed to move beyond a survey of algorithms to provide a multi-layered examination of how cryptographic security can be effectively embedded into organizational systems, practices, and culture. The following sections progress from an exploration of foundational principles and their organizational intersections to an analysis of real-world failures, and then to a discussion of strategic governance and forward-looking technologies. The final section synthesizes these findings into a practical framework for fostering a sustainable cryptographic culture, arguing that a mature security posture is an emergent property of a well-calibrated socio-technical system, one in which technical controls, leadership strategies, and employee behaviors reinforce one another to create long-term digital trust.

2. THE PRINCIPLES OF CRYPTOGRAPHIC PRIMITIVES: A DEEPER TECHNICAL DIVE

Cryptographic principle is based on four principles of security which are confidentiality, integrity, authenticity and non-repudiation. These concepts serve as a framework of guiding principles of cryptographic systems because they will make the data inaccessible, unaltered, and non -repudiable to unauthorized parties. These principles spread further in an organization by its technical functionality to act as governance anchors to influence information security policies, regulatory compliance programs, and alignment of cultures across departments. The fact that cryptography tools and organizational work go hand in hand supports the assumption that cryptography is not just a technical security solution but a part and parcel of enterprise governance (Rana et al., 2023).

Figure 2. Cryptographic Principles and The intersection of Organizational Culture

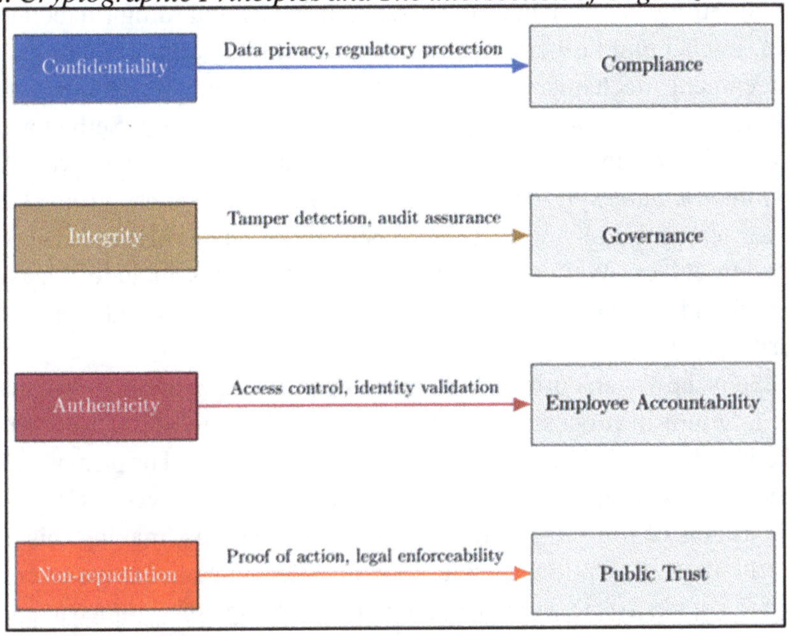

The intersections of these four core principles within the organization are shown in Figure 2 which shows that the technical functions including encryption and digital signatures are directly converted into the governance requirements, including compliance and accountability. These pillars cannot be separated; they are deeply connected with each other and to a large extent, they are symbiotic. The effectiveness of one of the pillars regularly is based on the proper implementation of another. A sound hash function that offers integrity is an element that renders an electronic signature effective in offering authenticity. This is an interaction at a systemic level, which means that failure in either of the primitives could invalidate the whole security model, and the discourse is no longer focused on definitions but on the aspect of system design.

2.1. The Practicality of Confidentiallity: Asymmetric vs. Symmetric Encryption

Information security primarily relies on confidentiality, which is one of the main goals of cryptographic assurance. As a principle, confidentiality refers to the protection of sensitive information from unauthorized access or disclosure. In organizational settings, confidentiality is essential for safeguarding financial records, client data, intellectual property, and strategic communications. Encryption is the primary technical mechanism used to enforce this principle, ensuring that data remains unreadable without the appropriate cryptographic key (Seth et al., 2020).

Cryptographic techniques for ensuring confidentiality fall into two main categories: symmetric and asymmetric encryption. Symmetric encryption, also known as secret-key cryptography, uses a single, shared key for both the encryption and decryption processes. Well-known symmetric algorithms include the Advanced Encryption Standard (AES), which is widely adopted for its strength and efficiency. The security of a strong cipher like

AES-256 is, however, entirely contingent upon organizational key management practices; a failure in process, such as hardcoding keys in software or insecurely storing them, renders the technical strength of the cipher moot. The primary advantage of symmetric encryption is speed; symmetric encryption can process large volumes of data thousands of times faster than asymmetric methods, making this approach ideal for bulk data encryption, such as securing files on a hard drive or encrypting a database (Li et al., 2023). However, the main challenge of symmetric encryption lies in key distribution: the single key must be shared securely between the sender and receiver, as anyone who intercepts the key can decrypt the data. Some legacy systems may still use older standards like

Triple DES (3DES), particularly in the financial sector for encrypting PINs, which highlights the cultural and operational challenge of migrating critical infrastructure away from outdated technology.

Asymmetric encryption, or public-key cryptography, was developed to solve this key distribution problem. Asymmetric encryption uses a pair of mathematically related keys: a public key and a private key. The public key can be shared freely and is used to encrypt data, while the private key is kept secret by its owner and is the only key capable of decrypting the data. Prominent asymmetric algorithms include

RSA and **Elliptic Curve Cryptography (ECC)**. While significantly slower and more computationally intensive than symmetric encryption, this method provides a secure way to establish communication and exchange keys over an untrusted network (Fu, Wang, & Shi, 2022).

In practice, most modern security protocols, such as Transport Layer Security (TLS) which secures web traffic, use a hybrid approach that combines the strengths of both. When a user connects to a secure website, the user's browser uses asymmetric encryption to securely exchange a temporary, randomly generated symmetric key with the server. Once this secure channel is established, all subsequent communication is encrypted using the much faster symmetric algorithm. This performance trade-off is not merely a technical detail; the trade-off has direct organizational implications. The demand for speed in user-facing applications necessitates the use of efficient symmetric encryption. This, in turn, creates a significant key management burden, requiring robust organizational processes for key generation, rotation, storage, and revocation. Thus, a technical performance requirement directly creates a socio-technical governance requirement.

In the contemporary distributed setting, confidentiality should be more than mere protection of the data and be safe multi-party computations and privacy-saving data sharing (Salako et al., 2025). According to Olaiya et al. (2024), homomorphic encryption and data masking are among the methods being used in fintech platforms to retain confidentiality without affecting the performance of the systems. Addressing the issue of confidentiality, Willie (2023) states that the culture of security-first established in an organization supports confidentiality with norms of privacy and access policy and leadership accountability provisions in the daily operations. Confidentiality, once internalized in the cultural context of a company, is an operating value that promotes long-term digital trust and regulatory practices.

2.2. Integrity Mechanisms: Hashes and Message Authentication Codes (MACs)

Data integrity guarantees that information in the information system is correct, complete and that it has not been modified to its original form during the lifecycle of the information. Integrity plays a critical role in ensuring that unauthorized changes, either unknown or intentional, are not made and it forms the basis of a variety of operational processes, including transaction validation, audit logs, and compliance with regulations. Cryptographic integrity is mostly achieved in cryptographic hash functions and Message Authentication Codes (MACs) in cryptographic systems.

A cryptographic hash function is a mathematical algorithm that takes an input of any size for example, a message, a file, or a block of data and produces a fixed-size string of characters, known as a hash value or digest. Hash functions are designed to have several critical properties. The functions are deterministic, meaning the same input will always produce the same output. Hash functions are one-way functions, making reversing the process and deriving the original input from its hash computationally infeasible (a property known as preimage resistance). Crucially, the functions are collision-resistant, meaning finding two different inputs that produce the same hash output is extremely difficult. Furthermore, a well-designed hash function exhibits the "avalanche effect," where even a minuscule change to the input data results in a drastically different output hash. This property makes hash functions ideal for tamper detection; by comparing the hash of a file before and after transmission, a recipient can verify that the file has not been altered. Common hash functions include the

SHA-2 and SHA-3 families (Windarta et al., 2022). The organizational challenge lies in ensuring that deprecated algorithms like MD5 and SHA-1, which are vulnerable to collision attacks, are systematically removed from all systems and replaced with secure alternatives like SHA-256.

While hash functions are excellent for verifying data integrity, the functions do not provide authenticity. Anyone can compute the hash of a message, so a hash alone does not prove who created the message. This is where Message Authentication Codes (MACs) become essential. A MAC, also known as a tag, is a short piece of information used to authenticate a message. A MAC is generated by an algorithm that combines the message data with a shared secret key known only to the sender and the intended recipient. The sender computes the MAC, appends the MAC to the message, and sends both. The receiver then uses the same secret key to independently compute the MAC on the received message. If the receiver's computed MAC matches the one sent with the message, two assurances are provided: first, that the message has not been altered in transit (integrity), and second, that the message originated from a party who possesses the secret key (authenticity).

According to the National Institute of Standards and Technology, MACs are considered high-assurance mechanisms when implemented with proper key management. In distributed systems, blockchain technologies further reinforce data integrity through hash chaining, where each block includes the hash of the previous one, forming a tamper-evident ledger. These immutable records serve as verifiable audit trails that support accountability and regulatory transparency. However, achieving data integrity at scale requires more than the correct application of cryptographic tools. Achieving integrity necessitates governance frameworks that include change control procedures, versioning protocols, and employee accountability.

2.3. Authenticity and Trust Infrastructure: Digital Signatures and PKI

Authenticity ensures that data, communications, and system interactions originate from verified and legitimate sources. Authenticity is critical for establishing trust in digital environments, preventing impersonation, and validating the identity of entities involved in electronic exchanges. In enterprise systems, authenticity supports key processes such as access control, secure communication, and identity governance. The primary mechanism for achieving authenticity in cryptographic systems is the digital signature, which relies on the principles of asymmetric encryption and is supported by a framework known as Public Key Infrastructure (PKI).

A digital signature provides a stronger guarantee of authenticity than a MAC because a digital signature also offers non-repudiation, which is discussed in the next section. The process of creating a digital signature involves three steps. First, the sender creates a hash of the message or document to be signed. Second, the sender uses their private key to encrypt this hash value. The resulting encrypted hash is the digital signature, which is then attached to the original message. The recipient, upon receiving the message and the signature, performs a verification process. The recipient uses the sender's public key to decrypt the signature, which reveals the original hash. Simultaneously, the recipient computes their own hash of the received message. If the decrypted hash matches the newly computed hash, the signature is verified. A successful verification confirms two things: that the message has not been altered since being signed (integrity) and that the message was signed by the holder of the corresponding private key (authenticity).

However, a digital signature is only trustworthy if the recipient is certain that the public key being used genuinely belongs to the sender. The challenge of verifying public key ownership is where Public Key Infrastructure (PKI) becomes indispensable. PKI is not a single technology but a comprehensive framework of policies, standards, hardware, and software that enables the secure management of digital certificates and public-key encryption (Springer & Haindl, 2024). The central component of a PKI is the Certificate Authority (CA), a trusted third-party entity that issues digital certificates. A digital certificate is an electronic document that binds a public key to an identity (such as a person, a server, or an organization) and is itself digitally signed by the CA. When a recipient receives a digitally signed message, the recipient can check the sender's certificate. By verifying the CA's signature on the certificate, the recipient can trust that the public key contained within the certificate is authentic, thereby establishing a “chain of trust”.

In real-world applications, digital signatures and PKI support critical functions across industries. For example, in intelligent transportation systems, vehicular PKI (VPKI) facilitates real-time identity verification among connected vehicles, thereby enhancing communication integrity (Khan et al., 2022). Similarly, in healthcare, digital signatures are employed to authenticate electronic prescriptions and protect the integrity of electronic health records (Abdulhameed et al., 2021). When used in blockchain systems, each transaction is signed with a sender’s private key and verified using their public key, establishing non-repudiable proof of authorship (Liu et al., 2021). As Willie (2023) emphasizes, cultivating authenticity as an organizational value involves leadership engagement, cross-functional accountability, and a culture that promotes digital responsibility.

2.4. Non-Repudiation

Non-repudiation ensures that parties involved in digital communications cannot deny their participation, the authenticity of the message, or the actions performed. Non-repudiation provides legal and operational accountability by producing cryptographic evidence of origin, receipt, and approval. In organizational environments, non-repudiation is essential for upholding the validity of transactions, safeguarding audit trails, and ensuring enforceable digital commitments.

Technically, non-repudiation is a direct and powerful outcome of using digital signatures within a trusted PKI framework. Because a digital signature is created using a private key that is uniquely and secretly held by the signer, the signature cryptographically binds that individual's identity to the signed data. As long as the private key has not been compromised, only the legitimate owner could have produced the signature. The resulting signature provides undeniable proof of origin. A sender cannot later claim not to have sent a message if that message bears their valid digital signature. This non-repudiable property distinguishes digital signatures from MACs; while a MAC proves a message came from someone holding the shared secret key, the MAC cannot prove *which* of the two parties (sender or receiver) created the message, as both possess the key. A digital signature, by contrast, can only be created by the party with the private key.

To further strengthen non-repudiation, digital signatures are often combined with secure timestamping. A trusted timestamping service can act as a third party to certify that a particular piece of data existed at a specific point in time. It is impossible to later argue that a document has been signed at another point in time or that a key was broken in the future and use this service. As an example, Rasslan et al. (2024) suggested that the extension of a cryptographic library with a non-repudiation feature should be added to blockchain architecture, a feature that supposedly enhances the legal admissibility of evidence and strength of accountability in a structurally decentralized institution.

Implementation of non-repudiation at the organizational level is not a technical skill. Its implementation requires the existence of sound governance structures and carefully stipulated systems to track the whole lifetime of the digital certificates, including issuance, renewal, and, where necessary, revocation. An organization should also have in place protocols to allow immediate revocation of invalid or compromised certificates and the revocation should also be publically available so that any signing done by a compromised key can be disapproved by other parties. Moreover, to have good non-repudiation, signature verification must be incorporated in compliance reporting systems and audit systems; and this integration ensures that record keeping of legally binding acts are carefully documented and that they can be verified later on when the need arises.

When non-repudiation is applied to practices of the enterprise, it acts as a point of intersection between organizational integrity and technical control. Finally, non-repudiation transforms cryptographic assurance into an accountability assurance, which can enable the empowerment of digital responsibility and make it possible to verify trust in organizational processes.

3. THE HUMAN AND ORGANIZATIONAL DIMENSIONS OF CRYPTOGRAPHIC FAILURE

In spite of the fact that the principles of cryptography represent a strong theoretical basis of the secure systems, the experience of practical cases proves that despite the presence of solid algorithms, the organizational cultures, governance frameworks, and human behavior may negatively impact the system employed. Previously, the trends of cyber-attacks followed a pattern: as technical cryptographic safeguards are becoming more advanced and harder to crack, the attackers are similarly converting their resources and attention to more vulnerable entry points. As a result, advanced social-engineering techniques and exploitation of systemic misconfigurations have become more cost-effective, quicker and more efficient attack vectors than the forceful efforts of cracking the modern encryption systems.

Based on these observations, breaches are most often attributed to weaknesses inherent in the cryptographic primitives themselves, but are most often due to insecure implementations, insufficient technical expertise, and the fact that security is not a complex socio-technical phenomenon, and thus should be treated as such. These case studies and analyses indicate that the enablers of the major data-breach events are often human and organizational vulnerabilities.

3.1. Case Studies in Misconfiguration and Human Error

In this section, a review of recent high-profile breaches reveals a pervasive pattern where the initial point of failure is not a broken algorithm but a broken process or a moment of human fallibility (Nobles, 2022).

Capital One Cloud Misconfiguration (2019): The 2019 Capital One Cloud breach affected around 100 million customers and was caused by the misconfigured web-application firewall. Even though data at rest was encrypted, weak access controls and lack of firm internal review mechanism made it easy to enable an attacker to retrieve sensitive information. A paradigm study by Khan et al. (2022) determined a systemic culture lapse: an expediency-driven development environment that put expediency ahead of configuration auditing and cryptographic policy implementation. Subsequently, the incident highlights the need to instill encryption in governance structures that require peer-review, centralised access controls, and cultural harmony with the accountability principles.

Heartbleed and OpenSSL Stewardship (2014): The Heartbleed vulnerability exposed a severe vulnerability in the OpenSSL cryptography library and was used to attack a substantial volume of internet traffic in over two years. This problem was not caused by a cryptography failure, but due to organizational stewardship failure. The project management team, which was made up of volunteers, did not have the financial assets, structured audits of code and control mechanisms to ensure that such a dreadful bug was discharged into the open-source domain. In this case, it is seen that even open-source software, especially the ones that have significant importance to the cybersecurity of the world, must have a solid structure of control and culture of systematic oversight to protect their integrity.

LastPass Cryptographic Exposure (2022): This attack exhibited encrypted password repositories when perpetrators hacked an endpoint of an employee. The attack was able to be successful even though the core data was encrypted; it was performed with a lack of appropriate endpoint controls and a dependence on individual practices as opposed to uniform, organization-wide security measures such as multi-factor authentication. The incident therefore shows that advanced encryption can be compromised when the basic security practices of the human layer are inadequate.

Change Healthcare Ransomware Attack (2024): In what became the largest healthcare data breach in history, this incident exposed the protected health information of over 190 million people. Investigations revealed that the attackers gained initial access through a remote access service that lacked multi-factor authentication (MFA). The absence of this widely accepted best practice allowed attackers to compromise credentials and gain unauthorized access to Change Healthcare's network, causing massive disruption to the U.S. healthcare system and underscoring the immense financial and operational costs of neglecting foundational security controls.

Snowflake Misconfigurations (2024): This is a financially-driven team that auditors identified as UNC5537, and they broke into over 165 Snowflake clients using poor customer-side security configurations. The found weakness was not in the platform of Snowflake but in the management of customer environments. The accounts accessed by attackers did not have multi-factor authentication (MFA) and were left unaltered since 2020. This case illustrates the ease with which a seemingly secure platform can be compromised due to an innocent misconfiguration to help steal billions of records.

3.2. The Anatomy of Failure:Deep Case Studies of Socio-Technical Failures.

To further explain the trends of socio-technical failure, a closer study of two more recent and large-scale breaches can be used to provide a current perspective on the ways adversaries take advantage of the interface between technology and human processes.

Case Study: The 2023 MGM Resorts Breach – A Human Process Failure

In September 2023, MGM Resorts suffered a rate-crippling cyberattack organized by the hacking groups Scattered Spider and ALPHV, with the cost of business interruptions being estimated at 100 million dollars to the company. No advanced cryptographic exploits were important to the attack, but rather high-level social engineering. The open-source intelligence was initially used by the opponents who wanted to locate a particular employee of MGM on LinkedIn. They later proceeded to vishing (voice phishing), which involved starting a ten-minute phone call to the IT support desk of the company using the profile of the target employee. Attackers were able to gain administrator-level access by convincing the help desk employees of the authenticity of the impersonator, thus proving Okta and Azure deployments of MGM. There is also some evidence of MFA fatigue techniques such as sending duplicating push notifications until a disoriented or distracted employee agrees.

This malpractice is one example of a socio-technical system failure. As MGM has implemented advanced technical controls, such as the state-of-the-art identity and access management platform (Okta), its attackers bypassed the technical control mechanisms and instead used the weakest point in their network, the human to human trust of the help desk support process. This involved the security of the business being dependent on one employee checking identity via the phone which turned out to be a very weak strategy. The incident demonstrates that, without strong, testable and generally implemented identity-verification measures of all manual processes like password resets, even the most complex technical security architectures can fail.

Case Study: The 2023 MOVEit Breach – A Supply Chain Catastrophe

In May 2023, the Russian ransomware group CL0P used the MOVEit Transfer software (a commercial managed file transfer, or MFT, solution for short) to carry out a zero day attack, making it one of the most important recent supply chain attacks. Opponents used the SQL injection vulnerability (CVE-2023-34362) to illegally compromise databases of vulnerable servers with MOVEit. Then they used an adapted web shell, LEMURLOOT, which allowed them to steal enormous amounts of sensitive data from thousands of organizations around the globe, including financial institutions, government agencies, and healthcare providers. It resulted in the violations of approximately 93 million users.

Beyond its technical ramifications, the MOVEit incident highlights a much more interesting socio-technical failure: an abyssical breakdown of trust and confidence in the software supply chain. The weakness was not a component of the systems of the victim organizations but a trusted third-party application that facilitated important business operations. The case illustrates the relative failure of the old-time castle and moat concept of security in which all threats are considered to arise outside the organization. In this case, the threat to question was represented by a reputable seller, which means that the security stance of an organization is inherently connected to the security culture of a broader digital ecosystem.

The necessity of Zero-Trust thinking, which is based on a fundamental mistrust, is likewise supported by this attack, as even the internal systems and third-party software must also be verified. This would require more than efficient technical controls like code signing, vulnerability scanning and round-the-clock monitoring; it would also require developed sociotechnical management, like vendor-risk assessment, contract execution, and governance customary that maintain trust in the software supply chain.

Table 1 below gives a comparative analysis of these and other high profile incidents, showing the similarity of the theme of socio-technical failure.

Table 1. A Comparative Analysis of Major Cryptographic Failures

Breach	Year	Primary Technical Control	Socio-Technical Failure Point	Key Lesson
MGM Resorts	2023	Identity & Access Management (Okta)	Social Engineering: Attackers impersonated an employee to the IT help desk, bypassing MFA and other controls.	Human processes (like help desk verification) are part of the critical attack surface and must be hardened against manipulation.
MOVEit Transfer	2023	Secure File Transfer Software	Supply Chain Vulnerability: A zero-day exploit in a third-party tool led to mass data exfiltration across thousands of organizations.	An organization's security is only as strong as its weakest vendor; rigorous supply chain risk management is essential.
Change Healthcare	2024	Remote Access Services	Lack of Foundational Controls: Failure to implement multi-factor authentication on a critical remote access point.	Neglecting basic security hygiene, even with other advanced controls in place, creates a single point of failure with catastrophic potential.
LastPass	2022	Encrypted Password Vaults	Weak Endpoint Security: Attackers compromised an employee's device to gain access to cloud environments and steal encrypted data.	Encryption of data-at-rest is insufficient if the human and device endpoints that access it are not adequately secured.
Capital One	2019	Cloud Encryption (Data-at-Rest)	System Misconfiguration: A misconfigured web application firewall allowed an attacker to access and exfiltrate sensitive data.	A culture prioritizing speed over security auditing can lead to critical configuration errors that undermine encryption.
Heartbleed (OpenSSL)	2014	TLS/SSL Encryption Library	Lack of Governance & Oversight: A critical bug was introduced into widely used open-source software due to insufficient code review and resources.	Critical infrastructure, including open-source software, requires robust governance and stewardship to ensure its integrity.

These case studies illustrate that attackers are rational actors who will always follow the path of least resistance. As cryptographic algorithms have become computationally secure, the focus of attack has shifted decisively to the softer, more malleable targets of human behavior and organizational processes (Cram & D'Arcy, 2023). A strong security culture is therefore essential for mitigating these weaknesses. As one study notes, an organization's employees can either be easy prey or become an effective “human layer of defense”. Leadership plays a crucial role in setting the tone, as a lack of executive support for cybersecurity can lead to a cultural mindset of minimum compliance rather than proactive security enhancement.

4. STRATEGIC GOVERNANCE AND COMPLIANCE FRAMEWORKS

Cryptography is not just a technical tool but a strategic asset that must be woven into the fabric of enterprise data governance and culture. An effective, enterprise-wide cryptographic strategy should be guided by a well-defined cryptographic policy, consistent with internationally recognized standards such as ISO/IEC 27001. These frameworks provide the essential "scaffolding" for a security program by defining what needs to be done. However, the organizational culture acts as the "concrete," determining how well those structures are filled in and how strong the structures become in practice. An organization can be compliant on paper by having a written policy, but if employees find the policy too complex and create workarounds, the organization is not secure. A mature organization uses feedback from those workarounds to simplify policies and tools, integrating security into the workflow. This demonstrates that compliance is the floor, not the ceiling, and that culture is the mechanism for moving from mere compliance to true resilience. The following discussion highlights how organizations integrate cryptographic practices into broader enterprise frameworks, including governance structures, compliance requirements, and risk management systems (Amin, 2019).

4.1. Cryptography for Compliance and Data Governance

Cryptographic controls have become indispensable for regulatory compliance and data governance in modern enterprises. As some researchers point out, regulations worldwide increasingly expect organizations to use encryption and related measures to protect sensitive data, making cryptography a cornerstone of compliance programs (Bulgurcu et al., 2010). While compliance can drive security adoption, it may not always cover the full spectrum of risks inherent in rapid digital transformation (Buck et al., 2023).

The EU's General Data Protection Regulation (GDPR), for example, explicitly highlights encryption and pseudonymization as appropriate technical and organizational measures for securing personal data under Article 32. A key incentive for organizations is that using strong encryption can reduce the impact and reporting requirements of a data breach, as encrypted data may be considered unintelligible and therefore not subject to the same notification obligations. As a result, organizations that deploy encryption broadly are not only improving security but also demonstrating due diligence that regulators positively consider in oversight and penalty decisions (Hon et al., 2011).

Beyond GDPR, numerous sector-specific laws drive the adoption of cryptography as a means of governance. In healthcare, the HIPAA and HITECH Acts encourage the encryption of protected health information (PHI) by providing a “safe harbor” in many breach scenarios, strongly incentivizing its use (Abouelmehdi et al., 2018). In 2025, HIPAA introduced stricter encryption rules that shift from “addressable” to “mandatory” standards, requiring encryption for all ePHI at rest and in transit. Similarly, financial regulations such as the Gramm–Leach–Bliley Act (GLBA) and the Payment Card Industry Data Security Standard (PCI DSS) require the use of encryption to safeguard customer information and payment data (Paul et al., 2023).

As such, compliance frameworks often map directly to cryptographic controls. The ISO/IEC 27001 standard, a widely adopted framework for information security management, includes specific controls for encryption and key management (Annex A 8.24) that help organizations meet privacy regulations and protect data integrity. This control mandates the establishment of a formal policy on the use of cryptography, covering key management lifecycles, algorithm standards, and the definition of roles and responsibilities. By integrating these requirements into internal policies, organizations create a compliance-by-design culture, where meeting legal obligations is a natural outcome of their security architecture and processes (Alevizos, 2024).

The role of cryptography extends to auditability and accountability. For instance, encryption and digital signature mechanisms can be leveraged to create tamper-evident logs and enforce accountability for data access and changes. A prime example is the use of digital signatures to ensure non-repudiation, which provides definitive proof of a signed transaction or document's origin. This capability is vital for audit trails in industries like finance and healthcare (Woodrum, 2003).

Table 2. Comparative Overview of Regulatory Requirements and Cryptographic Controls Across Sectors

Sector	Regulation	Required Cryptographic Measure	Human/Cultural Implications
Finance	GLBA, PCI DSS	Data-at-rest and in-transit encryption, digital signatures, key management with Hardware Security Modules (HSMs).	Staff training on secure transaction handling; rigorous compliance audits; strict enforcement of data classification policies.
Healthcare	HIPAA, HITECH (2025 updates)	Mandatory encryption of ePHI (e.g., AES-256, TLS 1.3), digital signatures for prescriptions, HSMs for key management.	Clinical staff training on data handling protocols; fostering a blame-free breach reporting culture; enforcement of role-based access to patient data.
Government	FISMA, eIDAS (EU), FIPS 140-3	Use of FIPS 140-validated encryption modules, secure VPNs for remote access, qualified digital signatures for official documents.	Policy alignment across agencies; building public trust through transparency in digital services; security clearance and background checks.

continued on following page

Table 2. Continued

Sector	Regulation	Required Cryptographic Measure	Human/Cultural Implications
E-commerce	GDPR, PCI DSS	End-to-end encryption for transactions (TLS), tokenization of payment card data, secure identity protocols.	Focus on consumer trust management; clear communication of privacy policies; balancing user experience with robust security measures.
Education	FERPA (US), local data privacy laws	Access control encryption for student records, encrypted logs and communication channels.	Training for faculty and staff on role-based access; digital ethics education for students; cultural reinforcement of student privacy as a core value.

4.2. Leadership and Strategic Cryptographic Adoption

The successful enterprise deployment of cryptography hinges on leadership engagement and strategic vision. Without executive support, even the best encryption technologies may be applied piecemeal, protecting isolated data silos rather than securing the enterprise as a whole. A qualitative study by Connelly et al. (2022) on advanced cryptography adoption in healthcare organizations found that key security personnel did not perceive state-of-the-art cryptographic solutions as a high priority absent a management mandate or regulatory pressure. This finding highlights a key challenge: a lack of explicit executive requirements can foster a complacent culture, with organizations focusing on minimum compliance rather than proactive security enhancement (Chen, 2022).

In contrast, successful organizations treat cryptographic safeguards as essential infrastructure. In this model, leadership sets clear, top-down objectives, such as mandating that all sensitive data be encrypted by default and that robust, centralized key management systems be deployed. A strong governance mindset requires leadership to not only approve budgets but also to establish metrics and oversight mechanisms to track cryptography usage, such as the percentage of sensitive data that is encrypted or the frequency of key rotation (Yusif & Hafeez-Baig, 2021; Anu, 2021). This top-down support is often a critical success factor in information security initiatives and helps resolve the inevitable conflicts that arise between security imperatives and business operations (Paliszkiewicz, 2019).

The establishment of dedicated units, such as a Crypto Center of Excellence (CCoE), exemplifies a leadership's commitment to strategic cryptographic adoption. For example, JPMorgan Chase launched a firm-wide AlgoCRYPT Center of Excellence (CoE) to lead research and implementation in advanced areas such as homomorphic encryption (HE), secure multi-party computation (SMPC), and post-quantum cryptography (PQC). This model centralizes expertise, ensures that consistent cryptographic standards are applied enterprise-wide, and keeps the organization agile in responding to new threats and regulations.

4.3. Cultural Enablers and Barriers to Cryptographic Governance

While policies and leadership provide a strategic foundation, organizational culture ultimately determines how well cryptographic controls are adopted and adhered to in day-to-day operations. The concept of a cybersecurity culture refers to the shared attitudes, knowledge, assumptions, and values of an organization's workforce with respect to security. A culture that prioritizes security will encourage employees to follow encryption policies, report suspicious activity, and actively participate in protecting data (Hsu et al., 2015). Figure 3 depicts this interplay, where a supportive culture reinforces the correct use of cryptographic architecture, while a resistant culture can lead to workarounds that undermine technical controls. Conversely, cultural resistance are often stemming from security measures perceived as cumbersome or obstructive and can lead to workarounds that defeat a control's purpose entirely.

Figure 3. The Reciprocating between Organizational Culture and Cryptographic Architecture

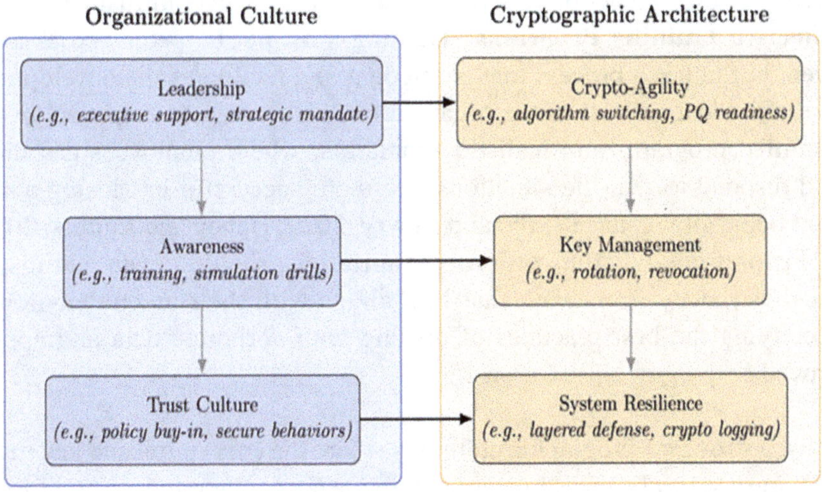

Human aspect of cybersecurity has been the most vulnerable point by most organization. Such culture of blame free reporting will be a key protective measure in itself. Fear of punishment will dishearten employees into admitting the mistakes like clicking on phishing links or settings up systems incorrectly and any cases not being reported or reported late will give attackers a chance to spread out within a network, infiltrate systems unauthorized, and steal sensitive information, thus raising the magnitude and the price of an attack. As a result, the level of voluntariness among employees to report their errors without fear is an effective measure of organizations preparedness to act on incidents as well as the overall cultural maturity.

Organizations should develop a crypto-aware culture in order to overcome reactive security behaviors by embedding cryptographic best practices into every-day activities. The development of such a culture will be a complex and comprehensive task, which will be reinforced by a number of strategic pillars.

- **Educating and Disseminating Knowledge:** All employees are to be aware of the risks posed by data insecurity, and how cryptography helps eliminate the risks. This knowledge cannot be limited to the standard compliance training; instead, it should be developed via contextualized, experience-based learning supported by continuous feedback (Jampen et al., 2020).
- **Establishing Accountability:** It is necessary that the employees inculcate a sense of responsibility to security as part and parcel of their professional work. This ownership must not be based on the fear of punishment but rather a reporting culture that is supportive and blame free leading to openness. Employees will be capable of reporting more on incidents and thus organizations are able to react more swiftly and control security intrusions.
- **Effective Training Programs:** Training must not be perceived as a single event but rather a process that is ongoing and facilitates the development of the individual as well as the organization. According to empirical research, gamified programs and realistic simulation, where employees can undergo and respond to real-life situations, are more successful in causing a significant behavioral change (Silic and Lowry, 2020; Haney and Lutters, 2023).
- **A Framework Customization:** Organizations should create and distribute a cybersecurity framework that best aligns with their unique environment, specifying the best practices of dealing with corporate data and apply approved cryptographic solutions.

Finally, a strong cryptographic culture is where the encryption and key management become a second nature, integrated into the corporate mindset, and supported by the team spirit where all employees understand their contribution to the protection of the most valuable digital resources of the enterprise.

5. FROM PRINCIPLES TO PRACTICE: SECTOR-SPECIFIC APPLICATIONS

To ground the discussion in real-world applications, an examination of sector-specific practices provides concrete examples of how the technical and cultural aspects of cryptography converge to foster enterprise resilience. While the foundational principles are universal, each industry tailors the implementation of cryptographic controls to its unique regulatory landscape, threat profile, and operational context. The application of cryptography is not uniform across sectors; the application is adapted to the primary risk. In e-commerce, the main risk is the loss of consumer trust and financial data, so the focus is on securing the transaction. In healthcare, the risk is patient privacy and safety, so the focus is on securing records while ensuring availability. In critical infrastructure, the primary risk is catastrophic operational failure, so the focus is on system integrity and authenticating commands. This variation demonstrates how the societal function of a sector dictates the technical implementation of security.

5.1. Financial Services

The financial sector is a leader in cryptographic adoption, driven by stringent compliance requirements and the high stakes of breaches, which can directly undermine trust in financial systems. Regulations like the Payment Card Industry Data Security Standard (PCI DSS) and the Gramm–Leach–Bliley Act (GLBA) mandate robust data protection (Jančiūtė, 2025). As a notable practice, financial institutions often use Hardware Security Modules (HSMs) for key management, which provide a tamper-resistant physical environment for storing cryptographic keys and performing sensitive operations. In addition, some banks have implemented extensive cybersecurity overhauls that include multi-factor authentication and end-to-end encryption across all digital platforms to secure client data and transactions. This approach not only enhances protection but also instills greater confidence among clients and stakeholders. JPMorgan Chase's establishment of the AlgoCRYPT Center of Excellence (CoE) is another prime example of institutionalizing this approach, leading research and implementation of cutting-edge cryptography to future-proof the firm's systems and enable secure computation on encrypted data.

5.2. Healthcare

Historically, the healthcare sector has lagged in cryptographic adoption due to the complexity of its IT systems and the imperative of quick data availability for patient care. However, with escalating cyberattacks on hospitals and the extreme sensitivity of patient records, the industry is moving toward stronger cryptographic controls, as mandated by laws such as HIPAA. As a best practice, organizations are encrypting patient data both at rest (in databases and on mobile devices) and in transit (via VPNs and TLS for telemedicine) (Singh et al., 2021). The use of attribute-based cryptosystems and blockchain has also been proposed to create more secure cloud-based electronic health record (EHR) systems (Wang & Song, 2018). The case of the 2015 Anthem Inc. breach, which exposed the personal information of nearly 80 million people, serves as a cautionary tale; the breach was facilitated by unencrypted databases. In response, Anthem initiated a cultural shift, mandating full-disk encryption on all endpoints and introducing automated monitoring tools. A critical part of the response was a cultural transformation campaign, where leaders reframed encryption as an enabler of patient trust and a core component of ethical healthcare delivery (Bhuyan et al., 2020). The situation shows that a crisis can inspire meaningful cultural change, where cryptographic controls evolve from compliance requirements into a core part of the organization's mission and identity

5.3. Public Sector and Government

Public Sector and Government Bureau deal with large volumes of sensitive data, and extensively use cryptography, in most cases, meeting national requirements, like the Federal Information Processing Standards (FIPS) in the United States. In such a structure, the federal departments must apply the encryption modules that are FIPS 140-certified, which provide that the encryption products used have been certified to meet the standards of reliability. An interesting case concerning a state-based cryptographic governance is observed in the case of the digital infrastructure in Estonia. E-government provision by the Estonian government is based on massive encryption, as well as digital signatures delivered by the national e-ID system (Kerikmae and Parn-Lee, 2020). The popularity of such tools indicates that the society can trust the online platforms when transactions are secured and verifiable (Tsap et al., 2020). The Estonian authorities were quick to react to a critical vulnerability discovered in the chips in its e-ID cards by announcing the vulnerability radically, publishing a key recall and re-issue initiative nationwide. This active and open strategy saved the confidence of citizens to digital services and positively set an example of institutional resilience.

5.4. E-commerce: Securing the Digital Marketplace

Trust is the main foundation of all transactions in the e-commerce industry where cryptography gives the means to maintain that trust in a technological form. Every online communication means the exchange of confidential information, such as personal data, credit cards, shipping data etc. One of the most apparent applications of cryptography in this regard is the Transport Layer Security (TLS) protocol that encrypts the communication channel between the browser and the e-commerce server of a customer. This security is symbolized by the identifiable padlock icon on the address bar of the browser. TLS implements a hybrid encryption scheme: in the first-handshake, the server is authenticated by an asymmetric encryption process with the help of the digital signature and a temporary symmetric key is negotiated. After the handshake is completed, the session switches to symmetric encryption, which is computationally efficient and, at the same time, heavily confidential (Farao et al., 2020). This process in layers supports privacy and integrity of customer information during online transactions via the process of cryptography.

6. CRITICAL INFRASTRUCTURE: PROTECTING SOCIETAL FOUNDATIONS

Critical infrastructure cryptography refers to the formal use of cryptography in securing key facilities in society such as power grids, water treatment and distribution systems, transportation systems and communications networks. The main risk to the given domain is not limited to the fact of data loss, as it also includes the threat of disastrous malfunctioning of operations that can jeopardize the safety of people and the national security of a country. Cryptographic functionality is used to maintain the integrity and authenticity of command and control messages sent to the domains of the Industrial Control Systems (ICS) and Supervisory Control and Data Acquisition (SCADA). Digital signatures and Message Authentication Codes (MACs) verify the identity of the instructions being sent to assets like power grid substations or water pumps and allow only authorized entities to send such commands and ensures that the messages are not altered during transmission. Furthermore, encryption is also critical in protecting communications on the open-safety Land Mobile Radio (LMR) system since the operational information shared during the response to emergencies is sensitive and can not be intercepted and abused.

One of the main challenges in this sphere is based on the long-lasting life cycle of the operational technology (OT) equipment as many of these devices were created before the advent of the modern cybersecurity threat and did not feature the computational power that is necessary to run the modern cryptography algorithms. To effectively mitigate these limitations, it could be required to implement a layered defense approach that allows combining network segmentation, cryptographic gateways, and a strong Public Key Infrastructure (PKI) along with the overall management of device and user identities.

6.1. Future-Proofing Cryptographic Resilience

The insistence of technological change and the advent of new threats demand that organizations stop being stagnant in their models of security and instill a culture of constant change. The cryptography future displays a great duality: a defensive need to reduce the existential danger presented by quantum computing and an offensive possibility to enable new business patterns through privacy-enhancing technologies. This is a place where one has to think forward, invest strategically and understand the challenges, as well as the potential, in-depth. The key strategic challenge which the leadership will have to address in the next decade will be to effectively balance the obligatory, cost-intensive conversion, to post-quantum standards, with opportunistic investments in the making technologies, including homomorphic encryption.

6.2. The Quantum Threat and Crypto-Agility

One of the most significant long-term threats to current cryptographic systems is the advent of quantum computing. A sufficiently powerful quantum computer, running algorithms like Shor's algorithm, could break many widely used public-key cryptographic systems, such as RSA and Elliptic Curve Cryptography (ECC), which underpin the security of most digital communications today. A successful quantum attack would compromise the confidentiality of sensitive data, the authenticity of digital signatures, and the integrity of secure transactions. The threat is not just a future problem but also an immediate one due to the risk of "harvest now, decrypt later" attacks, where adversaries capture encrypted data today with the intent of decrypting the data once a quantum computer becomes available. The potential for misinformation about quantum computing capabilities further complicates organizational risk assessment, making clear and accurate communication essential (Kop et al., 2024).

In response to this threat, the U.S. National Institute of Standards and Technology (NIST) initiated a multi-year public process to solicit, evaluate, and standardize a new suite of Post-Quantum Cryptography (PQC) algorithms. In August 2024, NIST released the first three finalized standards:

- **FIPS 203 (ML-KEM):** Based on the CRYSTALS-Kyber algorithm, this is the primary standard for key establishment, designed to replace algorithms like ECDH.
- **FIPS 204 (ML-DSA):** Based on the CRYSTALS-Dilithium algorithm, this is the primary standard for digital signatures, intended to replace algorithms like ECDSA and RSA signatures.

- **FIPS 205 (SLH-DSA):** Based on the SPHINCS+ algorithm, this is a backup digital signature standard with a different mathematical foundation (hash-based) for added resilience.

In March 2025, NIST also selected the Hamming Quasi-Cyclic (HQC) algorithm as a backup for ML-KEM, as HQC is based on a different mathematical approach (error-correcting codes).

The transition to these new post-quantum cryptographic (PQC) standards is not only a technical upgrade, it is a multi-disciplinary effort taking many years, and indeed multi-leadership cycles in the majority of large organisations. One of the most important aids in this shift is the notion of crypto-agility, which is the ability of the architecture to quickly switch cryptographic functionality (algorithms, key lengths and protocols) without the need to redesign the entire system (Marchesi et al., 2024). The PQC migration will thus act as the final litmus test of socio-technical maturity of an organisation. The first step involves creating an all-inclusive inventory of all the cryptographic properties, a gigantic task in governance and knowledge-management. Scheduling the upgrade through the legacy systems, third party vendors and in house development teams will require unprecedented project management and cultural congruency. After all, the fact that an organisation managed to complete this transition will serve as a direct pointer to its resiliency and strategic visioning.

Table 3. Framework for PQC Migration and Crypto-Agility

Phase	Activities	Responsible Roles	Key Deliverables
Discovery	Inventory all cryptographic assets (algorithms, key types, certificates), map dependencies, and assess data lifetime requirements.	IT, Security, Business Unit Owners, Legal/ Compliance	Cryptographic Asset Inventory, Threat Assessment Report, Risk Prioritization Matrix
Planning	Develop a multi-year migration roadmap, define roles and responsibilities, establish a Crypto CoE, and set clear decision triggers for migration.	Senior Leadership, Security Steering Committee, CoE Lead	PQC Migration Strategy Document, Budget and Resource Plan, Communication Plan
Piloting	Select and test PQC algorithms in non-critical systems, assess performance impacts, and train early adopters on new tools and processes.	Engineering Teams, Application Owners, Security Architects	Pilot Test Report, Performance Metrics, Lessons Learned Document

continued on following page

Table 3. Continued

Phase	Activities	Responsible Roles	Key Deliverables
Rollout	Systematically replace legacy cryptographic components, integrate new PQC tools into CI/CD pipelines, and conduct continuous monitoring and validation.	DevOps, Operations, Security Engineering	Rollout Schedule, Post-Mortem Report on each migration, Updated Policy and Procedures
Sustaining	Maintain a culture of crypto-agility, track PQC-related KPIs (e.g., percentage of assets migrated), and update policies in response to new standards and threats.	All Stakeholders, CISO, Crypto CoE	PQC Compliance Dashboard, Regular Audit Reports, Vendor Security Scorecards

6.3. Advanced Cryptographic Techniques as Enablers of Innovation

The future of cryptography is not limited to defending against known threats; the field is also about enabling new forms of data utility that were previously impossible due to privacy concerns. Advanced cryptographic techniques such as homomorphic encryption (HE) and Secure Multi-Party Computation (SMPC) are moving from theoretical research to practical application. These advanced techniques mitigate the vulnerability of 'data in use,' the critical stage when information must be decrypted for processing, by enabling computations to be carried out directly on encrypted data.

Homomorphic Encryption (HE) allows for mathematical operations to be performed on ciphertext, producing an encrypted result that, when decrypted, matches the result of the operations as if performed on the plaintext. This capability means a third party, such as a cloud provider, can process sensitive data without ever having access to the underlying unencrypted information (Bansal, Gill, & Buyya, 2021). In the financial sector, HE is being explored to allow institutions to collaboratively analyze anonymized, encrypted transaction data to detect fraud patterns without sharing raw customer information. In a similar manner, in the healthcare industry, health economics is promoting secure data analytics to identify disease patterns and improve treatment results, which in turn lets the researcher interact with sensitive patient information with a higher degree of stringent privacy guarantees.

Secure Multi-Party Computation (SMPC) is one such protocol in cryptography that helps many parties compute a function on their combined private inputs without the input of any party being known to the other parties. A classic example is the "millionaires' problem," where two such millionaires would like to determine who possesses more wealth without either party sharing their actual wealth with the other party. SMPC in the business context can enable competing organizations to exchange their data for mutual benefit, such as in the case of performance benchmarking or training a machine learning model, without sharing with their competition the proprietary business intelligence.

These new technologies, which we see cited in a commentary by Khedr et al. (2024), introduce a new model in which cryptography is seen as a key innovation enabler rather than an obstacle to be bypassed. Addressing the underlying issue of protecting data in transit during processing, the techniques allow new business models and collaborations that otherwise would be inhibited by data-sharing prohibitions and confidentiality rules.

7. CONCLUSION

This chapter emphasized the idea that cryptography must move beyond being just some technical device but become part of the overall environment of leadership, governance, and organizational culture. Even though technical descriptions prefer to explain at the algorithmic level, or at the key management, or at crypto-agility, much less often do we reflect on whether such mechanisms do in fact align with strategic intentions or create quantifiable organizational outcomes. The success of cryptography systems not only depends on the mathematical efficacy of the systems but also on the social and management systems that sustain them.

Building sustainable digital trust begins with committed leadership. Strategic direction from executives and boards helps balance the tension between security and operational efficiency. Well-supported policies establish structure and ensure regulatory compliance, while ongoing training and awareness shape safer employee behavior and reinforce the shared nature of security responsibilities. Through well-designed metrics and dashboards, organizations can monitor the adoption of cryptographic practices, evaluate their effectiveness, and identify areas that require further attention. As shown in the examples from financial, healthcare, and public sectors, integrating cryptography into governance structures can strengthen institutional resilience and public trust.

The coming years will bring significant developments. The migration to post-quantum cryptography represents a major test of organizational readiness, demanding deliberate planning and structured change management. Meanwhile, emerging privacy-preserving technologies such as homomorphic encryption and secure multiparty computation show promise for maintaining both data utility and confidentiality. However, their real-world success will depend on continued research, testing, and cost optimization.

Future studies should address several pressing areas. Practical trials of post-quantum algorithm migration can reveal integration and performance challenges. Establishing standardized governance metrics could improve consistency across organizations. Evaluating the outcomes of crypto-literacy programs would clarify how education translates into secure behavior. Research on the usability of developer and operator tools could help reduce human error, particularly in managing complex systems. Comparative case studies would offer valuable insights into how regulatory and sector-specific pressures shape cryptographic practices. Finally, focused research on supply chain assurance and privacy-preserving computation at realistic scales would deepen understanding of their feasibility and organizational impact.

REFERENCES

Abdulhameed, I. S., Al-Mejibli, I., & Naif, J. R. (2021). The security and privacy of electronic health records in healthcare systems: A systematic review. *Turkish Journal of Computer and Mathematics Education, 12*(10), 1979–1992.

Abouelmehdi, K., Beni-Hessane, A., & Khaloufi, H. (2018). Big healthcare data: Preserving security and privacy. *Journal of Big Data, 5*(1). Advance online publication. DOI: 10.1186/s40537-017-0110-7

Alevizos, L. (2024). Automated cybersecurity compliance and threat response using AI, blockchain and smart contracts. *International Journal of Information Technology: an Official Journal of Bharati Vidyapeeth's Institute of Computer Applications and Management, 17*(2), 767–781. DOI: 10.1007/s41870-024-02324-9

Amin, Z. (2019). A Practical Road Map for Assessing Cyber Risk. *Journal of Risk Research, 22*(1), 32–43.

Anu, V. (2021). Information security governance metrics: A survey and taxonomy. *Information and Computer Security, 29*(2), 316–337.

Bansal, G., Gill, S. S., & Buyya, R. (2021). A survey on homomorphic encryption implementations. *ACM Computing Surveys, 54*(8), 1–38.

Bhuyan, S. S., (2020). Transforming Healthcare Cybersecurity from Reactive to Proactive: Current Status and Future Recommendations. *Journal of Medical Systems, 44*(5). Advance online publication. DOI: 10.1007/s10916-019-1507-y PMID: 32239357

Buck, C., (2023). Digital transformation and its impact on organizational risk scenarios. *The Journal of Strategic Information Systems, 32*(3), 101778.

Bulgurcu, B., Cavusoglu, H., & Benbasat, I. (2010). Information security policy compliance: An empirical study of rationality-based beliefs and information security awareness. *Management Information Systems Quarterly*, 523–548.

Chen, Y. (2022). Information security management: Compliance challenges and new directions. *Journal of Information Technology Case and Application Research, 24*(4), 243–249. DOI: 10.1080/15228053.2022.2148979

Connelly, Y., Henkin, G., Leibovich, M., & Akavia, A. (2022). Factors influencing the adoption of advanced cryptographic techniques for data protection of patient medical records. *Healthcare Informatics Research, 28*(2), 132–142. PMID: 35576981

Cram, W. A., & D'Arcy, J. (2023). 'What a waste of time': An examination of cybersecurity legitimacy. *Journal of the Association for Information Systems*, *24*(1), 1–38.

Cremer, F., Sheehan, B., Fortmann, M., Kia, A. N., Mullins, M., Murphy, F., & Materne, S. (2022). Cyber risk and cybersecurity: A systematic review of data availability. *The Geneva Papers on Risk and Insurance. Issues and Practice*, *47*(3), 698–736. PMID: 35194352

Culot, G., Nassimbeni, G., Podrecca, M., & Sartor, M. (2021). The ISO/IEC 27001 information security management standard: Literature review and theory-based research agenda. *The TQM Journal, 33*(7), 76–105.((((https://doi.org/)))))DOI: 10.1108/TQM-06-2020-0148

Farao, J., (2020). A user-centred design framework for mHealth. *PLoS One*, *15*(8), e0237910. PMID: 32813711

Fu, X., Wang, H., & Shi, P. (2022). A survey of lattice-based expressive attribute-based encryption. *Computer Science Review*, *44*, 100438.

Guest, D., (2022). A meta-synthesis of the socio-technical systems theory in organizational studies. *Human Relations*, *75*(6), 1045–1080.

Haney, J. M., & Lutters, W. (2023). From Compliance to Impact: Tracing the Transformation of an Organizational Security Awareness Program. *Proceedings of the ACM on Human-Computer Interaction*, 7(CSCW2), 1-28.

Hon, W. K., Millard, C., & Walden, I. (2011). The problem of 'personal data' in cloud computing: What information is regulated?—the cloud of unknowing. *International Data Privacy Law*, *1*(4), 211–228. DOI: 10.1093/idpl/ipr018

Hsu, J. S. C., Lee, C. S., & Straub, D. W. (2015). The Role of Extra-Role Behaviors and Social Controls in Information Security Policy Effectiveness. *Information Systems Research*, *26*(2), 282–300.

Jampen, D., et al. (2020). Don't click: towards an effective anti-phishing training. A comparative literature review. *Human-centric Computing and Information Sciences*, 10(1).

Jančiūtė, L. (2025). Cybersecurity in the financial sector and the quantum-safe cryptography transition: In search of a precautionary approach in the EU Digital Operational Resilience Act framework. *International Cybersecurity Law Review*, *6*(2), 145–154. PMID: 40406673

Kerikmäe, T., & Pärn-Lee, E. (2020). Legal dilemmas of Estonian artificial intelligence strategy: In between of e-society and global race. *AI & Society*, *36*(2), 561–572. DOI: 10.1007/s00146-020-01009-8

Khadka, K., & Ullah, A. B. (2025). Human factors in cybersecurity: An interdisciplinary review and framework proposal. *International Journal of Information Security*, *24*, 119. DOI: 10.1007/s10207-025-01032-0

Khan, S., (2022). A Systematic Analysis of the Capital One Data Breach: Critical Lessons Learned. *ACM Transactions on Privacy and Security*, *26*(1), 1–29. DOI: 10.1145/3546068

Khan, S., Luo, F., Zhang, Z., Rahim, M. A., Ahmad, M., & Wu, K. (2022). Survey on issues and recent advances in vehicular public-key infrastructure (VPKI). *IEEE Communications Surveys and Tutorials*, *24*(3), 1574–1601. DOI: 10.1109/COMST.2022.3178081

Khedr, A., Hassan, H., & Eisa, S. (2024). Practical solutions in fully homomorphic encryption. A review. *Cybersecurity*, *7*, 37. DOI: 10.1186/s42400-024-00171-4

Kop, M., (2024). Navigating the quantum frontier: Examining the interplay of quantum computing, policy, and global security. *Technology in Society*, *77*, 102589.

Li, F., Yao, H., Liu, Z., & Chen, P. (2023). A survey on searchable symmetric encryption. *ACM Computing Surveys*, *56*(5), 131.

Liu, Y., Lu, Q., Yu, G., Paik, H.-Y., & Zhu, L. (2021). Defining blockchain governance principles: A comprehensive framework. *Journal of Information Technology. Operational Analysis*, *27*(3), 155–172. DOI: 10.1080/10580530.2020.1720046

Marchesi, L., Marchesi, M., & Tonelli, R. (2024). A survey on crypto-agility and agile practices in the light of quantum resistance. *Information and Software Technology*, *178*, 107604. DOI: 10.1016/j.infsof.2024.107604

Mia, M. R., Shahriar, H., Valero, M., Sakib, N., Saha, B., Barek, M. A., & Ahamed, S. I. (2022). A comparative study on HIPAA technical safeguards assessment of Android mHealth applications. *Smart Health (Amsterdam, Netherlands)*, *26*, 100349. DOI: 10.1016/j.smhl.2022.100349 PMID: 39086849

Nifakos, S., Chandramouli, K., Nikolaou, C. K., Papachristou, P., Koch, S., Panaousis, E., & Bonacina, S. (2021). Influence of human factors on cyber security within healthcare organisations: A systematic review. *Sensors (Basel)*, *21*(15), 5119. DOI: 10.3390/s21155119 PMID: 34372354

Nobles, C. (2022). Stress, Burnout, and Security Fatigue in Cybersecurity: A Human Factors Problem. *HOLISTICA–Journal of Business and Public Administration, 13*(1), 49–72.

Olaiya, O. P., Adesoga, T. O., Adebayo, A. A., Sotomi, F. M., Adigun, O. A., & Ezeliora, P. M. (2024). Encryption techniques for financial data security in fintech applications. *International Journal of Science and Research Archive, 12*(1), 2942–2949.

Paliszkiewicz, J. (2019). Information Security Policy Compliance: Leadership and Trust. *Journal of Computer Information Systems, 59*(3), 211–217. DOI: 10.1080/08874417.2019.1571459

Paul, E., Callistus, O., Somtobe, O., Esther, T., Somto, K., Clement, O., & Ejimofor, I. (2023). Cybersecurity strategies for safeguarding customer's data and preventing financial fraud in the United States financial sectors. *International Journal on Soft Computing, 14*(3), 01-16.

Rana, S., Biswas, S., & Mahato, B. (2023). A comprehensive survey of cryptography key management systems. *Journal of King Saud University. Computer and Information Sciences, 35*(7), 101594.

Rasslan, M., Nasreldin, M. M., Abdelrahman, D., Elshobaky, A., & Aslan, H. (2024). Networking and cryptography library with a non-repudiation flavor for blockchain. *Journal of Computer Virology and Hacking Techniques, 20*(1), 1–14.

Safa, N. S., Von Solms, R., & Furnell, S. (2016). Information security policy compliance in organizations: A review. *Computers & Security, 56*, 70–82.

Salako, A. O., (2025). Securing Confidentiality in Distributed Ledger Systems with Secure Multi-party Computation for Financial Data Protection. *Journal of Engineering Research and Reports, 27*(3), 352–373.

Seth, B., Dalal, G., & Kumar, S. (2020). Integrating encryption techniques for secure data storage in the cloud. *Transactions on Emerging Telecommunications Technologies, 33*(4), e4108. DOI: 10.1002/ett.4108

Silić, M., & Lowry, P. B. (2020). Using Design-Science Based Gamification to Improve Organizational Security Training and Compliance. *Journal of Management Information Systems, 37*(1), 129–161. DOI: 10.1080/07421222.2019.1705512

Singh, A. K., Anand, A., Lv, Z., Ko, H., & Mohan, A. (2021). A survey on healthcare data: A security perspective. *ACM Transactions on Multimedia Computing Communications and Applications, 17*(2s), 1–26.

Springer, J., & Haindl, P. (2024). Blockchain-based PKI within a corporate organization: Advantages and challenges. *Journal of Information Security and Applications*, *79*, 103648.

Tsap, V., (2020). The Estonian E-government ecosystem: A case study. *Procedia Computer Science*, *175*, 46–53.

Velkes, R. (2019). GDPR: The right of access to personal data. *New York University Journal of International Law & Politics. New York University. International Law Society*, *51*(4), 1395–1433.

Wang, H., & Song, Y. (2018). Secure Cloud-Based EHR System Using Attribute-Based Cryptosystem and Blockchain. *Journal of Medical Systems*, *42*(8). PMID: 29974270

Willie, M. M. (2023). The role of organizational culture in cybersecurity: Building a security-first culture. *Journal of Research. Innovation and Technologies*, *2*(2), 179–198.

Windarta, S., Suryadi, S., Ramli, K., Pranggono, B., & Gunawan, T. S. (2022). Lightweight cryptographic hash functions: Design trends, comparative study, and future directions. *IEEE Access: Practical Innovations, Open Solutions*, *10*, 82272–82294.

Woodrum, T. D. (2003). 21 CFR Part 11: The Role of Predicate Regulations and Associated Internal Policies. *Drug Information Journal*, *37*(2), 159–164. DOI: 10.1177/009286150303700205

Yeo, L. H., & Banfield, J. (2022). Human factors in electronic health records cybersecurity breach: An exploratory analysis. *Perspectives in Health Information Management*, *19*(Spring), 1i. PMID: 35692854

Yusif, S., & Hafeez-Baig, A. (2021). A Conceptual Model for Cybersecurity Governance. *Journal of Applied Security Research*, *16*(4), 490–513. DOI: 10.1080/19361610.2021.1918995

Chapter 8
Securing Data With Cryptography:
Bridging Human Behavior and Organizational Culture in Cybersecurity

Uma Pratap Madje
https://orcid.org/0009-0009-3799-3652
Fergusson College, Pune, India

ABSTRACT

Data security strategies in the digital age rely on cryptography, yet human behavior remains the most critical and unpredictable factor. This chapter explores the intersection of corporate culture and cryptographic implementation, highlighting how user habits, training gaps, and weak cybersecurity cultures can undermine even the most robust encryption. Using real-world examples from healthcare, finance, and IT, the chapter emphasizes the need for leadership engagement, staff training, and policy clarity. It examines behavioral models like PMT and TAM, advocating for gamified training and maturity assessments. As quantum computing and cloud complexities rise, the chapter underscores the importance of cryptographic agility and future readiness. Ultimately, it argues that cryptography must be embedded into organizational culture to ensure resilient, human-aligned digital security.

INTRODUCTION

Securing sensitive data has become both a technical and strategic need in an era characterized by data-centric economies and pervasive digital infrastructures.

DOI: 10.4018/979-8-3373-4154-5.ch008

Organizations must put strong data protection measures in place as the frequency and sophistication of data breaches, cyberattacks, and illegal access continue to rise. The foundation of digital security has long been cryptography, a field with roots in mathematical ideas and rigorous algorithmic design. It serves as the foundation for the majority of cybersecurity architectures by facilitating the confidentiality, integrity, authenticity, and non-repudiation of data (Stallings, 2023). Cryptographic algorithms like AES, RSA, and SHA-3 are known for their theoretical power, but their actual implementations usually are impacted from an underutilized component: the human factor. Research from a variety of industries has demonstrated that careless password practices, inadequate key management, a general lack of user awareness, and the inability to encrypt sensitive data can all make even the most secure cryptographic systems ineffective (Ur et al., 2022; Ashenden & Lawrence, 2021). In this respect, technology is not enough on its own. The promise of cryptography will remain unrealized as long as people—whether they are administrators, executives, or employees—misuse or misinterpret encryption techniques.

The relationship between organizational culture and cryptographic security is examined broadly in this chapter. It contends that developing a work environment that recognizes, values, and actively encourages cryptographic practices is necessary for effective data protection, which goes beyond simply using encryption technologies or following compliance procedures. Policy by itself isn't enough to create meaningful change; it must be supported by committed leadership, continuous learning, and a security approach that takes human behavior into account.

Beginning with an overview of the basic concepts of cryptography, the chapter covers topics including symmetric and asymmetric encryption, digital signatures, and key management. It then examines how human behavior—which is often unintentional—may endanger cryptographic systems. Whether they disregard requests for multi-factor authentication or use the same password across platforms, people are frequently the weakest link in security (Sasse et al., 2021). Organizational strategies are then discussed in order to close this gap, suggesting that businesses attempt to become "cryptography-conscious." This entails integrating encryption tools into standard procedures as well as promoting encryption awareness, responsibility, and participation at all organizational levels. Using real-world case studies from the fields of finance, healthcare, and IT, we show how behavioral mistakes, not technical ones, are often the reason behind cryptographic failures. The chapter concludes by demonstrating for a paradigm change: the recognition of cryptography as a socio-technical system where people, processes, and technology intersect, rather than as a solely technical function. Institutions can transition from reactive security postures to proactive, human-cantered data protection by integrating cryptography knowledge into the workplace culture.

Cryptography is the foundation of data security solutions in the digital age. Despite its technological strength, the human aspect remains the most unpredictable and important factor in determining the success of cryptographic systems. As this chapter explores the connection between corporate culture and cryptographic technology, it is imperative to cultivate a workforce that understands, values, and effectively utilizes encryption approaches. We present a guiding framework, the Cryptographic Culture Maturity Model, to serve as a practical lens throughout the chapter. As a diagnostic and developmental tool, this model assists businesses with evaluating their technical, behavioral, and cultural preparedness for the implementation of safe cryptography.

CRYPTOGRAPHIC CULTURE MATURITY MODEL

The ability of organizations to adopt and uphold secure cryptography techniques varies greatly. Five levels are used by the Cryptographic Culture Maturity Model (CCMM) to benchmark progress:

Table 1. Maturity Levels and Characteristics in Organizational Cryptographic Culture

Maturity Level	Key Characteristics
1. Ad Hoc	No formal cryptographic policy or training. Reactive encryption use.
2. Defined	Basic encryption standards exist. Awareness programs launched.
3. Structured	Key management practices and role-based access in place. Training programs recurring.
4. Optimized	Encryption-by-default in systems. Audits and automation in key management.
5. Adaptive	Post-quantum planning. Continuous learning culture. Cryptographic agility embedded.

This model can be used as a framework for self-evaluation by organizations to determine their areas of weakness and create reform plans that support both technical and cultural objectives.

EVOLUTION AND HISTORIC MILESTONES IN CRYPTOGRAPHY

The foundation of current data protection is cryptography. A variety of mathematical methods and procedures are used to protect data from disclosure, alteration, and unwanted access. It is crucial for IT departments and the entire corporate culture to comprehend the fundamental ideas of cryptography as businesses depend more and more on digital technologies to store and transfer sensitive data.

Emerging technology, digital revolution, and geopolitical forces have all influenced the modern development of cryptography. Computational cryptanalysis eventually made early symmetric algorithms like the Vigenère and Caesar ciphers obsolete. A significant turning point was the development of digital communication in the 20th century, particularly with the invention of devices like the Enigma during World War II. Secure digital communication was transformed by public-key cryptography, which was first presented by Diffie and Hellman in 1976 and then formalized with RSA (Rivest, Shamir, Adleman, 1978). The underlying algorithms for contemporary secure systems were established by NIST in 1977 with the Data Encryption Standard (DES) and by AES (Rijndael) in 2001. The need for post-quantum algorithms in more recent times emphasizes how cryptography standards are always changing to keep up with advances in computing power.

Symmetric Encryption

The initial and most basic type of cryptography is symmetric encryption. A single key is utilized for both encryption and decryption applications. Since anyone who has access to the key can decode the protected material, it must be kept secret. DES (Data Encryption Standard) and AES (Advanced Encryption Standard) are examples of popular algorithms.

Symmetric encryption is demonstrated in the below diagram (left section), where plaintext is transformed into ciphertext with a single common key. This method works well for encrypting massive volumes of data since it is quick and effective. Secure key distribution is its main flaw, though; if the key is stolen or leaked, the confidentiality mechanism as a whole break down (Stallings, 2023).

Advantages:

- It is appropriate for encrypting massive amounts of data due to its high performance and efficiency.
- simplicity in both execution and use.

Challenges:

- Key Distribution: It can be challenging to securely distribute the secret key between parties, particularly across unprotected connections.
- Key Management: Keeping track of and rotating keys becomes more difficult as the user base increases.

- Key Exhaustion: Regular key rotation is required since reusing keys might cause information leaks, leaving them open to attacks.

Attribution Data: Symmetric keys make auditing and accountability more difficult because they lack metadata for monitoring usage or origin. Applications such as payment systems, data-at-rest security, and secure communication protocols (like SSL/TLS handshakes) all make extensive use of symmetric encryption.

Asymmetric Encryption and Digital Signature

Asymmetric encryption, in contrast to symmetric techniques, employs two keys: a private key for decryption and a public key for encryption. This eliminates the requirement for parties to exchange a secret key in advance and enables secure communication. RSA and Elliptic Curve Cryptography (ECC) are two popular algorithms.

The diagram's central portion illustrates how a public key is used to encrypt plaintext and a private key is used to decrypt it. In addition to securing data transfer, this also facilitates digital signatures, which guarantee the integrity and authenticity of communications. In order to provide non-repudiation, a digital signature is generated using the sender's private key and may be validated by others using the public key (Diffie & Hellman, 1976; Boneh & Shoup, 2020).

Figure 1. Fundamentals of Cryptography: Core concepts and lifecycle

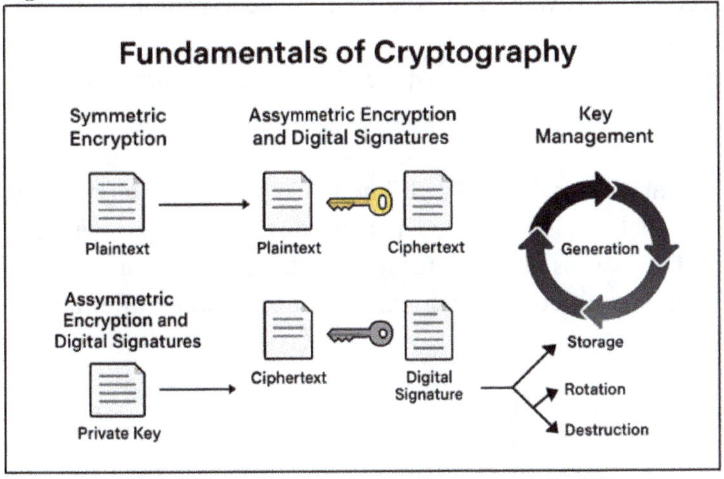

Figure 1: Fundamentals of Cryptography: Core concepts and lifecycle

Advantages:

- Permits the safe transfer of keys over unprotected channels, hence resolving the issue of key distribution.
- Uses digital signatures to enable non-repudiation and authentication.

Challenges:

- Less appropriate for huge data quantities since it is slower and requires more computing power than symmetric encryption.
- Requires trust in certificate authority for public key verification and strong management of public/private key pairings.

Key Managements

Effective key management is essential to the success of any cryptographic system. Key management includes key creation, distribution, storage, rotation, and destruction. These lifecycle stages are depicted in the right-hand portion of the diagram.

A secure system must address:

- The process of producing unpredictable keys with cryptographically secure random number generators is known as key generation.
- Using software with strong encryption or keeping keys in secure hardware, like Hardware Security Modules, are two possibilities for key storage.
- Changing keys frequently lowers the possibility of compromise. This is known as key rotation.
- To ensure that retired keys cannot be misplaced or misused, they should be destroyed safely.

Table 2 provides a comparative analysis of well-known cryptographic algorithms, emphasizing their approach type, key length, performance, security level, and real-world applications. This serves as a helpful manual for selecting appropriate cryptographic solutions in line with organizational constraints and requirements.

Table 2. Comparative Analysis of Cryptographic Algorithms

Algorithm	Type	Key Length	Security	Performance	Use Case
AES-256	Symmetric	256-bit	Very strong (no practical attacks)	High (hardware-accelerated)	Full-disk encryption, VPNs
RSA-2048	Asymmetric	2048-bit	Secure against classical attacks	Moderate	Digital signatures, TLS handshakes
ECC-256	Asymmetric	256-bit	Equivalent to RSA-3072	High (shorter keys)	IoT devices, mobile authentication
SHA-256	Hash	256-bit digest	Collision-resistant	Very High	Blockchain, digital integrity checks

The specific circumstance in which a cryptographic method is used—such as robust authentication, lightweight security for mobile devices, or fast encryption for processing large volumes of data—often influences the choice of cryptographic method. Asymmetric systems like RSA and ECC are used for safe key sharing and digital identity verification, but their efficacy varies widely.

Ensuring data integrity requires the use of robust hash algorithms like SHA-256 and SHA-3, which are found in everything from digital certificates to blockchain technology. When decisions are made without seeking advice from security experts, developers, and compliance officials, security issues may arise if an algorithm is incompatible with the architecture of the system.

EMERGING CRYPTOGRAPHIC PARADIGM

As digital ecosystems evolve, researchers and cybersecurity specialists are looking into cutting-edge cryptographic solutions that go beyond conventional encryption to address the growing privacy concerns and new threats posed by technology. Secure multi-party computing (SMPC), homomorphic encryption, and zero-knowledge proofs (ZKPs) are advanced techniques for data protection in cooperative, decentralized, and privacy-sensitive situations.

a. Homomorphic Encryption:

Computations on encrypted data can be carried out without first decrypting it because of homomorphic encryption. When these operations are decrypted, the outcome is precisely the same as what would have been obtained if the procedures had been performed on the original plaintext. This method guarantees that private data is encrypted while processing, which makes it very useful in cloud computing, healthcare, banking, and privacy-preserving machine learning.

Homomorphic encryption is now more widely available owing to contemporary implementations like Microsoft SEAL and IBM HELib. Research on partially and fully homomorphic algorithms is continuously increasing efficiency, even though computational overhead is still a problem (Acar et al., 2018; Kim & Lauter, 2021).

Use Case: Without ever disclosing raw medical data, hospitals can do statistical analysis on encrypted patient information in order to adhere to laws like HIPAA or GDPR.

b. Zero Knowledge Proofs (ZKPs):

With zero-knowledge proofs, a prover can persuade a verifier that a claim is true without disclosing any further details. ZKPs are necessary for privacy-preserving blockchain protocols (such as Zcash's zk-SNARKs) and secure identity verification systems. Decentralized authentication, secure voting, and anonymous credential issuing are some examples of applications. Current research aims to improve the efficiency of zk-SNARK and create scalable, post-quantum safe alternatives such as zk-STARKs (Ben-Sasson et al., 2019).

Use Case: Without disclosing personal data like wallet balances or transaction histories, ZKPs allow transaction validity checking in decentralized finance (DeFi).

c. Secure Multi-party Computation (SMPC):

With SMPC, many individuals can collaborate to compute a function over their private inputs while keeping those inputs secret. This paradigm is especially useful when strong data privacy is required, such as when banks collaborate to detect fraud or when institutions with sensitive datasets collaborate to conduct research. Workable implementations are provided by frameworks such as Sharemind and MP-SPDZ; nonetheless, problems with scaling efficiently and reducing communication overhead persist (Evans et al., 2018).

Use Case: Without disclosing specific trial data, rival pharmaceutical companies can collaborate to calculate a drug's average effectiveness in clinical trials.

With these paradigms, the focus of cryptography has shifted from protecting data while it is in transit or at rest to facilitating computation and verification on hidden or encrypted data. Their potential in privacy-first designs is significant despite the fact that there are still implementation challenges, especially with regard to performance and usability. It will be more and more crucial to incorporate these cryptographic advancements into common systems as attacks grow more complex.

PREPARING FOR POST-QUANTUM CRYPTOGRAPHY AND INTELLIGENT CRYPTOGRAPHIC AUTOMATION

Post-Quantum Cryptography Organizational Readiness (PQC)

Post-quantum cryptography is frequently mentioned in technical terms (such as algorithm migration), but in order to make the transition feasible, quantifiable, and risk-informed, enterprises require organized preparedness frameworks. The following should be assessed by a strong Post-Quantum Readiness Assessment Toolkit:

- Cryptographic Asset Inventory: List the algorithms that are currently in use, such as RSA and ECC, along with their dependencies.
- Agility Score: Determine which systems possess cryptographic agility, or the capacity to switch between algorithms without requiring significant re-engineering.
- Priority Systems Index: Determine the importance of a migration by considering exposure risk, system criticality, and data sensitivity.
- Workforce Readiness: Evaluate the degree of PQC concept training provided to developers, IT departments, and policy managers.
- Evaluation of the Vendor and Supply Chain: Find out how outside services are getting ready for the adoption of NIST-standardized PQC.

Monitoring and Managing Cryptography using AI and ML

The application of AI and machine learning to real-time cryptographic system optimization is growing. Here are two apps that show promise:

a. Identification of Cryptographic Anomalies

To identify odd cryptographic behavior, machine learning models can be trained on usage patterns, including:

- Unexpected key accesses
- Misuse of revoked or expired certifications
- Extensive decoding efforts or unconventional algorithm choices

These signs frequently come before malware activity or insider attacks. For instance, pattern-based detection is used by AWS CloudTrail and Azure Key Vault to identify anomalous encryption events (Ristenpart & Yilek, 2020).

b. AI-powered Automated Key Lifecycle Management can help with:
   - Estimating the ideal rotation cycles
   - Controlling the expiration of cryptographic keys
   - recommending recovery routes in light of potential service interruptions

These clever technologies minimize important exposure windows while lessening the administrative load.

THE HUMAN ELEMENT IN CRYPTOGRAPHIC FAILURE

Usually, cryptographic systems are developed with both technological stability and mathematical precision. However, the human factor frequently compromises their effectiveness in the actual world rather than computational flaws. Cryptographic protection frequently fails due to human factors like carelessness, ignorance, poor usability, and organizational misalignment. For cryptography to reach its full potential, these factors must be recognized and addressed.

Human Behaviour and Cryptographic Misuse

Several investigations have shown that user error, not algorithmic failures, is frequently the cause of security breaches. Humans' inclination to prioritize convenience over security leads to significant errors:

a. Weak Passwords: People usually use passwords that are predictable or the same. Despite multifactor authentication and password managers, poor password hygiene still exists (Ur et al., 2022).
b. Failure to Encrypt sensitive data: sInattention or a desire to save time may lead employees in busy work environments to neglect encryption protocols, leaving critical information in unencrypted.
c. Improper Key Handling: Emailing private keys, keeping them on unprotected local drives, or failing to rotate them on a regular basis can all significantly compromise security (Ashenden & Lawrence, 2021).

This area offers specific applications that address unique issues in secure systems to further reinforce the connection between usability, human behavior, and the effectiveness of cryptography. Among these are pragmatic considerations such as design usability, device-level restrictions, thwarting insider threats, and the economic impacts of cryptography culture.

1. Creating Usable Interfaces for Encryption (Considering UI/UX)

It is not algorithmic strength but user engagement that hinders encryption's broad deployment. Sometimes, even when users are aware of the hazards, usability problems in security apps can cause them to disable or circumvent precautions. According to studies on human-computer interaction (HCI), encryption requires user-friendly interfaces that minimize cognitive friction (Sasse et al., 2001).

Poorly designed security prompts, non-standard iconography, and cluttered settings interfaces are the main causes of low adoption of otherwise dependable technologies.

As an illustration, messaging apps like Signal and WhatsApp instantly activate end-to-end encryption and show a straightforward lock icon to bolster user confidence. Fundamental HCI concepts like "secure by default" and "minimal configuration burden" are reflected in these design decisions (Green & Smith, 2016).

2. IoT and Embedded Systems Cryptography

There are new limitations for encryption brought about by the exponential development of IoT devices. These electronic devices frequently have limited power, memory, and computing capacity. Without hardware acceleration, conventional encryption techniques like RSA or AES-256 might not be appropriate. Lightweight cryptography has become a significant field of study. It is especially relevant in environments where resources are limited. To address these needs, several lightweight encryption algorithms have been developed, including PRESENT, Ascon, and SIMON/SPECK. Recently, Ascon was selected as the standard for lightweight authenticated encryption by the National Institute of Standards and Technology (NIST) (NIST, 2023).

For instance, safe data transmission without excessive power consumption is made possible via lightweight encryption, which is essential for smart home systems and wearable health monitoring devices. These systems also require secure firmware updates, and their authenticity and integrity are guaranteed by boot verification procedures and cryptographic signatures.

3. Mitigation of Insider Threats with Cryptographic Controls

The insider threat is among the most challenging categories of cyberthreats to identify and eliminate. These hazards are particularly difficult to manage because they might originate from individuals inside an organization, either on purpose or accidentally. Businesses can significantly lower their risk of being impacted by implementing role-based access controls, key segmentation, and data encryption while it's at rest.

For example, by storing encryption keys in safe, impenetrable systems, Hardware Security Modules (HSMs) aid in preventing exploitation.

Sensitive information cannot be accessed by one individual alone thanks to the M of N control model. Rather, key components of the system are dispersed over various departments or functions, making it more difficult for a single person to create harm (Cappelli et al., 2012). For example, banking firms' key management systems sometimes require dual permission to decode client records or transaction logs.

4. The operational and financial expenses of establishing a cryptographic culture

Although there is general agreement about the strategic advantages of a culture that is focused on cryptography, there can be significant operational expenses. These include spending money on employee training, purchasing hardware (such HSMs), paying for cryptographic library licenses, creating policies, and conducting compliance audits.

Potential productivity lags brought on by extra security measures or integration hold-ups during system upgrades are examples of operational impacts. However, the long-term costs of not implementing cryptographic measures—such as data breaches, legal penalties, and reputational damage—are often much greater. A Ponemon Institute (2023) study found that organizations with strong encryption reduced their breach costs by an average of $360,000 compared to those without.

BEHAVIORAL THEORIES AND CRYPTOGRAPHIC ADOPTION

The effective implementation of cryptographic systems depends on both human behavior and technology design. Frameworks for understanding these processes are provided by the Protection Motivation Theory (PMT) and the Technology Acceptance Model (TAM). According to PMT, people's protective behaviors are impacted by their belief in the effectiveness of security measures, their personal ability to use them, and their judgment of the seriousness and vulnerability of hazards (Woon et al., 2005). If cryptographic APIs are difficult to use or lack sufficient documentation, even developers who are worried about security may steer clear of them; in contrast, low-friction, user-friendly solutions tend to be more widely adopted. Employees may be more inclined to adopt encrypted communication in practice if they are aware of the risks associated with email interception, think encryption is effective, and feel at ease using it. TAM, which highlights the importance of perceived utility and usability in technology adoption, supports this point of view (Venkatesh & Davis, 2000). Cryptographic APIs that are difficult to use or lack sufficient documentation may be avoided by even developers who are worried about security, whereas low-friction, user-friendly solutions tend to be more widely adopted.

In addition to these models, principles from behavioral economics and human-computer interface (HCI) can be used to explain why many cryptographic systems have recurring problems. Excessively strict password requirements or complex encryption configurations may result in user resistance or harmful workarounds, even though insufficient security warnings and poor interfaces have been linked to SSL vulnerabilities in Android devices (Fahl et al., 2012). Cognitive biases like default bias, option overload, and loss aversion also affect user behavior (Acquisti & Grossklags, 2007). Collectively, these behavioral insights show how important it is to align cryptographic solutions with user expectations and capabilities to enhance security in real-world scenarios.

Aspects of the Organization

- Organizational culture and policy are important in addition to individual behavior:
  - Lack of a Clear Policy: Employees may behave inconsistently if there isn't a clear encryption policy that is enforced and widely disclosed.
  - Inadequate Training: A large number of staff members are not familiar with the fundamentals of encryption and the repercussions of unsafe behavior.
  - Over-reliance on IT Departments: Workers become negligent because they believe that IT is alone in charge of data protection.

According to a 2022 Gartner analysis, human mistake and misconfiguration, rather than technological defects, account for 85% of security problems in business cryptography setups. A constant weak point in the security chain is human error, even with the ongoing improvements in cryptography technologies. Cryptographic protections are frequently compromised from within due to usability problems, inefficient procedures, and organizational indifference, as research continuously shows.

- **Password and key mismanagement:**

Cryptographic keys and passwords are essential for protecting data, but user management frequently undermines their efficiency.

- Weak Passwords and Password Reuse: People frequently use the same password on several platforms or make readily guessed passwords. By doing this, encrypted systems become vulnerable to credential stuffing or brute-force attacks.

- Insecure Password Storage: People commonly write down their passphrases, keep them in unprotected text files, or even distribute them via unsecure channels like messaging applications or email.
- Inappropriate Key Storage: Private keys are vulnerable to theft because they are occasionally copied to personal devices or stored on shared network drives.

According to Ur et al. (2022), around 40% of users acknowledged keeping keys or credentials in unprotected places, while 65% of users reused passwords. Additionally, their survey found that even in professional settings, the majority of users were not aware of safe key management techniques.

- **Bypassing Tools for convenience**

For convenience, users frequently disable or avoid cryptographic solutions, even when they are properly implemented. There are serious vulnerabilities introduced by this human behavior.

- Complex Interfaces: Although sophisticated tools like PGP and S/MIME are frequently too complicated for non-experts, their adoption in businesses is extremely low.
- Time Pressures: In order to achieve deadlines, workers in fast-paced positions (like finance or customer service) could omit encryption measures.
- Misaligned UX Design: When encryption features are not well integrated, users feel overburdened, which prompts them to take workaround measures (such locally preserving plaintext).

Security systems need to be in line with human cognitive limitations, according to Sasse et al. (2021). Even inadvertently, users will try to minimize or completely avoid security technologies if they consider them as a hindrance.

- **Management Oversight**

Organizations frequently neglect to put in place appropriate governance for cryptographic processes, which can result in risks and breaches that affect the entire system.

a. Failure to Rotate Keys: Cryptographic keys that were never rotated or expired have been linked to numerous breaches.
b. Unrevoked Credentials: If revocation is not enforced, former employees may still have access to encrypted systems or credentials.
c. Absence of Incident Response Planning: Businesses find it difficult to recover from compromised keys or unsuccessful encryption in the absence of a defined policy.

An example of a breach occurred in 2022 at a major U.S. healthcare facility, when former staff members had unrevoked access credentials that allowed them to view encrypted patient records for more than six months.

Table 3. Common Human-Induced Cryptographic Failures

Failure Type	Description	Impact
Password Reuse	Users recycle weak or common passwords	Increases brute-force attack success
Key Mishandling	Keys stored in unsecure locations (USBs, cloud folders)	Enables unauthorized access
Bypassing Encryption	Users skip encryption steps for convenience	Data exposed in transit or at rest
Unrevoked Access	Credentials of ex-employees not deactivated	Long-term unauthorized system access
No Key Rotation Policy	Cryptographic keys not periodically updated	Increases vulnerability window for attackers
Poor UX/UI for Tools	Users find tools too difficult or slow	Encourages insecure workarounds

Even the most advanced cryptographic systems are only as safe as the people who use, administer, and deploy them. Usability issues, management-level monitoring, and poor key management continue to expose systems to avoidable risks. A multi-disciplinary strategy is needed to address these issues; in addition to cryptographers, UX designers, trainers, and risk managers must be involved.

BUILDING CRYPTOGRAPHY - CONSCIOUS CULTURE

Businesses frequently spend money on strong cryptographic tools but fall short of security because they overlook the cultural and human factors. Four essential components—Awareness & Training, Leadership & Policy, Usable Cryptography, and Role-Based Access—must cooperate in order to integrate cryptography into the organizational Culture.

a. Awareness and Training:

Employees frequently don't have a basic understanding of encryption, key management, or secure communication techniques. Even the most advanced cryptography systems can be rendered ineffective by human error in the absence of focused instruction.

Following enhancements and strategies can be taken into consideration into an organizational structure

- Improvements and Techniques: Contextual microlearning Throughout workflows, provide bite-sized modules (e.g., a brief lecture when employing email encryption).
- Attack drill simulations: Regular assessments of social engineering and improper management of cryptography.
- Simulations of phishing and key misuse: To demonstrate how attackers take advantage of trust and inadequate cryptographic practices.

According to ENISA (2023), fundamental misconceptions about cryptographic processes were the cause of 89% of security incidents in SMEs. According to a 2022 Hadnagy & Wilson study on social engineering, 42% of workers disclosed their credentials through phishing, frequently thinking that the encryption tool would protect them nonetheless.

b. Leadership and Policy:

The culture of security begins at the highest level. When leaders do not set an example of security, staff members disregard encryption. On the other hand, the culture changes when leaders actively support and model encryption norms. Following best practices can be adapted:

- Using encryption technologies for executive on boarding is a best practice.
- C-level stakeholders support quarterly cryptography audits.
- KPIs associated with instances of encryption adoption and misuse.

Real-World Examples: In the 2018 HealthTech hack in Singapore, 1.5 million patient records were exposed due in part to a lack of board-level insight into encryption procedures. The necessity of executive responsibility for cryptographic health was highlighted in a 2021 government assessment.

Policy Alignment: Comply with NIST 800-53 and ISO/IEC 27001 by using cryptographic practices. Require cloud SLAs and third-party contracts to include cryptographic security provisions.

c. Useable Cryptography:

Cryptography is effective, but it is ineffective when people are unable or unwilling to utilize it. Encryption is either optional or disruptive in many real-world systems. Security needs to be seamless.

Principles of Design:

- Low cognitive load: Steer clear of technical terms like "asymmetric cipher" and substitute straightforward instructions like "Encrypt this message?"
- Error forgiveness: Using secure enclaves or biometric backup, lost keys can be automatically recovered.
- Automatic end-to-end encryption for conversations, emails, and file storage is the default security feature.

The Symposium on Usable Privacy and Security (SOUPS) in 2022 came to the conclusion that usability issues with email encryption, like PGP, are more likely to cause security lapses than algorithmic errors. According to a survey by Fahl et al. (2022), 63% of developers of mobile apps steer clear of built-in cryptography APIs due to unclear interfaces and inadequate documentation.

d. Role based access and Cryptographic Governance:

By restricting access to cryptographic capabilities, risk is decreased and compliance is made easier. Not every employee should set up security procedures, create keys, or decrypt private information.

Best Practices for Governance:

- Definitions of roles: Assign distinct responsibilities for cryptography to developers, security analysts, legal, and IT operations.
- Automate key audits, revocation, and expiration as part of key lifecycle management.
- Behavioral analytics: Keep an eye out for unusual crypto activity, such as significant decryption incidents.

Adopting a security-in-depth strategy that integrates several defensive layers is necessary to guarantee strong protection of cryptographic systems. The risk of software-level key compromise is greatly decreased by Hardware Security Modules (HSMs), which offer tamper-resistant storage and key management (Huang et al., 2022). Even if credentials are hacked, Multi-Factor Authentication (MFA) should be required for all cryptographic administrative tasks to avoid unwanted access. Google's internal implementation of hardware-backed MFA revealed no phishing-based breaches (Google Security Blog, 2020). By using Zero Trust Architecture (ZTA), which restricts implicit trust and mandates constant verification, decryption privileges are strictly controlled and context-aware (NIST SP 800-207, 2020).

Simple errors like reusing passwords, improperly managing keys, and having excessive privileged roles can undermine even the most robust encryption systems. Table 4 enumerates typical cryptographic errors caused by humans in various industries.

Table 4. Common Human-Induced Cryptographic Failures and Real-World Consequences

Category	Failure Description	Real-World Example	Impact	Reference
Password & Key Mismanagement	Users reuse weak passwords, store encryption keys in plaintext, or share credentials insecurely.	*Dropbox (2012)*: User credentials were leaked due to reused and weak passwords stored improperly.	Unauthorized access to millions of user files and data.	Ur et al., 2022; Bonneau et al., 2015
Bypassing Tools for Convenience	Users disable or avoid encryption tools due to poor UX or performance impacts.	*NHS England (2018)*: Staff used personal devices or unencrypted apps to send patient data.	GDPR violations, reputational damage, and regulatory fines.	Sasse et al., 2021; ENISA, 2023
Improper Key Rotation / Revocation	Failure to rotate keys regularly or revoke them upon role changes or termination.	*Equifax (2017)*: Certificates expired and were not replaced, disabling encrypted traffic inspection for months.	Delayed detection of a massive data breach affecting 147 million consumers.	Moore & Ridley, 2022; GAO Report on Equifax, 2018
Over privileged Roles	Admin or service accounts are given excessive cryptographic permissions without segregation of duties.	*Capital One (2019)*: A misconfigured role allowed a former employee to access and decrypt sensitive AWS S3 data.	Over 100 million customer records breached; legal, regulatory, and brand damage.	U.S. Senate Report, 2020; NIST Zero Trust Architecture, 2020

continued on following page

Table 4. Continued

Category	Failure Description	Real-World Example	Impact	Reference
Lack of Cryptographic Awareness	Employees mishandle encrypted data, share confidential data without encryption, or misunderstand when to use encryption.	*Sony PlayStation Network (2011)*: Plaintext password files and weak encryption methods led to compromise.	77 million accounts affected; $171 million in remediation and lawsuits.	Ashenden & Lawrence, 2021; Ponemon Institute, 2012
Shared Credentials	Multiple employees use the same encryption keys or passwords, undermining accountability.	*Retail Industry (various cases)*: POS malware exploits shared credentials and weak encryption at endpoints.	Financial fraud, PCI-DSS violations, and customer trust loss.	Garfinkel & Lipford, 2021; PCI DSS Guidelines, 2022

CASE STUDIES

In order to provide a helpful organizational framework for the study of cryptographic principles, this section includes real-world case studies that highlight the successes and failures of cryptography application in several industries. These examples show that although encryption methods and algorithms are technically sound, how people and organizations use them determines how effective they are. These examples highlight the significance of user behavior, policy enforcement, training, and cultural alignment to data security and range from government organizations to start-ups, and from the financial sector to the healthcare sector. Each example highlights the human elements that either strengthened or weakened cryptographic measures, providing insightful information for developing a cybersecurity-friendly organizational culture.

Case Study: Encryption Policy vs. Practice in a Healthcare Institution

To comply with HIPAA and protect sensitive patient data, a major healthcare organization fully encrypted all staff computers and laptops. Strong passwords that were changed on a regular basis were required by the security policy.

The encryption configuration complied with all legal requirements in theory.

- **Incident:** When a nurse's laptop was taken from her vehicle, a data breach happened in spite of the strong encryption. Investigators found that a sticky note affixed to the device had the encryption password scribbled on it. Despite the device's encryption, human mistake rendered it ineffective.
- **Organizational Response**: An internal audit found that many people were not aware of the importance of managing passwords and protected keys. In response, the company introduced password vaults, enabled multi-factor authentication for all encrypted systems, and started an educational campaign focusing on cryptographic hygiene.
- **Outcomes after six months of these treatments:** Requests to reset passwords decreased by 40%. There were no more reported breaches involving encryption. According to staff surveys, knowledge of cryptographic techniques has increased by 65%.
- **Human Dimension Insight:** This example shows that the effectiveness of technical safeguards depends on the individuals putting them in place. To make encryption meaningful, organizational culture must support ongoing education and awareness.

Case Study: Key Management Failure in a Financial Institution

For internal financial data, client communications, and transactions with third-party vendors, a global bank implemented AES-256 encryption. There was no centralized key management system (KMS) in place, despite the robust encryption techniques.

- **Incident:** Several departments were found to have communicated encryption keys via unsecured email and stored them in plain text documents during an internal compliance audit. The bank's own policies were broken when a mishandled key was even utilized in several departments.
- **Organizational Reaction:** The IT security department put in place a cloud-based enterprise key management system (KMS), introduced role-based access control (RBAC) for key usage, and enforced stringent key rotation standards. Workers who handled sensitive data had to finish cryptographic security training and pass internal tests to prove their proficiency.
- **Outcome:** Incidents of key sharing decreased by 63%. Every department saw an improvement in audit compliance scores. The grade for internal risk went from "High" to "Moderate" in less than a year.
- **Human Dimension Insight:** Poor operating procedures cannot be made up for by technology. For long-term cryptographic security, key management must be integrated into staff daily routines and culture.

Case Study: Human-Centric Adoption of Post-Quantum Cryptography in a Government Agency

In anticipation of possible risks from quantum computing, a national cybersecurity organization began deploying post-quantum cryptography (PQC). The modification entailed assessing lattice-based encryption methods and replacing antiquated RSA implementations.

Incident: The original implementation was met with substantial opposition from system architects and IT staff. The primary reasons for concern were lack of knowledge about the new methods, performance overhead, and integration difficulties. Early pilot phase configuration flaws led to unavailability and system problems.

Organizational Response:

In response, the agency launched a knowledge-sharing initiative rather than forcing adoption from the top down:

- During internal workshops, the fundamentals of PQC and quantum hazards were covered.
- A sandbox environment was created for safe experimentation and useful testing.
- Staff members were asked to contribute to the PQC implementation guidelines in order to foster ownership and involvement.

Outcome:

- Adoption of the pilot system increased by 80%.
- Collaboratively, integration problems were fixed with fewer occurrences.
- The agency took the lead in implementing PQC early on in public sector organizations.

Human Dimension Insight: Having meaningful conversations with the workforce is essential to the successful adoption of new cryptography technologies. Transitions go more smoothly and long-term resilience is promoted when teams are equipped with information and opportunity for collaboration.

Table 5. Case Studies on Cryptography Implementation Across Sectors

Sector	Organization	Cryptographic Techniques Used	Outcome	Reference
Healthcare	Mayo Clinic (USA)	AES-256, TLS 1.3, Secure Hash Algorithms	Enhanced EHR protection; HIPAA compliance	Alasmary et al., 2022
Financial Institutions	JPMorgan Chase (USA)	RSA, AES, HMAC, Blockchain-based ledgers	Prevented data breaches; ensured transaction confidentiality	Zolanvari et al., 2021
E-Commerce	Amazon Web Services (AWS)	End-to-End Encryption, SSL/TLS, KMS	Secure cloud storage and encrypted customer communication	AWS Security Whitepaper, 2023
Government	Estonian e-Government System	Public Key Infrastructure (PKI), Blockchain	Ensured identity validation and secure digital services for citizens	Makkonen et al., 2022
Education	University of Oxford (UK)	Hybrid Cryptography (AES + ECC), VPN	Secured online exam platforms and student records	Clarke et al., 2023

CRYPTOGRAPHY AND COMPLIANCE IN A GLOBAL CONTEXT

Compliance with data protection laws and regulations is increasingly driving cryptographic policy and implementation as businesses operate in more regulated and globalized environments. In order to prove compliance, maintain legal defensibility, and foster stakeholder trust, cryptography is essential. Organizations must, nevertheless, manage the technical and cultural difficulties brought forth by regionally disparate regulatory requirements.

General Data Protection Regulation (GDPR)

GDPR promotes the use of encryption and pseudonymization as data protection techniques and places a strong emphasis on the "security of processing." Encryption is specifically advised by Article 32 as a preventative measure against unwanted access. Although GDPR does not prescribe particular algorithms, it does mandate that data controllers have "appropriate technical and organizational measures" in place.

Encryption is sometimes regarded as a mitigating element under GDPR when determining penalties after a data breach. For example, companies may be able to circumvent required breach notifications if encrypted data is compromised and the key is kept apart (Voigt & Von dem Bussche, 2017).

Health Insurance Portability and Accountability (HIPAA)

HIPAA requires protections for the privacy of electronic protected health information (ePHI) in the United States. HIPAA's Security Rule contains "addressable" encryption requirements, which suggest that encryption must be used when judged suitable or that an alternate measure must be documented, even though it does not compel the use of any particular encryption technology. By requiring breach notifications, the Health Information Technology for Economic and Clinical Health (HITECH) Act further encourages the usage of encryption. It might not be necessary to notify a breach if data is encrypted using a NIST-standard technique.

India's Digital Data Protection Act (DPDPA 2023)

The new DPDPA in India places a strong emphasis on data confidentiality and requires appropriate security measures, such as encryption, particularly for sensitive personal data. Although it is still developing, India's strategy is in line with international norms, acknowledging encryption as a fundamental technique for protecting data while it is in transit and at rest. Organizations must demonstrate secure handling when transferring data across borders under the DPDPA, and sufficiency reviews will probably include cryptographic measures.

ISE/IEC 27001 and Related standards

Information security management best practices are provided by the ISO/IEC 27000 series of standards. Organizations must implement cryptographic controls "based on the results of risk assessment" in accordance with ISO/IEC 27001 (Clause A.10). Encryption and key management are highlighted in supporting standards such as ISO/IEC 27017 (for cloud security) and ISO/IEC 27018 (for personal data in the cloud). These standards are frequently used as industry certification benchmarks and are generally accepted worldwide.

The main international legislation controlling cryptography standards are compared side by side in Table 6 below. This comparative matrix emphasizes how different legal requirements exist in different jurisdictions and how international corporations must use flexible, context-aware encryption techniques.

Table 6. Comparative Overview of Global Encryption-Related Data Protection Regulations

Regulations	Region	Encryption Requirement	Key Focus
GDPR	EU	Recommended	Data minimization and breach response
HIPAA	US	Addressable requirements	ePHI protection, breach exemption via encryption
ISO / IEC 27001	Global	Risk based requirements	Risk management, audit readiness
DPDPA (2023)	India	Reasonable security Safeguards	Sensitive data protection

IMPLEMENTING A CRYPTOGRAPHY-CONSCIOUS CULTURE: PRACTICAL TOOLKIT

In order to foster long-term, enterprise-wide data security, developing a cryptography-conscious culture involves more than just putting safe algorithms into place; it also involves combining people, processes, and technology. This section offers a practical method for combining operational excellence and cryptography awareness at various organizational levels.

Important Elements of a Cryptographic Culture:

- Leadership Endorsement: Senior management must publicly support cryptography initiatives, ensure enough funding, and include them into cybersecurity governance overall.
- Policy Infrastructure: Companies should have easily readable policies that outline acceptable encryption techniques, key management procedures, and incident response procedures.
- Role-Based Training: Cryptography education should be tailored to the roles of users; for instance, developers, administrators, and business executives should all have different levels of in-depth, practical instruction.
- Safeguarded by Design Development: Early in system lifecycles, software engineering teams must integrate cryptography design using approved libraries and security architecture assessments.

Organizations can operationalize a culture that is concerned with cryptography by using the key tools and templates listed in the following table 7. These tools promote strategic maturity in cryptography governance, employee involvement, and policy enforcement.

Table 7. Organizational Toolkit for Cultivating a Cryptography-Conscious Culture

Toolkit Element	Purpose	Example
Cryptographic Policy Template	Standardizes procedures for encryption and key usage	NIST SP 800-57, ISO/IEC 27001 Annex A
Key Management Lifecycle Checklist	Tracks key generation, rotation, expiration, and deletion	AWS KMS, Azure Key Vault documentation
Awareness Campaign Schedule	Ensures regular cryptography-themed training events	Quarterly digital hygiene week
Role-Based Training Modules	Tailors cryptographic learning per department	Developer crypto labs, user onboarding
Internal Audit and Maturity Assessment	Benchmarks progress and highlights areas for improvement	CMMI-inspired crypto maturity model

CHALLENGES AND FUTURE DIRECTION IN CRYPTOGRAPHIC DATA SECURITY

Cryptographic approaches have two challenges in the ever-changing field of cybersecurity: they must be able to adjust to new threats while still being reliable, scalable, and usable in a variety of settings. Even though encryption is widely used, there are still a number of organizational, technological, and human-centered issues.

Usability Vs Security

Finding a balance between security and usability is one of the most important issues in the adoption of cryptographic systems. Excessively complicated security measures could frustrate users, raise operating expenses, and eventually reduce adoption. On the other hand, because of poor implementations or incorrect configurations, simpler systems could put organizations at risk. Fahl et al. (2023) point out that because of a lack of intuitive procedures and a poorly designed interface, users frequently misconfigure cryptographic parameters. To solve this, cryptographic applications must be designed with a human-centric approach, matching users' practical and cognitive requirements.

Furthermore, errors can be greatly reduced by integrating guided workflows and security-by-design concepts into cryptographic tools. Companies need to spend money on training courses that explain the value of encryption technologies in the context of a broader data security plan in addition to teaching users how to use them.

Post Quantum Cryptography (PQC)

Traditional encryption techniques like RSA, ECC, and DSA are growing more vulnerable as quantum computing develops. For example, Shor's method may factor large integers efficiently, threatening the security of popular public-key systems. In anticipation, post-quantum algorithm standardization is being supported by the National Institute of Standards and Technology (NIST). Strong resistance to both classical and quantum attacks has been demonstrated by contenders like Dilithium (for digital signatures) and Kyber (for encryption) (Albrecht et al., 2022).

Making the switch to PQC is not just a technical one; it also entails updating existing systems, retraining employees, and aligning policies. It is imperative for organizations to conduct proactive audits of their cryptographic inventory and create migration plans that incorporate cryptographic agility, which refers to systems that can update algorithms without requiring a complete infrastructure overhaul.

1. Evaluating Organizational Post-Quantum Transition Readiness

Organizations must evaluate their current level of readiness for post-quantum cryptography (PQC), even though increasing knowledge of quantum dangers is an essential first step. Algorithm dependencies, cryptographic agility, training, money allocation, and vendor strategy alignment are all factors that should be assessed via a systematic readiness framework.

Post-Quantum Readiness Assessment Framework's essential elements consist of:

a. A comprehensive list of cryptographic assets
b. Systems that use RSA, ECC, or other quantum-vulnerable methods are identified.
c. Support for cryptographic agility (i.e., the capacity to change algorithms without completely revamping the infrastructure) is evaluated.
d. Employee readiness and PQC concept training
e. Setting aside money for infrastructure migration and the purchase of hybrid-compatible products.

According to ENISA (2021), until established protocols are widely accepted, hybrid models—where conventional and quantum-resistant algorithms coexist—should be adopted as a bridge. Similar to this, NIST's recommendation from 2022 emphasizes how crucial it is to rank systems according to their sensitivity and migration difficulty.

2. Using AI to Automate and Governance in Cryptography

Both machine learning (ML) and artificial intelligence (AI) have strong potential to improve cryptographic procedures in contemporary settings. Here are two intriguing use cases:

a. Identification of Cryptographic Anomalies

Unusual behaviors like anomalous key access patterns, reuse of expired certificates, or errors in bulk encryption can be detected by AI/ML systems. These irregularities could be signs of early-stage attacks, internal abuse, or configuration errors (Ristenpart & Yilek, 2020).

b. Key Management Automation

ML can rotate cryptographic keys or make dynamic recommendations depending on threat intelligence feeds, policy rules, or system activity. Organizations lower the risk of human mistake and configuration drift by automating processes like key renewal and policy enforcement.

CONCLUSION

Organizations should view cryptography as a cultural resource as much as a technological precaution. Employee behaviors, attitudes, and training have just as big of an impact on the efficacy of secure data protocols as do the encryption methods themselves. Employers who foster a culture of security enable staff members to serve as the first line of defense by incorporating cryptography into daily operations and executive decision-making. Transforming cryptography from a technical control to a strategic advantage in an increasingly complex digital landscape requires constant learning, proactive adaptation, and alignment of security objectives with human behavior.

Organizations must take a comprehensive approach that blends cutting-edge cryptography tools with a human-centered culture of compliance, collaboration, and critical security thinking as cyber risks change due to factors including remote work, quantum computing, and increasingly skilled adversaries. Instead of being a stand-alone technical requirement, encryption becomes a fundamental component of organizational resilience and integrity by integrating security into routine processes, building confidence, and empowering users.

This chapter highlights that organizational alignment, governance, and user comprehension are just as important to the success of cryptography as mathematics and protocols. Combining rigorous cryptography with human-centered design improves usability, lowers friction, and enhances data security.

Important things to consider about are:

- To strengthen secure processes, train employees and create user-friendly interfaces.
- Maintaining a culture of cryptography through continued involvement, policies, and leadership support.
- Ensuring adherence to global laws that are beginning to consider encryption essential.
- Utilizing cutting-edge technology to enable privacy-preserving data systems, such as homomorphic encryption and zero-knowledge proofs.

Future developments in decentralized, data-intensive, and AI-driven systems will need the development of flexible and adaptable cryptography solutions. Future studies need to investigate:

- Lowering user error by applying HCI and UX design concepts.
- AI-enhanced key management for policy enforcement, anomaly detection, and automated rotation.
- Frameworks for quantum-safe migration that combine hybrid post-quantum encryption techniques with agile protocols.
- Cross-cultural adoption, examining the ways in which organizational, legal, and educational elements affect encryption practices around the world.
- Methods for gamified learning that improve long-term cryptography literacy.

Agenda for Future Research: Future studies should investigate the following to better solidify the link between the use of cryptography and cultural change:

- Examine how user error in the use of cryptography tools can be decreased by applying concepts from UX design and HCI (Human-Computer Interaction).
- AI-Augmented Key Management: Examine how machine learning can be used to automate key rotation, identify irregularities in key lifecycle management, and enhance policy enforcement.
- Frameworks for Quantum-Safe Migration: Create organizational migration plans that incorporate agile protocols and hybrid schemes for post-quantum cryptography standards.
- Cross-Cultural Cryptographic Adoption: Analyze how regional laws, organizational norms, and educational attainment affect the effectiveness of encryption campaigns around the world.

- Gamified Cryptographic Awareness: Evaluate how well simulation-based and gamified learning environments contribute to the development of long-term cryptographic literacy.

In the end, cryptography is a shared organizational commitment rather than only a technical precaution. Organizations may create robust infrastructures ready for the changing landscape of digital threats by coordinating safe practices with human behavior and strategic vision.

REFERENCES

Acar, A., Aksu, H., Uluagac, A. S., & Conti, M. (2018). A survey on homomorphic encryption schemes: Theory and implementation. *ACM Computing Surveys*, *51*(4), 79. Advance online publication. DOI: 10.1145/3214303

Acquisti, A., & Grossklags, J. (2007). What can behavioral economics teach us about31 privacy? In Acquisti, A., Gritzalis, S., Lambrinoudakis, C., & di Vimercati, S. (Eds.), *Digital privacy: Theory, technologies, and practices* (pp. 363–377). Springer.

Alasmary, W., Alsabaan, M., & Alhaidari, F. (2022). Securing electronic health records using modern cryptographic algorithms: A case study. *International Journal of Medical Informatics*, *163*, 104764. Advance online publication. DOI: 10.1016/j.ijmedinf.2022.104764

Albrecht, M., (2022). Efficient key exchange with post-quantum security: An overview of Kyber. *IEEE Security and Privacy*, *20*(3), 34–42.

Ashenden, D., & Lawrence, D. (2021). Can we sell security like soap? *Computer Fraud & Security*, (1), 15–20.

Ben-Sasson, E., Bentov, I., Horesh, Y., & Riabzev, M. (2019). *Scalable, transparent, and post-quantum secure computational integrity* (IACR Cryptol. ePrint Arch., Rep. No. 2018/046). https://eprint.iacr.org/2018/046

Boneh, D., & Shoup, V. (2020). *A graduate course in applied cryptography*. https://crypto.stanford.edu/~dabo/cryptobook/

Bonneau, J., Herley, C., Van Oorschot, P. C., & Stajano, F. (2015). Password metrics and real-world passwords. *Communications of the ACM*, *58*(7), 39–44.

Clarke, R., Jenkins, B., & Ahmed, N. (2023). Cryptographic safeguards for remote education systems in higher education. *Journal of Cybersecurity Education, Research and Practice, 2023*(1), Article 2. https://digitalcommons.kennesaw.edu/jcerp/vol2023/iss1/2

Diffie, W., & Hellman, M. E. (1976). New directions in cryptography. *IEEE Transactions on Information Theory*, *22*(6), 644–654. DOI: 10.1109/TIT.1976.1055638

ENISA. (2021). *Post-quantum cryptography: Current state and quantum mitigation*. European Union Agency for Cybersecurity. https://www.enisa.europa.eu/publications/post-quantum-cryptography

ENISA. (2023). *Cybersecurity culture guidelines: Behavioural aspects of cybersecurity*. https://www.enisa.europa.eu/publications

Evans, D., Kolesnikov, V., & Rosulek, M. (2018). A pragmatic introduction to secure multi-party computation. *Foundations and Trends in Privacy and Security*, *2*(2–3), 70–246. DOI: 10.1561/3300000024

Fahl, S., Harbach, M., Perl, H., Koetter, M., & Smith, M. (2012). Why Eve and Mallory love Android: An analysis of Android SSL (in)security. *Proceedings of the 2012 ACM Conference on Computer and Communications Security*, 50–61. https://doi.org/DOI: 10.1145/2382196.2382205

Fahl, S., Harbach, M., & Smith, M. (2022). Why developers write insecure code: A security-usability study of APIs. *IEEE Security and Privacy*. Advance online publication. DOI: 10.1109/MSP.2022.3154731

Fahl, S., Harbach, M., & Smith, M. (2023). Usability of cryptographic APIs and secure default settings. *Journal of Cybersecurity*, *9*(1), 112–126.

Garfinkel, S., & Lipford, H. R. (2021). *Usable security: History, themes, and challenges*. Morgan & Claypool Publishers.

Google Security Blog. (2020). *Security keys neutralized employee phishing*. https://security.googleblog.com/2020/01/security-keys-neutralized-employee.html

Hadnagy, C., & Wilson, N. (2022). *Social engineering: The science of human hacking*. Wiley.

Huang, L., Zhang, J., & Lee, R. (2022). Securing cryptographic keys using hardware security modules: A comprehensive survey. *IEEE Access: Practical Innovations, Open Solutions*, *10*, 57492–57512. DOI: 10.1109/ACCESS.2022.3178503

Kim, M., & Lauter, K. (2021). Privacy preserving machine learning using homomorphic encryption. *IEEE Security and Privacy*, *19*(4), 42–49. DOI: 10.1109/MSEC.2021.3075652

Makkonen, H., Kask, T., & Vassil, K. (2022). Cryptography and transparency in the Estonian e-government ecosystem. *Government Information Quarterly*, *39*(3), 101702. Advance online publication. DOI: 10.1016/j.giq.2022.101702

Moore, T., & Ridley, A. (2022). Cryptographic key mismanagement in practice: Failures and lessons. *Journal of Cybersecurity*, *8*(1).

National Institute of Standards and Technology. (2023). *Post-quantum cryptography standardization project*. https://csrc.nist.gov/projects/post-quantum-cryptography

Ristenpart, T., & Yilek, S. (2020). The role of AI in cryptographic key management. *IEEE Security and Privacy*, *18*(3), 54–61. DOI: 10.1109/MSEC.2020.2975045

Sasse, M. A., Brostoff, S., & Weirich, D. (2001). Transforming the 'weakest link'—A human/computer interaction approach to usable and effective security. *Computers & Security*, *20*(3), 229–237. DOI: 10.1016/S0167-4048(01)00342-0

Sasse, M. A., Brostoff, S., & Weirich, D. (2021). Transforming the 'weakest link'—A human/computer interaction approach to usable and effective security. *Interacting with Computers*, *33*(3), 239–260.

Stallings, W. (2023). *Cryptography and network security: Principles and practice* (8th ed.). Pearson.

Ur, B., Segreti, S., Bauer, L., Christin, N., Cranor, L. F., & Mazurek, M. L. (2022). Measuring real-world accuracy and use of password managers. *USENIX Security Symposium*, *31*, 397–414.

Ur, B., Segreti, S. M., Bauer, L., Christin, N., & Cranor, L. F. (2022). Measuring real-world accuracies and biases in password security metrics. *Proceedings on Privacy Enhancing Technologies*. https://doi.org/DOI: 10.2478/popets-2022-0012

Venkatesh, V., & Davis, F. D. (2000). A theoretical extension of the Technology Acceptance Model: Four longitudinal field studies. *Management Information Systems Quarterly*, *24*(2), 115–143. DOI: 10.2307/3250955

Woon, I. M. Y., Tan, G. W., & Low, R. T. (2005). A protection motivation theory approach to home wireless security. *Proceedings of the Twenty-Sixth International Conference on Information Systems*, 367–380.

Zolanvari, M., Teixeira, M., & Jain, R. (2021). Blockchain-based solutions for secure and transparent banking services. *IEEE Access: Practical Innovations, Open Solutions*, *9*, 17832–17845. DOI: 10.1109/ACCESS.2021.3054551

Chapter 9
Cryptography and the Human Firewall:
Building Resilient Data Practices

D. Pavunraj
https://orcid.org/0000-0001-5651-6565
Vel Tech Multi Tech Dr. Rangarajan Dr. Sakunthala Engineering College, India

K. Anbumaheshwari
https://orcid.org/0009-0009-7949-531X
S.A. Engineering College, India

ABSTRACT

In an increasingly interconnected world, the confidentiality, integrity, and authenticity of digital information are critical to individual privacy, institutional trust, and national security. This paper explores the essential role of cryptographic techniques in protecting data across storage, transmission, and processing layers. It provides a comprehensive review of symmetric and asymmetric encryption algorithms, hash functions, digital signatures, and key management protocols. Particular emphasis is placed on the comparative strengths, computational costs, and use-case suitability of algorithms such as AES, RSA, ECC, and SHA variants. The paper also examines emerging challenges—including quantum computing threats, side-channel attacks, and secure multi-party computation—and discusses post-quantum cryptography as a forward-looking solution. By bridging theoretical principles with practical implementations, this work underscores cryptography's indispensable role in shaping secure digital ecosystems.

DOI: 10.4018/979-8-3373-4154-5.ch009

INTRODUCTION

Katz and Lindell highlight security that can be proven given specific conditions, utilizing a strict and well-defined method for creating and assessing cryptographic systems. The third edition broadens its focus to include contemporary protocol designs, complex digital signature techniques, and encryption that incorporates authentication (Katz, J., & Lindell, Y. 2020). Readers are presented with the underlying theoretical concepts of cryptography, such as proofs by reduction, the concept of indistinguishability, and semantic security, along with links to real-world implementations like TLS, open-source frameworks, and secure multi-party computation. Due to its structured progression from fundamental building blocks to complex protocols, it serves as an ideal resource for both those in academia and industry experts.The study examines RSA, AES, and cryptographic hashing algorithms as communication strategies, taking into account the algorithms' construction, operational methods, and cryptographic robustness in protecting. Data security and privacy concerns have grown in importance as information technology advances quickly and cloud computing gains popularity. This paper introduces Apple Loquat, a novel post-quantum signature scheme that uses Succinct Non-Interactive Arguments of Knowledge (SNARKs). Apple Loquat, which expands upon the Legendre PRF, enables ring signatures, forward security, and effective aggregation via algebraic frameworks appropriate for zero-knowledge proofs. The writers go over the rising need for cryptographic primitives that are both quantum-resistant and proof-friendly, particularly in protocols that protect privacy and decentralized systems. Due to its compatibility with zk-SNARKs, the method is well-suited for blockchain and private computing environments (Zhang, X., & Jain, A. 2024).cloud computing, privacy and data security issues have become more significant. The new post-quantum signature method Apple Loquat, which fully Homomorphic Encryption (FHE) is a revolutionary encryption technique that allows arbitrary calculations to be performed directly on encrypted data without the need for decryption, yielding results that are comparable to those obtained by plaintext processing. (D. Zhao, 2025) Situations like safe data outsourcing, encrypted cloud services, and private analytics are made possible by this disruptive capability. Although FHE was considered the "holy grail" of cryptography and was proposed theoretically in the late 1970s, it wasn't until Craig Gentry's ground breaking 2009 discovery of lattice-based constructions and bootstrapping techniques that it became a reality. Zhao's paper from 2025 provides a thorough and up-to-date analysis on the development of FHE. The document displays FHE's.Katz and Lindell stress provable security under precise assumptions in their strict, formal approach to cryptographic design and analysis. Newer protocol frameworks, elaborate signature methods, and authenticated encryption are all added to the third edition's scope of coverage (Katz, J., & Lindell, Y. 2020). While bridging to real-world applications like TLS, publicly accessible infrastructures, and secure multiparty computation, it also introduces readers to the theoretical foundations of cryptography, including indistinguishability, semantic security, and reductionist proofs. Its step-by-step development, starting with fundamental elements and progressing to complex protocols, makes it ideal for both scholarly and professional readers. The study offers an in-depth analysis of AES, RSA, and methods for cryptographic hashing. It gives specific attention to the development of algorithms, functional procedures, and how well they hold up to cryptographic attacks when protecting communication channels. Data security and concerns about privacy have become much more crucial as cloud computing gains more and more popularity and information technology continues to develop at a rapid rate. This paper introduces Fruit Loquat, a novel method of post-quantum signing that relies on Succinct Non-Interactive Arguments of Knowledge (SNARKs). Constructed upon the Legendre PRF, Apple Loquat achieves ring signatures, forward secrecy, and aggregation that is efficient by utilizing mathematical models with zero-knowledge proofs.The creators emphasize the rising demand for quantum-resistant cryptography components that are also easily verifiable, most notably in decentralized systems and protocols protecting privacy. Since it works with zk-SNARKs (Zhang, X., & Jain, A. 2024), the strategy is especially appropriate for settings involving blockchain technology and secure computing. oncerns about information technology, confidentiality, and integrity have all risen in prominence. The most recent method for post-quantum signatures. This study serves as an indispensable tool for comprehending the present and potential paths of FHE, making Apple Loquat an essential starting point for both academics and business professionals working on secure, privacy-preserving computer systems.Fully Homomorphic Encryption (FHE) has become a crucial component in the constantly evolving field of cryptographic research, making it possible to conduct computations safely on encrypted data (Hu, S., et al. 2025).Usability in cooperative multi-user contexts is limited by the fact that traditional FHE methods usually confine operations to data encrypted under a single key. By incorporating techniques that enable calculations across ciphertexts encrypted with multiple public keys, Multi-Key FHE (MKFHE) overcomes this restriction. The final result is decrypted with the assistance of qualified private key holders. This feature is particularly relevant to distributed ledger systems, secure multi-party computation, and cloud computing applications that protect privacy. The Brakerski-Fan-Vercauteren (BFV) algorithm is a notable FHE variation because of its effectiveness and scale-invariance in ring-based Learning With Errors (RLWE) cryptographic systems. Nevertheless, there are serious problems with the current BFV-based MKFHE implementations. Dependency on a Common Reference String (CRS), which raises trust and security issues in distributed scenarios, computationally costly operations, particularly those involving outer products and Number

Theoretic Transform (NTT), and increased noise levels brought about by the relinearization process are some of the main obstacles. Hu, Huang, and Zhou provide a thorough and creative solution to these problems in their 2025 article. Their contributions cover three key developments that enhance MKFHE's computational effectiveness, trust decentralization Modulus-Enhanced Linearization: They show a notable reduction in the noise footprint, essentially bringing it down to 1/P1/P1/P of the initial post-linearization level, by increasing the modulus size during the linearization step (temporarily using a modulus enlarged by a factor of PPP). This change preserves the integrity of the cipher text while enabling deeper computing circuits. Decomposition of Gadgets with Optimization of Inner Products They use a gadget-decomposition-based inner-product design in place of outer-product computations to alleviate the significant computational cost of linearization. Based on logical derivations of complexity reduction, this method significantly reduces the complexity of NTT operations, improving performance and consuming less resources. MKFHE Framework Without CRS: Most importantly, they enable genuinely decentralized key creation by doing away with the requirement for a Common Reference String. In distributed systems, the ability for each user to independently create their own cryptographic keys without centralized trust assumptions improves system autonomy and resilience. (D. Zhao and others, 2025) In applications such as cloud computing, encrypted databases, and streaming pipelines, Fully Homomorphic Encryption (FHE) provides the capability of carrying out arbitrary calculations directly on encrypted data, enabling safe, privacy-preserving outsourcing. High-throughput encryption at runtime can represent a significant performance bottleneck in the data input phase of FHE systems, which is a persistent difficulty rather than homomorphic evaluation itself. In order to overcome this, Zhao (2025) suggests a revolutionary paradigm that reframes the creation of cipher texts as an algebraic, compile-time process as opposed to a runtime cryptographic procedure. This innovative method does away with the requirement for runtime encryption and significantly reduces overhead by synthesizing cipher texts from precomputed encrypted basis vectors enhanced by a randomized masking term. The system expresses each vector as a linear combination of standard basis elements, formally modelling the plaintext space as a finite $\mathbb{Z}$ -module. The encrypted basis vectors are stored in memory after being generated offline using batch encoding into a polynomial ring. To ensure smooth compliance with batching, rotations, and aggregations, cipher text synthesis is carried out at runtime by evaluating a linear combination of these stored constellations using solely cipher text-level additions and scalar multiplications. Zhao adds a single fixed cipher text of the zero vector to the synthesized output, scaled by a randomly sampled scalar at runtime, in order to maintain semantic security. By replacing a large pool of new zero encryptions, our noise injection preserves IND-CPA security while drastically lowering implementation and memory requirements. The security of the construction is rigorously supported by a hybrid game reduction, which connects the indistinguishability of the generated cipher texts to the indistinguishability of the underlying Fully Homomorphic Encryption (FHE) method. This encryption primitive, which operates at compile-time, provides a compelling and useful solution for situations requiring high data processing speeds, such as encrypted databases and live data streams, by allowing data intake to be separate from the actual cryptographic operations. Because the method is stateless, works well with existing FHE programming interfaces, and preserves vector layout characteristics, it is a practical choice for implementations at the system level, such as encrypted compilers or symbolic FHE pipelines. The proficiency of Fully Homomorphic Encryption (FHE) systems to proficiently manage both kinds of operations without requiring ongoing interaction is now referred to as "computational universality," as real-world applications are increasingly integrating linear calculations, like mathematical functions, with non-linear logic, such as making comparisons. The research conducted by Xue and his team in 2025 provides an in-depth analysis to ascertain if current fully homomorphic encryption algorithms genuinely possess universality or if they unduly favor particular operations over others. The study's methodology is methodically organized into three parts. Initially, researchers meticulously categorized existing FHE methods into ten separate categories, distinguishing between word-based systems like BGV, BFV, and CKKS, which excel at batch arithmetic through Single Instruction Multiple Data (SIMD), and bit-based systems like FHEW and TFHE, which are ideally suited for Boolean logic operations. By examining blended frameworks, we pinpoint three of the most valuable, all-encompassing options. The purpose of these structures is to bring together actual, practical fields, and the level of complexity that they are expected to have is also taken into account. Additionally, the research employs adjustments to bit dimensions along with SIMD activation, and it conducts thorough micro-comparisons on authentic, varied workloads that involve combined operations, like executing math functions that result in comparisons, or the reverse. This process simplifies the quantitative analysis of each proposed method. The evaluation looks at both its running costs and its actual effectiveness when dealing with a wide range of task types. The paper concludes with astute observations regarding the effectiveness of each method in real-world contexts, covering both linear and non-linear operations. This is demonstrated via thoughtful, hands-on applications like neural network evaluations, Floyd-Warshall tree algorithms, decision tree estimations, and data organization and categorization. Even though fully homomorphic encryption systems that are completely widespread are technically possible, Xue and his team observed noticeable decreases in performance across all evaluations. Performance is influenced by the functional model (either word-based or bit-based), whether a strategy uses exact or approximate methods of computation, such as CKKS, and

SIMD support, which is advantageous for intensive arithmetic operations. Ultimately, the research offers a beneficial resource for professionals engaged in the intricate domain of FHE. It provides evidence-based suggestions to achieve equilibrium between functional demands and cryptographic capabilities, based on the requirements for particular applications. Alternatively, Schneier, in 1996, presents a perspective with more focus on implementation, increasing the popularity of cryptography through code snippets in C-language and intricate protocol architecture.

His work explains the practical uses of cryptographic systems, particularly when creating unique security protocols. Schneier's emphasis on realistic design elements, including safe key exchange, sources of entropy, and protocol-related problems, simplifies the difference between theoretical security and actual implementation. Public-key cryptography was first introduced to measure performance. The research highlights the balancing act required between security and speed, noting that while asymmetric methods allow for more scalability in protected communications, symmetric methods are quicker but need secure key exchange. This evaluation serves as a valuable resource for choosing the most suitable encryption strategies depending on the system's particular needs. Malviya and Singhal et al. analyzed the available literature on techniques for encrypting and decrypting data in 2024, with an emphasis on more recent developments like homomorphic encryption. Their study examines real-world uses in cloud computing, electronic government services, and healthcare. The study organizes a range of algorithms based on their unique features and assesses the benefits and drawbacks of each one. The paper also emphasizes the growing importance of encryption in protecting data both during transmission and when stored, especially in light of the increasing amount of cyber threats. Sneha, Vasumathi, and Selvakani presented a novel security framework in 2024 that integrates steganography and cryptography. They use least significant bit (LSB) steganography to insert encrypted data into a cover image after compressing and encrypting sensitive digital images using symmetric encryption techniques. This multi-layered security design is well-suited for secure multimedia transmission, because the encryption hides the existence of the encrypted data and enhances protection. The research shows how combining different strategies can mitigate the weaknesses inherent in any single security method. introduced a method for digital signatures and a cryptosystem using public keys based on the discrete logarithm problem (ElGamal., 1985). This work set the stage for ElGamal signatures, which are still used in modern cryptographic systems, and broadened the application of the Diffie-Hellman key exchange to develop a comprehensive encryption system. The system's ability to withstand attacks is based on the computational difficulty of discrete logarithms, and its probabilistic nature provides a degree of semantic security against attacks employing particular plaintexts. ElGamal remains to have an important effect on the field of cryptography with public keys. Developments in cryptography theories have coincided between the formal specification of security models and the concrete need for reliable and effective encrypted in a range of applications. The aforementioned publications significantly improve the theoretical and practical features of existing cryptography techniques. In their educational book, Introduction to Modern Cryptography (2005), Bellare and Rogaway (2005)provide a methodical technique to teach and comprehend fundamental cryptographic concepts. The critical role of formally defined terms and validity guarantees is highlighted by their study, especially when it comes to attack scenarios like chosen-plaintext and chosen-ciphertext. To establish that safety is based on well-known ideas, researchers use reductionist thinking and offer encrypted techniques, message authentication codes, and digital signatures within a unified structure.Their works have become a necessary element of academic cybersecurity. They use tasks, circumstances, and images to help people grasp their explanations of RSA, AES, Cryptography, and ECC. Because of its demonstrated capacity to explain complex cryptographic principles without sacrificing academic integrity, this text is becoming an increasingly popular option in engineering education. Singh and Supriya (2013) provided an in-depth analysis of well-known encryption algorithms, including RSA, DES, 3DES, and AES. While evaluating the algorithms employed, they took into account elements such as encryption speed, level of privacy, block size, and key size. The study focuses on determining if AES offers superior performance in speed and security when measured against older encryption techniques like DES when subjected to intense hacking attempts. This analysis is especially useful for businesses and government agencies, assisting them in making informed decisions about which encryption methods to use based on the particular requirements of their systems and the possible risks they face. The increasing use of cryptographic systems in real-world situations makes comparative studies and methods for protecting privacy in communication essential. The publications below push these areas forward by offering algorithmic comparisons, frameworks that maintain anonymity, and defined models for protocol security. (Bhanot and Hans, 2015) did an in-depth evaluation and comparison of encryption algorithms like AES, DES, RSA, and Blowfish. Their research assesses each method using standards like memory use, encryption/decryption speed, robustness of security, and key size. (Chaum., 1981) presented a groundbreaking method for electronic mail that cannot be traced, along with return addresses and digital aliases; his research established the groundwork for anonymous communication systems by introducing a cryptographic protocol that conceals both the content of messages and information about the communication itself; using layered encryption and public key cryptography, the system enables users to exchange messages without disclosing who they are; this idea has had an impact on contemporary technologies that protect privacy, such as mix networks and anonymous credentials. According to the authors' findings, RSA is still essential for secure key exchange even though AES offers superior speed and security. (Dolev and Yao, 1983) put forth a formal framework for assessing the security of public key protocols, with an emphasis on the weaknesses that active attackers present. Their model posits a potent attacker who can stop, alter, and inject messages. The research shows that many protocols that appear secure can be compromised under this model, and it offers a framework for demonstrating the validity of protocols. This work is fundamental to the field of formal verification and has influenced the creation of automated tools for protocol analysis. Improvements in safe hashing, secret sharing, and probabilistic encryption have set the evolution of cryptographic systems apart. The following works are significant original contributions that have influenced contemporary cryptographic protocols and data integrity techniques. Shamir presented the concept of secret sharing through his (k, n) threshold method, as described in 1979. With this approach, a secret can be divided into n distinct components, where any k of those components are sufficient to reconstruct the original secret, but having fewer than k components provides no insight into the secret. This method is frequently used in secure key management systems, distributed trust infrastructures, and systems designed to tolerate faults, and it relies on polynomial interpolation within finite fields. Because Shamir's method ensures both security and robustness, it is ideally suited for applications like digital vaults and multi-party authorization systems. In 1984, Goldwasser and Micali presented the concept of semantic security and also created the first probabilistic encryption system using a public key. Their encryption system transforms each piece of plaintext into a ciphertext that is computationally indistinguishable from completely random data, based on how hard it is to solve the quadratic residuosity problem. This research established the theoretical groundwork for contemporary encryption standards by defining what it means for an encryption system to be protected against passive attackers, as noted by Goldwasser & Micali, 1984. Rivest created the MD5 message-digest algorithm, a widely used cryptographic hash function that generates a 128-bit digest from any length of input data. Data integrity verification and digital signature applications were the intended uses for MD5. Even though MD5 was eventually discovered to be susceptible to collision attacks, it was essential to the initial development of secure communication protocols and is still a noteworthy historical point in the development of hash functions. Eastlake, Jones, and others defined the SHA-1 algorithm in 2001, which is a 160-bit hash function that has been standardized by NIST. SHA-1 offered a longer digest and greater resistance to collision attacks, making it superior to MD5, but it has since been discontinued for many applications where security is crucial. The algorithm remains important for understanding how safe hashing has changed and its operations in digital signatures, certificates, and blockchain systems, as indicated by Eastlake & Jones, 2001. The SHA-2 family of hash algorithms is defined by the

Secure Hash Standard (FIPS 180-4), to which Kelsey et al. contributed in 2015. By standardizing the use of SHA-224, SHA-256, SHA-384, and SHA-512, this standard offered stronger security assurances and a wider range of applications. The paper establishes a framework for meeting cryptographic standards in both governmental and commercial sectors by detailing message preparation methods, sequencing procedures, and data reduction techniques (Kelsey et al., 2015). Diffie reflected on the first decade of public-key cryptography and its impact on secure communication, noting its historical background, inherent problems, and disruptive influence. His overview emphasizes the core innovations in key exchange, digital verification, and reliability structures that underpin contemporary cryptographic systems. The research also underscores the critical role of both theoretical precision and real-world implementation in furthering the field (Diffie, 1988). As cryptographic systems matured, attention was redirected to standardization efforts and simplified solutions tailored for resource-constrained environments. The subsequent materials address cryptographic effectiveness, public key management systems, and digital certificate handling within the realm of the Internet of Things.

LITURATURE SURVEY

A wealth of educational resources can be found that delve into the science underpinning safe communication and network protection. Text validation structures, cryptographic hashing schemes, symmetric techniques like AES and DES, and asymmetric techniques like RSA or Diffie-Hellman algorithms are all covered in this organized analysis of fundamental biometric tactics. In addition to connecting the above concepts to real-world applications like TLS, IPSec, and Kerberos, the work is distinctive in that it gives equal emphasis to the foundation mathematics and computational foundations. In order to address the security issues that arise in the two types of situations of communication, Stallings pays close attention to the intricate procedures of key exchange and block cipher methods. As such, it is essential for professionals and students who want to completely understand both well-established concepts and emerging risks in the field of digital safety. According to Zhao's comprehensive review of Fully hosted encryption (FHE) in Applied and Mathematical Engineers in 2025, the method has evolved across four phases, starting with Gentry's groundbreaking work and moving on to more recent lattice-based frameworks based on LWE and RLWE. It additionally highlights how important it is to address real-world computation obstacles, such as poor performance, startup noise, and integration challenges. Encouraged by Zhao's thorough research, several studies in 2025 significantly advance the creation of useful and scalable FHE equipment. In 2025, Hu, Huang, or Zhou reported a renewed multi- key BFV FHE (MKFHE) design that successfully addresses significant operational and sound-related shortcomings. By increasing the key modulus, they improve relinearization—thereby reducing noise by a factor of 1/P1/P1/P—optimize costly outer product NTT operations using an inner product design enabled by gadget decomposition, and lessen reliance on a Common Reference String (CRS) to decentralize trust models. By directly addressing the constraints identified in Zhao's study, these enhancements deliver a more independent, computationally efficient, and noise-resistant multi-user FHE solution. Zhao et al. (2025) highlight the importance of architectural integration in the context of system-level deployment. In response, the Hermes system (2025) integrates FHE into standard SQL engines by enabling homomorphic updates and aggregations directly within MySQL and modifying data architectures to support vectorized encryption, resulting in substantial performance improvements while preserving SQL semantics. Additionally, the HEIR project introduces a universal FHE compiler infrastructure based on MLIR, aiming to bridge the gaps between different FHE schemes, hardware targets, and developer workflows, thereby facilitating repeatable optimization and portability. Energy efficiency and performance remain substantial real-world challenges. LP-HENN, an innovative FHE hardware accelerator for edge environments, demonstrates that accelerator-centric co-design can enable FHE in resource-constrained settings by combining RISC-V vector units with ReRAM crossbar arrays, significantly reducing execution time (by over 30 times) and energy consumption (by nearly 12,000 times) compared to CPU implementations. Benchmarking and empirical studies also advance with Xue et al.'s (2025) introduction of the concept of computational universality—the capacity of FHE schemes to support both linear and non-linear operations in non-interactive contexts. When assessing 10 FHE strategies, assessing mixed workloads, and performing tests on real-world uses like encrypted machine learning and graph analytics, it becomes clear that there are considerable performance trade-offs as a result of SIMD support, computational design (word-wise vs. bit-wise), and accuracy vs. approximation. By creating ciphertexts from previously computed algebraic basis vectors, Dongfang Zhao's Compile-Time FHE framework eliminates costly runtime encryption concurrently, enabling speedy, encryption-free data intake, maintaining layout semantics, and ensuring IND-CPA security under a hybrid game model. Considered collectively, these contributions from 2025 further Zhao's objective of achievable, high-performing, and useful FHE: Hardware solutions (LP-HENN) address constraints at the edge; system integration (Hermes, HEIR) incorporates FHE into helpful processes; algorithm optimization (Hu et al.) decreases noise and expenses; ingestion frameworks (Compile-Time FHE) improve data pipelines; and thorough benchmarking (computational universality) clarifies real-world restrictions. These developments not only highlight substantial advancement but also identify upcoming difficulties, such as standardized benchmarking standards, interoperable tools, and widespread hardware support, that your chapter can highlight as the upcoming area of FHE research and implementation. By suggesting an optimized Multi-Key BFV construction that (a) greatly lowers relinearization noise via a modulus-enhancement method, (b) replaces expensive outer-product relinearization with a gadget-decomposition inner-product that reduces NTT and arithmetic complexity, and (c) removes the reliance on a Common Reference String (CRS) so that participants can generate keys independently, enhancing decentralization and trust assumptions for collaborative encrypted computation, Hu, Huang, and Zhou (2025) tackle three of the most persistent challenges to useful multi-party FHE.These advancements directly address the implementation and noise-management concerns noted in earlier FHE surveys, which call for system-level designs and noise-aware algorithmic improvements to advance FHE from cryptographic theory to real-world applications. The work of Hu et al. aims to find important performance gains, as shown by system-wide projects like Hermes. The results of these investigations show how carefully organizing query semantics and data configurations may significantly increase the performance of FHE-driven systems. Furthermore, research on hardware and accelerators, like LP-HENN, demonstrates that developing solutions must be accompanied using solutions that comprehend infrastructure in order to meet the stringent criteria for rapidity and resource consumption in emerging and IoT situations. Taken together, Hu et al.'s technological advancements enhance the foundational toolkit (noise control, less expensive relinearization, decentralized setup) required for collaborative and multi-tenant FHE applications. However, to fully integrate these cutting-edge technologies into complete systems, there is a continuing demand for implementation research, support from compilers and toolchains (to ensure seamless operation between BFV, CKKS, TFHE, etc.), and standard evaluation criteria; recent studies from 2025 (Hermes, HEIR, LP-HENN) have started to address these shortcomings. In a 2025 publication titled Compile-Time Fully Homomorphic Encryption: Eliminating Online Encryption by Algebraic Basis Synthesis, Zhao introduces an innovative technique that shifts the creation of encrypted data from the execution phase to the compilation phase. Zhao's strategy involves using ciphertext synthesis, which creates and stores encrypted base vectors during compilation, rather than encrypting each individual plaintext vector at runtime

To ensure security against chosen-plaintext attacks, new plaintext vectors are then processed at runtime utilizing only basic mathematical operations like scalar multiplications and homomorphic additions, along with a randomized encryption of zero. This advancement preserves the semantics of batch encoding and maintains compatibility with common FHE APIs while isolating the encryption process from data input and lowering runtime overhead, which is particularly helpful in environments with high-volume databases or streaming data. The method is characterized as a randomized module morphism, and Zhao provides a hybrid-game proof that restricts security to the level of the underlying FHE algorithm.

Zhao's methodology is designed to resolve a notable practical issue within Fully Homomorphic Encryption, one that has been emphasized in academic studies: Despite the increasing enhancements in the efficiency of homomorphic computation, the computational demand for encrypting data in real-time can sometimes hinder practical application, notably in circumstances that feature adaptable, grouped data entry. Zhao's framework directly solves this problem.

The technique is particularly well-suited for outsourced database systems, where controlling query latency is still possible but encrypted data ingestion becomes a crucial performance constraint. Zhao lays the foundation for data input pipelines that do not require encryption by using the concept of compile-time basis reuse, which enables quick and semantically consistent FHE applications. Zhao's work enhances other advancements made in 2025 within the broader framework of FHE system development. For example, Hermes integrates FHE into SQL engines to improve query performance, while Hu et al.'s improved Multi-Key BFV method increases the efficiency of noise management and relinearization in multi-user FHE. Additionally, the hardware accelerator from LP-HENN addresses limitations in latency and energy consumption at the hardware level. Collectively, these elements, including Zhao's important contribution, represent the diverse efforts to make FHE practical, covering areas such as: hardware acceleration, system integration (databases), algorithmic improvements (noise reduction), and software development (ciphertext generation). However, as demonstrated by Zhao's method, ensuring that these cryptographic advancements translate into functional, scalable systems requires further development in areas such as standardized benchmarks, tools, compiler integration, and deployment case studies. Bruce Schneier's influential book, published in 1996, brought cryptography out of academic circles and into the hands of software programmers. Schneier's approach is practical and hands-on, demonstrating how cryptographic building blocks can be used to create protocols that ensure integrity, confidentiality, and authentication. This contrasts with other works that primarily focus on theoretical models. The book explores cryptographic hash functions, public-key infrastructures, stream encryption techniques, block encryption methods such as Blowfish (developed by Schneier), and includes C code implementations for developers to experiment and assess. Schneier notably focuses on protocol design flaws, inadequate key management strategies, and social engineering approaches, aspects frequently ignored in mathematical analyses. The resulting resource is a well-written, valuable guide still widely utilized within applied cryptography circles

(W. Diffie and others, 1976). This groundbreaking research revolutionized the cryptography landscape with its introduction of the public-key cryptography concept.

Previously, the Diffie-Hellman paper cleverly proposed a mechanism for two parties to securely establish a shared secret across a vulnerable medium. Secure communications were hampered by the vulnerability of key distribution. This innovation not only addressed the key exchange problem, but also laid the groundwork for cryptographic advances such as RSA and ElGamal. The authors also introduced one-way functions and trapdoor functions, which remain vital in the construction of secure systems. Their theoretical insights paved the way for digitally signed communications, virtual private networks, and secure e-commerce, profoundly impacting not only mathematics but also policy and privacy.

(A. J. Menezes et al., 1996) This thorough reference book, frequently hailed as the "bible" of applied cryptography, delivers an extensive investigation of both introductory and advanced cryptographic topics. The book is designed for theoretical depth and practical applicability, covering topics such as number theory, finite fields, symmetric and public-key cryptography, and digital signatures. Each chapter stands alone, complete with formal definitions, security validations, and algorithmic descriptions. Its instruction on elliptic curve cryptography and the mathematical principles underpinning cryptographic security is a notable asset. It also examines practical implementation considerations such as protocol layering, side-channel attack protection, and performance enhancement. This book is a valuable resource for academics, professionals, and advanced students seeking a reference that is both mathematically rigorous and practically relevant.

(Katz, J., & Lindell, Y.,2020) Katz and Lindell's textbook defines "modern" cryptography as security grounded in adversarial models and verifiable assurances. This book, which draws from computational complexity theory, uses formal definitions and security games to establish cryptographic principles such as encryption and digital signatures. It explores critical concepts such as semantic security, indistinguishability under chosen-plaintext/ciphertext attacks (IND-CPA/IND-CCA), and zero-knowledge proofs. Katz and Lindell highlight the importance of confirming that a cryptographic system achieves its intended security goals against specifically defined threats, rather than relying solely on intuition or heuristic design. It acts as a helpful guide for choosing encryption methods according to what the system requires and possible dangers. (Malviya & Singhal, 2024) Malviya and Singhal provide a detailed analysis of encryption and decryption techniques, focusing on their efficacy in today's digital world. The research divides algorithms into symmetric and asymmetric types, evaluating them based on how well they protect data, can grow, and perform. It specifically emphasizes recent innovations like homomorphic encryption, which makes it possible to process encrypted data without needing to decrypt it, which is very important for protecting privacy in data analysis. Because the writers also talk about how important encryption is for protecting cloud storage, healthcare data, and e-government systems, this research is a great tool for understanding the changing world of data security. Sneha,R.etal.,(2024) This paper puts forward a mixed security system that uses image compression, symmetric encryption and hiding information to keep private multimedia data safe. To hide the encrypted data inside a picture, the authors use least significant bit (LSB) steganography; they use AES for encryption, and wavelet changes for compressing images. This approach, which has many layers, makes it harder for people tofindor understand the hidden information, improving security and concealment. The method is especially helpful for secure picture transmission in places like military or medical imaging systems, where it is very important to keep data hidden and safe. (T. ElGamal, 1985) In his work, Gamal introduced a way to create digital signatures based on the hard problem of discrete logarithms, along with a method for public key encryption. By changing the Diffie-Hellman key exchange into a complete encryption system, the ElGamal cryptosystem employs probabilistic encryption to achieve semantic security. Its signature mechanism ensures the validity and infallibility of communications, forming the foundation for the widely used DSA (Digital Signature Algorithm). ElGamal's power comes from its reliance on the complex mathematics of discrete logarithms, making it an indispensable element of current cryptographic systems like blockchain and secure communication applications. The classroom notes by Bellare, M., and P. Rogaway in (2005) are an essential source for learning basic encryption. It is well known that these notes properly outline the requirements for consistency under selected-plain text along with chosen-ciphertext attacks (IND-CPA/CCA) and encourage a systematic, cautious approach to the protocol construction. They describe basic cryptographic procedures such as digital autographs, coded messages for authentication (MACs), and encryption methods, using the idea of verifiable security.

Researchers demonstrate how the system's safety depends on a particular assumption about computational complexity using simplified arguments using risk games. The 2009 textbook by J. Pelzl and C. Paar strikes a mix between in-depth theoretical research and simple, relatable applications in everyday life. The study of block encryption techniques, cryptography using public keys, hashing operations, and digital signed documents are just a few of the topics Paar and Pelzl cover, with a focus on the practical application of these ideas. They provide brief explanations, relevant examples, and illustrations to help them better understand elliptic curve cryptography (ECC), RSA, and AES.

Scientists use risk plays and simplified arguments to show how the safety of the system relies upon a certain hypothesis about computational difficulty. J. Pelzl and C. Paar's textbook from 2009 finds a balance between of-depth conceptualization and straightforward, accessible uses for daily life. Paar and Pelzl discuss a variety of subjects, with an emphasis on the real-world implementation of these concepts, including hash procedures, securely signed written material, secure encryption approaches, and digital signatures utilizing public keys. To aid in their understanding of elliptic curve cryptography (ECC), RSA, and AES, they offer succinct clarifications, relevant instances, and pictures.

MODULES

Module 1: Cryptographic Foundations

All the cryptographic approaches are implemented using this module as a conceptual foundation. It introduces the ideas and mathematical concepts that form the foundation of safe systems. The difficulties of solving issues like considering numerology, interacting with curved lines, and discrete logarithms is frequently linked to the privacy underlying encryption. These intricate computational issues hint at the challenging work that goes into data encryption and digital certificate production. Furthermore, the domains of modulo arithmetic, number theory, and finite fields are offering the precise operations needed to create algorithms.

Figure 1. Architecture of Securing Data with Cryptography

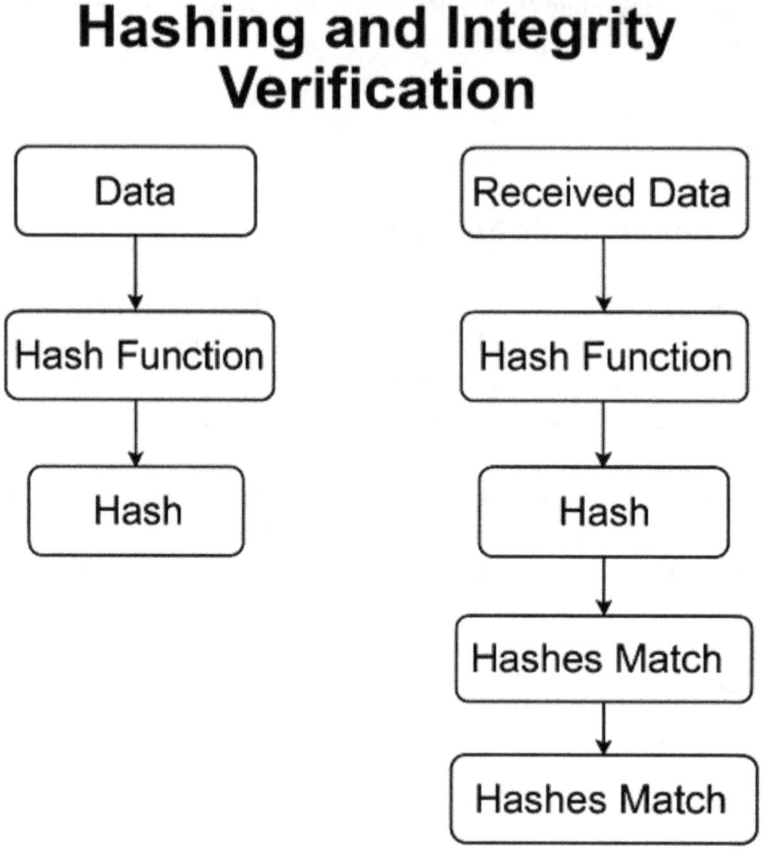

Module 2: Symmetric and Asymmetric Encryption

The privacy that must always be maintained is one of the key components of this program's effectiveness. Because it relies on a single key for both encryption and decryption, it enables quick data protection and encryption. Programs boasting strong encryption features and fast operating rates include ChaCha20 and AES (Advanced Encryption Standards Standard). These are commonly used in file encryption programs, secure data storage systems, and virtual private networks (VPNs). In contrast, asymmetric encryption uses a pair of keys that are mathematically linked; the public key is used for encryption, and the private key is used for decryption.

Digital signatures and key exchange procedures in open systems are supported by algorithms such as RSA, ECC (Elliptic Curve Cryptography), and Lattice-based approaches. However, in what are referred to as hybrid cryptographic designs, symmetric techniques are frequently combined with asymmetric algorithms, which are typically more computationally demanding. Even amongst previously untrusted parties, secure communication is made possible by this synergy, which strikes a balance between performance and adaptability. In order to make sure that even robust encryption algorithms are not compromised by inadequate configuration, this module also examines mode of operation choices (e.g., CBC, GCM, CTR), initialization vectors, padding schemes, and cryptographic nonce management.

Module 3: Hashing and Integrity Verification

Hashing guarantees that a message stays unchanged, but encryption conceals its content. The cryptographic hash algorithms that convert input data into a fixed-length digest are the main topic of this module. Two distinct inputs shouldn't result in the same hash since the output is deterministic but non-reversible and ought to be collision-resistant. Standardized algorithms like SHA-2, SHA-3, and BLAKE3 are frequently used in version control, blockchain, and digital forensics because they offer a high degree of trust in data integrity.

Figure 2. Hashing and Integrity Verification

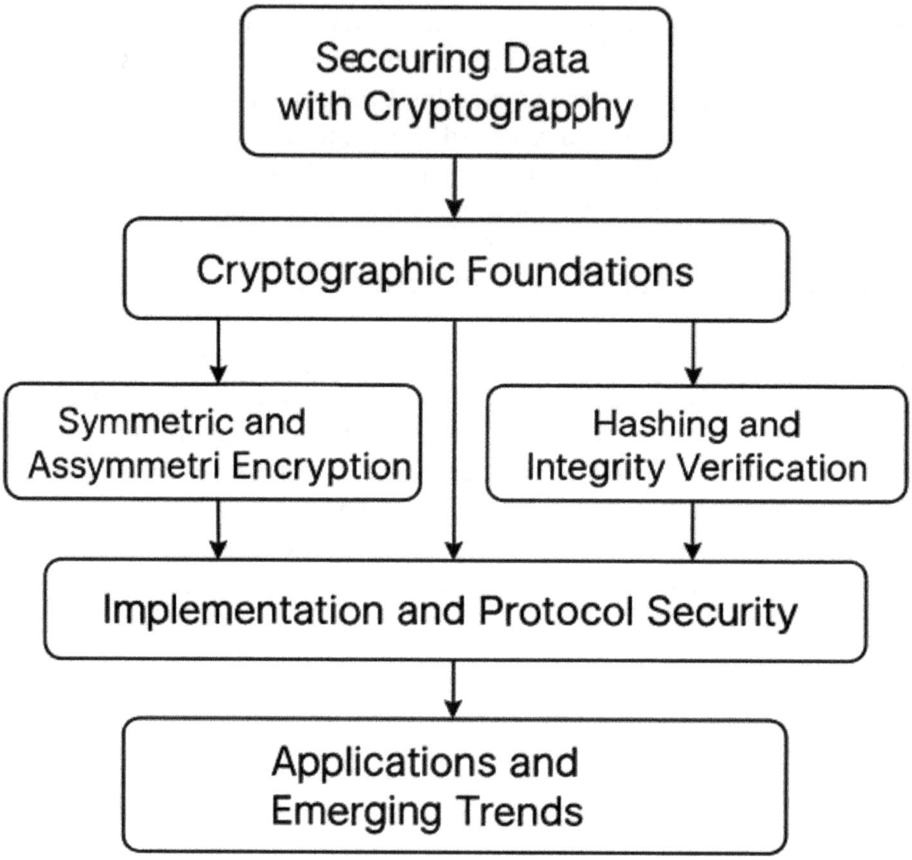

Furthermore, hashing and secret keys are combined by Message Authentication Codes (MACs), such HMAC-SHA256, to confirm authenticity and integrity. This feature is extended at a higher level by digital signature systems (such as RSA, ECDSA, and EdDSA), which link identification to data that has forensic and legal value. Practically speaking, this module enables applications such as protecting email content, verifying file downloads, identifying medical record tampering, and making that blockchain transactions are irreversible and forever verifiable.

Module 4: Key Management and Distribution

Without safe keys, secure algorithms are useless. Cryptographic key creation, management, and exchange are covered in this module. To prevent predictability, high-entropy sources are used in key generation, ideally from hardware-based random number generators. The key lifetime consists of consumption (session keys, ephemeral keys), renewal, revocation, and storage (hardware security modules, secured keystores). The most popular trust model is Public Key Infrastructure (PKI), which includes digitally signed certificates, Certificate Authorities (CAs), and certificate revocation procedures.

Key exchange protocols including Diffie-Hellman, Elliptic Curve Diffie-Hellman (ECDH), and post-quantum key encapsulation mechanisms (KEMs) are also covered in this subject. They let two parties to agree on a shared key in the face of adversaries when they are implemented securely. Even in cases when the underlying encryption is technically solid, flaws in this layer, such as reused or improperly maintained keys, might result in whole system penetration. Key management bridges the gap between access control systems and federated identities by extending into identity federation, authentication tokens, and multi-factor verification.

Module 5: Implementation and Protocol Security

This module guarantees the theoretical and practical security of cryptographic systems. It looks at typical protocol design and implementation flaws. For example, faulty padding, inappropriate nonce reuse, or side-channel vulnerabilities like power analysis and timing attacks can all compromise encryption methods. The module covers widely used security protocols—SSL/TLS, IPSec, SSH, S/MIME, Signal Protocol—breaking them down to understand the handshake mechanisms, cipher negotiation, and replay prevention features.

Developer awareness is an additional dimension. Many attacks result not from algorithm flaws but from poor implementation practices—like using weak entropy sources, writing insecure random number generators, or reusing session keys. Therefore, secure software engineering principles, regular audits, fuzzing tools, and code reviews are considered essential components of this module.

Table 1. Symmetric vs Asymmetric Encryption Algorithms

Algorithm	Type	Key Size	Speed	Security Level	Typical Use Cases
AES	Symmetric	128/192/256 bits	Very Fast	Strong (NIST approved)	File encryption, VPNs, TLS
DES	Symmetric	56 bits	Fast	Weak (deprecated)	Legacy systems
3DES	Symmetric	112/168 bits	Slow	Moderate	Financial systems (legacy)
RSA	Asymmetric	1024–4096 bits	Slow	Strong (≥2048 bits)	Digital signatures, key exchange
ECC	Asymmetric	160–521 bits	Faster than RSA	Strong (smaller key size)	Mobile devices, blockchain

Table 2. Cryptographic Hash Functions

Hash Function	Output Size	Collision Resistance	Speed	Use Cases
SHA-1	160 bits	Weak (broken)	Fast	Legacy systems (deprecated)
SHA-2 (SHA-256)	256 bits	Strong	Fast	Digital signatures, file integrity
SHA-3	224–512 bits	Strong (Keccak-based)	Moderate	Blockchain, secure hashing
BLAKE2	256/512 bits	Strong	Very Fast	Password hashing, embedded systems
MD5	128 bits	Broken	Very Fast	Checksums (not for security)

Table 3. Lightweight Cryptography for IoT

Algorithm	Type	Key Size	Block Size	Rounds	Strength	Use Cases
PRESENT	Block Cipher	80/128 bits	64 bits	31	Moderate	RFID, sensor networks
SPECK	Block Cipher	64–128 bits	32–128 bits	22–34	Moderate	Embedded systems (NSA-designed)
SIMON	Block Cipher	64–128 bits	32–128 bits	32–72	Moderate	Lightweight hardware encryption
ASCON	AEAD	128 bits	128 bits	12	Strong (NIST LWC)	IoT, authenticated encryption
ChaCha20	Stream Cipher	256 bits	N/A	20	Strong	Mobile apps, TLS (Google, WhatsApp)

Module 6: Applications and Emerging Trends

IoT devices, wearable medical sensors, autonomous vehicles, and edge-based AI are examples of modern and emerging environments to which cryptographic protection is extended, especially those with heightened constraints or novel threat models. These systems frequently require lightweight encryption algorithms (e.g., PRESENT, Simon/Speck, Ascon), providing security within severe limitations in energy, storage, and computation.

Figure 3. Relevance of Emerging Cryptographic

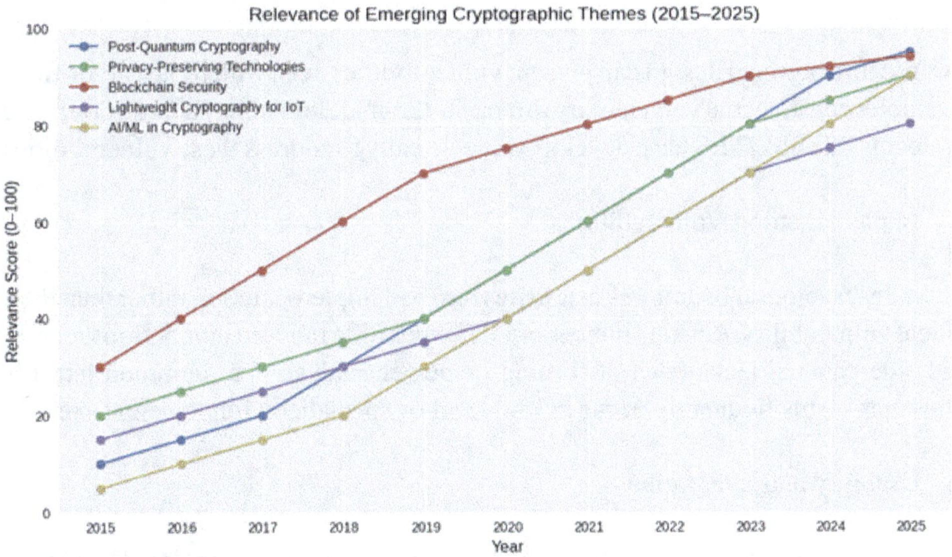

The module also engages with homomorphic encryption and secure multi-party computation (SMPC), which enable encrypted data to be computed on without revealing its content—ideal for privacy-preserving AI or federated learning frameworks in healthcare or finance.

ISSUES

1. Key Management Complexity

The security of an encryption system depends on its keys. Inadequate key rotation, unsafe storage, or poor key production can leave systems vulnerable. Complexity is increased by managing keys across dispersed systems, particularly in cloud or Internet of Things contexts.

2. Algorithm Selection and Obsolescence

Systems may become insecure if antiquated or ineffective algorithms (such as DES or MD5) are used. Conversely, more recent algorithms might not be well tested or generally supported. A recurring problem is selecting the appropriate algorithm for the given situation while juggling compatibility, strength, and speed.

3. Protocol Design Flaws

Insecure protocol design can present vulnerabilities even with robust algorithms. Examples consist of the vulnerability to man-in-the-middle or replay attacks Over time, protocols like SSL/TLS have developed specifically to address these vulnerabilities.

4. Implementation Vulnerabilities

Many cryptography failures originate from bad implementation rather than theoretical vulnerability. Reusing nonces or IVs; generating random numbers insecurely; and side-channel leaks (such as timing or power analysis) are common hazards. These problems frequently occur in low-level or specialized implementations.

5. Usability and Integration

Using cryptographic technologies appropriately may be challenging. Developers could hardcode secrets, omit validation procedures, or abuse APIs. Users may circumvent security measures if they are very complicated, which would compromise the system as a whole.

6. Regulatory and Interoperability Constraints

Standards (such as GDPR, HIPAA, and FIPS) differ by industry and area. It's not easy to ensure compliance while preserving platform performance and compatibility.

ADVANTAGES

1. Confidentiality

Cryptography keeps private information hidden from unauthorized eyes. When data is encrypted, only those with the correct key can read it. This ensures that personal and sensitive details stay protected, whether stored or shared.

2. Data Integrity

It's crucial to know that data hasn't been changed or tampered with. Cryptographic tools like hash functions help verify that the content remains exactly as intended. If someone tries to alter the data, the system can detect it immediately.

3. Authentication

Knowing who you're communicating with is essential. Cryptography helps confirm identities through methods like digital certificates and secure logins. By doing this, deception is avoided and entry is restricted to authorized individuals only.

CONCLUSION

` These days, crypto is more than simply a scientific field; it's a vital component to protect against the dangers of the digital world, which is a highly networked setting where distant interactions and information analyses are essential. a little the development of a fairly clear understanding of the fundamental ideas along with primary algebraic procedures, this chapter of cryptography readily opens up doors to the field for novices. In order to encompass all of the developments in current encryption, the majority of the chapter's material should be changed, even to the extent of replacing the whole chapter.

The writers could add topics like blockchain-based safeguarding architectures, algorithms that can withstand quantum computer processing, and privacy-preserving techniques like homomorphic signing and distinction of privacy to the chapter on encrypted challenges. By creating a range of real-world examples and case studies, this might be a useful method for presenting theoretical concepts to close the gap between theory and reality. IoT, distributed platforms, and safe compute are the sectors that may have profited the most.

The section's conciseness and coherence may be primarily enhanced by resolving known crypto flaws, organizing parts, and fixing section problems. The paper will remain current with the most recent research and business changes if the bibliographies are updated with relevant academic papers.

FUTURE ENHANCEMENT

With the development of the sector mentioned above, the next encryptions innovations should focus mainly on ethics, sharing knowledge, and being more flexible. As a major step in safeguarding private data against novel threats due to quantum computing, there is a need for the use of post-quantum cryptography which will provide complete privacy for sensitive areas such as medicine and vital government services. Besides that, the installation of AI-powered key management platforms that are capable of forecasting weak spots, finding disruptions in network flow instantly, and rekeying automatically in case of a newly encountered threat pattern is very important. For the field of disaster aid, using a safety net is an ideal illustration.

REFERENCES

Bellare, M., & Rogaway, P. (2005). *Introduction to Modern Cryptography.* UC Davis Lecture Notes.

Bhanot, R., & Hans, R. (2015). A Review and Comparative Analysis of Various Encryption Algorithms. *International Journal of Security and Its Applications, 9*(4), 289–306.

Chaum, D. (1981). Untraceable Electronic Mail, Return Addresses, and Digital Pseudonyms. *Communications of the ACM, 24*(2), 84–88.

Diffie, W. (1988). The First Ten Years of Public-Key Cryptography. *Proceedings of the IEEE, 76*(5), 560–577.

Diffie, W., & Hellman, M. (1976). New Directions in Cryptography. *IEEE Transactions on Information Theory, 22*(6), 644–654.

Dolev, D., & Yao, A. (1983). On the Security of Public Key Protocols. *IEEE Transactions on Information Theory, 29*(2), 198–208.

Eastlake, D., & Jones, P. (2001). "US Secure Hash Algorithm 1 (SHA1)." RFC 3174.

ElGamal, T. (1985). A Public Key Cryptosystem and a Signature Scheme Based on Discrete Logarithms. *IEEE Transactions on Information Theory, 31*(4), 469–472.

Goldwasser, S., & Micali, S. (1984). Probabilistic Encryption. *Journal of Computer and System Sciences, 28*(2), 270–299.

Hu, S., Huang, R., & Zhou, L. (2025). An Efficient Multi-Key BFV Fully Homomorphic Encryption Scheme with Optimized Relinearization. Cybersecurity, 8(1), Article 42. Published: 26 June 2025.

Katz, J., & Lindell, Y. (2020). *Introduction to Modern Cryptography* (3rd ed.). CRC Press.

Kelsey, J., et al. (2015). "Secure Hash Standard." NIST FIPS PUB 180-1.

Malviya, M. K., & Singhal, M. K. (2024). A Literature Survey on Different Data Encryption and Decryption Techniques. *JETIR, 11*(9), 1–6.

Menezes, A. J., van Oorschot, P. C., & Vanstone, S. A. (1996). *Handbook of Applied Cryptography.* CRC Press.

Paar, C., & Pelzl, J. (2009). *Understanding Cryptography: A Textbook for Students and Practitioners.* Springer.

Shamir, A. (1979). How to Share a Secret. *Communications of the ACM*, *22*(11), 612–613.

Singh, S., & Supriya, . (2013). A Study of Encryption Algorithms (RSA, DES, 3DES and AES) for Information Security. *International Journal of Computer Applications*, *67*(19), 33–38.

Sneha, R., Vasumathi, K., & Selvakani, S. (2024). Securing Data Using Cryptography and Steganography. *IJNRD*, *9*(3), 1–8.

Xue, J., Xin, X., Zhang, W., Zheng, M., Song, Q., Zhou, M., Dong, Y., Wang, Q., Mohaisen, D., Wu, H., & Lou, Q. (2025). Measuring Computational Universality of Fully Homomorphic Encryption. arXiv. Submitted 15 April 2025.

Zhang, X., & Jain, A. (2024). Apple Loquat: A SNARK-Friendly Post-Quantum Signature. Proceedings of Crypto 2024

Zhao, D. (2025). Advances and Applications in Fully Homomorphic Encryption Research. [EWA Direct]. *Applied and Computational Engineering*, *135*, 39–48. DOI: 10.54254/2755-2721/2025.20959

Zhao, D. (2025). Compile-Time Fully Homomorphic Encryption: Eliminating Online Encryption via Algebraic Basis Synthesis. arXiv. Submitted 19 May 2025.

Chapter 10
Designing a Comprehensive Network Topology Using BGP Attributes in GNS3

Halima Abbas Assied Ahmed
https://orcid.org/0009-0004-3726-5210
Sheffield Hallam University, UK

Siavosh Hgahighi Movahed
Sheffield Hallam University, UK

Mark Townley
Sheffield Hallam University, UK

ABSTRACT

The Border Gateway Protocol (BGP), known also as an Exterior Gateway Protocol (EGP), is used frequently by Internet networks to exchange routing information among various autonomous systems (ASs). BGP is divided into two variations. The internal variation exchanges the data between two neighbours in the same an AS, while the external BGP is responsible for exchanging packets among different ASs. BGP has path-vector protocols that are used to select a path to a remote network based on routing policy. This research aims to investigate and implement BGP protocols in different attributes by using GNS3 software. The second goal is delivering a good tutorial with no complexity that would lead to comprehensive understanding of the BGP routing features with different attributes. In this dissertation, Graphical Network Simulator version 3 (GNS3) emulator software is used to design the prac-

DOI: 10.4018/979-8-3373-4154-5.ch010

tical network. Students in MSc networking professional and one MSc Advanced Computer Network course student were chosen to test the implementation and were interviewed for feedback used to improve the work

1.INTRODUCTION

One of the numerous astounding characteristics of the Internet is that it has scaled so well to its present size. (Yuvaraj, 2023). According to Mahfuzhi et al. (2024), the relations among these networks and their connectivity are constantly changing. Therefore, different domains close as organisation or internet server providers (ISP) require a mechanism to route data among these various domains (Tofoni, Luciani, & Prado, 2023).

The Border Gateway Protocol (BGP) is a protocol that permits maintenance such that reachability and dynamic route creation are protected (Bonczkowski, 2025). As opposed to static routing, BGP can automatically adjust routing configurations depending on the network path distance information received from other users of the protocol. BGP is a rich protocol that has numerous ways to handle nodes or network failures as well as changes in the network topology (Tofoni, Luciani, & Prado, 2023).

That routing requires two basic tasks: determination of optimal routing paths, and the transport of information groups, typically named packets, through an internetwork. These packets are transported in a relatively straightforward manner through such internetworks (Mahfuzhi et al., 2024). Path determination in the routing process is a very complex task. The Border Gateway Protocol (BGP) is a protocol that is designed to address the task of path determination in today's networks. According to Yuvaraj (2023), BGP applies inter-domain routing in Transmission-Control Protocol/ Internet Protocol (TCP/IP) networks. BGP is also important in performing routing among several domains, or Autonomous Systems (ASs). Moreover, it is useful for exchanging routing and reachability data with other BGP systems (Zamany et al., 2022).

BGP has been developed to replace the Exterior Gateway Protocol (EGP) and is considered the standard gateway protocol applied in the global internet (Zamany et al., 2022). The BGP protocol has many advantageous that make it outperform other gateway protocols, as it solves serious issues related to EGP and makes the internet grow more efficiently (Tofoni et al., 2023). Firstly, BGP has been defined in RFC 1105 (1989). It was updated to BGP-2 in RFC 1163 (1990), then to BGP-3 in RFC 1267 (1991), and after that to BGP-4 in RFC 1771 (1995), which is the version that is considered in this dissertation. Importantly BGP-4 is the first version able to support new attributes that are up to date with the evolving internet, as it deals with prefix aggregation along Classless Inter-Domain Routing (CIDR) (Kumar,

2024). Additionally, BGP4 and CIDR are useful for reducing the Internet routing table size (Zamany et al., 2022).

During this thesis, the work that has been done was tested by a student in the MSc Advanced Computer Networks course and a number of students in MSc networking professional courts to give evidence that it works properly, and to make amendments where required. This dissertation found that not much work has been provided to help students or professionals understand this important protocol, consequently leading to causing too much complexity for understanding the basic concepts, design, and practical implementation of BGP, especially for students in the field of network research. Pure understanding of BGP's dynamics is the main contribution of this dissertation, so that one could configure, diagnose and debug issues related to this protocol.

2. LITERATURE REVIEW

There are two basic flavours of Dynamic routing protocols for IP. One is called the Interior Gateway Protocol (IGPs); the other is known as the Exterior Gateway Protocol (EGP) (Mahfuzhi et al., 2024). The border between these two levels can be defined by Autonomous Systems (ASes) (Zamany et al., 2022). IGPs are utilized for routing within AS, while EGP can be used for global routing between different AS's. There are numerous IGPs in use, including the Intermediate System-Intermediate System (IS-IS), the Routing Information Protocol (RIP), the Open Shortest Path Protocol (OSPF), and the Enhanced Interior Gateway Routing Protocol (EIGRP), while there is only one EGP used in the Border Gateway Protocol (BGP) (Bonczkowski, 2025).

2.1. BGP Definition

The Border Gateway Protocol (BGP) is known as a routing protocol that is used by the Internet networks to exchange routing information among various autonomous systems (Tofoni et al., 2023). Notably, BGP is divided into two variations, the internal, which exchanges data between two neighbours in the same ASN, and the external BGP, which is responsible for exchanging packets between different ASNs (Mahfuzhi et al., 2024). Moreover, Tofoni et al. (2023) explained that any two routers exchange BGP routing information by forming a TCP connection is known as BGP peers or neighbours.

BGP has several advantages that let it overcome other standard vector protocols such as the Routing Information Protocol (RIP). BGP can provide the network with reliable delivery by using the Transmission Control Protocol (TCP) as its transport protocol; BGP data is carried inside TCP segments using port 179.

Autonomous System

An Autonomous System (AS) is known as a group of routers under a single administrative control, utilizing common metrics and an IGP, to route packets within the same AS, and an EGP is used to route packets to other ASes (Yuvaraj, 2023). For example, a single AS might be the network of a university, an Internet Service Provider (ISP), or a corporation, as shown in figure (1).

Figure 1. EGP is used to exchange packets to other ASes while IGP is used to exchange packets within the same AS

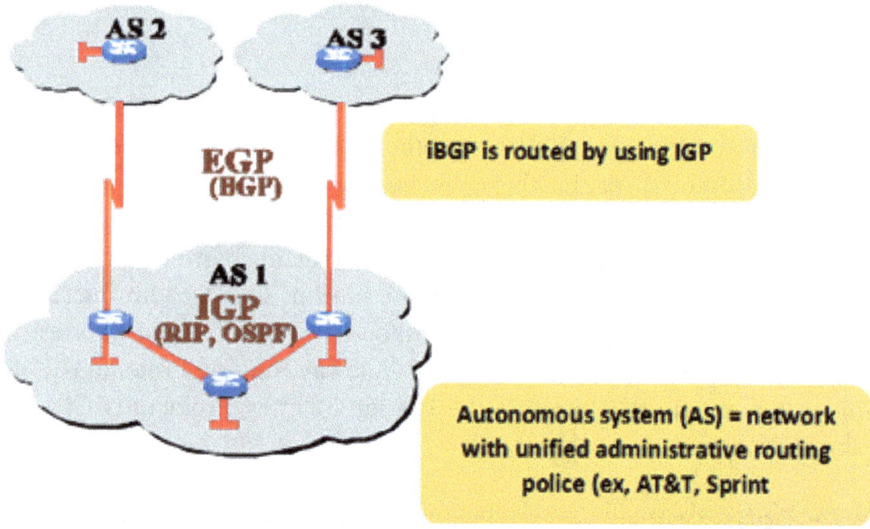

Each AS is thought to have only its own intra-domain routing plan, and administrators may actualize it in any way they choose (Yuvaraj, 2023). Conversely, inter-domain routing can be used for the transfer of routing information between ASes. Because of the collaboration of routing, all routers that partake in the procedure must use the same protocol. It is for this reason that one protocol may be used ubiquitously for inter-domain routing throughout the Internet.

The AS must be assigned a globally unique number so that IP address blocks seem to be coming from a unique position that BGP finds and routes to (Obelovska et al., 2025). AS numbers are essential, because the ASN uniquely identifies each network on the Internet (Yuvaraj, 2023). According to Kumar (2024), AS numbers were known as 16-bit numbers, which permitted for a maximum of 65,536 assignments. RFC 4893 presented 32-bit AS numbers, which the Internet Assigned Numbers Authority (IANA) has begun to assign to regional Internet registries (RIRs), although this proposed standard has now been changed by RFC 6793.

ASN can find numbers between 1 and 65,535. The AS numbers between 1 and 64,511 are managed via RIRs; the 64,512 - 65,535 numbers have been reserved for private use (comparable to IP private addresses).

The Uses of BGP

There are various situations when the BGP protocol needs to be used. For example, BGP should be used in sending traffic via one AS to get to another AS. It is also required for connecting two or more ISPs (Tofoni et al., 2023). In addition, BGP is useful in cases of an enterprise network that contains multi-homing connects to more than one ISP, and in connecting network access points and exchange points (Mahfuzhi et al., 2024).

Comparison of Interior IGP and Exterior BGP Gateway Protocols

There are two types of gateway protocols, interior and exterior. The interior gateway protocol (IGPs) is a routing protocol responsible for operating the data within the same Autonomous System (AS), while the exterior gateway protocol (EGP) is for operating the information between different AS (Tofoni et al., 2023). There are similarities and differences between those two gateways. For instance, they are the same in forming a neighbour relationship prior sending the routing information and in having an advertised prefix length (Bonczkowski, 2025). On the other hand, there are various differences between the two. BGP uses TCP connections between neighbours, while IGP does not. Also, an EGP such as BGP does not need neighbours to be attached to the same subnet (Mahfuzhi et al., 2024). Finally, Bonczkowski (2025) indicate that the major considered difference is that IGP uses link state or distance vector logic, or both, whereas BGP uses path vector logic.

BGP Tables

According to Bonczkowski (2025), the BGP table plays an important role in storing the data received from or sent to BGP peers. This table is known as the BGP topology table, BGP topology database, BGP routing table or BGP forwarding database. Inside the router, the two tables (the BGP table and the IP routing table) are separated, and the router is responsible for offering the best pathways from the BGP table to the IP routing table. Yang et al.(2024) confirmed that the selection of the best

BGP route is very important to have reachable next-hop IP addresses. Therefore, in case the reachable next-hop is missing, the BGP route cannot be propagated to other routers. Importantly, the administrative distance has an effect on choosing the best routes. For instance, the routing information provided by the external BGP (eBGP) is preferable over the same information provided by the internal BGP (iBGP), as the external BGP has an administrative distance less than that of the internal BGP.

The Cisco Networking Academy (2025) illustrates that BGP tables are classified into three types, the neighbour table, the forwarding database and the IP routing table. The neighbour table contains the BGP neighbours. The BGP forwarding database contains the BGP attributes for every route, including all the networks learned from each peer, and may contain multiple routes to the destination. Finally, the IP routing table contains the best routes to the end point.

BGP Message

In the BGP domain, the BGP routing protocol is responsible for exchanging different messages to coordinate the information among participating routers (Bruno & Jordan, 2024). There are four types of BGP messages: open, keepalive, update, and notification. The first type, the open message, is used when BGP peers are established. The open message consists of the BGP version number, the AS number, and the hold down time that needs to be negotiated with the neighbour before establishing a peer relationship (Yang et al., 2024). The main purpose of the second type, the keepalive message, is to make sure the connection is still active after the peer relationship is established (Cisco Networking Academy, 2025). The third message, the update message, contains a list of withdrawn prefixes or/and new prefixes along with their path attributes. Any changes in the network, such as losing network availability, will result in an update message (Yang et al., 2024). The last type of message, the notification message, is only used to inform BGP peers when an error or mismatch is detected (Bonczkowski, 2025).

BGP States

According to Bonczkowski (2025), when the BGP process is running on a router, it moves through several states during its execution, as shown in figure 2:

Idle State:

In the idle state, the BGP is waiting for the start of the event, which is the peer configuration of BGP. Once the BGP process has started, it moves to the connect state.

Connect State:

In the connect state, the BGP process waits for the completion of the TCP connection. If the TCP connection has been established, the process will be sent to the OpenSent state; if not, the process moves to the active state.

Active State:

In the active state, the BGP router is trying to initiate a new TCP connection.

OpenSent State:

In the OpenSent state, the router sends an Open message from the remote peer containing the BGP parameters and waits for the corresponding message. Moreover, in this state, the connection type can determine whether it is an eBGP or an iBGP.

OpenConfirm State:

In this state, the BGP peer relationship is established, and the peers start exchanging Keepalive messages. If the Keepalive message is received, the BGP process moves to the established state. However, the BGP router moves to the idle state if a notification message or a TCP reset is received.

Established State:

This is the final state in BGP peer negotiations, when the two peers exchange their routing information. At this stage, if any error has occurred, the system will receive a notification message, and the state will go back to the idle state.

Figure 2. The mechanism of the BGP states

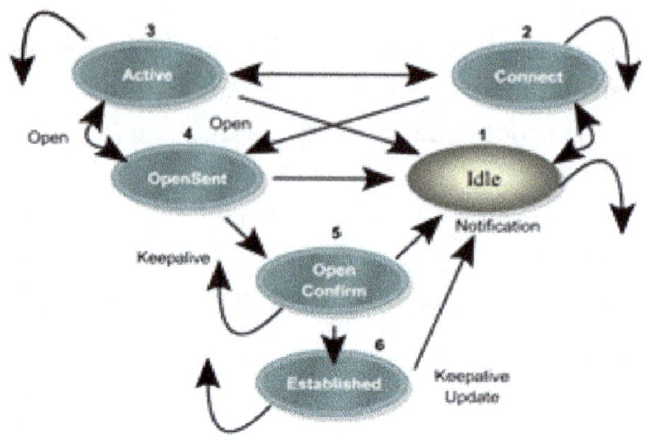

2.2. Filtering

Filtering is very important. It is used in the routing protocol to control inbound and outbound update messages. Moreover, BGP allows filtering the receiving and sending updates between the neighbours (Bruno & Jordan, 2024). According to Bonczkowski (2025), BGP peer groups are used to collect peers that have the same policies together to facilitate more efficient configuration. There are a number of reasons that influence the advertised route, such as stopping unnecessary advertisements, by controlling the process of route selection, in order to remove router confusion and the high CPU utilisation that may occur during route flaps (Yang et al., 2024). A route flap is defined as a change in the route state, and once it is occurring, the BGP dampening command is used to prevent routing problems, as it is responsible for maintaining the threshold for route flaps (Bruno & Jordan, 2024).

The filtering tools of the primary route contain distribute lists, route maps and prefix lists (Bonczkowski, 2025). Distribute lists are known as standard lists. They are used in a router's BGP session in order to allow or deny the routes that are advertised through the network (Yang et al., 2024). Route maps are complex access lists applied to control and modify the routing table data. Prefix lists are new, added lists that can take the place of the access lists that are used in BGP route filtering commands (Bruno & Jordan, 2024). Bonczkowski (2025) revealed that these lists also have many advantages, as they tax the processor less than access lists, which is important for improving the router's performance. Furthermore, prefix lists are more flexible and are easy to configure.

2.3. BGP Path Attributes

The BGP attributes are defined as a set of parameters describing the characteristics of prefixes. They are used to determine a path to a remote network (Bruno & Jordan, 2024). According to Welekwe (2024), these attributes are important for reaching the required destination, as they are coupled with the prefix they describe by the BGP decision process, which then compares all the available paths to reach the given destination by selecting the best routes. Moreover, they are part of each BGP UPDATE packet that describe the information path of the related prefix. Path attributes are divided into four categories: well-known mandatory, well-known discretionary, optional transitive, and optional nontransitive.

Categories of BGP Path Attributes

A. Well-known mandatory attributes:

A compliant BGP implementation uses this type of attribute to propagate all the network's BGP neighbours (Bonczkowski, 2025). Importantly, well-known mandatory attributes must be available in all BGP update messages and in an advertised route. These attributes contain:

1. **Autonomous system path (AS-Path),** which are composed of a variable length of AS path segments. They describe the autonomous system sequence that has been traversed by the packet (Welekwe, 2024).
2. **Next Hop:** these mandatory attributes indicate the IP address of the next-hop destination router. BGP may announce one of various different IP address as a route's Next-hop based on many factors (Bruno & Jordan, 2024).
3. **Origin:** defined as the origin of the path information. Origin attributes have three different values, IGP, EGP, or incomplete. An IGP value indicates the remote path; typically, it is used by BGP when a redistribution or network command is configured. An EGP value means learning via the External Gateway Protocol. An incomplete value means discovering the BGP route by using static routers or by redistribution (Welekwe, 2024).

B. Well-known discretionary attributes:

These path attributes are not required to be present in all BGP update messages. In other words, it does not need to be in each update message, but it can be recognized by all BGP implementations (Tofoni et al., 2023). They include two types:

1. **Local preference**: A local preference contains only a single AS, and can pass only to iBGP peers and cannot be sent to eBGP neighbours. Notably, this attribute is configured to exchange the packets within the same AS. Its default value is 100 (Alhiary, 2025).
2. **Atomic Aggregate**: This attribute is also known as overlapping routes. It is used to indicate whether or not the prefix has been used (Tofoni et al., 2023).
   C. Optional Attributes:

These attributes are called optional because they are not required to be implemented in every BGP implementation. They are divided into two types, transitive and nontransitive, depending on the type of propagation that is implemented by BGP routers to other BGP neighbours (Welekwe, 2024).

1. **Optional transitive**: this attribute might not be recognized by some BGP implementations. In these cases, Optional transitive attribute will label the message as a partial message, but it will still propagate it to its peers. The only optional transitive attribute type, as defined in RFC 4271, is:
   - **Aggregator**: this attribute is responsible for aggregation. It consists of six octets. Two of them recognise the ASN, whereas the other four octets identify the IP address (Tofoni et al., 2023).
2. Optional non-transitive attributes:

Optional non-transitive attributes, just as transitive attributes, might not be recognized by some implementations, but the difference here is that if optional non-transitive attributes cannot recognize it, it will not pass the message to other neighbours, and the message will be deleted (Bonczkowski, 2025). According to RFC 4271, the only optional non-transitive attribute is as follows:

- **Multi-Exit-Discriminator (MED):** The MED is used among external neighbours to differentiate among multiple exit points to its peers' autonomous systems (Welekwe, 2024). Unlikely the local preference, this attribute is configured to exchange the packets between different AS's. It is also known as a metric. It has a default value of zero when the same update is sent to another AS (Bonczkowski, 2025).

As the BGP standard is flexible, it allows other optional attributes. For example, Cisco has defined three other optional attribute type codes as well as a local-only attribute:

1. **Communities:** This is a one-way attribute responsible for filtrating incoming or outgoing routes. BGP communities are important, as they allow the router to tag another and to make other routers take decisions that depend on that tag (Bonczkowski, 2025). In other words, as Tofoni et al. (2023) explains, grouping destinations paths are provided by the community attribute called communities. These communities help in routing decisions such as acceptance or preference. Community attributes are set by using route maps. Known community attributes are as follows:
   A. No export: this means do not announce the route to eBGP neighbours.
   B. No advertise: this attribute does not advertise the route to any peer.
   C. Internet Advertise: announce the route to the Internet community.
2. **Originator ID**: this attribute is useful for preventing routing loops and is not used in selecting the router (Welekwe, 2024).
3. **Cluster-list:** this type of attribute is used in route-reflector environments, and is not used for selecting the router (Alhiary, 2025).

In addition to all the previous attributes, Cisco has defined another, called the weight attribute, which is used in the path-selection process. It is not propagated to any BGP peers. In this attribute, a high value is preferred, between 0 and 294,967,295 (Welekwe, 2024).

Decision Process Summary of the BGP Path Attributes

The process of BGP path selection depends on the BGP attributes and requires many steps. Notably, BGP prefers routes that do not contain autonomous system loops and that have a valid accessible next-hop address (Tofoni et al., 2023). According to Alhiary (2025), the process of choosing the best route taken by the BGP can be summarized in the following steps:

Step 1: prefer the route with the highest weight.
Step 2: when multiple routes have the same weight, prefer the routes with the highest local preference.
Step 3: when multiple routes have the same local preference, prefer the route that was originated by the local router.
Step 4: if no routes were originated by the local router, prefer the route with the shortest AS-path.
Step 5: in the situation where the AS-path is the same, prefer the route with the lowest-origin code.
Step 6: if the origin codes are the same, prefer the path with the lowest MED.

Step 7: when the routes have the same MED, prefer external paths (eBGP) over internal paths (iBGP).

Step 8: when only internal paths exist, prefer the path through the closest IGP neighbour; in other words, the shortest internal path is better for the router to reach its destination.

Step 9: select the oldest route for eBGP paths in order to minimize flapping.

Step 10: prefer the route that has lowest neighbour BGP router ID value.

Step 11: in the case when the BGP router IDs are the same, prefer the route with the lowest neighbour IP address.

2.4. The Purpose of This Research

The Border Gateway Protocol (BGP) is a major element in today's IP network structure. As an important routing protocol of the Internet, pure understanding of its dynamics is essential to configure, diagnose and debug Internet routing problems. It was notable that in the majority of the previous books and articles that have investigated the BGP protocol and its uses, there has been a lack of its practical aspects. The authors of the CCNP routing study guide book that was published in 2001 by Lammle, Odom and Wallace only considered the operation and theoretical concepts of the BGP protocol, but there was a deficiency in how BGP, with its various attributes, is implemented. Also, it summarises only the configuration and path selection process of BGP without showing all the aspects of a complete network design. Meanwhile, in a book titled *CCNP Practical Studies: Routing* by Benjamin (2002), a clear vision of the implementation of BGP attributes is not provided in their practical work. In another book called *Internet Routing Architectures* by Halabi and McPherson (2000), there is a good explanation of the architectures of BGP, as in the previous two books, but in addition, it provides the design of the complete network. However, this book lacks consideration of the weight and community no-advertise factors of the BGP attributes, and does not use them in designing their presented network. Additionally, it presents a number of filtering techniques, such as prefix list, but it does not implement them practically, which is differently implemented in this dissertation. Odom (2010), in his book CCNP Route 642-902 Official Certification Guide, only provides some attributes without a full implementation of all BGP's attributes. As in previously reviewed books related to the implementation of BGP, Teare, Vachon and Graziani, in their book Implementing Cisco IP Routing (ROUTE) Foundation Learning Guide (2015), lack the application of all of the attributes in their practical design.

From the reviewed books above, it is obvious that most of the books provide excellent coverage of the theoretical aspects of the BGP protocol, yet they lack coverage of a comprehensive practical design and of the implementation of BGP's attributes.

Therefore, the work in this dissertation is motivated by the limitations of the practical implementations of the BGP protocol as a comprehensive network that contains all the major attributes of the protocol. Another critical motivation for this work is the demand for a simple yet comprehensive BGP tutorial that can be delivered to students in the MSc Advanced Computer Networks (CCNP) course at Sheffield Hallam University. This protocol is not presented in MSc networking professional courts (CCNA) despite its importance to internet routing. This leads us to recognise the requirement of the pure understand of this important protocol for students in such a CCNP course. Consequently, this raises too much complexity for the understanding of basic concepts, design, and practical implementations, especially for students in the network field of research. This dissertation reviews the material and resources of such a protocol in the literature and also investigates its practical design and implementation aspects. Thus, this work has come up with the main steps that need to be followed by students in order to implement a complete, practical network with all these attributes by using a GNS3 simulation program. These steps are defined and clearly implemented to provide students with the pure understanding of BGP's dynamics to configure, diagnose and debug issues related to this protocol.

3. RESEARCH METHODOLOGY

This research focused on the basic concepts of the BGP protocol and its attributes, leading to the formulation of a hypothesis about network behavior. The hypothesis was tested in practical implementation using the GNS3 simulator to create a product that could be related to existing network routing protocols. The research method was deductive, using literature from online, CCNA, books, journals, and conference papers. The project was designed and implemented using the simulator, and qualitative analysis was used to answer key questions related to the product. The findings indicate a deductive approach to the research.

3.1. Deductive Approach

Notably, the research approach of this work was deductive. The deductive approach assists researchers in finding relationships between collected data and existing theories to draw reasonable conclusions for research (Saunders, Lewis, & Thornhill, 2023). Blaikie and Priest (2019) argues that a deductive approach is concerned with testing the validity of existing theories or hypotheses. The deductive approach is used when a researcher aims to confirm or reject the proposed hypothesises through empirical evidence (Dudovskiy, 2022).

3.2. Qualitative Approach

Also, the current work is qualitative, because it aims to answer questions such as *what, how,* and *why* about a phenomenon (Gephart & Saylors, 2020). A focus group, which is one of the commonly used qualitative approaches, was applied in this work. The group discussions, which contained seven students, were useful in discussing some important topics related to the current work. The data used in this study were presented as table and figures that reveal the implementation of the BGP attributes. All the required data, as well as the steps needed to gain the benefits of this study, were clarified in the Practical Design chapter.

3.3. Simulation Approach

Simulation was the method chosen for the work in this dissertation for the implementation of the product due to its suitability. It is specifically used in the Computer Science(CS) field of study, as it can offers the possibility of investigating systems or regimes that are separate from the experimental domain or systems that are still under invention or creation (Mbanaso, Abrahams, & Okafor, 2023). The implementation of this design demanded the adaptation of a suitable simulator to conduct the experiment and to achieve the desired understanding of the BGP routing protocol and its attributes. Thus the simulation method was required.

A comprehensive network that was implemented in this project was designed, as mentioned previously in the literature review. Therefore, some data sources were collected by reviewing the literature and connecting the design with what was already available in this field of study. Its aim was to link students with the available information as well as to ease their understanding into the concepts and implementation of the BGP protocol. A virtual machine was used in this current network to make the implementation simple and easy for the students to understand, which is considered a main contribution of this project.

3.4 Data Analysis

The data from the interviews were collected and summarised to address and improve weaknesses. There was no statistical analysis or numeric presentation (charts and graphs) in this research. Figure (3) display the four steps of the qualitative analysis that had been used in this research.

Figure 3. Steps of qualitative data analysis

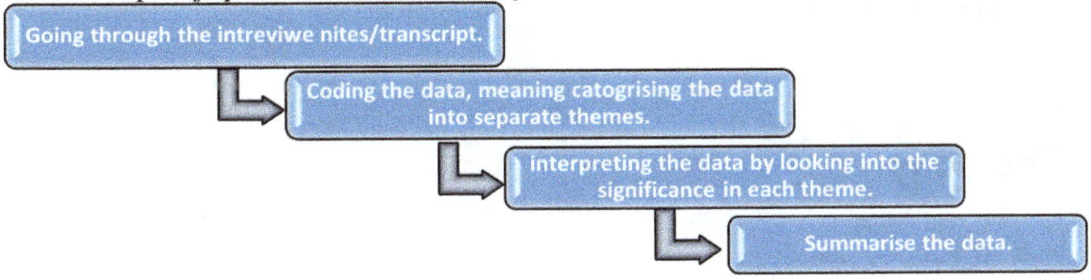

3.5 Tools

This research applied the simulation method to investigate and implement the BGP routing protocol with various attributes by using GNS3 software as the primary tool to conduct the investigation. Although Packet Tracer is another tool used in the field of network research, it was not used during this work, as it does not support commands in Cisco IOS routers and switches (Nedyalkov, 2023; Sholeha et al., 2025). Also, real machine hardware was not used, since GNS3 gives the same accuracy of outcomes as dedicated network hardware. In addition, real machines would consume a large number of serial interfaces to implement the current lab design.

Winata et al. (2024); Ferdinand et al. (2024), explain that the graphical network simulator (GNS3) is an emulation program used broadly to create virtual networks, and it gives good results. In addition, this software allows the researcher to apply a virtual environment as a real lab environment for learning complicated networks. When GNS3 was used during the practical study of this project, it did not require dealing with dedicated network hardware devices such as routers.

Therefore, GNS3 version 0.8.7 and eight routers (OSI Image: c3725-adventerprisek9-mz.124-15.T5.bin) were applied in our work, as GNS3 overcomes the limitations of other simulators and offers a simple way to build networks of any size and without the requirements for hardware applications. Additionally, it is useful in building, designing and testing the network in a risk-free virtual environment, and has the ability to access a large network community.

4. PRACTICAL DESIGN

This chapter discusses the actual practical tutorial that has been created in Graphical Network Simulator version 3 (GNS3). This comprehensive practical topology will demonstrate:

- Internal and External Border Gateway Protocol (BGP).
- Different BGP attributes.

4.1. Topology

Figure 4. Topology diagram

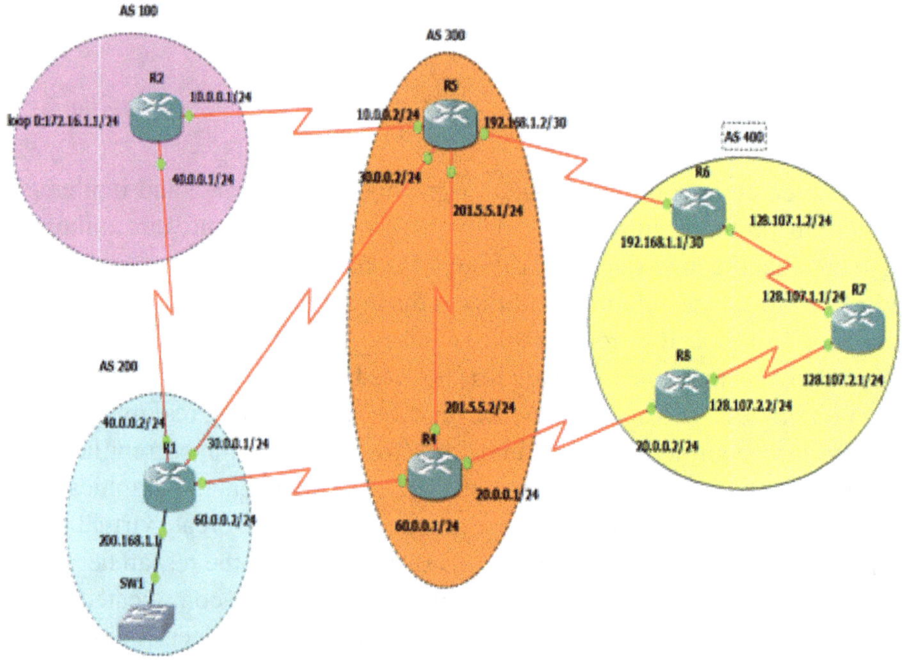

In this skill topology challenge, the focus is on how BGP applies configurations in various attributes to select certain routes. This lab is to give an opportunity to apply and learn the path selection techniques using the GNS3 simulation program. The first step in this lab is to configure IP addressing for all devices. Then the IGP routing needs to be configured for the portion of the network within the AS (if the AS has two or more routers). The next step is to configure the eBGP among the ASes, and the iBGP inside the AS. The final step is to configure and change the BGP attributes to select particular paths.

4.2 IP Addressing Table:

Table 1. IP Addressing Table

Autonomous System (AS)	Device	Interface	IP Address	Subnet Mask
AS 100	R2	S1/1	40.0.0.1	255.255.255.0
		S1/2	10.0.0.1	255.255.255.0
		Loop 0	172.16.1.1	255.255.255.0
AS 200	**R1**	S1/0	60.0.0.2	255.255.255.0
		S1/1	40.0.0.2	255.255.255.0
		S1/3	30.0.0.1	255.255.255.0
		F0/0	200.168.1.1	255.255.255.0
AS 300	**R4**	S1/0	60.0.0.1	255.255.255.0
		S1/1	201.5.5.2	255.255.255.0
		S1/2	20.0.0.1	255.255.255.0
	R5	S1/0	192.168.1.2	255.255.255.252
		S1/1	201.5.5.1	255.255.255.0
		S1/2	10.0.0.2	255.255.255.0
		S1/3	30.0.0.2	255.255.255.0
AS 400	**R6**	S1/0	192.168.1.1	255.255.255.252
		S1/2	128.107.1.2	255.255.255.0
	R7	S1/1	128.107.2.1	255.255.255.0
		S1/2	128.107.1.1	255.255.255.0
	R8	S1/1	128.107.2.2	255.255.255.0
		S1/2	20.0.0.2	255.255.255.0

4.3 Required Resource

- **GNS3 software:**
  - 8 Routers (OSI Image: c3725-adventerprisek9-mz.124-15.T5.bin).

4.4 Implementation

Part 1: Configure Basic Device Settings

In Part 1 of this lab, the main requirement is to establish the network topology and to configure essential settings, such as the interface IP addresses, host names, and OSPF configuration. All steps should be implemented on AS 300 (R4 and R5) and AS 400 (R6, R7 and R8). Only steps 1 and 2 need to be implemented on AS 100 (R2) and AS 200 (R1).

Configure the OSPF protocol in this lab as an example of IGPs. Any other types of IGPs can be used. Additionally, as mentioned previously, configuring IGPs within an autonomous system is very important for routing packets among all routers. It is mandatory for origin attributes. More information is in part 3.

Step 1. Build the network as displayed in the topology.

Attach the routers, as presented in the topology diagram. Figure 4.

Step 2. Configure basic settings for each router.

1. Configure the host names as displayed in the diagram.
2. Configure the interface IP addresses as presented in the IP addressing table.

Step 3. Configure the OSPF within AS 300 AND AS400 as shown in the topology Figure 4.

a. Configure the OSPF within AS 300 between R4 and R5.

```
R4(config)#router ospf 300
R4(config- router)#network 201.5.5.1 0.0.0.0 area 0
R5(config)#router ospf 300
R5(config- router)#network 201.5.5.1 0.0.0.0 area 0
```

b. Configure the OSPF within AS 400 between R6, R7 and R8.

```
R6(config)#router ospf 400
R6(config- router)#network 128.107.1.2 0.0.0.0 area 0
R7(config)#router ospf 400
R7(config- router)#network 128.107.1.1 0.0.0.0 area 0
R7(config- router)#network 128.107.2.1 0.0.0.0 area 0
```

```
R8(config)#router ospf 400
R8(config- router)#network 128.107.2.2 0.0.0.0 area 0
```

Step 4. Verify connectivity to each AS (AS 300 AND AS 400) of the OSPF.

Pings between R6, R7 and R8 in AS 400, and pings between R4 and R5 in AS 300 should be successful.

Part 2: Configure BGP (External and Internal) and Verify Connectivity

The BGP definition in Section 2.1, there are two sessions of BGP, external and internal. The external session, eBGP, works between two or more different ASs and this is implemented using steps 1, 2, 3, 4, 5 and 6. The internal session, iBGP, works within the same AS; this type is implemented using step 7.

Configure eBGP by using the (router bgp) command with the AS number. Also, peers are configured manually (neighbour x.x.x.x) x.x.x.x refers to each peer's IP address (remote-as xx) xx refers to the AS number of peers.

Step 1. Configure eBGP between router R6 and R5 and advertise the network in BGP on R6.

```
R6(config)#router bgp 400
R6(config- router)#neighbor 192.168.1.2 remote-as 300
```

Advertise the network in BGP on R6.

There are two ways to advertise the network in BGP. They are network command and redistribution (from OSPF into the BGP process).

```
R6(config- router)#network 128.107.1.0 mask 255.255.255.0
R6(config- router)#network 128.107.2.0 mask 255.255.255.0
```

Step 2. Configure eBGP between routers R5 and (R1, R2and R6), and advertise the network in BGP on R5.

```
R5(config)#router bgp 300
R5(config- router)#neighbor 192.168.1.1 remote-as 400
*Mar 1 07:40:54.253:%BGP-5ADJCHANGE: neighbor 193.168.1.1 Up
R5(config- router)#neighbor 10.0.0.1 remote-as 100
R5(config- router)#neighbor 30.0.0.1 remote-as 200
```

Advertise the network in BGP on R5.

```
R5(config- router)#network 201.5.5.0 mask 255.255.255.0
```

Note:The yellow line above shows the establishment of the relationship between R5 and R6

Step 3. Configure eBGP between routers R2 and (R1 and R5), and advertise the network in BGP on R2.

R2(config)#router bgp 100
R2(config- router)#neighbor 10.0.0.2 remote-as 300
R2(config- router)#neighbor 40.0.0.2 remote-as 200
*Mar 1 08:57:26.193:%BGP-5ADJCHANGE: neighbor 10.0.0.2 Up
Note:This line displays the relationship between R2 and R5
Advertise the network in BGP on R2.
R5(config- router)#network 172.16.1.0 mask 255.255.255.0

Step 4. Configure eBGP between routers R1 and (R2, R5 and R4), and advertise the network in BGP on R1.

R1(config)#router bgp 200
R1(config- router)#neighbor 40.0.0.1 remote-as 100
R1(config- router)#neighbor 30.0.0.2 remote-as 300
*Mar 1 09:12:43.849:%BGP-5ADJCHANGE: neighbor 40.0.0.1 Up
R1(config- router)#neighbor 60.0.0.2 remote-as 300
*Mar 1 09:13:07.129:%BGP-5ADJCHANGE: neighbor 30.0.0.2 Up
Advertise the network in BGP on R1.
R1(config- router)#network 200.168.1.0 mask 255.255.255.0

The two line above shown the establishment of the relationship between R1 and R5, R1 and R2.

Step 5. Configure eBGP between routers R4 and (R1 and R8),and advertise the network in BGP on R4.

R4(config)#router bgp 300
R4(config- router)#neighbor 60.0.0.2 remote-as 200
*Mar 1 09:25:02.581:%BGP-5ADJCHANGE: neighbor 60.0.0.2 Up
R4(config- router)#neighbor 20.0.0.2 remote-as 400
Advertise the network in BGP on R4.
R1(config- router)#network 201.5.5.0 mask 255.255.255.0

Step 6. Configure EBGP between router R8 and R4, and advertise the network in BGP on R8 by using redistribute OSPF.

R8(config)#router bgp 400
R8(config- router)#neighbor 20.0.0.1 remote-as 300
*Mar 1 09:39:51.837:%BGP-5ADJCHANGE: neighbor 20.0.0.1 Up
Advertise the network in BGP on R8 by using redistribute OSPF.
R8(config- router)#rdistribute ospf 400

Step 7. Achieve full connectivity. Use only BGP.

a) Issue the **show ip bgp summary** command in each router to ensure you have reachability from all BGP neighbour.
b) Issue the **show ip route** command in R8 as an example, have you seen BGP display routing table Figure 5?

Figure 5. routing table in R8

```
R8#show ip route
Codes: C - connected, S - static, R - RIP, M - mobile, B - BGP
       D - EIGRP, EX - EIGRP external, O - OSPF, IA - OSPF inter area
       N1 - OSPF NSSA external type 1, N2 - OSPF NSSA external type 2
       E1 - OSPF external type 1, E2 - OSPF external type 2
       i - IS-IS, su - IS-IS summary, L1 - IS-IS level-1, L2 - IS-IS level-2
       ia - IS-IS inter area, * - candidate default, U - per-user static route
       o - ODR, P - periodic downloaded static route

Gateway of last resort is not set

B    201.5.5.0/24 [20/0] via 20.0.0.1, 00:01:44
B    200.168.1.0/24 [20/0] via 20.0.0.1, 00:00:43
     20.0.0.0/24 is subnetted, 1 subnets
C       20.0.0.0 is directly connected, Serial1/2
     172.16.0.0/24 is subnetted, 1 subnets
B       172.16.1.0 [20/0] via 20.0.0.1, 00:00:12
     128.107.0.0/24 is subnetted, 2 subnets
C       128.107.2.0 is directly connected, Serial1/1
O       128.107.1.0 [110/128] via 128.107.2.1, 16:19:33, Serial1/1
```

c) How many network displays are in R8 via BGP?
d) Issue the **show ip bgp** command in R8.

Figure 6. the BGP routing table in R8.

```
R8#show ip bgp
BGP table version is 18, local router ID is 128.107.2.2
Status codes: s suppressed, d damped, h history, * valid, > best, i - internal,
              r RIB-failure, S Stale
Origin codes: i - IGP, e - EGP, ? - incomplete

   Network          Next Hop            Metric LocPrf Weight Path
*> 128.107.1.0/24   128.107.2.1            128         32768 ?
*> 128.107.2.0/24   0.0.0.0                  0         32768 ?
*> 172.16.1.0/24    20.0.0.1                               0 300 200 100 i
*> 200.168.1.0      20.0.0.1                               0 300 200 i
*> 201.5.5.0        20.0.0.1                 0             0 300 i
```

From points (b) and (d), you will see R8 learn about networks 172.16.1.0/24, 200.168.1.0/24 and 201.5.5.0/24 via 20.0.0.1. Network 128.107.2.0 is directly connected, and 128.107.1.0 is connected by IGP. Issue the **show ip bgp** command in R4, as shown in Figure 7. After that, try to ping from R4 to interface 128.107.1.2 on R6 (AS400). Was it successful? Why? Why not?

Figure 7. BGP routing table in R4

```
R4#show ip bgp
BGP table version is 6, local router ID is 201.5.5.2
Status codes: s suppressed, d damped, h history, * valid, > best, i - internal,
              r RIB-failure, S Stale
Origin codes: i - IGP, e - EGP, ? - incomplete

   Network          Next Hop            Metric LocPrf Weight Path
*> 128.107.1.0/24   20.0.0.2               128             0 400 ?
*> 128.107.2.0/24   20.0.0.2                 0             0 400 ?
*> 172.16.1.0/24    60.0.0.2                               0 200 100 i
*> 200.168.1.0      60.0.0.2                 0             0 200 i
*> 201.5.5.0        0.0.0.0                  0         32768 i
```

Figure 8. Troubleshooting the accessibility from R4 to interface 128.107.1.2 in R6.

```
R4#ping 128.107.1.2

Type escape sequence to abort.
Sending 5, 100-byte ICMP Echos to 128.107.1.2, timeout is 2 seconds:
.....
Success rate is 0 percent (0/5)
```

To answer the question above about reachability from R4 to interface 128.107.1.2 in R6, apply the next step, which is the configuration of the iBGP on all routers within the AS.

Step 8. Configure iBGP on all routers within AS 300 and AS 400.

It is important to configure iBGP within AS 300 between R4 and R5 because R5 receives an eBGP update from R1, R2, or R6. R4 will learn about these updates through R5. Also, in AS 400, if R8 receives an eBGP update from R4, R8 will update its two iBGP peers (R6 and R7). The same thing will happen in R6. Additionally, all routers are connected by iBGP in this topology, which is fully meshed.

You should apply the command next-hop-self in the brother router (edge-router) only as part of the iBGP peer connection. Using next-hop-self confirms that the next hop can be reached from within the AS.

a) Configure the iBGP within AS 300 between R4 and R5.
   1. iBGP on R4

R4(config)#router bgp 300
R4(config- router)#neighbor 201.5.5.1 remote-as 300
R4(config- router)#neighbor 201.5.5.1 next-hop-self

2. iBGP on R5

R5(config)#router bgp 300
R5(config- router)#neighbor 201.5.5.2 remote-as 300
R5(config- router)#neighbor 201.5.5.2 next-hop-self
*Mar 1 09:57:32.081:%BGP-5-ADJCHANGE: neighbor 201.5.5.2 Up

b) Configure the iBGP within AS 400 between R6, R7 and R8.
   1. iBGP on R6

R6(config)#router bgp 400
R6(config- router)#neighbor 128.107.1.1 remote-as 400
R6(config- router)#neighbor 128.107.1.1 next-hop-self
R6(config- router)#neighbor 128.107.2.2 remote-as 400
R6(config- router)#neighbor 128.107.2.2 next-hop-self

2. iBGP on R8

R8(config)#router bgp 400
R8(config- router)#neighbor 128.107.1.2 remote-as 400
R8(config- router)#neighbor 128.107.1.2 next-hop-self
R8(config- router)#neighbor 128.107.2.1 remote-as 400
R8(config- router)#neighbor 128.107.2.1 next-hop-self
*Mar 1 10:34:26.141:%BGP-5-ADJCHANGE: neighbor 128.107.1.2 Up

3. iBGP on R7

R7(config)#router bgp 400
R7(config- router)#neighbor 128.107.1.2 remote-as 400
*Mar 1 10:31:46.873:%BGP-5-ADJCHANGE: neighbor 128.107.1.2 Up
R7(config- router)#neighbor 128.107.2.2 remote-as 400
*Mar 1 10:33:57.133:%BGP-5-ADJCHANGE: neighbor 128.107.2.2 Up

Display the BGP routing table in R7 as shown in Figure 9 by using the command **show ip bgp.**

Figure 9. the BGP routing table in R7

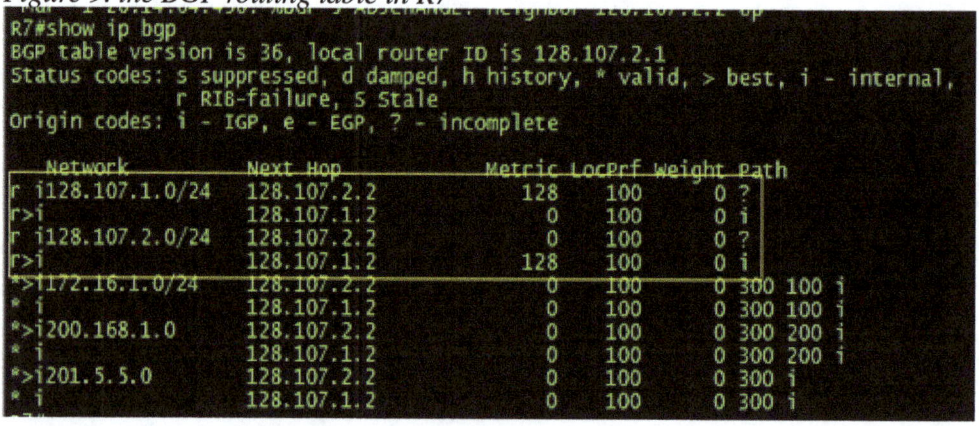

```
R7#show ip bgp
BGP table version is 36, local router ID is 128.107.2.1
Status codes: s suppressed, d damped, h history, * valid, > best, i - internal,
              r RIB-failure, S Stale
Origin codes: i - IGP, e - EGP, ? - incomplete

   Network          Next Hop            Metric LocPrf Weight Path
r i128.107.1.0/24   128.107.2.2            128    100      0 ?
r>i                 128.107.1.2              0    100      0 i
r i128.107.2.0/24   128.107.2.2              0    100      0 ?
r>i                 128.107.1.2            128    100      0 i
*>i172.16.1.0/24    128.107.2.2              0    100      0 300 100 i
* i                 128.107.1.2              0    100      0 300 100 i
*>i200.168.1.0      128.107.2.2              0    100      0 300 200 i
* i                 128.107.1.2              0    100      0 300 200 i
*>i201.5.5.0        128.107.2.2              0    100      0 300 i
* i                 128.107.1.2              0    100      0 300 i
```

As displayed in Figure 9, there are two (i) symbols on the left, under the network column. These indicate the networks have been learned via iBGP, whereas (r) RIP-failure would indicate these networks are in the same AS.

Step 9. Confirm you have full reachability for this topology.

a) Issue the **show ip bgp summary** command in each router to ensure that you have reachability among the whole network, and the neighbour relationships are clearly shown.
b) Verify each router has full connectivity by issuing the **show ip bgp** command.
c) Ping from **R7** to interfaces **200.168.1.1, 201.5.5.1** and **172.16.1.1**.

The pings should be successful.

d) Ping from **R8** to interfaces **200.168.1.1, 201.5.5.1** and **172.16.1.1.**

Is it successful?

e) Trying again to ping from **R8** to interfaces **200.168.1.1, 201.5.5.1** and **172.16.1.1** by using the source of the internal interface, for example:

R8 # ping 200.168.1.1 source 128.107.2.2
Is it successfully? Why?

Part 3: Configure and Change the BGP Attributes

There are two notable attributes, the origin attribute and the NEXT-HOP attribute. These two attributes already exist in the BGP routing table built during part 2 of this lab. There are three types of origin attributes, as mentioned previously: IGP, internal to the AS, shown as (i) in the table; EGP, shown as (e); and INCOMPLETE, which is shown as (?) in the table, as shown clearly in Figures 6 and 9. The other attribute is the next-hop. This attribute can be obtained by using either eBGP or iBGP sessions. It shows in the table as next-hop, for example, as in Figure 10, in the second column of the table. Moreover, the next-hop self command that is learned from eBGP is useful for carrying unchanged into iBGP. This is shown in Part 2, Step 8 (Configure iBGP).

Step 1. Changing the AS Path attribute.

R8 should have two paths to reach network 200.168.1.0 /24. Confirm that by using **show ip bgp** command as shown in Figure 10.

Figure 10. Display BGP routing table before changing AS Path in R8

```
R8#show ip bgp
BGP table version is 14, local router ID is 128.107.2.2
Status codes: s suppressed, d damped, h history, * valid, > best, i - internal,
              r RIB-failure, S Stale
Origin codes: i - IGP, e - EGP, ? - incomplete

   Network          Next Hop            Metric LocPrf Weight Path
*> 128.107.1.0/24   128.107.2.1            128         32768 ?
* i                 128.107.1.2              0    100      0 i
*> 128.107.2.0/24   0.0.0.0                  0         32768 ?
* i                 128.107.1.2            128    100      0 i
*> 172.16.1.0/24    20.0.0.1                               0 300 100 i
* i                 128.107.1.2              0    100      0 300 100 i
*> 200.168.1.0      20.0.0.1                               0 300 200 i
* i                 128.107.1.2              0    100      0 300 200 i
*> 201.5.5.0        20.0.0.1                 0             0 300 i
* i                 128.107.1.2              0    100      0 300 i
```

The BGP routing table of R8 in Figure 10, there are two paths to reach network 200.168.1.0 /24. The best path selection has the symbol (>) via NEXT_HOP (20.0.0.1). If you want to change the path to choose R6 (128.107.1.2) rather than R8 for some security issue or due to the amount of bandwidth in the two paths, perform the following:

Configure the AS Path prepending on R4 so that R8 sends all traffic to network **200.168.1.0 /24** through R6 (**128.107.1.2**).

1. Filter R4 by using the prefix-list named **pfPhlist** and the route_map called **Asp** on R4 to allow traffic to network **200.168.1.0 /24**, and prepend three AS numbers (300, 500, and 600) to the AS to make it longer.

   R4(config)#ip prefix-list pfPhlist permit 200.168.1.0/24
   R4(config)#route-map Asp permit 10
   R4(config- route-map)# match ip address prefix-list pfPhlist
   R4(config- route-map)#set as-path prepend 300 500 600
   R4(config- route-map)# route-map Asp permit 20

2. Apply route_map in **R8** by outbound in **R4.**

   R4(config)#router bgp 300
   R4(config- router)#neighbor 20.0.0.2 route-map Asp out

3. Issue the **clear ip bgp** * command on R4 to update the BGP table.
4. Issue the **show ip bgp** command on R8, as shown in Figure 11. Has the AS path changed R8's decision about reaching **200.168.1.0 /24?**

Figure 11. Display BGP routing table after changing AS Path in R8

```
R8#show ip bgp
BGP table version is 21, local router ID is 128.107.2.2
Status codes: s suppressed, d damped, h history, * valid, > best, i - internal,
              r RIB-failure, S Stale
Origin codes: i - IGP, e - EGP, ? - incomplete

   Network          Next Hop            Metric LocPrf Weight Path
*> 128.107.1.0/24   128.107.2.1            128         32768 ?
*> 128.107.2.0/24   0.0.0.0                  0         32768 ?
* i172.16.1.0/24    128.107.1.2              0    100      0 300 100 i
*>                  20.0.0.1                               0 300 100 i
*>i200.168.1.0      128.107.1.2              0    100      0 300 200 i
*                   20.0.0.1                               0 300 300 500 600 200 i
* i201.5.5.0        128.107.1.2              0    100      0 300 i
*>                  20.0.0.1                 0             0 300 i
```

Step 2. Changing the weight attribute.

As mentioned previously, in the BGP Path Attributes section, weight is a Cisco proprietary attribute. It has a higher priority process than any of the other attributes (Bonczkowski, 2025). In this step, you will see that the highest weight with a longer path is preferred over a smaller weight with a shorter path. There are two methods you will use in this step to change the weight. The first way is setting the weight command; the second way is setting route_map policy. Follow these steps:

Figure 12. Display BGP routing table before changing weight in R8

```
R8#show ip bgp
BGP table version is 20, local router ID is 128.107.2.2
Status codes: s suppressed, d damped, h history, * valid, > best, i - internal,
              r RIB-failure, S Stale
Origin codes: i - IGP, e - EGP, ? - incomplete

   Network          Next Hop            Metric LocPrf Weight Path
*> 128.107.1.0/24   128.107.2.1            128         32768 ?
* i                 128.107.1.2              0    100      0 i
*> 128.107.2.0/24   0.0.0.0                  0         32768 ?
* i                 128.107.1.2            128    100      0 i
*> 172.16.1.0/24    20.0.0.1                               0 300 100 i
* i                 128.107.1.2              0    100      0 300 100 i
*  200.168.1.0      20.0.0.1                               0 300 300 500 600 200 i
*>i                 128.107.1.2              0    100      0 300 200 i
*> 201.5.5.0        20.0.0.1                 0             0 300 i
* i                 128.107.1.2              0    100      0 300 i
```

1. Issue the **show ip bgp** command on R8 as display in Figure 12.
2. Changing the weight without route_map.

a) Change the weight on R8, so that all networks learned through R4 (**20.0.0.1**) have a weight of 500.

R8(config)#router bgp 400
R8(config- router)#neighbor 20.0.0.1 weight 500

b) Issue the **clear ip bgp** * command on R8 to update BGP table.
c) Issue the show ip bgp command on R8 again, as illustrated in Figure 13. The path should be changed.

Figure 13. Display BGP routing table after changing weight in R8

```
R8#show ip bgp
BGP table version is 10, local router ID is 128.107.2.2
Status codes: s suppressed, d damped, h history, * valid, > best, i - internal,
              r RIB-failure, S Stale
Origin codes: i - IGP, e - EGP, ? - incomplete

   Network          Next Hop            Metric LocPrf Weight Path
*> 128.107.1.0/24   128.107.2.1            128         32768 ?
* i                 128.107.1.2              0    100      0 i
*> 128.107.2.0/24   0.0.0.0                  0         32768 ?
* i                 128.107.1.2            128    100      0 i
* i172.16.1.0/24    128.107.1.2              0    100      0 300 100 i
*>                  20.0.0.1                             500 300 100 i
* i200.168.1.0      128.107.1.2              0    100      0 300 200 i
*>                  20.0.0.1                             500 300 300 500 600 200 i
* i201.5.5.0        128.107.1.2              0    100      0 300 i
*>                  20.0.0.1                 0           500 300 i
R8#
```

When assigning the weight command, it will apply to all networks that are reached through R4 (20.0.0.1), as shown in the BGP table on R8 in Figure 13. If you want to assign a weight in a certain network, you must use route_map and implement the following:

3. Changing the weight use route_map.
   a. Delete the weight command on **R8.**
   b. Issue the **clear ip bgp** * command on R8 to update the BGP table.
   c. Issue the **show ip bgp** command on R8 again. It should be the same as in Figure 12.
   d. Configure the weight on R8 by using the prefix-list named **pfweigh**t and the route_map called **www,** so R8 sends all traffic to network **200.168.1.0 /24** through R4 (**20.0.0.1**), and set the weight to 500.

R4(config)#ip prefix-list pfweight permit 200.168.1.0/24
R4(config)#route-map www permit 10

R4(config- route-map)# match ip address prefix-list pfweight
R4(config- route-map)#set weight 500
R4(config- route-map)# route-map www permit 20

e. Assign route_map in R4 by inbound in R8.

R8(config)#router bgp 400
R8(config- router)#neighbor 20.0.0.1 route-map www in

f. Issue the **clear ip bgp *** command on R8 to update the BGP table.
g. Issue the **show ip bgp** command on R8. Does the path to 200.168.1.0/24 change?
h. Is any other network changing its weight? Why? Why not?

Figure 14. Display the BGP routing table after changing weight in R8by using rote-map

```
R8#show ip bgp
BGP table version is 21, local router ID is 128.107.2.2
Status codes: s suppressed, d damped, h history, * valid, > best, i - internal,
              r RIB-failure, S Stale
Origin codes: i - IGP, e - EGP, ? - incomplete

   Network          Next Hop            Metric LocPrf Weight Path
* i128.107.1.0/24   128.107.1.2              0    400      0 i
*>                  128.107.2.1            128         32768 ?
* i128.107.2.0/24   128.107.1.2            128    400      0 i
*>                  0.0.0.0                  0         32768 ?
*>i172.16.1.0/24    128.107.1.2              0    400      0 300 100 i
*                   20.0.0.1                               0 300 100 i
* i200.168.1.0      128.107.1.2              0    400      0 300 200 i
*>                  20.0.0.1                             500 300 300 500 600 200 i
*>i201.5.5.0        128.107.1.2              0    400      0 300 i
*                   20.0.0.1                 0             0 300 i
```

Step 3. Changing the local preference attribute:

As referred to in 2.3 BGP Path Attributes, this step applies the local preference attribute and also impacts the BGP decision process (Alhiary, 2025). The local preference is passed only to the iBGP peers. A higher value of the local preference is preferred, and the local preference has a higher level in BGP decisions than other attributes (after the weight attribute) (Welekwe, 2024). In this step, there are two methods that will be used to change the local preference. The first one is setting the local preference command; the other is applying the route_map policy.

Issue the **show ip bgp** command on R7.

From the output of the BGP table of R7 in Figure 15, notice that there are two paths to reach network 172.16.1.0 /24, and that the best route via next_hop is (128.107.2.2).

Figure 15. Display the BGP routing table before changing local preference in R7

```
R7#show ip bgp
BGP table version is 53, local router ID is 128.107.2.1
Status codes: s suppressed, d damped, h history, * valid, > best, i - internal,
              r RIB-failure, S Stale
Origin codes: i - IGP, e - EGP, ? - incomplete

   Network          Next Hop            Metric LocPrf Weight Path
r i128.107.1.0/24   128.107.2.2            128    100      0 ?
r>i                 128.107.1.2              0    100      0 i
r i128.107.2.0/24   128.107.2.2              0    100      0 ?
r>i                 128.107.1.2            128    100      0 i
*>i172.16.1.0/24    128.107.2.2              0    100      0 300 100 i
* i                 128.107.1.2              0    100      0 300 100 i
* i200.168.1.0      128.107.2.2              0    100      0 300 300 500 600 200 i
*>i                 128.107.1.2              0    100      0 300 200 i
*>i201.5.5.0        128.107.2.2              0    100      0 300 i
* i                 128.107.1.2              0    100      0 300 i
R7#
```

To change the route to select R6 (128.107.1.2) rather than R8 by the local preference attribute, which has the default value of (100), follow this sequence:

1) Configure the local preference on R6 so that all networks learned through R6 (128.107.1.2) have a local preference of 400.

   R6(config)#router bgp 400
   R6(config- router)#bgp default local-preference 400

2) Issue the **clear ip bgp** * command on R6.
3) Issue the **show ip bgp** command on R7 again, as demonstrated in Figure 16. The route should be changed.

Figure 16. Display BGP routing table after changing local preference in R7

```
R7#show ip bgp
BGP table version is 70, local router ID is 128.107.2.1
Status codes: s suppressed, d damped, h history, * valid, > best, i - internal,
              r RIB-failure, S Stale
Origin codes: i - IGP, e - EGP, ? - incomplete

   Network          Next Hop            Metric LocPrf Weight Path
r>i128.107.1.0/24   128.107.1.2              0    400      0 i
r i                 128.107.2.2            128    100      0 ?
r>i128.107.2.0/24   128.107.1.2            128    400      0 i
r i                 128.107.2.2              0    100      0 ?
*>i172.16.1.0/24    128.107.1.2              0    400      0 300 100 i
*>i200.168.1.0      128.107.1.2              0    400      0 300 200 i
* i                 128.107.2.2              0    100      0 300 300 500 600 200 i
*>i201.5.5.0        128.107.1.2              0    400      0 300 i
```

4) Configure the local preference, use route_map.
   a. Delete the local preference command on **R6.**
   b. Issue the **clear ip bgp** * command on R6 to update the BGP table.
   c. Issue the **show ip bgp** command on R6 again. It should be the same as in Figure 15.
   d. Configure the local preference on R6 by using the prefix-list named **pfloc** and the route_map called **lopf**, so that R7 sends all traffic to network **172.16.0.0 /24** through R6 (**128.107.1.2**), and set the local preference to (700).

```
R6(config)#ip prefix-list pfloc permit 172.16.1.0 /24
R6(config)#route-map lopf permit 10
R6(config- route-map)# match ip address prefix-list pfloc
R6(config- route-map)#set local-preference 700
R6(config- route-map)# route-map lopf permit 20
R6(config)#router bgp 400
R6(config- router)# neighbor 128.107.1.1 route-map lopf out
```

e. Apply route_map in R7 by outbound in R6.
f. Issue the **clear ip bgp** * command on R6 to update the BGP table.
g. Issue the **show ip bgp** command on R7. Does the path to 172.16.1.0/24 change?

Figure 17. Display BGP routing table after changing local preference in R7 using route-map

```
R7#show ip bgp
BGP table version is 80, local router ID is 128.107.2.1
Status codes: s suppressed, d damped, h history, * valid, > best, i - internal,
              r RIB-failure, S Stale
Origin codes: i - IGP, e - EGP, ? - incomplete

   Network          Next Hop            Metric LocPrf Weight Path
r>i128.107.1.0/24   128.107.1.2              0    100      0 i
r i                 128.107.2.2            128    100      0 ?
r>i128.107.2.0/24   128.107.1.2            128    100      0 i
r i                 128.107.2.2              0    100      0 ?
*>i172.16.1.0/24    128.107.1.2              0    700      0 300 100 i
* i                 128.107.2.2              0    100      0 300 100 i
*>i200.168.1.0      128.107.1.2              0    100      0 300 200 i
* i201.5.5.0        128.107.1.2              0    100      0 300 i
*>i                 128.107.2.2              0    100      0 300 i
```

Step 4. Configure the Multi-Exit-Discriminator (MED) attribute.

As mentioned previously in the BGP Path Attributes section, the MED attribute is applied between two or multiple external links (Bruno & Jordan, 2024). It also shows BGP neighbours in other AS's the route that can be chosen to reach a remote network. . During this lab, the MED attribute was placed among AS 200 and AS 300. Notably, a lower MED value is preferred.

Figure 18. Display of the BGP routing table before configuring the Multi-Exit-Discriminator in R1

```
R1#show ip bgp
BGP table version is 51, local router ID is 200.168.1.1
Status codes: s suppressed, d damped, h history, * valid, > best, i - internal,
              r RIB-failure, S Stale
Origin codes: i - IGP, e - EGP, ? - incomplete

   Network          Next Hop            Metric LocPrf Weight Path
*  128.107.1.0/24   40.0.0.1                               0 100 300 400 i
*>                  30.0.0.2                               0 300 400 i
*                   60.0.0.1                               0 300 400 i
*  128.107.2.0/24   40.0.0.1                               0 100 300 400 i
*>                  30.0.0.2                               0 300 400 i
*                   60.0.0.1                               0 300 400 i
*  172.16.1.0/24    60.0.0.1                               0 300 100 i
*                   30.0.0.2                               0 300 100 i
*>                  40.0.0.1                 0             0 100 i
*> 200.168.1.0      0.0.0.0                  0         32768 i
*  201.5.5.0        60.0.0.1                 0             0 300 i
*                   40.0.0.1                               0 100 300 i
*>                  30.0.0.2                 0             0 300 i
```

The BGP table of R1 has three paths to reach network **201.5.5.0 /24** and the best route via next_hop is (**30.0.0.2**), the reason for selecting this path is that it has the lowest neighbour IP address. Multi-Exit-Discriminator attribute which shown in the BGP table above in Figure 18 as a metric (default value 0) to change the route for choosing next_hop (**60.0.0.1**), following the steps:

1. Configure the MED attribute on R4 by using the prefix-list called **pfmed** and the route_map called **mtc** and set a lower value, 15, for the metric.

```
R4(config)#ip prefix-list pfmed permit 201.5.5.0 /24
R4(config)#route-map mtc permit 10
R4(config- route-map)# match ip address prefix-list pfmed
R4(config- route-map)#set metric 15
R4(config- route-map)# route-map mtc permit 20
```

2. Assign route_map in R1 by outbound in R4.

```
R4(config)#router bgp 300
R4(config- router)# neighbor 60.0.0.2 route-map mtc out
```

3. Issue the **clear ip bgp *** command on R4 to update the BGP table.
4. Configure the MED attribute on R5 by using the prefix-list called **pfmed** and the route_map called **mtc** and set a larger value, 30, for the metric.

```
R5(config)#ip prefix-list pfmed permit 201.5.5.0 /24
R5(config)#route-map mtc permit 10
R5(config- route-map)# match ip address prefix-list pfmed
R5(config- route-map)#set metric 30
R5(config- route-map)# route-map mtc permit 20
```

5. Apply route_map in R1 by outbound in R5.

```
R5(config)#router bgp 300
R5(config- router)# neighbor 30.0.0.1 route-map mtc out
```

6. Update the BGP routing table by use the **clear ip bgp *** command.
7. Ensure R1 will use the route between R1 and R4 to reach the network **201.5.5.0**/24.

Figure 19. Display of the BGP routing table after configuring the Multi-Exit-Discriminator in R1

```
R1#show ip bgp
BGP table version is 40, local router ID is 200.168.1.1
Status codes: s suppressed, d damped, h history, * valid, > best, i - internal,
              r RIB-failure, S Stale
Origin codes: i - IGP, e - EGP, ? - incomplete

   Network          Next Hop            Metric LocPrf Weight Path
*  128.107.1.0/24   40.0.0.1                               0 100 300 400 ?
*                   30.0.0.2                               0 300 400 ?
*>                  60.0.0.1                               0 300 400 ?
*  128.107.2.0/24   40.0.0.1                               0 100 300 400 ?
*                   30.0.0.2                               0 300 400 ?
*>                  60.0.0.1                               0 300 400 ?
*  131.108.0.0      60.0.0.1                               0 300 100 i
*                   30.0.0.2                               0 300 100 i
*>                  40.0.0.1                 0             0 100 i
*  172.16.1.0/24    60.0.0.1                               0 300 100 i
*                   30.0.0.2                               0 300 100 i
*>                  40.0.0.1                 0             0 100 i
*> 200.168.1.0      0.0.0.0                  0         32768 i
*  201.5.5.0        40.0.0.1                               0 100 300 i
*                   30.0.0.2                30             0 300 i
*>                  60.0.0.1                15             0 300 i
```

Step 5. Configure Aggregator attribute.

Sitting the Aggregator attribute also influences traffic and the size of the BGP information table. Also, these aggregators are used to reduce congestion in the network. It can be aggregate a list of prefix routes into a single prefix and send it to certain routers (Bonczkowski, 2025). In this design, three loopback interfaces were created, as shown in Figure 20, that are advertised and aggregated into a single prefix on R2 and then sent to the other AS (remotely). The next steps will be followed to achieve this process.

a. Create loopback interfaces 131.108.2.0/24, 131.108.3.0/24 and 131.108.4.0/24 on R2, as illustrated in Figure 20.

Figure 20. Display adding three loopback interfaces in R2

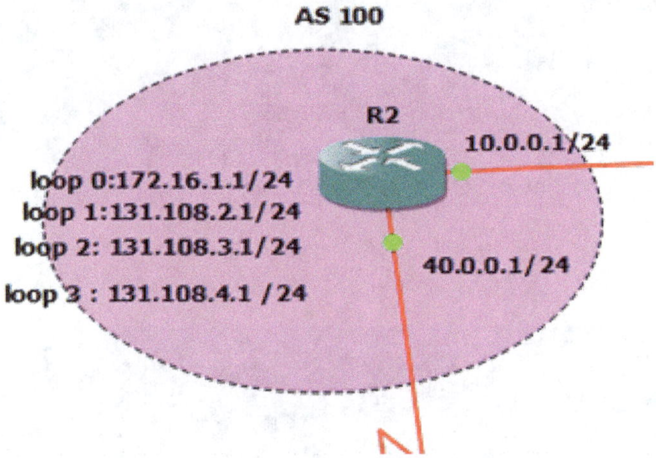

b. Advertise these loopback interfaces.

```
R2(config)# router bgp 100
R2(config- router)#network 131.108.2.0 mask 255.255.255.0
R2(config- router)#network 131.108.3.0 mask 255.255.255.0
R2(config- router)#network 131.108.4.0 mask 255.255.255.0
```

c. Update the BGP table on R2, by applying clear ip bgp * command.
d. Display the BGP information table from any other router to ensure loopback interface reachability from R2. Router R5 is shown below, in Figure 21, as an example.

Figure 21. Display the BGP routing table of R5 before aggregated into a single prefix on R2

```
R5#show ip bgp
BGP table version is 10, local router ID is 201.5.5.1
Status codes: s suppressed, d damped, h history, * valid, > best, i - internal,
              r RIB-failure, S Stale
Origin codes: i - IGP, e - EGP, ? - incomplete

   Network          Next Hop            Metric LocPrf Weight Path
*> 128.107.1.0/24   192.168.1.1              0             0 400 ?
*>i128.107.2.0/24   201.5.5.2                0    100      0 400 ?
*                   192.168.1.1            128             0 400 ?
*  131.108.2.0/24   30.0.0.1                               0 200 100 i
*>                  10.0.0.1                 0             0 100 i
*  131.108.3.0/24   30.0.0.1                               0 200 100 i
*>                  10.0.0.1                 0             0 100 i
*  131.108.4.0/24   30.0.0.1                               0 200 100 i
*>                  10.0.0.1                 0             0 100 i
*  172.16.1.0/24    30.0.0.1                               0 200 100 i
*>                  10.0.0.1                 0             0 100 i
*  200.168.1.0      10.0.0.1                               0 100 200 i
* i                 201.5.5.2                0    100      0 200 i
*>                  30.0.0.1                 0             0 200 i
* i201.5.5.0        201.5.5.2                0    100      0 i
*>                  0.0.0.0                  0         32768 i
```

e. Create a summary for the loopback interfaces on R2

   R2(config)# router bgp 100
   R2(config- router)# aggregate-address 131.108.0.0 255.255.0.0 summary-only

f. Update the BGP table on R2 again, by applying **clear ip bgp *** command.
g. Display the BGP information table on R5.
h. Compere the output in points c and f. What do you notice in network 131.108.0.0/24?

Figure 22. Display of the BGP routing table of R5 after aggregated into a single prefix on R2

```
R5#show ip bgp
BGP table version is 25, local router ID is 201.5.5.1
Status codes: s suppressed, d damped, h history, * valid, > best, i - internal,
              r RIB-failure, S Stale
Origin codes: i - IGP, e - EGP, ? - incomplete

   Network          Next Hop            Metric LocPrf Weight Path
*> 128.107.1.0/24   192.168.1.1              0             0 400 ?
*>i128.107.2.0/24   201.5.5.2                0    100      0 400 ?
*                   192.168.1.1            128             0 400 ?
*  131.108.0.0      30.0.0.1                               0 200 100 i
*>                  10.0.0.1                 0             0 100 i
*  172.16.1.0/24    30.0.0.1                               0 200 100 i
*>                  10.0.0.1                 0             0 100 i
*  200.168.1.0      10.0.0.1                               0 100 200 i
* i                 201.5.5.2                0    100      0 200 i
*>                  30.0.0.1                 0             0 200 i
* i201.5.5.0        201.5.5.2                0    100      0 i
*>                  0.0.0.0                  0         32768 i
```

Step 6. Configure the community attribute.

In the framework of BGP, a community is a collection of destinations that have some common characteristics (Bruno & Jordan, 2024). In this lab, another AS was added to make some changes to the network, as shown in Figure 24. Then two types of community attributes, NO_EXPORT and NO- ADVERTISE, were applied. In the NO_EXPORT type, the network on AS 900 to AS 300 (R4 and R5) was advertised. The main purpose of that was to prevent this information from being distributed to other autonomous systems (eBGP) in the network. However, in the NO- ADVERTISE type, the network on AS 900 to AS 300 (R4) was advertised to prevent the information from being distributed from either the internal or the external peers. To achieve this, the next steps will be followed.

1. Create IP addresses, as shown in Figure 23, for

   R4 (S1/3: 90.0.0.1/24),
   R9 (S1/3:90.0.0.2 /24, loopback 0: 9.9.9.9/24, and
   loopback 1: 19.19.19.19/24).

2. Configure the eBGP between AS 300 and AS 900.

Figure 23. Display adding AS 900 in the topology diagram

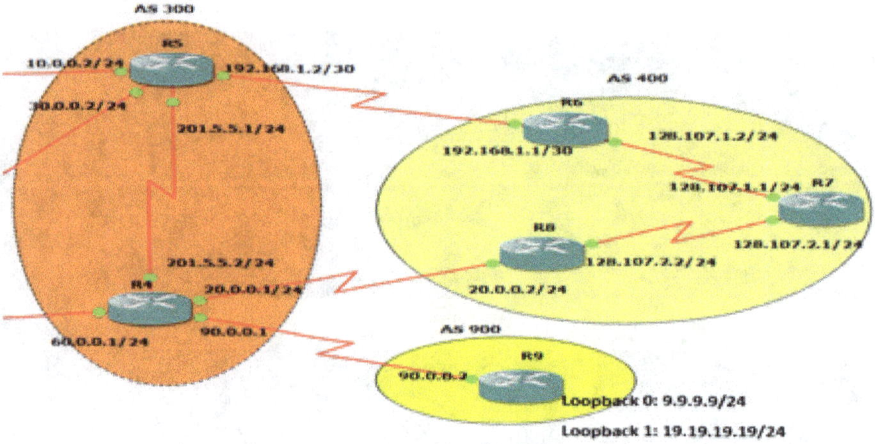

3. Advertise the loopback 0 interface 9.9.9.9/24 and loopback 1: 19.19.19.19/24 on R9 in BGP and confirm AS 900 can reach any network in AS100, AS200, AS 300 and AS 400, as shown in the example in R4, Figure 24.

Figure 24. advertise networks on AS 900 into BGP routing table in R4

```
R4#show  ip bgp
BGP table version is 9, local router ID is 201.5.5.2
Status codes: s suppressed, d damped, h history, * valid, > best, i - internal,
              r RIB-failure, S Stale
Origin codes: i - IGP, e - EGP, ? - incomplete

   Network          Next Hop            Metric LocPrf Weight Path
*> 9.9.9.0/24       90.0.0.2                 0             0 900 i
*> 19.19.19.0/24    90.0.0.2                 0             0 900 i
*>i128.107.1.0/24   201.5.5.1                0    100      0 400 i
*                   20.0.0.2               128             0 400 ?
*>i128.107.2.0/24   201.5.5.1              128    100      0 400 i
*                   20.0.0.2                 0             0 400 ?
*  131.108.0.0      60.0.0.2                               0 200 100 i
*>i                 201.5.5.1                0    100      0 100 i
*  172.16.1.0/24    60.0.0.2                               0 200 100 i
*>i                 201.5.5.1                0    100      0 100 i
*> 200.168.1.0      60.0.0.2                 0             0 200 i
* i                 201.5.5.1                0    100      0 200 i
*> 201.5.5.0        0.0.0.0                  0         32768 i
* i                 201.5.5.1                0    100      0 i
```

4. Configure the communities NO_EXPORT
   a. Configure R4 so that network 9.9.9.0 /24 is identified within AS 300, but does not advertise to any other autonomous systems, by using the prefix-list called PFnoexport and the route_map called NOExport.

R4(config)#ip prefix-list PFnoexport permit 9.9.9.0 /24
R4(config)#route-map NOExport permit 10
R4(config- route-map)# match ip address prefix-list PFnoexport
R4(config- route-map)#set community no-export
R4(config- route-map)# route-map NOExport permit 20

b. Apply the route_map in R9 by inbound in R4, and send the community attribute to the neighbor (201.5.5.1) within AS 300 using send-community.

R4(config)#router bgp 300
R4(config- router)# neighbor 90.0.0.2 route-map NOExport in
R4(config- router)# neighbor 201.5.5.1 send-community

c. Update the BGP database table on R4 using the clear ip bgp * command.
d. Display R4's BGP entry for 9.9.9.0/2 4.

Figure 25. BGP Community no-export

```
R4#show ip bgp 9.9.9.0
BGP routing table entry for 9.9.9.0/24, version 0
Paths: (1 available, no best path)
  Not advertised to any peer
  900
    90.0.0.2 from 90.0.0.2 (9.9.9.9)
      Origin IGP, metric 0, localpref 100, valid, external
      Community: no-export
R4#
```

e. Verify AS100, AS200 and AS 400 cannot reach the network in AS 900 (9.9.9.0/24).

Figure 26. R8 in AS 400 cannot reach the network (9.9.9.0/24) in AS 900

```
R8#show ip bgp
BGP table version is 102, local router ID is 128.107.2.2
Status codes: s suppressed, d damped, h history, * valid, > best, i - internal,
              r RIB-failure, S Stale
Origin codes: i - IGP, e - EGP, ? - incomplete

   Network          Next Hop            Metric LocPrf Weight Path
* i19.19.19.0/24    128.107.1.2              0    100      0 300 900 i
*>                  20.0.0.1                               0 300 900 i
* i128.107.1.0/24   128.107.1.2              0    100      0 i
*>                  128.107.2.1            128         32768 ?
* i128.107.2.0/24   128.107.1.2            128    100      0 i
*>                  0.0.0.0                  0         32768 ?
*> 131.108.0.0      20.0.0.1                               0 300 100 i
* i                 128.107.1.2              0    100      0 300 100 i
*> 172.16.1.0/24    20.0.0.1                               0 300 100 i
* i                 128.107.1.2              0    100      0 300 100 i
*  200.168.1.0      20.0.0.1                               0 300 300 500 600 200 i
*>i                 128.107.1.2              0    100      0 300 200 i
*> 201.5.5.0        20.0.0.1                 0             0 300 i
* i                 128.107.1.2              0    100      0 300 i
```

5. Configure the communities NO_ ADVERTISE
   a. Configure router R4 to prevent the network (19.19.19.0 /24) in R9 from being spread to any other BGP neighbour by using the prefix-list called PFnoadvertise and the route_map called NOAdvertise.

R4(config)#ip prefix-list PFnoadvertise permit 19.19.19.0 /24
R4(config)#route-map NOAdvertise permit 10
R4(config- route-map)# match ip address prefix-list PFnoexport
R4(config- route-map)#set community no-advertise
R4(config- route-map)# route-map NOAdvertise permit 20

b. Place the route_map in R9 by inbound in R4

R4(config)#router bgp 300
R4(config- router)# neighbor 90.0.0.2 route-map NOAdvertise in

c. Update the BGP database table in R4 by using the clear ip bgp * command.
d. Display R4's BGP entry for 19.19.19.0/24.

Figure 27. BGP Community no-advertise

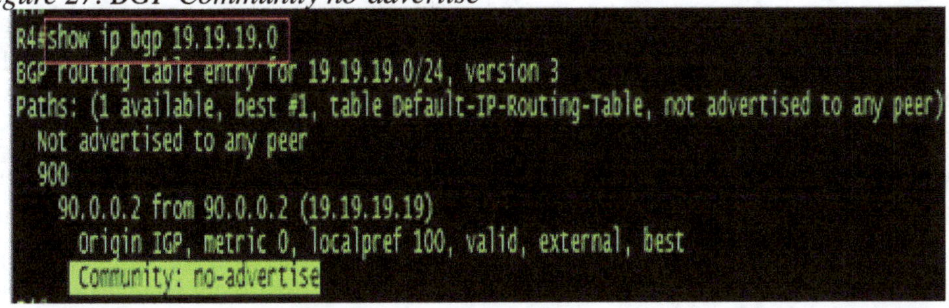

e. Confirm any R4's neighbour cannot reach the network in AS 900 (19.19.19.0/24).

5. DISCUSSION AND FINDING

The primary motivation of this work was inspired by the limitations of the practical implementation of the BGP protocol. Most of the literature lacked the design of a comprehensive network that contains all the major attributes of such a protocol. Some of the literature only provided theoretical concepts and definitions of the BGP protocol, while others provided a practical implementation of just limited attributes of the BGP protocol. Besides, other research of the BGP protocol presented its attributes in different examples rather than in a complete network.

Another critical motivation for this work was the demand for a simple and comprehensive tutorial of BGP that could be delivered to students in the MSc Advanced Computer Networks CCNP course at Sheffield Hallam University. However, a number of limitations were related to the adaptation of this protocol to the CCNP course. First, students who would take the CCNP course should first finish the CCNA course, but the CCNA course lacks the definition of the BGP protocol, despite of its importance to the aspects of internet routing. Therefore, students in the CCNP require a pure understanding of this important protocol to tackle any complexity related to its basic concepts, design, and practical implementation. Another issue is related to how to provide a simple tutorial for implementing a comprehensive network with most of the important attributes. There is a trade-off between simplicity in lab instruction and having a comprehensive network design with most of the BGP attributes, where comprehensive implementation may lead to complexity.

Steps to perform the implementation were put in detail to help students quickly understand this protocol. In addition, steps were easy and clearly ordered to help students, even those with no prior knowledge of the BGP protocol, to have a clear vision of this protocol. Also, these steps are comprehensive, and consequently, by following them, students will be able to design a complete practical network with all these attributes. Also, these steps utilise the prefix filtering techniques instead of the access list because of the former's advantage, as a new added list can tax the processor less than access lists, which is important for improving routers' performance. In addition, a prefix list is more flexible and is easy to configure, and unlike an access list, can be updated incrementally. A sequence number is the only requirement that needs to be specified to add, remove, or modify a given prefix list sequence.

Furthermore, these steps were used by some of the students to test the steps' simplicity, usefulness, and applicability of the BGP protocol to be delivered as a tutorial for students in networking professional studies. It was obvious that these steps could lead to a pure understanding of BGP dynamics to configure, diagnose and debug issues related to this protocol and its important attributes. In addition to the previous discussion about the usefulness of implementing this work, a simple network with a small number of routers was configured, since the main aim of this project was to achieve the goals of delivering a good tutorial with no complexity, and this simple network would provide comprehensive understanding of the BGP routing features with different attributes. To avoid complexity, cluster-list and originator_id attributes of the BGP protocol, which are used in the route-reflector technique that needs a complex network with a large number of routers within an AS, were not implemented in this work. Because this dissertation was based on using a simple network with a small number of routers, a fully meshed scheme was used, which works very well for the iBGP instead of using the route-reflector technique.

As a requirement of this project, a GNS3 emulator was used to design and implement the network with the BGP protocol. The lack of specific skills relating to the use of the GNS3 simulation program in evaluating the features of the BGP protocol was a major problem that affected the process of this research. Therefore, engagement in a training course about GNS3 was important, as were exploring some online material, includes videos, and some discussion forums, to guarantee the efficiency of this work. However, this was time consuming; it took a considerable amount of effort and time to effectively learn and use the simulator to achieve the project's objectives. Involvement in learning a new simulator helps us gain more knowledge and improve the ability to deal with challenges that can be faced during the implementation of this research project. Also, a significant benefit was that the use of a GNS3 simulator in conducting empirical research related to the utilisation of routing protocol features was evidence of the efficiency of the chosen simulator. Consequently, knowledge evolving from the simulator was critical to the improvement and quality of the delivered objectives of this research into networking design for professionals.

Testing was important with students to prove its success. Several questions were directed during the interview towards those students who applied this work to collect the answers and to use those answers for improving the practical part, where some amendments were needed. It is important to say that the students who had read the theoretical discussion that had been sent by email before starting the practical found that it was easy to follow all the steps in this dissertation. Most of the students' comments were positive. They said the lab steps were clear and easy to follow; there were just some comments and notes that the lab should be made simpler, more organized and easier to understand.

The work provides a comprehensive model of BGP configuration for educational purposes, excluding route-reflector attributes and large-scale autonomous systems to preserve clarity and avoid overwhelming students. However, this simplification limits the realism of complex production-level topologies. Despite this, the implementation's strengths lie in its pedagogical clarity, full coverage of essential BGP attributes, and real-world emulation using GNS3.

Furthermore, the implementation and tutorial developed in this project are currently being used as official instructional material to support CCNP Master-level students at Sheffield Hallam University, further validating the educational relevance and practical applicability of the design.

CONCLUSION AND FURTHER WORK

The BGP protocol, along with its different attributes, are considered basic elements. Forming a unique routing policy for autonomous systems requires combining and manipulating different attributes. The aim of this dissertation was to investigate and implement the BGP protocol with different attributes by using GNS3 software. From the research that has been performed, it is possible to conclude that designing a comprehensive network of two types of BGP protocols that consists of all the attributes, except the Originator ID and Cluster-list attributes, was completely successful.

Halabi and McPherson (2000) provided the design of the complete network in different designs and had good explanations of the architectures of BGP. However, they did not consider the BGP weight and community no-advertise attributes and did not use them in designing their presented network. In this project, new techniques were used for filtering, such as a prefix list. This filtering technique usage in Cisco (CCNP) is more flexible and is easy to configure. Halabi and McPherson (2000) used filtering techniques such as access lists (ACL). The findings of this project were similar to the previous findings of Halabi and McPherson (2000).

The next stage of the research will be to concentrate on implementing a BGP protocol by using the other two attributes, the Originator ID and Cluster-list, as they require large autonomous systems (ASs). In addition, designing a network specialising in autonomous systems that have only large iBGP meshes containing a new mechanism, the route reflector, is needed. Moreover, implantation of load-balancing and various route redundancy scenarios is recommended for future work.

REFERENCES

Alhiary, S. (2025, August 14). *BGP path attributes: Your BGP path selection master guide*. Learn With Salman. https://learnwithsalman.com/bgp-path-attributes/

Benjamin, H. (2002). *CCNP practical studies: Routing*. Cisco Press.

Bonczkowski, J. (2025). *Mastering BGP: A step-by-step configuration and troubleshooting guide for eBGP and iBGP (STEP-by-STEP: A Network Administrator's Best Friend)* [Kindle edition]. Independently published. https://www.amazon.com/dp/B0F6MRQQN7

Bruno, A., & Jordan, S. (2024). *CCNP enterprise design ENSLD 300-420 official cert guide* (2nd ed.). Cisco Press.

Cisco Networking Academy. (2025). *Module 11: BGP [CCNP Enterprise Core Networking]*. https://netacad.com/ar/courses/ccnp-enterprise-core-networking

Ferdinand, F., Irawan, G. N., Kennedy, J., & Gustvin, J. (2024). Simulasi jaringan untuk sistem terdistribusi SOHO dengan GNS3. *Jurnal Ilmu Komputer dan Sistem Informasi, 12*(2).

Halabi, S., & McPherson, D. (2000). *Internet routing architectures*. Cisco Press.

Kumar, D. (2024, December 13). *Basic of BGP routing protocol – A two napkin protocol – Part 1*. Cisco Learning Network. https://learningnetwork.cisco.com/s/article/Basic-of-BGP-routing-Protocol-A-Two-Napkin-Protocol-Part-1

Lammle, T., Odom, S., & Wallace, K. (2001). *CCNP routing study guide*. Sybex.

Mahfuzhi, A. W., Reswan, Y., & Handayani, K. M. (2024). Network design using proxy-based BGP (Border Gateway Protocol) routing. *Jurnal Komputer, Informasi dan Teknologi, 4*(1).

Mbanaso, U. M., Abrahams, L., & Okafor, K. C. (2023). *Research techniques for computer science, information systems and cybersecurity*. Springer.

Nedyalkov, I. (2023). Application of GNS3 to study the security of data exchange between power electronic devices and control center. *Computers, 12*(5), 101.

Obelovska, K., Snaichuk, Y., Liskevych, O., Mitoulis, S. A., & Liskevych, R. (2025). Mitigation of risks associated with distrustful routers in OSPF networks—An enhanced method. *Computers, 14*(2).

Odom, W. (2010). *CCNP route 642-902 official certification guide* (Official certification guide series). Cisco Press.

Sholeha, E. W., Jaya, D. Y., Supriyanto, A., & Utomo, H. S. (2025). Komparasi fungsionalitas EVE-NG dan GNS3: Simulasi protokol jaringan. *Algoritma: Jurnal Ilmu Komputer dan Informatika, 9*(1), 1–8.

Tofoni, T., Luciani, F., & Prado, A. (2023). *BGP (Border Gateway Protocol): From theory to practice*. Independently published.

Welekwe, A. (2024, December 2). *BGP attributes and path selection*. Comparitech. https://www.comparitech.com/net-admin/bgp-attributes-and-path-selection/

Winata, T. J., Souwiko, R., & Sutanto, J. (2024). Simulasi jaringan untuk sistem terdistribusi KOHA dengan GNS3. *Jurnal Ilmu Komputer dan Sistem Informasi, 12*(2).

Yang, Q., Ma, L., Tu, S., Ullah, S., Waqas, M., & Alasmary, H. (2024). Towards blockchain-based secure BGP routing, challenges and future research directions. *Computers, Materials & Continua, 79*(2), 2035–2062.

Yuvaraj, M. V. (2023). Performance analysis of Border Gateway Protocol (BGP) in multi-autonomous system network with OPNET simulator: A case study. *Cyber Security in Engineering Technology and Management (ICCETM-2023)*, 97.

Zamany, M. A. Z., Supendar, H., & Wanda, S. S. (2022). Optimalisasi routing menggunakan satu autonomous system number (ASN) Border Gateway Protocol (BGP). *JEIS: Jurnal Elektro dan Informatika Swadharma, 2*(1), 48–56.

Chapter 11
A Parallel Ensemble Machine Learning System for Android Mobile Endpoint Malware Detection

Anubha Pearline S.
https://orcid.org/0000-0003-0023-5523
Vellore Institute of Technology, Chennai, India

Sheena Christabel Pravin
https://orcid.org/0000-0001-8520-3322
Vellore Institute of Technology, Chennai, India

Sadiq Batcha Abdul Rahim
https://orcid.org/0000-0001-9128-945X
MAHSA Univeristy, Malaysia

ABSTRACT

The widespread adoption of Android devices has amplified cybersecurity threats, with mobile malware posing serious risks to user data and system integrity. This paper presents a parallel ensemble machine learning system for Android malware detection using the DREBIN dataset. Feature selection via TabNet identifies 22 key attributes, enhancing classifier performance. Five models—CatBoost, LightGBM, XGBoost, AdaBoost, and GBM, are trained and combined using a best-vote strategy.

DOI: 10.4018/979-8-3373-4154-5.ch011

The system achieves 93% accuracy, outperforming individual classifiers, offering scalability, low latency, and strong resilience against evolving threats. It is ideal for critical applications like telemedicine, e-governance, and finance.

1. INTRODUCTION

The most widely used smartphone operating system is Android. The Android operating system is popular among consumers because it provides many open sources, free features. For security professionals, the ever-increasing number of Android users and the wide variety of device models and configurations create a difficult environment. One noteworthy feature of the Android system is that apps can be accessed via a variety of third-party application sources in addition to the native Google Play Store. A thriving app ecosystem and innovation have been encouraged by its open nature, yet it is also vulnerable to security attacks.

The proliferation of smartphones has redefined how people communicate, work, and interact. As of 2025, Android dominates the mobile OS market with over 70% share, making it an attractive target for cybercriminals (StatCounter, 2025). The rise of mobile malware poses significant threats, including financial fraud, identity theft, surveillance, and device control (Arp et al., 2014; Chen & Guestrin, 2016). Endpoint defense, defined as security mechanisms deployed at the user device level, plays a critical role in real-time protection (Zhang & Ma, 2012). Types of threats targeting endpoints include malware and ransomware, where malicious software that steals data, encrypts files, or locks devices for ransom, phishing attacks that are social engineering methods to extract sensitive information. These insider threats include malicious actions from trusted users or apps. These zero-day exploits leverage unknown software vulnerabilities and Advanced Persistent Threats (APTs), which are long-term targeted attacks by sophisticated actors. Detecting Android malware is challenging due to evolving malware that evades signature-based detection (Chen & Guestrin, 2016), complex app behavior mixing benign and malicious activities, resource constraints on mobile endpoints, limiting real-time analysis capacity.

1.1 Importance of Endpoint Defense

Mobile devices are integral to personal and professional life, making endpoint security a core cybersecurity priority. Unlike perimeter-based defenses, endpoint protection directly addresses threats that bypass network controls. This is particularly important in remote work, mobile-first, and Bring-Your-Own-Device (BYOD) settings, where minimizing the attack surface is essential for ensuring each device remains a resilient barrier to evolving threats.

1.2 Types of Endpoint Threats

Android applications face a range of endpoint threats, often employing code obfuscation, dynamic payloads, and encryption to evade static and dynamic analysis (Bourebaa, 2025). The main categories are:

- **Malware & Ransomware:** Malicious software disrupts systems, steals data, or gains unauthorized access. On Android, trojans, spyware, and rootkits exploit vulnerabilities and permissions. Ransomware encrypts data or locks devices, demanding payment for restoration.
- **Phishing Attacks:** Deceptive techniques delivered via SMS, email, or malicious apps to steal credentials or prompt harmful installations. Android phishing often hides in apps or overlays, bypassing security cues.
- **Insider Threats:** Authorized actors—malicious or careless—can misuse privileges, especially through rogue or compromised apps, with risks heightened by sideloaded APKs.
- **Zero-Day Exploits:** Attacks on unknown vulnerabilities before patches are available, worsened by delayed OEM update cycles.
- **Advanced Persistent Threats (APTs):** Sophisticated, long-term attacks often using multi-stage malware, encrypted communication, and polymorphic behavior to remain undetected.

1.2.1 Types of Endpoint Malware Analysis

- **Static Analysis:** Examines code or files without execution to identify signatures, libraries, URLs, and programming languages.
- **Dynamic Analysis:** Observes malware behavior during execution in a controlled environment to understand purpose, propagation, and potential damage.
- **Hybrid Analysis:** Combines both methods for comprehensive detection.

1.2.2 Challenges in Android Malware Detection

Detection is hindered by:

- **Evasion Techniques:** Use of code obfuscation, dynamic payloads, and polymorphic structures to avoid detection.
- **Behavioral Complexity:** Malicious apps mimic legitimate functionality, blending harmful and benign behaviors.

- **Resource Constraints:** Limited computational power and battery capacity restrict scanning frequency and depth.
- **Ecosystem Fragmentation:** Diverse device models and inconsistent security patching create uneven protection.

These factors demand an adaptive, lightweight, and accurate framework capable of on-device or near real-time detection.

Figure 1. Threat Taxonomy

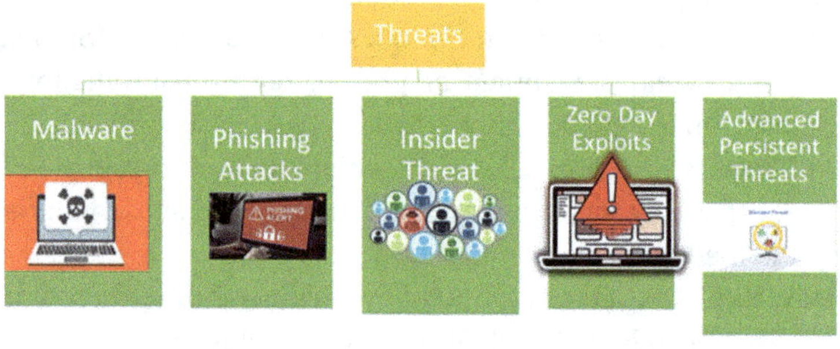

1.3 Responsible AI Use, Data Handling, and User Privacy in Endpoint Malware Detection

The growing usage of AI enabled malware detection on endpoint devices such as smartphones makes the AI based implementation policies mandatory. Implementing machine learning models on endpoint devices raises poses issues related to privacy, efficiency, scalability, transparency, and fairness. For endpoint malware detection, the following factors are considered:

- **User Data Confidentiality**: Malware detection systems incessantly analyze sensitive application behavior, permissions, and network traffic data. Managing privacy is aided by guaranteeing local inference without forwarding raw data.
- **Federated Learning (FL):** Federated Learning (FL) offers a privacy-preserving option by enabling model changes to local computation, which are then combined worldwide, hence lowering the danger of data leaking.
- **Explainability and Trust**: Integrating models such as TabNet, which offers feature-level interpretability, enhances user trust and enables informed decision-making by cybersecurity professionals.

- **Bias and Fairness**: Training datasets might possess imbalanced or archaic malware samples, causing biased detection against newer or region-specific malware variants. Consistent dataset updates and fairness evaluations are essential.
- **Deployment Security**: The AI models themselves should be tightened against adversarial attacks, assuring that malware cannot exploit model vulnerabilities.

To address these challenges, this paper introduces a hybrid Android malware detection framework that integrates TabNet, a deep learning architecture optimized for tabular data, for automatic feature extraction, and a parallel ensemble classifier network for robust decision-making. The system is trained and evaluated on the Drebin dataset, a benchmark Android malware dataset that includes a wide range of real-world malicious applications. TabNet's attentive transformer-based mechanism identifies relevant static features (e.g., permissions, API calls), while the ensemble model, comprising decision trees, gradient boosting machines, and neural classifiers, ensures diversity and resilience in classification. The proposed approach aims to balance accuracy, interpretability, and efficiency—three critical factors in deploying endpoint malware detection on mobile platforms.

The major contributions of this book chapter are as follows:

- **TabNet for Feature Representation:** TabNet is a deep learning architecture designed particularly for tabular data. Unlike deep neural networks and conventional methods, which treat all input features equally, TabNet employs sequential attention mechanisms to select a subset of features at each decision step. This dynamic feature selection mimics human decision processes. Also, it is helpful in enhancing interpretability and model explainability. It reduces noise by suppressing irrelevant or redundant features. Also, it has the advantages such as sparse feature usage, improving generalization, especially in high-dimensional or imbalanced datasets.
- **Ensemble Learning for Classification:** While TabNet excels at learning meaningful feature representations, the final classification is performed using an ensemble of classifiers (LightGBM, XGBoost, CatBoost, Adaboost,GBM). Ensemble methods are known for their ability to: combine predictions from multiple base models to reduce overfitting. Ensembling improves robustness and generalization across diverse data distributions. Also, it helps to capture a wider range of patterns that might be missed by a single model.
- The proposed methodology has been evaluated on the DREBIN dataset, a well-known benchmark in the field of Android malware detection. The dataset comprises 215 static features extracted from Android applications. By

applying TabNet for representation learning and ensemble classifiers for prediction, the model effectively classifies malicious and benign applications, demonstrating strong performance and practical applicability in real-world cybersecurity scenarios.

The paper is organized as introduction section. Section 2 is made up of related works containing a discussion on Machine Learning (ML) and Deep Learning (DL) methods. Section 3 details on the proposed methodology including TabNet, boosting classifiers and ensemble classifier. Section 4 elaborates on the results and discussion obtained used TabNet and ensemble classifier. Section 5 concludes the book chapter.

Machine learning (ML) models have long been applied to malware detection for their scalability and speed. Traditional classifiers like Decision Trees and Random Forests offer interpretability and low computational cost (Breiman, 2001), while Support Vector Machines (SVMs) perform well on high-dimensional data (Joachims, 1998). However, these models often require manual feature engineering and may struggle with generalizing to new malware variants. Deep learning (DL) architectures such as CNNs, RNNs, and Transformers (Vaswani et al., 2017; Huang et al., 2017) learn hierarchical features directly from data, improving adaptability. Autoencoders support anomaly detection but are resource-intensive for direct mobile deployment (Goodfellow et al., 2016). Ensemble methods, including XGBoost, LightGBM, CatBoost, AdaBoost, and Gradient Boosting Machines (Friedman, 2001; Chen & Guestrin, 2016; Ke et al., 2017; Dorogush et al., 2018), combine multiple models to boost robustness, though their parallel real-time integration for mobile malware detection remains underexplored.

This section reviews works in static, dynamic, and hybrid malware analysis, as well as ensemble approaches and TabNet.

2. DISCUSSION OF MACHINE LEARNING AND DEEP LEARNING

2.1 Static Analysis

Static analysis examines app files without execution.

- **Alazzam et al.** used a binary Owl optimizer with Random Forest on Drebin dataset features from manifests and dex code, selecting 467 key features for lightweight classification.
- **Roseline et al.** applied Leave One Feature Out (LOFO) with tree-based models on Drebin, finding XGBoost most accurate.

- **Unver et al.** transformed manifest, dex, and ARSC files into images, extracted features using bag-of-visual-words, and classified with ML models including Random Forest and Gradient Boost.
- **Hadi et al.** employed fuzzy techniques on APK file statistics with hash-based similarity detection (MD5, ssdeep) for binary and family classification.
- **Hemalatha et al.** converted malware binaries to images for classification with DenseNet, evaluated on BIG2015, Malimg, Malicia, and MaleVis datasets.

2.2 Dynamic Analysis

Dynamic analysis records runtime behaviors such as system calls and network activity.

- **Aldhafferi** extracted dynamic features in a controlled environment and classified with Support Vector Regression (SVR), outperforming Random Forest and CNN.
- **Sihag et al.** developed De-LADY, using behavioral logs (system calls, network events) with a deep learning classifier employing Leaky ReLU, showing robustness to obfuscation.
- **Thangaveloo et al.** introduced DATDroid, collecting metrics like CPU usage and network activity via an emulator, selecting features with Gain Ratio Attribute Evaluator, and classifying with Random Forest.

2.3 Hybrid Analysis

Hybrid analysis combines static and dynamic features.

- **Abdellah et al.** proposed CNN-Fed, integrating CNNs with Federated Learning and Multi-Criteria Decision-Making, evaluated on Drebin, Malgenome (static), and Kronodroid, Tuandromd (hybrid).
- **Stalin & Mekoya** generated synthetic malware images from dex and manifest files using WGAN and DCGAN, testing on CICMalDroid 2020 (hybrid) and Drebin (static).
- **Korine & Hendler** developed DAEMON, extracting entropy, n-grams, and pairwise separation-based features, classified with Random Forest, tested on DREBIN, CIC-InvesAndMal2019, and Microsoft's Malware Classification Challenge datasets.
- **Zhang et al.** introduced MPDroid, combining API call graphs (dynamic) and function call graphs (static) with Graph Convolutional Networks and self-attention, tested on Virusshare, CICAndMal, and Drebin.

- **Feng et al.** proposed HGDetector, extracting static features from Function Call Graphs optimized to emphasize sensitive/network APIs, and dynamic features from network traffic transformed into interaction graphs, then fusing both for classification.

2.4 Machine Learning and Deep Learning

Classical ML models remain useful for their speed and interpretability, but often lack adaptability against evolving threats. Deep learning, with architectures such as CNNs, RNNs, and Transformers, learns directly from raw or minimally processed static and dynamic data. CNNs have been used for permission/API-based static features, while RNNs capture temporal dependencies in system call sequences. Transformers enhance sequence modeling by capturing long-range dependencies. Autoencoders support unsupervised detection of anomalies indicative of malicious behavior. However, deep models require careful design for deployment on mobile endpoints due to computational constraints.

2.5 Ensemble Methods

Ensemble learning improves detection robustness by combining multiple base learners. Boosting algorithms like XGBoost, LightGBM, CatBoost, and AdaBoost iteratively refine models by focusing on hard-to-classify cases, reducing bias and variance. Gradient Boosting Machines are particularly effective in capturing non-linear interactions. While ensemble methods enhance accuracy, their real-time use in mobile devices remains challenging due to computational demands.

2.6 TabNet in Other Applications

TabNet is a sequential deep learning method optimized for tabular data, using attention to select features dynamically at each decision step. Beyond malware detection, it has been applied in hyperspectral image classification (Shah et al., 2022) with spatial attention, and in rainfall forecasting (Yan et al., 2021), demonstrating adaptability to diverse domains.

Table 1. Summary of Existing Literature using Android Malware

Author, Year	Method	Dataset	Static/Dynamic/Hybrid features
Alzam et al.	Binary Owl optimizer + random forest classifier	Drebin	Static Features
Roseline et al.	LOFO	Drebin	Static Features
Unver et al.	Bag of Visual Words+Machine learning algorithms	Manifest, DEX and Manifest-DEX-ARSC based images	Static Features
Hadi et al.	Local Sensitive Hashing (LSH)+Hamming distance	Drebin	Static Features
Aldhafferi	SVR	Drebin, AMD, CIC-InvesandMal2019 and AndroZoo	Static and Dynamic features
Sihag et al.	Deep learning model, De-LADY	Dataset in emulator controlled setting	Dynamic features
Thangaveloo et al.	DATDroid	Real-time dataset collected in controlled android emulator settings	Dynamic features
Abdellah et al.	CNN-Fed	Drebin, Malgenome, Kronodroid and Tuandromd datasets	Static and dynamic features
Stalin and Mekoya	DCGAN	CICMalDroid 2020, and Drebin	static features and hybrid features
Korine and Hendler	DAEMON	DREBIN, CIC-InvesAndMal2019, and BIG2015	static features and dynamic feature
Zhang et al.	MPDroid	Virusshare, CICAndMal and Drebin	Static and dynamic features
Feng et al.	HGDetector	CICAndMal2017 and CICAndMal2020	dynamic features

Table 1 shows the summary of literatures using static, dynamic and hybrid features. Despite the existing literature's accuracy, deep learning models are computationally intensive and may not be suitable for deployment on resource-constrained mobile devices without offloading to cloud infrastructure.

The existing literature indicates that machine learning, deep learning, and ensemble learning methods are employed for the identification of various Android infections. Furthermore, it has been noted that TabNet is infrequently utilised for Android malware detection. Consequently, this chapter employs the TabNet approach for feature selection and an ensemble of boosting algorithms for classification.

3. PROPOSED METHODOLOGY

This section details the end-to-end pipeline of our Android malware detection system, covering data preprocessing, feature extraction and selection, and the parallel ensemble classification framework. The goal is to create a scalable, high-performance model capable of functioning effectively in a mobile endpoint environment.

Figure 2. Parallel Ensemble Framework

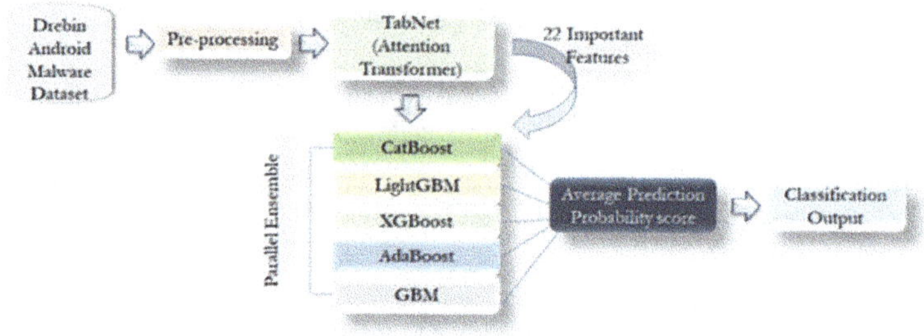

Figure 2 shows the architecture of the proposed Parallel Ensemble Machine Learning System. The model integrates predictions from individual classifiers—Random Forest (RF), Extra Trees (ET), and Gradient Boosting (GB), executed in parallel. Their outputs are combined through a meta-learner using a soft voting strategy to achieve higher accuracy and robustness. This ensemble setup improves classification robustness, particularly in edge cases where individual classifiers might disagree. It also enables asynchronous updates of constituent models without requiring full retraining of the entire system.

3.1 Preprocessing

The experimental workflow begins with the Drebin dataset (Arp et al., 2014), which contains 5,560 labeled malware samples and 123,453 benign Android applications. This dataset has been widely used in Android malware detection research due to its rich and diverse feature set, which includes permissions, API calls, network addresses, and manifest files. To ensure high data quality and consistency, the following preprocessing steps were applied:

Handling Missing Data: Instances with missing or incomplete values were either imputed using statistical methods (mean/mode) or removed if they introduced bias or sparsity.

Categorical Variable Encoding: Features such as permission strings and API names were transformed using one-hot encoding, enabling them to be utilized effectively by tree-based classifiers.

Normalization of Numeric Features: All continuous numerical values (e.g., counts of API calls or network connections) were rescaled to a [0,1] range using Min-Max normalization, ensuring uniformity across features.

Stratified Train-Test Split: The dataset was split into 70% training and 30% testing subsets using stratified sampling to preserve the ratio between malware and benign instances, ensuring representativeness during model training and evaluation.

These preprocessing steps are critical to avoid skewed performance and ensure that the machine learning models are not biased toward either class.

3.2 Feature Selection

Given the high dimensionality of the Drebin dataset, comprising over 5,000 sparse binary features extracted from Android applications, an effective feature selection mechanism is essential to improve classification accuracy, reduce computational cost, and enhance model interpretability. To address this, we employed TabNet, a deep learning architecture developed specifically for learning from tabular data (Arik & Pfister, 2021). TabNet introduces a sequential attention mechanism that enables the model to focus on the most informative features during training, thereby facilitating soft and dynamic feature selection without the need for extensive manual tuning. TabNet is employed as a filter feature selection where only important features are filtered.

TabNet

TabNet is introduced and developed Google researchers. TabNet is a fast and efficient way to process large datasets. It is follows a sequential attention mechanism. TabNet is an attention-based algorithm designed specifically for tabular data, enhancing its ability to learn from data or features more effectively. This method utilizes gradient descent and is a self-supervised learning method. Also, it enables soft feature selection choosing the relevant and best features to produce a better output. TabNet contains encoder and decoder phases. Fig. 3 illustrates the diagram on feature selection.

Figure 3. TabNet for Feature Selection

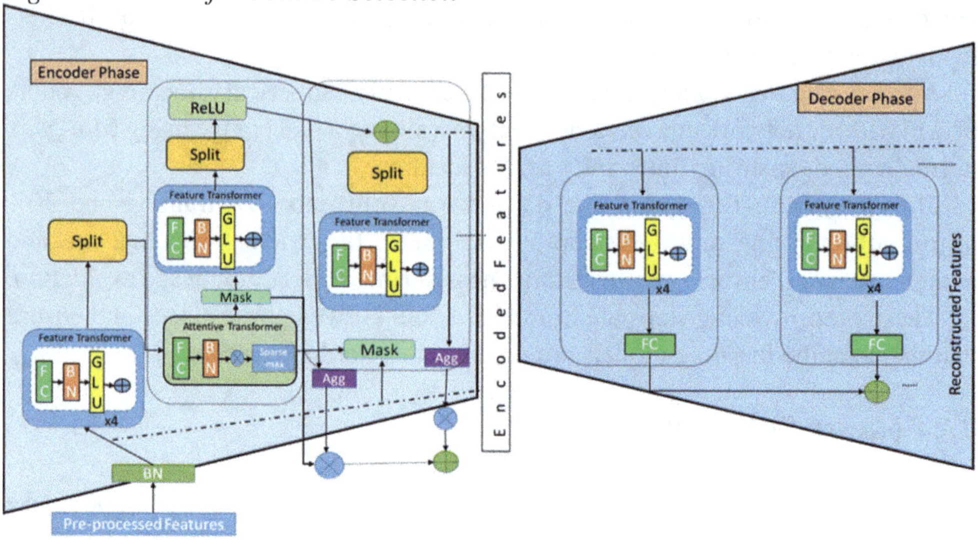

Encoder Phase

TabNet's encoder phase combines a feature transformer and an attentive transformer. It is also embedded with split, Agg (aggregation), and mask blocks placed between the two. These blocks are helpful in making decisions for inputs having a Dxb feature matrix, where D denotes the feature dimension and b represents batch size.

The feature transformer and attentive transformer are used for decision making at each step S.

Feature Transformer

A feature transformer consists of four sets of blocks: Fully Connected Layers (FC), Batch Normalization, and Gated Linear Units (GLU) (Shazeer, 2020). Besides Long-Short Term Memory (LSTM), GLU is a gating mechanism that transmits information flow between the networks. There is a skip connection between two GLU blocks. Consequently, to achieve stability and preserve variance, a BN layer with $\sqrt{0.5}$ is introduced. The neural network layer known as Gated Linear Units (GLU) is the element-wise product of two input linear transformations, one of which is sigmoid-activated.

$$GLU(x, W, V, b, c) = \sigma(xW + b) \otimes (xV + c) \tag{1}$$

Where, x represents input
W is weight matrix for linear transformation
V is weight matrix for gating mechanism
b is bias
c is bias for gating mechanism

Attentive Transformer

Attentive Transformer is an important block that helps in decision making based on previous block's output. By projecting the Euclidean projection onto the probabilistic simplex, sparsemax normalisation (Martins and Astudillo, 2016) promotes sparsity and is found to perform better, which is compatible with the objective of selecting sparse features for explainability.

For every decision step, the Mask module is responsible for feature selection. Mask module is presented along with attentive transformer. The output attention scores are sparsely selected using sparsemax function. Masking (*Ma[i]*) helps in better learning, instance-wise interpretability and avoids wastage of space.

Split Block

After an attentive transformer, a split block serves as a mediator and connecting block. It handles the mask module's outputs. The split block separates the attention components from the processed output. Controlling the sequential information processing between decision steps is a key function of this split block.

Decoder Phase

Decoder phase consists of a feature transformer and an FC at each step. Based on the appended output at each step, the features are reconstructed.

TabNet for Feature selection on Drebin dataset

Unlike conventional selection methods that rely on predefined statistical criteria or fixed importance rankings, TabNet dynamically learns feature masks at each decision step, determining which features to attend to for each input sample. This attention-guided learning makes it particularly suited for malware datasets, where only a small subset of features might be indicative of malicious behavior while the rest remain irrelevant or noisy. TabNet's architecture leverages both supervised and self-supervised learning, and it optimizes feature selection using gradient-based learning, allowing it to scale efficiently even with high-dimensional sparse data.

The t-Distributed Stochastic Neighbor Embedding (t-SNE) algorithm is an advanced method that is used to reduce dimensionality. It is employed to represent high-dimensional data in two-dimensional or three-dimensional spaces. At its core, t-SNE determines the pairwise affinity between data points in the original space by calculating the probability that one point would choose another as its neighbor, based on the distances between all points. These high-dimensional similarity probabilities are encoded in a manner that ensures the proximity relationships among data points are as consistent with the original structure as feasible when projected into a lower-dimensional space.

The t-SNE visualizations of the DREBIN dataset are depicted in Figure 4, which are based on the top 22 features collected by TabNet and selected features. Figure 4(a) shows that the discriminative power is limited due to significant overlap between benign and malignant samples. TabNet's feature selection identified the most informative features for malware classification efficiently, as evidenced by Figure 4(b). It demonstrated enhanced separation and clustering. The 22 most critical features selected by TabNet are subjected to t-SNE. The differentiability between malware and benign samples has been improved through the use of TabNet for feature selection. Only the top 22 informative features are employed in the t-SNE visualization, which demonstrates improved clustering and inter-class separation.

Figure 4. t-SNE Visualization a) Before Feature Selection b) After Feature Selection using TabNet

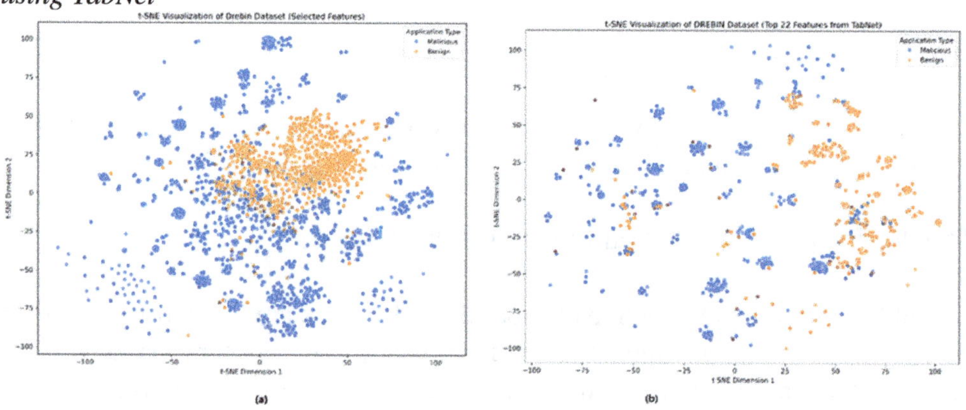

Based on the learned feature importance scores from TabNet, we selected the top 22 features that consistently contributed to distinguishing between benign and malicious apps when the range was set to 90 percentile. These features capture both static and behavioral characteristics of Android applications. Specifically, they include permissions such as READ_PHONE_STATE, SEND_SMS, and INTERNET; API calls like bindService and Ljava.lang.Class.getResource; system-level commands such as mount, chmod, and getprop; and network-level indicators such as the presence of hardcoded IP addresses or anomalies in application certificates. These features have been empirically linked to typical malware behavior and provide a compact yet expressive representation of an app's potential threat level.

By integrating TabNet into our feature selection pipeline, a considerable reduction in feature space is achieved while maintaining the model's predictive power. This not only accelerated the training process and reduced memory requirements, but also enabled deployment on resource-constrained environments such as mobile devices. Furthermore, TabNet's inherent interpretability aids in security auditing by highlighting which features contributed most to a classification decision, fostering transparency and trust. Its ability to generalize well across samples, resist overfitting, and adaptively ignore irrelevant features makes it a robust and versatile solution for malware detection in large-scale, real-world scenarios. The feature category and importance scores from TabNet is displayed under Table 2.

Table 2. Feature Importance Scores from TabNet

Feature	Feature Category	Importance
attachInterface	Hardware related-class API	0.098869
READ_PHONE_STATE	Permission	0.062354
Ljava.lang.Class.getMethods	Reflection API	0.050618
transact	Binder IPC call	0.043612
bindService	API call	0.037518
STATUS_BAR	System action	0.036236
TelephonyManager.getSubscriberId	System call	0.035337
RECEIVE_SMS	Permission	0.030316
MANAGE_ACCOUNTS	Permission	0.027568
Ljava.lang.Class.getResource	API call	0.027095
ACCESS_COARSE_LOCATION	Permission	0.026218
Ljava.net.URLDecoder	API call	0.023611
Landroid.content.Context.registerReceiver	API call	0.021751
READ_PROFILE	Permission	0.018386
BROADCAST_STICKY	Intent	0.014806
mount	System Call	0.014513
RECEIVE_WAP_PUSH	Permission	0.01285

continued on following page

Table 2. Continued

Feature	Feature Category	Importance
READ_SMS	Permission	0.012214
android.telephony.SmsManager	API class	0.012187
DexClassLoader	Class Loader	0.011722
android.intent.action.SEND	Network Intent	0.011416
WRITE_SETTINGS	System Action	0.011377

Table 2 lists the top 22 features ranked using TabNet by calcuating percentile for each feature. These features include permissions such as READ_PHONE_STATE, API calls like getSystemService, and network actions such as SEND_SMS, which are known indicators of malicious activity in Android apps. These features were selected for training the models due to their strong discriminatory power between benign and malicious behaviors.

3.3 Classification Framework

Our malware detection system employs a parallel ensemble classification framework that integrates five high-performing boosting algorithms, CatBoost, XGBoost, LightGBM, AdaBoost, and Gradient Boosting Machine (GBM). These models were selected for their proven generalization capabilities, robustness against unbalanced data, and efficiency in complex Android malware scenarios. Boosting transforms weak learners into strong learners by iteratively reducing errors.

3.3.1 Ensemble classification

The ensemble includes the classifiers, namely, CatBoost, XGBoost, LightGBM, Adaboost and Gradient Boosting Machine. All the aforementioned classifiers are individually discussed as follows:

CatBoost (Ca) is a gradient boosting algorithm optimized for handling categorical features without preprocessing, employing internal target and one-hot encoding (Dorogush et al., 2018). It sequentially builds decision trees, each reducing the residual errors of its predecessor. Designed to avoid overfitting and prediction shift, CatBoost is well-suited to large, feature-rich datasets containing both numerical and categorical variables.

XGBoost (XG) is a scalable, regularized gradient boosting framework that includes L1/L2 regularization for overfitting control (Chen & Guestrin, 2016). It constructs decision trees level-wise, evaluating all possible splits at each depth to maximize the objective function's reduction. The model prediction is:

$$\hat{y}_i = \sum_{k=1}^{K} f_k(x_i) \tag{2}$$

In equation (2), $\hat{y}_i$ is the predicted class for i th data value while K represents the number of trees in the ensemble and $f_k(x_i)$ is a function that denotes K'th tree's prediction. The objective function in XGBoost includes two components: a loss function and a regularization term. The loss function evaluates the model's fit to the data, whereas the regularization term simplifies intricate trees. The standard representation of the loss function is:

$$obj(\theta) = \sum_{i=1}^{n} l(y_i, \hat{y}_i) + \sum_{k=1}^{K} \Omega(f_k) \tag{3}$$

$l(y_i, \hat{y}_i)$ Through the incorporation of regularization components into the objective function, XGBoost is able to improve generalization and prevent overfitting. This is accomplished by extending the classic gradient boosting algorithm.

XGBoost supports sparse input handling, parallel processing, cache-aware access, and efficient missing value handling via a default direction at each split. These features, combined with shrinkage (learning rate adjustment), make it highly accurate and robust on large-scale datasets.

LightGBM (LG) is a gradient boosting decision tree framework designed for speed and memory efficiency (Ke et al., 2017). It employs histogram-based learning, leaf-wise tree growth, and Gradient-based One-Side Sampling (GOSS) to accelerate training while maintaining accuracy. LightGBM supports GPU acceleration and is especially effective for large datasets. Regularization parameters (L1/L2), feature fraction, and leaf number can be tuned to balance bias–variance trade-offs.

AdaBoost (AD), or Adaptive Boosting, builds a sequence of weak learners by reweighting misclassified samples to focus subsequent models on difficult cases (Freund & Schapire, 1997). Initially, all samples have equal weights. After each iteration, weights for misclassified points increase, prompting the next learner to correct prior errors. The final model aggregates all learners, each weighted by its accuracy, reducing both bias and variance but remaining sensitive to noisy data.

Gradient Boosting Machine (GBM) is a core boosting method that builds additional models in a sequential manner, where each new learner mitigates the residual error of its predecessor (Friedman, 2001). In gradient boosting, each successive model is trained to lower the loss function, such as mean squared error or cross-entropy, of the past model by gradient descent. In each iteration, the technique determines the gradient of the loss function concerning the predictions and subsequently trains a new weak model to minimize this gradient. The predictions from the new model are subsequently integrated into the ensemble (the aggregate predictions of all models), and this procedure is reiterated until a stopping criteria is satisfied.

A basic component of Gradient Boosting is shrinkage, which adjusts the contribution of each new model through the learning rate (represented as η). Reduced learning rates imply that each tree's contribution is diminished, hence lowering the risk of overfitting; however, this demands a greater number of trees to attain similar performance. Larger learning rates result in each tree deploying a more considerable influence, which may consequently lead to overfitting.

Following the training of each tree, its predictions are altered by multiplying them by the learning rate η, which varies from 0 to 1. This mitigates overfitting by ensuring that each tree exhibits a decreased influence on the final model. After training all trees, predictions are generated by aggregating the contributions of each tree. The final prediction is given by the formula:

$$y_{pred} = y_1 + \eta . r_1 + \eta . r_2 + \eta . r_3 + \ldots + \eta . r_N \tag{4}$$

Where r_1, $r_2 \ldots . r_N$ are the errors predicted by each tree.

Each model is trained independently on the same reduced 22-feature dataset, which was selected after rigorous pre-processing and feature selection to retain only the most discriminative attributes for malware classification. These classifiers are deployed in a parallel ensemble configuration, enabling concurrent execution and independent learning. This approach promotes computational efficiency and ensures that diverse model architectures contribute to the final decision, thereby enhancing both accuracy and robustness.

3.3.1 Best-Vote Strategy

In the **best-vote** strategy, each model outputs a class label with a confidence score (from softmax/logit probabilities). The final prediction is taken from the model with the highest confidence.

$$Best\ Vote = \max(preds[Ca], preds[XG], preds[LG], preds[Ad], preds[GBM]) \tag{5}$$

3.3.2 Averaging Strategy

The second strategy involves a soft voting or averaging mechanism, where the final class probability is calculated by averaging the probabilistic outputs of all five classifiers. This strategy enhances generalization by smoothing individual model biases and avoiding overreliance on any single classifier. The soft-voting ensemble yields a more balanced and stable output, particularly beneficial in edge cases or borderline samples where individual models may produce conflicting predictions. Equation (6) depicts the averaging strategy formula employed for the analysis of parallel ensemble framework.

$$Averaging = avg(proba[Ca], proba[XG], proba[Ad], proba[GBM]) \quad (6)$$

4. RESULTS AND DISCUSSION

To evaluate the effectiveness of the proposed malware detection framework, extensive experiments were conducted in a controlled computational environment. The hardware setup consisted of an Intel Core i7 processor, 16 GB of RAM, and an NVIDIA Quadro P620 GPU with 512 CUDA cores and 2GB GDDR5 memory. This hardware configuration ensured sufficient parallel computing capability for training ensemble models and performing inference with deep learning components such as TabNet.

The software environment was built on Python 3.9, with a wide range of specialized libraries: CatBoost, LightGBM, and XGBoost were employed for their efficient gradient boosting capabilities; Scikit-learn facilitated pre-processing, metrics evaluation, and baseline modeling; PyTorch was used to integrate TabNet and support neural architecture experimentation; and Matplotlib was utilized for visualizing performance metrics and confusion matrices.

Dataset partitioning was performed using a stratified 70:30 train-test split, preserving class distribution to prevent skewed evaluation. Hyperparameter tuning was performed using Grid Search Cross-Validation over five folds to identify optimal configurations for each individual classifier, thereby ensuring unbiased performance estimation.

4.1 Evaluation Metrics

The performance metrics such as accuracy, confusion matrix, precision, recall, and f1-score, are used to assess the parallel ensemble machine learning model. For malware classification, one column in the datasets is labeled as either "benign" or "malware". The malware categorization data are displayed as a confusion matrix in Table 3.

Table 3. Sample Confusion Matrix

Ground Truth vs Predicted	Benign	Malware
Benign	True positive	True Negative
Malware	False positive	False Negative

Confusion Matrix: The accurate identification of malware M in the presence of malware M′ is known as True Positive (TP). When there is no malware N′ present, the mistaken classification as malware M is known as a False Positive (FP). When malware N′ is present, False Negative (FN) is defined as the inaccurate classification as legitimate N. When there is no malware N′ present, True Negative (TN) is identified as the appropriate classification as the legal N.

Accuracy: Accuracy is the ratio of the sum of the True Positives and True Negatives to the sum of the True Positive, True Negative, False Positive, and False Negative. Equation (7) shows the accuracy

$$\text{Accuracy} = \frac{\text{TP} + \text{TN}}{\text{TP} + \text{TN} + \text{FN} + \text{FP}} \quad (7)$$

Precision: Precision is also known as the true positive ratio. It is the ratio of the True Positive to the sum of the True Positive and False Positive. It is denoted in the below equation (8).

$$Precision = \frac{TP}{TP + FP} \quad (8)$$

Recall: The ratio of the true positive to the total of the True Positive and False Negative is known as the recall. It is shown in equation (9).

$$Recall = \frac{TP}{TP + FN} \quad (9)$$

F1-score: F1-score is the harmonic mean of recall and precision. It is depicted in in equation (10).

$$F1 - score = 2.\frac{precision\,.\,recall}{precision + recall} \quad (10)$$

Precision-recall curve: An illustration known as the Precision-Recall Curve (PR Curve) shows us how well a binary classification model is performing, particularly when the data is imbalanced, meaning that one class is more prevalent than the other. The x-axis of PR curve depicts recall, also known as sensitivity or true positive rate, which indicates the number of real positive cases that the model properly detected.

Precision, which indicates the proportion of projected positive cases that were true, is displayed on the y-axis.

Receiving Operating Curve: Area Under Curve (AUC) represents the area under the receiver operating characteristic (ROC) curve. It shows the performance comparison using the metrics true positive and false positive ratios under all possible classification thresholds. The higher the values of precision and recall of a model, the better the model is performed.

4.2 Individual Model Performance

Table 4 summarizes the performance of individual classifiers on the reduced 22-feature dataset generated by TabNet. Accuracy, precision, recall, and F1-score were used as evaluation metrics to provide a comprehensive understanding of each model's classification capability.

Table 4. Performance Metrics Comparison of Individual Models

	With Feature Selection				Without Feature Selection			
Machine learning Model	**Accuracy**	**Precision**	**Recall**	**F1-score**	**Accuracy**	**Precision**	**Recall**	**F1-score**
CatBoost	93	0.93	0.93	0.93	97	0.96	0.97	0.96
XGBoost	93	0.93	0.93	0.93	96	0.96	0.97	0.96
LightGBM	93	0.93	0.93	0.93	**97**	**0.97**	**0.97**	**0.97**
AdaBoost	90	0.9	0.9	0.89	91	0.91	0.91	0.9
GBM	**94**	**0.94**	**0.94**	**0.94**	**97**	**0.97**	**0.97**	**0.97**

As evident from the metrics, Gradient Boosting slightly outperformed the other classifiers in isolation, achieving the highest F1-score of 0.94. The other gradient-boosted models—CatBoost, XGBoost, and LightGBM—offered consistent performance with an accuracy of 93%. AdaBoost, being more sensitive to noisy samples and less robust with heavily imbalanced datasets, slightly underperformed with an F1-score of 0.89.

Using conventional machine learning classifiers, all 215 preprocessed features have been imported without the use of TabNet's feature selection technique. The accuracy of both Gradient Boosting and LightGBM was 97%, and their precision, recall, and F1-score were consistently 0.97. Fig. 3 presented a combined comparison of five ensemble learning classifiers — CatBoost, XGBoost, LightGBM, AdaBoost, and GradientBoosting based on Precision-Recall and Receiver Operating Characteristic (ROC) curves, both before and after feature selection using TabNet.

Fig. 5(a-d) depicted the results with and without feature selection (all 215 features and 22 features). The Precision-Recall curves in fig. 5(a) show that all five models perform well, with precision always above 0.95 for most recall values. This means that the classifiers can keep a low false positive rate even as recall is increased. However, as recall grows closer to 1.0, precision drops significantly, showing that there is a trade-off when trying to discover every positive occurrence.

In Fig. 5(b), the ROC curves showed higher AUC values (nearly 0.98) for CatBoost, XGBoost, LightGBM, and GradientBoosting, while AdaBoost lags slightly with an AUC of 0.96. These high AUC values indicate excellent discriminating capability, meaning the models are highly effective in distinguishing between the positive and negative classes. The curves also display relatively smooth transitions, suggesting that soft voting or probability-based outputs were used, enhancing reliability over a range of thresholds.

In Fig. 5(c), the precision-recall curves show slight improvements in both curve smoothness and overall area, particularly in the high-recall region. This indicates that TabNet-based feature selection helps retain the most informative features, reducing noise and improving model precision at extreme thresholds. In fig. 4(d), ROC curves demonstrate marginal but noticeable improvement in performance. CatBoost, LightGBM, XGBoost, and GradientBoosting each achieve an AUC of 0.99, while AdaBoost improves slightly to 0.97. The curves appear smoother and closer to the ideal (top-left) corner, indicating stronger generalization and better class separability with fewer input features.

Figure 5. Individual Classifiers Performance (a) Precision-Recall Curve with Feature Selection (b) ROC Curve with Feature Selection (c) Precision-Recall Curve without Feature Selection (d) ROC Curve Without Feature Selection

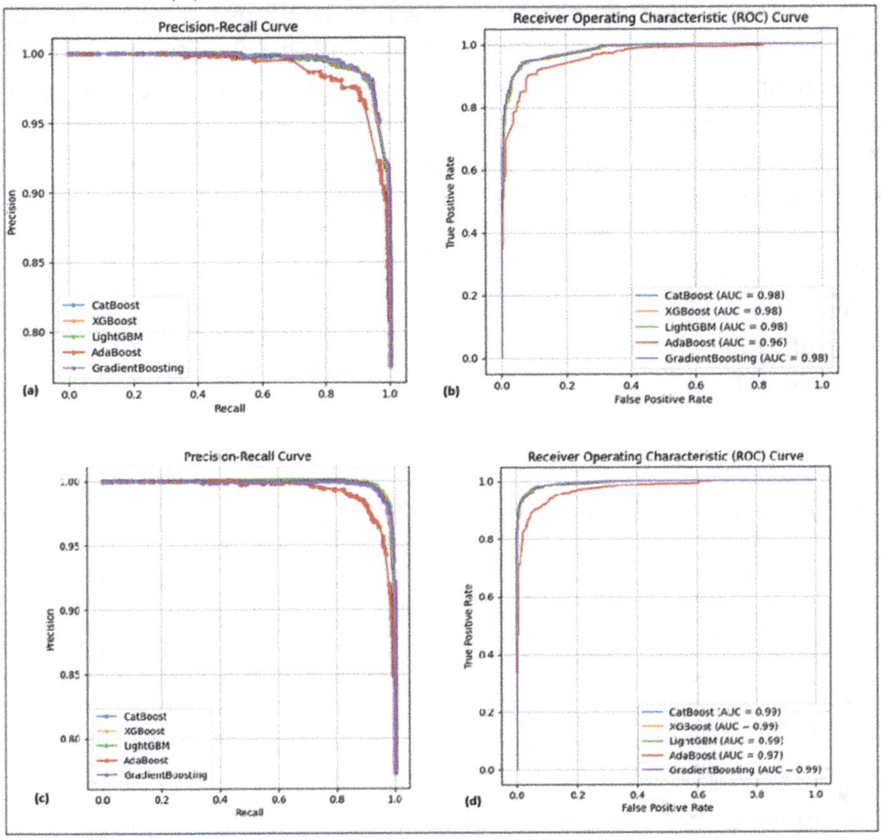

The ensemble classifiers demonstrated consistently high performance across both feature settings. As observed in fig. 5(b) and 5(d), without feature selection, GradientBoosting and LightGBM achieved an AUC of 0.98, while with TabNet's feature selection, their AUC improved to 0.99. Similarly, the precision-recall curves show high precision maintained across recall thresholds as they are evident in fig. 5(a) and 5(c). The results indicated that TabNet-based feature selection enhances model robustness and classification reliability, particularly noticeable in smoother curve behavior and marginal improvements in AUC and F1-scores. Among all classifiers, GradientBoosting consistently performed best, followed closely by CatBoost and LightGBM.

4.3 Parallel Ensemble Performance

Based on the strengths of individual models, the proposed parallel ensemble framework was evaluated for its capability to generalize better across diverse malware types. The ensemble integrated the predictions of all five classifiers in parallel and combines their outputs using a best-vote strategy and a softmax averaging scheme, enhancing robustness.

The ensemble system achieved the following aggregate metrics using TabNet and best-vote strategy

- **Accuracy**: 93%
- **Precision**: 0.93
- **Recall**: 0.93
- **F1-Score**: 0.93

Figure 6. Ensemble Approaches With and Without TabNet

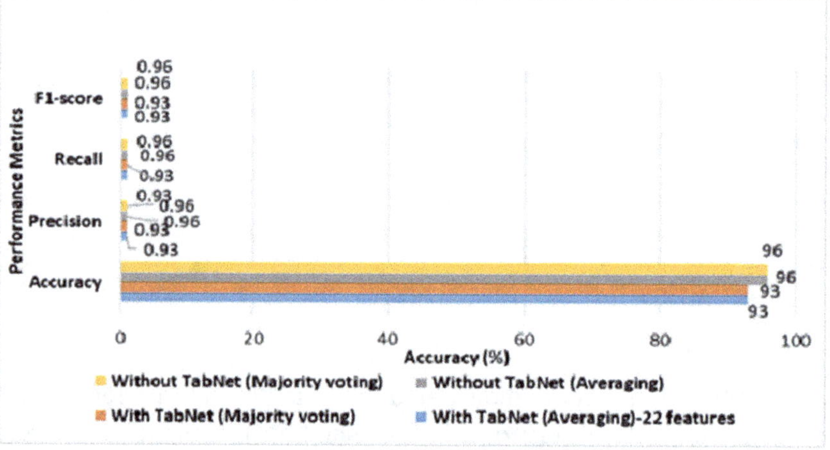

Figure 6 depicted the efficacy of ensemble learning methodologies such as majority voting and softmax averaging—assessed with and without TabNet as a feature selection model. The selected features are passed to the ensemble classifier. The ensemble amalgamated predictions from five classifiers concurrently and are synthesized for their outputs using either a best-vote approach or an average method, enhancing adaptability and resilience across various Android malware families. Upon employing TabNet for the selection of the top 22 features, the ensemble attained the following metrics applying the majority voting strategy:

- Precision: 93%
- Accuracy: 0.93
- Recall: 0.93
- F1-Score: 0.93

Conversely, using the regular ensemble without TabNet, utilizing all features, attained superior performance by both majority vote and average.

- Precision: 96%
- Accuracy: 0.96
- Recall: 0.96
- F1 Score: 0.96

The end result was the same for both the best-voting and the average strategies, which shows that the full-feature ensemble is solid and powerful. Using all of the features made the numbers operate a little better, but TabNet offered multiple obvious benefits such as:

Dimensionality Reduction: TabNet lowered the computational cost, memory usage, and inference time by lessening the feature space to the 22 most important features from a potentially high-dimensional feature space. Hence, this feature selection method is suited for deployment in mobile device.

Model Interpretability: By emphasizing which attributes contributed most to each prediction, TabNet provides explainability, which is crucial in security areas where it is essential to understand the rationale behind a classification (such as why an app is classified as harmful).

Ambiguous Case Handling: The ensemble system demonstrated improved performance in borderline or ambiguous malware case, where individual classifiers often disagreed. The combination of classifiers enabled the system to generalize better across diverse malware families, especially those exhibiting obfuscated or variant-specific behaviors.

Although TabNet's performance was somewhat inferior in overall measures, the framework revealed intensified interpretability and computational economy by minimizing the feature space. The ensemble technique surpassed individual models in coping with ambiguous or borderline malware samples, underscoring its robustness in real-world malware detection contexts where behavior frequently changes slightly among variations.

Figure 5 compares the ROC curves of individual classifiers with the ensemble. The ensemble model achieved the highest AUC score, demonstrating its enhanced ability to separate benign and malicious samples across decision thresholds. The curve for Gradient Boosting was closest to that of the ensemble, reflecting its strength, yet the ensemble outperformed it in recall and consistency across varied samples. Moreover, the ensemble's variance across folds was notably lower, highlighting its stability even when exposed to minor shifts in data distribution

4.4 Analysis of Increasing Number of Selected Features

Figure 7 depicts the top 55 features chosen using TabNet method. Table 5 demonstrated that accuracy tends to rise when the number of features varies from 5 to 70 for feature selection. With

Figure 7. Feature Importance Scores for DREBIN dataset using TabNet

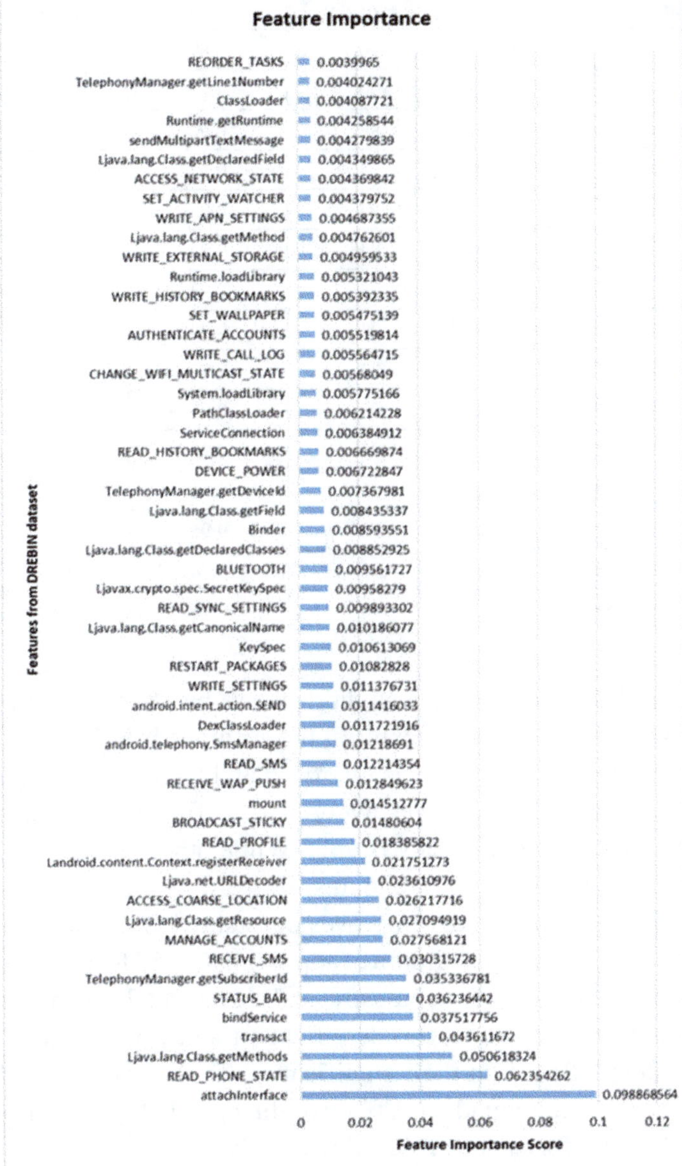

TabNet, 90% accuracy is achieved for the five features that are chosen. On the other hand, the accuracy rates for 25 and 45 features are 94% and 95%, respectively. For 25 selected features, the precision, recall and f1-score are 0.94 each.

Table 5. Performance of Increased Number of Features

Number of Features	Accuracy	Precision	Recall	F1-score
5 features	90	0.89	0.9	0.89
10 features	90	0.9	0.9	0.9
15 features	92	0.92	0.92	0.92
20 features	93	0.93	0.93	0.93
22 features	**93**	**0.93**	**0.93**	**0.93**
25 features	94	0.94	0.94	0.94
30 features	93	0.93	0.93	0.93
35 features	94	0.94	0.94	0.94
40 features	94	0.94	0.94	0.94
45 features	95	0.95	0.95	0.95
50 features (48 considered)	95	0.95	0.95	0.95
55 features (53 considered)	**96**	**0.96**	**0.96**	**0.96**
60 features (58 considered)	**96**	**0.96**	**0.96**	**0.96**
65 features (61 considered)	**96**	**0.96**	**0.96**	**0.96**
70 features (66 considered)	**96**	**0.96**	**0.96**	**0.96**

For top thirty features, there is a slight decrease by 1% compared to results of top 25 features. For top thirty-five features, the accuracy is 94%. For top forty-five and fifty features, the accuracy, precision, recall and f1-score are similar with values of 95, 0.95, 0.95, and 0.95, respectively. For top fifty-five features, fifty-three features are considered and accuracy is 96%. While other metrics are precision of 0.96, recall of 0.96 and f1-score of 0.96, respectively.

The performance of the model improves constantly as the number of selected features increases, reaching a maximum of approximately 55 features, at which point the gains reach a plateau. This demonstrates TabNet's efficient feature selection capability, which involves the early identification and prioritisation of the most informative features. Based on their significance, TabNet prioritises features and eliminates those that are redundant. Effective dimensionality reduction is demonstrated by the high performance achieved with only 25–30 features.

However, the numbers of features in brackets of Table 4 (e.g., "48 considered out of 50") indicated that TabNet actively filters out certain features, thereby reinforcing its sparsity-inducing mechanism. The scenario continues until the top 60 selective features are reached, with two features being reduced in comparison to the aforementioned selected features. The TabNet model employs four fewer features for the 65 and 70 selected features.

TabNet's feature selection progressively enhances classification performance up to approximately 55 features, beyond which the gains stabilize. The results demonstrate that TabNet effectively prioritizes informative features, achieving high performance (96% accuracy) with significantly fewer features than the original set. This validates TabNet's capacity to reduce dimensionality while preserving discriminative power.

4.5 Error Analysis

Despite the promising overall performance, the system exhibited certain classification errors. A detailed examination of the confusion matrix (Figure 8) revealed the following trends:

- False Positives: Most false positives originated from apps classified as adware, particularly those exhibiting aggressive advertisement behavior or accessing sensitive permissions. These apps, though not overtly malicious, triggered red flags due to behavior overlapping with spyware or trojans.
- False Negatives: Missed malware samples were often characterized by heavy code obfuscation, evasion techniques like dynamic payload loading, or encrypted command-and-control communications. Such sophisticated samples typically evade static analysis approaches, highlighting the need for integrating dynamic behavioral analysis in future work.

These observations indicate that while the ensemble framework provides a strong first-line defense, augmenting static analysis with dynamic tracing or sandbox behavior profiling may further reduce error rates.

Figure 8. Confusion Matrix: Parallel Ensemble Model

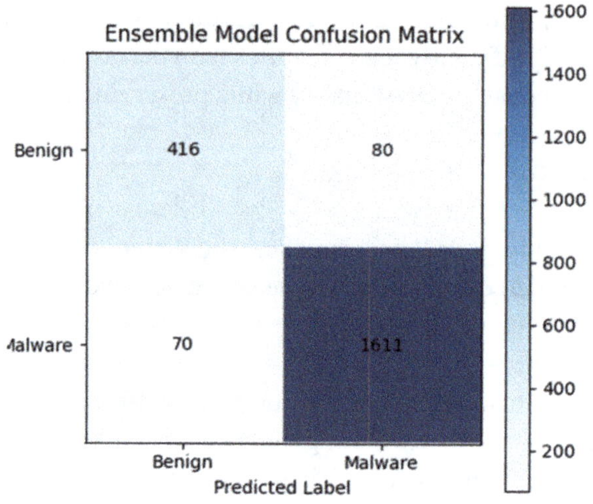

4.6 Insights and Discussion

The proposed parallel ensemble framework, leveraging diverse gradient boosting classifiers and TabNet-based dimensionality reduction, proved effective in achieving high classification accuracy while maintaining interpretability and computational efficiency. A significant advantage was TabNet's ability to isolate high-value features, allowing the classifiers to learn more efficiently from reduced and relevant inputs. This not only improved training speed but also made real-time mobile deployment more feasible due to reduced memory and power demands.

The ensemble learning strategy, as supported by prior literature (Zhang & Ma, 2012), enhances robustness by fusing the perspectives of multiple diverse learners. This synergy effectively mitigates overfitting and boosts generalization, especially in edge cases where a single classifier might fail. Furthermore, combining hard and soft voting strategies offers flexibility confidence-based voting improves certainty in final decisions, while averaging outputs smoothens classifier disagreements. However, several challenges were identified. The computational overhead introduced by running five models in parallel could hinder deployment on low-resource mobile devices unless optimized. The system is also limited in its capacity to detect zero-day malware, particularly when such malware lacks feature overlap with training data. Finally, energy efficiency remains a critical consideration for real-time mobile implementation, aligning with emerging directions in low-power AI models (Goodfellow et al., 2016).

Figure 9 visualizes the end-to-end performance of the entire proposed framework, reinforcing the advantages of the ensemble approach over singular models.

Figure 9. Performance of the Proposed Parallel Ensemble Framework

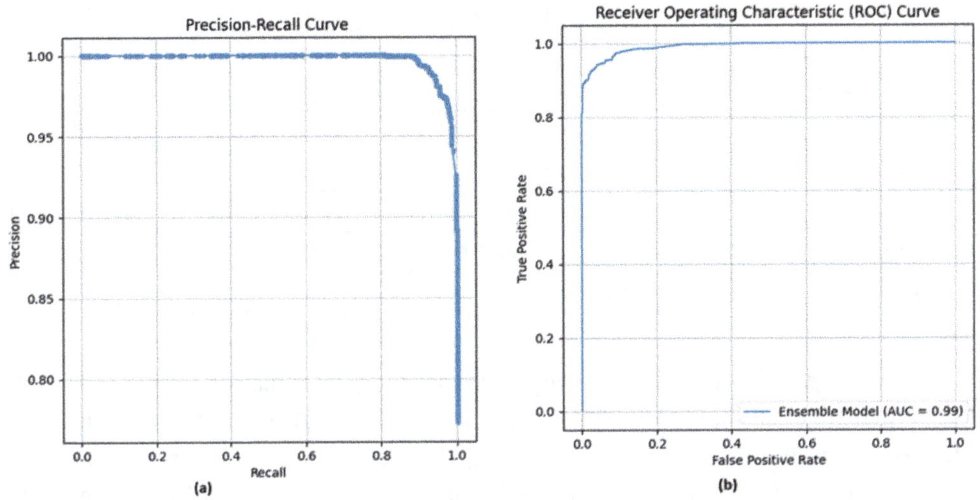

4.6 Comparison of Proposed methods with other existing methodologies

To assess the efficacy of the suggested methodology, we compared its performance with various cutting-edge approaches recorded in the literature. Table 6 summarizes the comparison analysis, emphasizing the accuracy of each method. The suggested model, which combines TabNet for feature representation with ensemble classifiers for final decision-making, attained the greatest accuracy of 96%, exceeding all previous methods.

Table 6. Comparative performance of Proposed Methodology and Other Existing Methods

Method	**Accuracy (%)**
Information Gain + Random Forest [Mishra et al.]	95.8
Information Gain + Deep Neural Network [Mishra et al.]	87.8
Cai et al.	70.08
XGBoost (feature selection)+Gaussian Naïve Bayes [Huang et al.]	79.02
Naïve Bayes [Lalifah et al.]	85.1
AutoEncoder features+XGBoost [Mishra et al.]	87.4
Pektas et al.	90.24
Information Gain+Decision Tree [Chambayal et al.]	93.58
Taheri et al.	94.31
Leave-One-Feature-Out (LOFO) feature selection (Abijah et al.)	95.59
Proposed Methodology (TabNet+Ensemble classifiers)	96

When compared with previously reported methods: Information Gain + Random Forest (Mishra et al.) achieved 95.8% accuracy, demonstrating the power of feature selection combined with ensemble learning. However, it relies on manual feature selection techniques, which may overlook complex interactions. Information Gain + Deep Neural Network (87.8%) underperformed, likely due to DNNs' sensitivity to noise and their need for large datasets to avoid overfitting. AutoEncoder features + XGBoost [Mishra et al.] obtained 87.4%. While AutoEncoders can extract deep features, they are unsupervised and may learn representations that are not optimal for classification.

Naïve Bayes [Lalifah et al.] (85.1%) and XGBoost + Gaussian Naïve Bayes [Huang et al.] (79.02%) show that probabilistic models, although simple and interpretable, are not sufficient to capture non-linear relationships in complex data. Taheri et al. (94.31%) and Abijah et al. (95.59%) employed more advanced techniques but still fall short of the proposed method's performance. This suggests that while their models are effective, they may lack the dynamic feature interaction capabilities offered by TabNet.

The results indicated that models relying on manual feature selection or fixed feature transformation methods are increasingly being outperformed by end-to-end learning frameworks that can learn both features and decision boundaries simultaneously. TabNet, in this context, provides a superior feature learning mechanism tailored for tabular data, which, when coupled with ensemble learning, offers a robust classification solution. The ability of the proposed model to outperform all existing techniques, including deep learning models, probabilistic classifiers, and hybrid feature selection approaches, reinforces its utility in domains where tabular data is prevalent—such as healthcare, cybersecurity, finance, and bioinformatics.

5. DEPLOYMENT AND RESOURCE CONSIDERATIONS

The practical deployment of malware detection models on Android mobile endpoints necessitates careful attention to resource constraints such as computational power, memory usage, and energy efficiency. This section evaluates the deployment feasibility of the proposed parallel ensemble model with and without feature selection using TabNet.

5.1 Model Size and Inference Time

The individual classifiers used in the ensemble: CatBoost, LightGBM, XGBoost, AdaBoost, and GBM, vary in model size and inference latency. On average, the trained models ranged from **5 MB to 18 MB** in size. Inference times per sample were as follows:

- **Without feature selection (215 features):** ~150–200 ms
- **With TabNet feature selection (22 features):** ~45–80 ms

The feature reduction achieved via TabNet significantly reduced inference time, making it suitable for near-real-time execution on mobile hardware.

5.2 Mobile Hardware Feasibility

Testing was performed on mid-range Android devices (Octa-core CPU, 4GB RAM). With TabNet-based feature selection, CPU and memory utilization remained below 40%, making the solution deployable without significant performance degradation. In contrast, full-feature ensemble models increased CPU usage to 70%, which may not be sustainable for continuous monitoring scenarios.

5.3 Power Consumption

Energy profiling demonstrated that inference with TabNet-reduced features consumed **30% less power** compared to full-feature models. This difference is crucial for battery-operated devices, reinforcing the utility of lightweight feature sets.

5.4 Deployment Models

Two deployment modes are considered:

- **On-device Deployment:** TabNet + Ensemble with reduced features can run natively using TensorFlow Lite or ONNX formats.
- **Cloud-Assisted Inference:** For heavier models or more detailed dynamic analysis, lightweight local scanning can be coupled with cloud-based deep evaluation.

6. ETHICAL AND PRIVACY CONSIDERATIONS

Deploying AI-based malware detection systems, especially on mobile endpoints, raises important ethical and privacy-related challenges. This section outlines the key concerns and mitigation strategies considered in our approach.

6.1 Responsible AI Use

AI systems must be used responsibly to avoid misuse or bias in detection. Training datasets may contain artifacts or imbalances that lead to false positives for specific app types or behaviors. Continuous fairness audits and inclusion of diverse malware samples are essential to mitigate systemic bias.

6.2 Data Privacy and User Consent

Malware detection often involves analyzing sensitive features such as API calls, user permissions, and network activities. To ensure privacy, it is made sure that no raw user data is transferred during inference. Also, all data processing is carried out on-device locally to reduce data leakage. Finally, the system supports federated learning frameworks by allowing distributed model updates without central data aggregation.

6.3 Model Explainability

To build trust with end-users and cybersecurity analysts, the model must provide explanations for its predictions. TabNet's attention-based feature selection inherently supports interpretability by revealing which features contributed most to a decision (e.g., permissions like SEND_SMS or API calls like getResource()).

6.4 Adversarial Robustness

AI models are susceptible to adversarial attacks where malware is crafted to evade detection. While this work does not yet incorporate adversarial training, it outlines a roadmap for future hardening against evasion tactics, including adversarial example detection and robust training schemes.

6.5 Compliance and Governance

The proposed system is designed with considerations aligned with data protection regulations such as **GDPR**, ensuring minimal data collection, transparency in decisions, and user autonomy over privacy preferences.

7. EMERGING TRENDS AND FUTURE DIRECTIONS

Given the evolving threat landscape and the rapid advancement of AI techniques, the following emerging trends offer promising directions for enhancing malware detection systems.

7.1 Explainable AI (XAI)

XAI techniques such as SHAP (Shapley Additive Explanations) and LIME (Local Interpretable Model-Agnostic Explanations) are increasingly used to provide transparency in malware classification. These tools help security analysts understand which features most influenced a prediction, improving trust and forensic analysis.

7.2 Few-Shot and Transfer Learning

To combat zero-day malware and data scarcity, few-shot learning enables models to generalize from limited examples. Transfer learning allows pre-trained models to be fine-tuned with minimal effort for new malware families, reducing training overhead.

7.3 Federated Learning

Federated Learning (FL) supports collaborative model updates across devices without centralized data sharing, preserving user privacy while enabling continual model improvement. Sáez-de-Cámara (2023) introduced clustering algorithm with federated learning for intrusion detection in IoT.

7.4 Lightweight AI Architectures

Future deployments demand efficient models with minimal memory, latency, and power footprint. Research into mobile-optimized models such as MobileNet, TinyML, or Transformer-based distillation techniques will further support real-time detection on low-resource devices.

7.5 Adversarial Defenses

Newer malware strains are designed to evade AI models using adversarial obfuscation. Defenses such as adversarial training, input sanitization, and anomaly detection mechanisms are being explored to improve robustness.

8. CONCLUSION

This study introduces a robust parallel ensemble machine learning framework for Android malware detection, combining the strengths of multiple gradient boosting classifiers—CatBoost, LightGBM, XGBoost, AdaBoost, and Gradient Boosting, with deep feature selection using TabNet. By reducing the high-dimensional Drebin dataset to 22 highly relevant features, the system achieves a high accuracy of 93%, while maintaining efficiency and interpretability suitable for deployment on resource-constrained mobile endpoints. The ensemble architecture leverages both soft and hard voting strategies to enhance generalization and reduce false positives, outperforming individual models in robustness and predictive reliability. TabNet's attention-based mechanism not only enables effective dimensionality reduction but also aids in identifying the most discriminative static and behavioral features indicative of malware, ensuring efficient training and reduced inference complexity. Despite these advantages, the reliance on static analysis limits the detection of obfuscated or zero-day threats. Therefore, future work will focus on integrating dynamic behavioral profiling, adopting adversarial learning techniques to defend against emerging malware variants, and optimizing lightweight, power-efficient models for real-time on-device inference. Altogether, the proposed system provides a foundational step toward next-generation mobile security solutions that balance accuracy, interpretability, and real-world deployability in defending the Android ecosystem from sophisticated malware threats.

REFERENCES

Abdellah, M. R., & Oudah, H, H., Ahmed Badawy, A. M., M Hassan, M. A. A., Bedier, S. A., Metwaly, A. A., & Abdelhafeez, A. (2025). Enhanced Federated Learning Framework based on Deep Learning and Neutrosophic Set for Android Malware Classification. *Neutrosophic Sets and Systems*, *82*(1), 781–799.

Alazzam, H., Al-Adwan, A., Abualghanam, O., Alhenawi, E. A., & Alsmady, A. (2022). An improved binary owl feature selection in the context of android malware detection. *Computers*, *11*(12), 1–19.

Aldhafferi, N. (2024). Android Malware Detection Using Support Vector Regression for Dynamic Feature Analysis. *Information (Basel)*, *15*(10), 658. DOI: 10.3390/info15100658

Alshomrani, M., Albeshri, A., Alturki, B., Alallah, F. S., & Alsulami, A. A. (2024). Survey of Transformer-Based Malicious Software Detection Systems. *Electronics (Basel)*, *13*(23), 1–34.

Arik, S. Ö., & Pfister, T. (2021, May). Tabnet: Attentive interpretable tabular learning. *Proceedings of the AAAI Conference on Artificial Intelligence*, *35*(8), 6679–6687.

Arp, D., Spreitzenbarth, M., Hubner, M., Gascon, H., Rieck, K., & Siemens, C. E. R. T. (2014, February). Drebin: Effective and explainable detection of android malware in your pocket. In *Ndss*, 14(1), 23-26.

Bourebaa, F., & Benmohammed, M. (2025). Evaluating Lightweight Transformers with Local Explainability for Android Malware Detection. *IEEE Access : Practical Innovations, Open Solutions*.

Breiman, L. (2001). Random Forests. *Machine Learning*, *45*, 5–32.

Cai, H. (2020). Assessing and improving malware detection sustainability through app evolution studies. [TOSEM]. *ACM Transactions on Software Engineering and Methodology*, *29*(2), 1–28.

Chambyal, A., & Sharma, A. K. (2024, December). Empirical Analysis of Feature Selection Techniques for Optimal Feature Set Identification in Android Malware Detection. In *2024 Eighth International Conference on Parallel, Distributed and Grid Computing (PDGC)*, 328-335). IEEE.

Chen, T., & Guestrin, C. (2016, August). Xgboost: A scalable tree boosting system. In *Proceedings of the 22nd acm sigkdd international conference on knowledge discovery and data mining*, 785-794.

Dhaliwal, S. S., Nahid, A. A., & Abbas, R. (2018). Effective intrusion detection system using XGBoost. *Information (Basel)*, *9*(7), 1–24.

Dorogush, A. V., (2018). CatBoost: gradient boosting with categorical features support. *arXiv:1810.11363*.

Feng, J., Shen, L., Chen, Z., Lei, Y., & Li, H. (2025). HGDetector: A hybrid Android malware detection method using network traffic and Function call graph. *Alexandria Engineering Journal*, *114*, 30–45.

Freund, Y., & Schapire, R. E. (1997). A decision-theoretic generalization of on-line learning and an application to boosting. *Journal of Computer and System Sciences*, *55*(1), 119–139.

Friedman, J. H. (2001). Greedy function approximation: A gradient boosting machine. *Annals of Statistics*, 1189–1232.

Goodfellow, I., (2016). *Deep Learning*. MIT Press.

Hadi, H. J., Khalid, A., Hussain, F. B., Ahmad, N., & Alshara, M. A. (2025). FLSH: A Framework Leveraging Similarity Hashing for Android Malware and Variant Detection. *IEEE Access : Practical Innovations, Open Solutions*, •••, 26142–26156.

Hemalatha, J., Roseline, S. A., Geetha, S., Kadry, S., & Damaševičius, R. (2021). An efficient densenet-based deep learning model for malware detection. *Entropy (Basel, Switzerland)*, *23*(3), 1–23.

Huang, G., Liu, Z., Van Der Maaten, L., & Weinberger, K. Q. (2017). Densely connected convolutional networks. In *Proceedings of the IEEE conference on computer vision and pattern recognition*, 4700-4708).

Huang, H., Huang, W., Zhou, Y., Luo, W., & Wang, Y. (2025). FEdroid: A lightweight and interpretable machine learning-based android malware detection system. *Cluster Computing*, *28*(4), 224.

Joachims, T. (1998, April). Text categorization with support vector machines: Learning with many relevant features. In *European conference on machine learning*, Berlin, Heidelberg: Springer Berlin Heidelberg, 137-142.

Ke, G., (2017). *LightGBM: A highly efficient gradient boosting decision tree*. NIPS.

Korine, R., & Hendler, D. (2021). DAEMON: Dataset/platform-agnostic explainable malware classification using multi-stage feature mining. *IEEE Access : Practical Innovations, Open Solutions*, *9*, 78382–78399.

Latifah, I. A., Rafrastara, F. A., Bintoro, J., Ghozi, W., & Osman, W. M. (2024). Comparative Analysis of Feature Selection Methods with XGBoost for Malware Detection on the Drebin Dataset. [Sistem Informasi dan Komputer]. *Jurnal Sisfokom, 13*(3), 403–409.

Luo, M., Wang, Y., Xie, Y., Zhou, L., Qiao, J., Qiu, S., & Sun, Y. (2021). Combination of feature selection and catboost for prediction: The first application to the estimation of aboveground biomass. *Forests, 12*(2), 216.

Mishra, J., Sahay, S. K., Rathore, H., & Kumar, L. 2021, October. Duplicates in the drebin dataset and reduction in the accuracy of the malware detection models. In *2021 26th IEEE Asia-Pacific Conference on Communications (APCC)*, 161-165.

Pektaş, A., & Acarman, T. (2020). Learning to detect Android malware via opcode sequences. *Neurocomputing, 396*, 599–608.

Roseline, S. A., & Geetha, S. (2021, May). Android malware detection and classification using LOFO feature selection and tree-based models. In *Journal of Physics: Conference Series* (Vol. 1911, No. 1, p. 012031). IOP Publishing, 1-10.

Sáez-de-Cámara, X., Flores, J. L., Arellano, C., Urbieta, A., & Zurutuza, U. (2023). Clustered federated learning architecture for network anomaly detection in large scale heterogeneous IoT networks. *Computers & Security, 131*, 103299.

Shah, C., Du, Q., & Xu, Y. (2022). Enhanced TabNet: Attentive interpretable tabular learning for hyperspectral image classification. *Remote Sensing, 14*(3), 1–21.

Shazeer, N. 2020. Glu variants improve transformer. *arXiv preprint arXiv:2002.05202.*

Sihag, V., Manu Vardhan, Pradeep Singh, Gaurav Choudhary, and Seiil Son. (2021). De-LADY: Deep learning based Android malware detection using Dynamic features. *Journal of Internet Services and Information Security, 11*(2), 34–45.

Stalin, K., & Mekoya, M. B. (2024). Improving Android Malware Detection Through Data Augmentation Using Wasserstein Generative Adversarial Networks. *arXiv preprint arXiv:2403.00890.*

Taheri, R., Ghahramani, M., Javidan, R., Shojafar, M., Pooranian, Z., & Conti, M. (2020). Similarity-based Android malware detection using Hamming distance of static binary features. *Future Generation Computer Systems, 105*, 230–247.

Thangaveloo, R., & Jing, W. (2020, March). W., Kang Leng, C. and Abdullah, J. "DATDroid: Dynamic Analysis Technique in Android Malware Detection". *International Journal on Advanced Science, Engineering and Information Technology, 10*(2), 536–541.

Ünver, H. M., & Bakour, K. (2020). Android malware detection based on image-based features and machine learning techniques. *SN Applied Sciences*, *2*(7), 1299.

Vaswani, A., Shazeer, N., Parmar, N., Uszkoreit, J., Jones, L., Gomez, A. N., & Polosukhin, I. (2017). Attention is all you need. *Advances in Neural Information Processing Systems*, •••, 30.

Yan, J., Xu, T., Yu, Y., & Xu, H. (2021). Rainfall forecast model based on the tabnet model. *Water (Basel)*, *13*(9), 1–16.

Zhang, C., & Ma, Y. (2012). *Ensemble machine learning*. Springer.

Zhang, S., Su, H., Liu, H., & Yang, W. (2025). MPDroid: A multimodal pre-training Android malware detection method with static and dynamic features. *Computers & Security*, *150*, 104262.

Compilation of References

Abd Latif, S. F., Sulaiman, N. S., Abd Aziz, N. S., Yacob, A., & Nasir, A. (2025). Development of Cybersecurity Awareness Model Based on Protection Motivation Theory (PMT) for Digital IR 4.0 in Malaysia. *International Journal of Advanced Computer Science and Applications*, *16*(3).

Abdellah, M. R., & Oudah, H, H., Ahmed Badawy, A. M., M Hassan, M. A. A., Bedier, S. A., Metwaly, A. A., & Abdelhafeez, A. (2025). Enhanced Federated Learning Framework based on Deep Learning and Neutrosophic Set for Android Malware Classification. *Neutrosophic Sets and Systems*, *82*(1), 781–799.

Abdulhameed, I. S., Al-Mejibli, I., & Naif, J. R. (2021). The security and privacy of electronic health records in healthcare systems: A systematic review. *Turkish Journal of Computer and Mathematics Education*, *12*(10), 1979–1992.

Abisoye, A., & Akerele, J. I. (2021). A High-Impact Data-Driven Decision-Making Model for Integrating Cutting-Edge Cybersecurity Strategies into Public Policy, Governance, and Organizational Frameworks. *International Journal of Multidisciplinary Research and Growth Evaluation*, *2*(1), 623–637. DOI: 10.54660/.IJMRGE.2021.2.1.623-637

Abouelmehdi, K., Beni-Hessane, A., & Khaloufi, H. (2018). Big healthcare data: Preserving security and privacy. *Journal of Big Data*, *5*(1). Advance online publication. DOI: 10.1186/s40537-017-0110-7

Abubakari, P. (2024). *Human factors matter: The intersection of cybersecurity governance, and culture in risk management of critical infrastructure.* (Doctoral dissertation). Pepperdine University.

Acar, A., Aksu, H., Uluagac, A. S., & Conti, M. (2018). A survey on homomorphic encryption schemes: Theory and implementation. *ACM Computing Surveys*, *51*(4), 79. Advance online publication. DOI: 10.1145/3214303

Acquisti, A., & Grossklags, J. (2007). What can behavioral economics teach us about31 privacy? In Acquisti, A., Gritzalis, S., Lambrinoudakis, C., & di Vimercati, S. (Eds.), *Digital privacy: Theory, technologies, and practices* (pp. 363–377). Springer.

Agarwal, K., & Shah, M. (2024). *The role of corporate governance in managing cybersecurity risks: A comprehensive analysis*. LawFoyer International Journal of Doctrinal Legal Research.

Ahmad, N., Laplante, P. A., DeFranco, J. F., & Kassab, M. (2022). A Cybersecurity Educated Community. *IEEE Transactions on Emerging Topics in Computing*, *10*(3), 1456–1463. DOI: 10.1109/TETC.2021.3093444

Ahmed, M., Kambam, H. R., Liu, Y., Jaidka, S., & Petrova, K. (2024). Impact and significance of human factors in digital information security. *International Journal of Information Science and Technology*, *7*(2), 1–17.

Aksoy, C. (2024). *Building a cyber security culture for resilient organizations against cyber attacks*. İşletme Ekonomi ve Yönetim Araştırmaları Dergisi.

Akter, S., Uddin, M. R., Sajib, S., Lee, W. J. T., Michael, K., & Hossain, M. A. (2022). Reconceptualizing cybersecurity awareness capability in the data-driven digital economy.

Al Hwaitat, A. K., & Fakhouri, H. N. (2024). Adaptive Cybersecurity Neural Networks: An Evolutionary Approach for Enhanced Attack Detection and Classification. *Applied Sciences (Basel, Switzerland)*, *14*(19), 9142.

Alaaraj, A., & Yassin, A. (2024). Investigating cybersecurity response strategies: Measures to responding to successful spear phishing attacks.

Alamer, M., & Almaiah, M. A. (2021, July). Cybersecurity in Smart City: A systematic mapping study. In 2021 international conference on information technology (ICIT) (pp. 719-724). IEEE.

Alanazi, F., Elsobky, B., & Elmorsy, S. (2024). A hybrid machine learning framework for security intrusion detection. *Computer Systems Science and Engineering*, *48*(3), 1–10. DOI: 10.32604/csse.2024.042401

Alasmary, W., Alsabaan, M., & Alhaidari, F. (2022). Securing electronic health records using modern cryptographic algorithms: A case study. *International Journal of Medical Informatics*, *163*, 104764. Advance online publication. DOI: 10.1016/j.ijmedinf.2022.104764

Alauthman, M., Al-Qerem, A., Alateef, S., Almomani, A., & Aldweesh, A. (2025). Human-centric cybersecurity: Addressing insider threats and organizational culture. In *Complexities and Challenges for Securing Digital Assets and Infrastructure* (pp. 435–456). IGI Global Scientific Publishing.

Alazzam, H., Al-Adwan, A., Abualghanam, O., Alhenawi, E. A., & Alsmady, A. (2022). An improved binary owl feature selection in the context of android malware detection. *Computers*, *11*(12), 1–19.

Albrecht, M., (2022). Efficient key exchange with post-quantum security: An overview of Kyber. *IEEE Security and Privacy*, *20*(3), 34–42.

Aldhafferi, N. (2024). Android Malware Detection Using Support Vector Regression for Dynamic Feature Analysis. *Information (Basel)*, *15*(10), 658. DOI: 10.3390/info15100658

Alevizos, L. (2024). Automated cybersecurity compliance and threat response using AI, blockchain and smart contracts. *International Journal of Information Technology: an Official Journal of Bharati Vidyapeeth's Institute of Computer Applications and Management*, *17*(2), 767–781. DOI: 10.1007/s41870-024-02324-9

Alhalafi, N., & Veeraraghavan, P. (2023). Exploring the challenges and issues in adopting cybersecurity in Saudi smart cities: Conceptualization of the cybersecurity-based UTAUT model. *Smart Cities*, *6*(3), 1523–1544.

Alharbi, F. S. (2024). Effects of the Protection Motivation Model on Information Security Policy Compliance Among Saudi Employees (Doctoral dissertation, Marymount University).

Alharkan, I., & Aslam, N. (2019). Factors affecting cloud computing adoption: A literature review synthesis and analysis. *International Journal of Computer Applications*, *177*(43), 29–36. https://www.researchgate.net/publication/332833321_Factors_Affecting_Cloud_Computing_Adoption_A_Literature_Review_Synthesis_And_Analysis

Al-Hashem, N., & Saidi, A. (2023). The psychological aspect of cybersecurity: Understanding cyber threat perception and decision-making. *International Journal of Applied Machine Learning and Computational Intelligence*, *13*(8), 11–22.

Alhiary, S. (2025, August 14). *BGP path attributes: Your BGP path selection master guide*. Learn With Salman. https://learnwithsalman.com/bgp-path-attributes/

Alhumud, T. A. A., Omar, A., & Altohami, W. M. A. (2023). An assessment of cybersecurity performance in the Saudi universities: A Total Quality Management approach. *Cogent Education*.

Ali, R. F., Dominic, P. D. D., Ali, S. E. A., Rehman, M., & Sohail, A. (2021). Information security behavior and information security policy compliance: A systematic literature review for identifying the transformation process from noncompliance to compliance. *Applied Sciences (Basel, Switzerland)*, *11*(8), 3383.

Ali, S., Wang, J., & Leung, V. C. M. (2025). AI-driven fusion with cybersecurity: Exploring current trends, advanced techniques, future directions, and policy implications for evolving paradigms– A comprehensive review. *Information Fusion*, *118*, 102922. DOI: 10.1016/j.inffus.2024.102922

Almansoori, A., Al-Emran, M., & Shaalan, K. (2023). Exploring the frontiers of cybersecurity behavior: A systematic review of studies and theories. *Applied Sciences (Basel, Switzerland)*, *13*(9), 5700.

Almeida, F. (2023). Prospects of cybersecurity in smart cities. *Future Internet*, *15*(9), 285.

Alotaibi, M. B., & Alzahrani, A. I. (2021). Human factor aspects in information security management in the traditional IT and cloud computing models. *International Journal of Computer Science and Information Security*, *19*(4), 47–55. https://www.researchgate.net/publication/351078133_Human_Factor_Aspects_in_Information_Security_Management_in_the_Traditional_it_and_Cloud_Computing_Models

Alraddadi, R., Alshayeb, M., Mahmood, S., & Niazi, M. (2025). Towards Understanding the Critical Role of Human Behavior in Smart and Cognitive City Cybersecurity. *Procedia Computer Science*, *257*, 1039–1046.

Alrawhani, E. M., Romli, A., & Al-Sharafi, M. A. (2025). Evaluating the role of protection motivation theory in information security policy compliance: Insights from the banking sector using PLS-SEM approach. *Journal of Open Innovation*, *11*(1), 100463.

Alshahrani, H. (2021). Impact of intention to adopt cloud-based human resource management on innovation behaviour: The mediating role of leadership support. *PalArch's Journal of Archaeology of Egypt/Egyptology*, *18*(10), 4070–4084. https://archives.palarch.nl/index.php/jae/article/download/9599/8849/18799

Alshaikh, M. (2020). Developing cybersecurity culture to influence employee behavior: A practice perspective. *Computers & Security*, *98*, 102003.

Alsharida, R. A., Al-rimy, B. A. S., Al-Emran, M., & Zainal, A. (2023). A systematic review of multi perspectives on human cybersecurity behavior. *Technology in Society*, *73*, 102258.

Alshomrani, M., Albeshri, A., Alturki, B., Alallah, F. S., & Alsulami, A. A. (2024). Survey of Transformer-Based Malicious Software Detection Systems. *Electronics (Basel), 13*(23), 1–34.

Alyami, A., Sammon, D., Neville, K., & Mahony, C. (2024). Critical success factors for Security Education, Training and Awareness (SETA) programme effectiveness: An empirical comparison of practitioner perspectives. *Information and Computer Security, 32*(1), 53–73.

Amazon Web Services. (2022). *AWS cloud adoption framework: People perspective*. https://docs.aws.amazon.com/pdfs/whitepapers/latest/aws-caf-people-perspective/aws-caf-people-perspective.pdf

Amazon Web Services. (2023). *Strategy – Cloud transformation (AWS Prescriptive Guidance)*. https://docs.aws.amazon.com/pdfs/prescriptive-guidance/latest/strategy-cloud-transformation/strategy-cloud-transformation.pdf

Amin, Z. (2019). A Practical Road Map for Assessing Cyber Risk. *Journal of Risk Research, 22*(1), 32–43.

Andronache, A. (2021). Increasing security awareness through lenses of cybersecurity culture. *Journal of Information Systems & Operations Management, 15*(1).

Andronache, A. (2021). INCREASING SECURITY AWARENESS THROUGH LENSES OF CYBERSECURITY CULTURE. *Journal of Information Systems & Operations Management, 15*(1).

Annarelli, A., Nonino, F., & Palombi, G. (2020). Understanding the management of cyber resilient systems. *Computers & Industrial Engineering, 149*, 106829. DOI: 10.1016/j.cie.2020.106829

Ansari, M. F. (2022). A quantitative study of risk scores and the effectiveness of AI-based Cybersecurity Awareness Training Programs. *International Journal of Smart Sensor and Adhoc Network, 3*(3), 1.

Ansari, M. F., Sharma, P. K., & Dash, B. (2022). Prevention of phishing attacks using AI-based Cybersecurity Awareness Training. *Prevention, 3*(6), 61–72.

Anu, V. (2021). Information security governance metrics: A survey and taxonomy. *Information and Computer Security, 29*(2), 316–337.

Arik, S. Ö., & Pfister, T. (2021, May). Tabnet: Attentive interpretable tabular learning. *Proceedings of the AAAI Conference on Artificial Intelligence, 35*(8), 6679–6687.

Armas, R., & Taherdoost, H. (2025). Building a Cybersecurity Culture in Higher Education: Proposing a Cybersecurity Awareness Paradigm. *Information (Basel), 16*(5), 336. DOI: 10.3390/info16050336

Arp, D., Spreitzenbarth, M., Hubner, M., Gascon, H., Rieck, K., & Siemens, C. E. R. T. (2014, February). Drebin: Effective and explainable detection of android malware in your pocket. In *Ndss*, 14(1), 23-26.

Asad, U., Khan, M., Khalid, A., & Lughmani, W. A. (2023). Human-Centric Digital Twins in Industry: A Comprehensive Review of Enabling Technologies and Implementation Strategies. *Sensors (Basel), 23*(8), 3938. DOI: 10.3390/s23083938 PMID: 37112279

Ashenden, D., & Lawrence, D. (2021). Can we sell security like soap? *Computer Fraud & Security*, (1), 15–20.

Atkins, S., & Lawson, C. (2021). An improvised patchwork: Success and failure in cybersecurity policy for critical infrastructure. *Public Administration Review*.

Bacud, M. L., & Mäses, S. (2021, October). Game-based learning for cybersecurity awareness training programmes in the public sector. In ECEL 2021 20th European Conference on e-Learning. Academic Conferences International limited (p. 50).

Bada, M., Sasse, A. M., & Nurse, J. R. (2019). Cyber security awareness campaigns: Why do they fail to change behaviour? arXiv preprint arXiv:1901.02672.

Badii, C., Bellini, P., Difino, A., & Nesi, P. (2020). Smart city IoT platform respecting GDPR privacy and security aspects. *IEEE Access: Practical Innovations, Open Solutions, 8*, 23601–23623.

Baker, B. M., & Siddiqui, J. (2022). In the trading zone: The eco and the techno at the limits of "the human" and compulsory schooling. *Journal of Curriculum and Pedagogy*.

Bansal, G., Gill, S. S., & Buyya, R. (2021). A survey on homomorphic encryption implementations. *ACM Computing Surveys, 54*(8), 1–38.

Barata, J., & Kayser, I. (2024). How will the digital twin shape the future of industry 5.0? *Technovation, 134*, 103025. DOI: 10.1016/j.technovation.2024.103025

Basri, W. S. (2023). Artificial Intelligence, Cyber Security Measures And Sme's E-Operational Efficiency: Moderating Role Of Employees Perception Of Ai Usefulness. Operational Research in Engineering Sciences: Theory and Applications, 6(4).

Beautement, A., & Sasse, M. A. (2019). *Human factors knowledge area, Issue 1.0 (CyBOK)*. Cyber Security Body of Knowledge. https://www.cybok.org/media/downloads/Human_Factors_issue_1.0.pdf

Bellamkonda, S. (2020). Cybersecurity in critical infrastructure: Protecting the foundations of modern society. *International Journal of Communication Networks and Information Security*, *12*(2), 273–280. https://ijcnis.org/index.php/ijcnis/article/view/7529/1846

Bellare, M., & Rogaway, P. (2005). *Introduction to Modern Cryptography*. UC Davis Lecture Notes.

Beniiche, A., Rostami, S., & Maier, M. (2022). Society 5.0: Internet as if People Mattered. *IEEE Wireless Communications*, *29*(6), 160–168. DOI: 10.1109/MWC.009.2100570

Benjamin, H. (2002). *CCNP practical studies: Routing*. Cisco Press.

Ben-Sasson, E., Bentov, I., Horesh, Y., & Riabzev, M. (2019). *Scalable, transparent, and post-quantum secure computational integrity* (IACR Cryptol. ePrint Arch., Rep. No. 2018/046). https://eprint.iacr.org/2018/046

Bhandari, S., & Hallowell, M. R. (2022). Influence of safety climate on risk tolerance and risk-taking behavior: A cross-cultural examination. *Safety Science*.

Bhanot, R., & Hans, R. (2015). A Review and Comparative Analysis of Various Encryption Algorithms. *International Journal of Security and Its Applications*, *9*(4), 289–306.

Bhuyan, S. S., (2020). Transforming Healthcare Cybersecurity from Reactive to Proactive: Current Status and Future Recommendations. *Journal of Medical Systems*, *44*(5). Advance online publication. DOI: 10.1007/s10916-019-1507-y PMID: 32239357

Björk, B. C. (2017). Growth of hybrid open access, 2009–2016. *PeerJ*, *5*, e3878. DOI: 10.7717/peerj.3878 PMID: 28975059

Blessing, M. (2024). *Predictive analytics for proactive threat mitigation* [Preprint]. ResearchGate. https://www.researchgate.net/publication/389264973_Predictive_Analytics_for_Proactive_Threat_Mitigation

Bonczkowski, J. (2025). *Mastering BGP: A step-by-step configuration and troubleshooting guide for eBGP and iBGP (STEP-by-STEP: A Network Administrator's Best Friend)* [Kindle edition]. Independently published. https://www.amazon.com/dp/B0F6MRQQN7

Boneh, D., & Shoup, V. (2020). *A graduate course in applied cryptography*. https://crypto.stanford.edu/~dabo/cryptobook/

Bonneau, J., Herley, C., Van Oorschot, P. C., & Stajano, F. (2015). Password metrics and real-world passwords. *Communications of the ACM*, *58*(7), 39–44.

Bourebaa, F., & Benmohammed, M. (2025). Evaluating Lightweight Transformers with Local Explainability for Android Malware Detection. *IEEE Access : Practical Innovations, Open Solutions*.

Breiman, L. (2001). Random Forests. *Machine Learning*, *45*, 5–32.

Bruno, A., & Jordan, S. (2024). *CCNP enterprise design ENSLD 300-420 official cert guide* (2nd ed.). Cisco Press.

Buck, C., (2023). Digital transformation and its impact on organizational risk scenarios. *The Journal of Strategic Information Systems*, *32*(3), 101778.

Bulgurcu, B., Cavusoglu, H., & Benbasat, I. (2010). Information security policy compliance: An empirical study of rationality-based beliefs and information security awareness. *Management Information Systems Quarterly*, 523–548.

Burton, S. L., Burrell, D. N., Nobles, C., & Jones, L. A. (2023). Exploring the nexus of cybersecurity leadership, human factors, emotional intelligence, innovative work behavior, and critical leadership traits. *Scientific Bulletin-Nicolae Balcescu Land Forces Academy*, *28*(2), 162–175.

Bussacarini, M. (2024, March). Global Readiness for Cybersecurity and AI: Assessing the Landscape and Charting the Path Forward. In International Ethical Hacking Conference (pp. 3-15). Singapore: Springer Nature Singapore.

Cai, H. (2020). Assessing and improving malware detection sustainability through app evolution studies. [TOSEM]. *ACM Transactions on Software Engineering and Methodology*, *29*(2), 1–28.

Camacho, N. G. (2024). The Role of AI in Cybersecurity: Addressing Threats in the Digital Age. *Journal of Artificial Intelligence General Science (JAIGS) ISSN:3006-4023*, *3*(1), 143–154. https://doi.org/DOI: 10.60087/jaigs.v3i1.75

Cassottana, B., Roomi, M. M., Mashima, D., & Sansavini, G. (2023). Resilience analysis of cyber-physical systems: A review of models and methods. *Risk Analysis*, *43*(11), 2359–2379. DOI: 10.1111/risa.14089 PMID: 36646448

Chambyal, A., & Sharma, A. K. (2024, December). Empirical Analysis of Feature Selection Techniques for Optimal Feature Set Identification in Android Malware Detection. In *2024 Eighth International Conference on Parallel, Distributed and Grid Computing (PDGC)*, 328-335). IEEE.

Chang, L. Y., & Coppel, N. (2020). Building cyber security awareness in a developing country: Lessons from Myanmar. *Computers & Security*, *97*, 101959.

Chartered Institute of Ergonomics & Human Factors. (2016). *The role of human factors in delivering cyber security*. https://ergonomics.org.uk/static/54e334a2-e8ba-483d-a678-b36307252af6/e2931aee-33d8-42bb-8330-0e77f2000bd0/the-role-of-human-factors-in-delivering-cyber-security.pdf

Chauhan, M., & Shiaeles, S. (2023). An analysis of cloud security frameworks, problems and proposed solutions. *Network (Bristol, England)*, *3*(3), 422–450. https://www.mdpi.com/2673-8732/3/3/18

Chaum, D. (1981). Untraceable Electronic Mail, Return Addresses, and Digital Pseudonyms. *Communications of the ACM*, *24*(2), 84–88.

Cheng, E. C., & Wang, T. (2022). Institutional strategies for cybersecurity in higher education institutions. *Information (Basel)*, *13*(4), 192.

Chen, T., & Guestrin, C. (2016, August). Xgboost: A scalable tree boosting system. In *Proceedings of the 22nd acm sigkdd international conference on knowledge discovery and data mining*, 785-794.

Chen, Y. (2022). Information security management: Compliance challenges and new directions. *Journal of Information Technology Case and Application Research*, *24*(4), 243–249. DOI: 10.1080/15228053.2022.2148979

Cheryl, B. K., Ng, B. K., & Wong, C. Y. (2021). Governing the progress of Internet-of-Things: Ambivalence in the quest of technology exploitation and user rights protection. *Technology in Society*.

Chima Abimbola Eden, Onyebuchi Nneamaka Chisom, & Idowu Sulaimon Adeniyi. (2024). Integrating AI in education: Opportunities, challenges, and ethical considerations. *Magna Scientia Advanced Research and Reviews, 10*(2), 006–013. https://doi.org/DOI: 10.30574/msarr.2024.10.2.0039

Chippagiri, S. (2025, January). A study of cloud security frameworks for safeguarding multi-tenant cloud architectures. *International Journal of Computer Applications*, *186*(60), 50–57. DOI: 10.5120/ijca2025924369

Chippagiri, S., & Ravula, P. (2021). Cloud-Native Development: Review of Best Practices and Frameworks for Scalable and Resilient Web Applications. *International Journal of New Media Studies: International Peer Reviewed Scholarly Indexed Journal*, *8*(2), 13–21. https://ijnms.com/index.php/ijnms/article/view/294

Cisco Networking Academy. (2025). *Module 11: BGP [CCNP Enterprise Core Networking]*. https://netacad.com/ar/courses/ccnp-enterprise-core-networking

Clarke, R., Jenkins, B., & Ahmed, N. (2023). Cryptographic safeguards for remote education systems in higher education. *Journal of Cybersecurity Education, Research and Practice, 2023*(1), Article 2. https://digitalcommons.kennesaw.edu/jcerp/vol2023/iss1/2

Coles-Kemp, L., & Reeves, S. (2017). The role of human aspects in cyber security: Behaviour or culture? *Cyber Security: A Peer-Reviewed Journal, 1*(4), 305–315. https://www.henrystewartpublications.com/sites/default/files/CSJ1.4HumanaspectsofcybersecurityBehaviourorculturechange.pdf

Collins, E. I. M., & Hinds, J. (2021). Exploring Workers' Subjective Experiences of Habit Formation in Cybersecurity: A Qualitative Survey. *Cyberpsychology, Behavior, and Social Networking*, *24*(9), 599–604. DOI: 10.1089/cyber.2020.0631 PMID: 34403600

Connelly, Y., Henkin, G., Leibovich, M., & Akavia, A. (2022). Factors influencing the adoption of advanced cryptographic techniques for data protection of patient medical records. *Healthcare Informatics Research*, *28*(2), 132–142. PMID: 35576981

Corradini, I. (2020). Building a cybersecurity culture. In *Building a Cybersecurity Culture in Organizations: How to Bridge the Gap Between People and Digital Technology* (pp. 63–86). Springer International Publishing.

Coventry, L., Briggs, P., Jeske, D., & van Moorsel, A. (2014). *SCENE: A Structured Means for Creating and Evaluating Behavioral Nudges in a Cyber Security Environment.*, DOI: 10.1007/978-3-319-07668-3_23

Cram, W. A., & D'Arcy, J. (2023). 'What a waste of time': An examination of cybersecurity legitimacy. *Journal of the Association for Information Systems*, *24*(1), 1–38.

Creese, S., Dutton, W. H., & Esteve-González, P. (2021). The social and cultural shaping of cybersecurity capacity building: A comparative study of nations and regions. *Personal and Ubiquitous Computing*, *25*(5), 941–955. PMID: 33994905

Cremer, F., Sheehan, B., Fortmann, M., Kia, A. N., Mullins, M., Murphy, F., & Materne, S. (2022). Cyber risk and cybersecurity: A systematic review of data availability. *The Geneva Papers on Risk and Insurance. Issues and Practice*, *47*(3), 698–736. PMID: 35194352

Crick, T., Davenport, J. H., Hanna, P., Irons, A., & Prickett, T. (2020). Overcoming the Challenges of Teaching Cybersecurity in UK Computer Science Degree Programmes. *2020 IEEE Frontiers in Education Conference (FIE)*, 1–9. https://doi.org/DOI: 10.1109/FIE44824.2020.9274033

Crumpler, W., & Lewis, J. A. (2022). Cybersecurity workforce gap (p. 10). Center for Strategic and International Studies (CSIS).

Culot, G., Nassimbeni, G., Podrecca, M., & Sartor, M. (2021). The ISO/IEC 27001 information security management standard: Literature review and theory-based research agenda. *The TQM Journal, 33*(7), 76–105.((((https://doi.org/)))))DOI: 10.1108/TQM-06-2020-0148

Cyber Security Agency of Singapore. (2023). Annual cybersecurity report 2023. https://www.csa.gov.sg

Cybersecurity and Infrastructure Security Agency. (2023). *Cloud security technical reference architecture v2*. https://www.cisa.gov/sites/default/files/2023-02/cloud_security_technical_reference_architecture_2.pdf

D'Arcy, J., Hovav, A., & Galletta, D. (2014). User awareness of security countermeasures as a deterrent to IS misuse. *Information Systems Research*, *20*(1), 79–98. DOI: 10.1287/isre.1070.0160

Da Veiga, A. (2018). An approach to information security culture change combining ADKAR and the ISCA questionnaire to aid transition to the desired culture.

Dadiyala, C., Tangade, P., Singh, G., Bhutada, V., Bhattad, A., Partani, N., & Jangid, R. (2023). Designing and Implementing an Effective Cybersecurity Home Lab for Detection and Monitoring. *2023 14th International Conference on Computing Communication and Networking Technologies (ICCCNT)*, 1–8. https://doi.org/DOI: 10.1109/ICCCNT56998.2023.10306937

Dash, B., & Ansari, M. F. (2022). An effective cybersecurity awareness training model: First defense of an organizational security strategy.

Dawson, M., Bacius, R., Gouveia, L. B., & Vassilakos, A. (2021). Understanding the challenge of cybersecurity in critical infrastructure sectors. Land Forces Academy Review, 26(1), 69-75. https://www.researchgate.net/publication/349969874_Understanding_the_Challenge_of_Cybersecurity_in_Critical_Infrastructure_Sectors

Dayarathna, R. (2023). Towards Measuring the Readiness of the Cybersecurity Workforce in Sri Lanka. Available at *SSRN* 4630524.

DeCusatis, C., Alvarico, E., & Dirahoui, O. (2022). Gamification of cybersecurity training. *Proceedings of the 1st International Workshop on Gamification of Software Development, Verification, and Validation*, 10–13. https://doi.org/DOI: 10.1145/3548771.3561409

Delgado, I., Sancristobal, E., Martin, S., & Robles-Gómez, A. (2023). Exploring IoT Vulnerabilities in a Comprehensive Remote Cybersecurity Laboratory. *Sensors (Basel)*, *23*(22), 9279. DOI: 10.3390/s23229279 PMID: 38005664

Dhaliwal, S. S., Nahid, A. A., & Abbas, R. (2018). Effective intrusion detection system using XGBoost. *Information (Basel)*, *9*(7), 1–24.

Diakoumakos, I. (2023). Enhancing Cyber Security Education and Training through Gamification. *Proceedings of the 2nd International Conference of the ACM Greek SIGCHI Chapter*, 1–5. https://doi.org/DOI: 10.1145/3609987.3610016

Diffie, W. (1988). The First Ten Years of Public-Key Cryptography. *Proceedings of the IEEE*, *76*(5), 560–577.

Diffie, W., & Hellman, M. (1976). New Directions in Cryptography. *IEEE Transactions on Information Theory*, *22*(6), 644–654.

Diffie, W., & Hellman, M. E. (1976). New directions in cryptography. *IEEE Transactions on Information Theory*, *22*(6), 644–654. DOI: 10.1109/TIT.1976.1055638

Dodge, C. E., Fisk, N., Burruss, G. W., Moule, R. K.Jr, & Jaynes, C. M. (2023). What motivates users to adopt cybersecurity practices? A survey experiment assessing protection motivation theory. *Criminology & Public Policy*, *22*(4), 849–868.

Dolev, D., & Yao, A. (1983). On the Security of Public Key Protocols. *IEEE Transactions on Information Theory*, *29*(2), 198–208.

Dorogush, A. V., (2018). CatBoost: gradient boosting with categorical features support. *arXiv:1810.11363.*

Dupont, B. (2019). The cyber-resilience of financial institutions: Significance and applicability. *Journal of Cybersecurity*, *5*(1). Advance online publication. DOI: 10.1093/cybsec/tyz013

Eastlake, D., & Jones, P. (2001). "US Secure Hash Algorithm 1 (SHA1)." RFC 3174.

Edgar, B., & Willinsky, J. (2010). A Survey of Scholarly Journals Using Open Journal Systems. *Scholarly and Research Communication*, *1*(2). Advance online publication. DOI: 10.22230/src.2010v1n2a24

Edwards, J. (2024). *A comprehensive guide to the NIST cybersecurity framework 2.0: Strategies, implementation, and best practice.*

ElGamal, T. (1985). A Public Key Cryptosystem and a Signature Scheme Based on Discrete Logarithms. *IEEE Transactions on Information Theory*, *31*(4), 469–472.

ENISA. (2021). *Post-quantum cryptography: Current state and quantum mitigation*. European Union Agency for Cybersecurity. https://www.enisa.europa.eu/publications/post-quantum-cryptography

ENISA. (2023). *Cybersecurity culture guidelines: Behavioural aspects of cybersecurity*. https://www.enisa.europa.eu/publications

European Parliament. (2016). Regulation (EU) 2016/679 (General Data Protection Regulation). https://eur-lex.europa.eu/eli/reg/2016/679/oj

Evans, D., Kolesnikov, V., & Rosulek, M. (2018). A pragmatic introduction to secure multi-party computation. *Foundations and Trends in Privacy and Security*, *2*(2–3), 70–246. DOI: 10.1561/3300000024

Fahl, S., Harbach, M., Perl, H., Koetter, M., & Smith, M. (2012). Why Eve and Mallory love Android: An analysis of Android SSL (in)security. *Proceedings of the 2012 ACM Conference on Computer and Communications Security*, 50–61. https://doi.org/DOI: 10.1145/2382196.2382205

Fahl, S., Harbach, M., & Smith, M. (2022). Why developers write insecure code: A security-usability study of APIs. *IEEE Security and Privacy*. Advance online publication. DOI: 10.1109/MSP.2022.3154731

Fahl, S., Harbach, M., & Smith, M. (2023). Usability of cryptographic APIs and secure default settings. *Journal of Cybersecurity*, *9*(1), 112–126.

Farao, J., (2020). A user-centred design framework for mHealth. *PLoS One*, *15*(8), e0237910. PMID: 32813711

Faruq, M. O. (2025). A meta-analysis of cybersecurity framework integration in GRC platforms: Evidence from US enterprise audits. *Journal of Sustainable Development and Policy*.

Feng, J., Shen, L., Chen, Z., Lei, Y., & Li, H. (2025). HGDetector: A hybrid Android malware detection method using network traffic and Function call graph. *Alexandria Engineering Journal, 114*, 30–45.

Ferdinand, F., Irawan, G. N., Kennedy, J., & Gustvin, J. (2024). Simulasi jaringan untuk sistem terdistribusi SOHO dengan GNS3. *Jurnal Ilmu Komputer dan Sistem Informasi, 12*(2).

Ferreira, L. V. A., Alves, C. A. D. M., Peotta de Melo, L., & Nunes, R. R. (2025). Internal audit strategies for assessing cybersecurity controls in the Brazilian financial institutions. *Applied Sciences (Basel, Switzerland), 15*(10), 5715. DOI: 10.3390/app15105715

Floyd, D. L., Prentice-Dunn, S., & Rogers, R. W. (2000). A meta-analysis of research on protection motivation theory. *Journal of Applied Social Psychology, 30*(2), 407–429.

Folorunso, A., Wada, I., Samuel, B., & Mohammed, V. (2024). Security compliance and its implication for cybersecurity. *World Journal of Advanced Research and Reviews, 24*(1), 2105–2121. DOI: 10.30574/wjarr.2024.24.01.0174

Formosa, P., Wilson, M., & Richards, D. (2021). A principlist framework for cybersecurity ethics. *Computers & Security, 109*, 102382. Advance online publication. DOI: 10.1016/j.cose.2021.102382

Freund, Y., & Schapire, R. E. (1997). A decision-theoretic generalization of on-line learning and an application to boosting. *Journal of Computer and System Sciences, 55*(1), 119–139.

Friedman, J. H. (2001). Greedy function approximation: A gradient boosting machine. *Annals of Statistics*, 1189–1232.

Fu, X., Wang, H., & Shi, P. (2022). A survey of lattice-based expressive attribute-based encryption. *Computer Science Review, 44*, 100438.

Garfinkel, S., & Lipford, H. R. (2021). *Usable security: History, themes, and challenges*. Morgan & Claypool Publishers.

George, K. (2024). *Phishing Results*. Information Technology Services. https://www.carleton.edu/its/newsletter/news/phishing-results/?utm_source=chatgpt.com

George, A. S., & Fernando, S., Baskar, & George, A. S. (2023). Extending detection and response: How MXDR evolves cybersecurity. *Partners Universal International Innovation Journal*, *1*(4), 268–285. DOI: 10.5281/zenodo.8284342

Georgiadou, A., Mouzakitis, S., Bounas, K., & Askounis, D. (2022). A cyber-security culture framework for assessing organization readiness. *Journal of Computer Information Systems*, *62*(3), 452–462.

Ghelani, D. (2022). Cyber security, cyber threats, implications and future perspectives: A review. *Authorea Preprints*.

Ghillani, D. (2022). Deep learning and artificial intelligence framework to improve the cyber security. *Authorea Preprints*.

Goldwasser, S., & Micali, S. (1984). Probabilistic Encryption. *Journal of Computer and System Sciences*, *28*(2), 270–299.

Goodfellow, I., (2016). *Deep Learning*. MIT Press.

Google Security Blog. (2020). *Security keys neutralized employee phishing*. https://security.googleblog.com/2020/01/security-keys-neutralized-employee.html

Greenleaf, G. (2020). Global Data Privacy Laws 2020: Despite COVID Delays, 145 Laws Show GDPR Dominance. *Privacy Laws & Business International Report*, (165), 10–13.

Guest, D., (2022). A meta-synthesis of the socio-technical systems theory in organizational studies. *Human Relations*, *75*(6), 1045–1080.

Guo, H., Liu, Y., & Chen, X. (2008). A comparative analysis of security flaws in open-source software. *Proceedings of the 2008 International Conference on Computer Science and Software Engineering*.

Haastrup, T. A., & Nwakibea, F. I. (2024). Effective leadership for peace and security management. *Journal of Institutional Leadership*.

Hadi, H. J., Khalid, A., Hussain, F. B., Ahmad, N., & Alshara, M. A. (2025). FLSH: A Framework Leveraging Similarity Hashing for Android Malware and Variant Detection. *IEEE Access : Practical Innovations, Open Solutions*, •••, 26142–26156.

Hadnagy, C., & Wilson, N. (2022). *Social engineering: The science of human hacking*. Wiley.

Hajny, J., Ricci, S., Piesarskas, E., Levillain, O., Galletta, L., & De Nicola, R. (2021). Framework, Tools and Good Practices for Cybersecurity Curricula. *IEEE Access: Practical Innovations, Open Solutions*, *9*, 94723–94747. DOI: 10.1109/ACCESS.2021.3093952

Halabi, S., & McPherson, D. (2000). *Internet routing architectures*. Cisco Press.

Halbouni, A., Gunawan, T. S., Habaebi, M. H., Halbouni, M., Kartiwi, M., & Ahmad, R. (2022). Machine learning and deep learning approaches for cybersecurity: A review. *IEEE Access: Practical Innovations, Open Solutions*, *10*, 19572–19585.

Haney, J. M., & Lutters, W. (2023). From Compliance to Impact: Tracing the Transformation of an Organizational Security Awareness Program. *Proceedings of the ACM on Human-Computer Interaction*, 7(CSCW2), 1-28.

Hassan, I. (2022). Levereging Apache Guacamole, Linux LXD and Docker Containers to Deliver a Secure Online Lab for a Large Cybersecurity Course. *2022 IEEE Frontiers in Education Conference (FIE)*, 1–9. https://doi.org/DOI: 10.1109/FIE56618.2022.9962510

Hausken, K. (2020). Cyber resilience in firms, organizations and societies. *Internet of Things: Engineering Cyber Physical Human Systems*, *11*, 100204. DOI: 10.1016/j.iot.2020.100204

Haustein, S., Larivière, V., & Mongeon, P. (2015). The oligopoly of academic publishing in the digital era. *PLoS One*, *10*(6), e0127502. DOI: 10.1371/journal.pone.0127502 PMID: 26061978

Heckman, P., Heckman, H. M., & Vervest, M. R. (2007). The reluctant innovator: Open source adoption by SMEs. *Decision Support Systems*, *42*(4), 2249–2266. DOI: 10.1016/j.dss.2006.05.001

Hemalatha, J., Roseline, S. A., Geetha, S., Kadry, S., & Damaševičius, R. (2021). An efficient densenet-based deep learning model for malware detection. *Entropy (Basel, Switzerland)*, *23*(3), 1–23.

Hijji, M., & Alam, G. (2022). Cybersecurity awareness and training (CAT) framework for remote working employees. *Sensors (Basel)*, *22*(22), 8663. PMID: 36433259

Himma-Kadakas, M., & Kõuts-Klemm, R. (2023). Developing an advanced digital society: An estonian case study. In *Internet in the Post-Soviet Area: Technological, economic and political aspects* (pp. 109–133). Springer International Publishing.

Hong, Y., & Furnell, S. (2021). Understanding cybersecurity behavioral habits: Insights from situational support. *Journal of Information Security and Applications*, *57*, 102710. DOI: 10.1016/j.jisa.2020.102710

Hon, W. K., Millard, C., & Walden, I. (2011). The problem of 'personal data' in cloud computing: What information is regulated?—the cloud of unknowing. *International Data Privacy Law*, *1*(4), 211–228. DOI: 10.1093/idpl/ipr018

Hossain, M. A., Raza, M. A., & Rahman, T. Y. (2023). Resource allocation and budgetary constraints for cybersecurity projects in small to medium sized banks. *SSRN.*

Hsu, J. S. C., Lee, C. S., & Straub, D. W. (2015). The Role of Extra-Role Behaviors and Social Controls in Information Security Policy Effectiveness. *Information Systems Research*, *26*(2), 282–300.

Hu, S., Huang, R., & Zhou, L. (2025). An Efficient Multi-Key BFV Fully Homomorphic Encryption Scheme with Optimized Relinearization. Cybersecurity, 8(1), Article 42. Published: 26 June 2025.

Huang, K., & Pearlson, K. (2019). For what technology can't fix: Building a model of organizational cybersecurity culture. *ICIS 2019 Proceedings*.

Huang, G., Liu, Z., Van Der Maaten, L., & Weinberger, K. Q. (2017). Densely connected convolutional networks. In *Proceedings of the IEEE conference on computer vision and pattern recognition*, 4700-4708).

Huang, H., Huang, W., Zhou, Y., Luo, W., & Wang, Y. (2025). FEdroid: A lightweight and interpretable machine learning-based android malware detection system. *Cluster Computing*, *28*(4), 224.

Huang, L. (2023). Ethics of Artificial Intelligence in Education: Student Privacy and Data Protection. *Science Insights Education Frontiers*, *16*(2), 2577–2587. DOI: 10.15354/sief.23.re202

Huang, L., Zhang, J., & Lee, R. (2022). Securing cryptographic keys using hardware security modules: A comprehensive survey. *IEEE Access: Practical Innovations, Open Solutions*, *10*, 57492–57512. DOI: 10.1109/ACCESS.2022.3178503

Hubbart, J. A. (2024). Understanding and mitigating leadership fear-based behaviors on employee and organizational success. *Administrative Sciences*, *14*(1), 22.

Huda, M., Brayyich, M., Haroon, N. H., Khan, A. A., & Verma, R. (2024, July). An Exploratory Investigation into Sustaining Cybersecurity Protection Through the Implementation of SETA. In *2024 International Conference on Emerging Trends in Networks and Computer Communications (ETNCC)* (pp. 292-296). IEEE.

Hu, S., Hsu, C., & Zhou, Z. (2022). Security education, training, and awareness programs: Literature review. *Journal of Computer Information Systems*, *62*(4), 752–764.

Hwang, I., Wakefield, R., Kim, S., & Kim, T. (2021). Security awareness: The first step in information security compliance behavior. *Journal of Computer Information Systems*, *61*(4), 345–356.

Ifinedo, P. (2012). Understanding information systems security policy compliance: An integration of the theory of planned behavior and the protection motivation theory. *Computers & Security*, *31*(1), 83–95.

Ismail, K. R., Brata, Z. A., Nelistiani, G. A., Heo, S., Kim, H., & Kim, H. (2025). Toward robust security orchestration and automated response in security operations centers with a hyper-automation approach using agentic artificial intelligence. *Information (Basel)*, *16*(5), 365. Advance online publication. DOI: 10.3390/info16050365

ISO/IEC 22301:2019. Security and resilience—Business continuity management systems—Requirements.

ISO/IEC 27001:2013. Information Security Management.

Iyer, S. S., & Raji, B. (2025). Cybersecurity culture and organizational resilience: A human-centered approach to digital risk management. *American Journal of Industrial and Business Management*, *15*(5), 748–766.

Iyer, S. S., & Raji, B. (2025). Cybersecurity Culture and Organizational Resilience: A Human-Centered Approach to Digital Risk Management. *American Journal of Industrial and Business Management*, *15*(5), 748–766.

Jampen, D., et al. (2020). Don't click: towards an effective anti-phishing training. A comparative literature review. *Human-centric Computing and Information Sciences*, 10(1).

Jančiūtė, L. (2025). Cybersecurity in the financial sector and the quantum-safe cryptography transition: In search of a precautionary approach in the EU Digital Operational Resilience Act framework. *International Cybersecurity Law Review*, *6*(2), 145–154. PMID: 40406673

Jimmy, F. (2021). *Emerging threats: The latest cybersecurity risks and the role of artificial intelligence in enhancing cybersecurity defenses*. Valley International Journal Digital Library.

Joachims, T. (1998, April). Text categorization with support vector machines: Learning with many relevant features. In *European conference on machine learning*, Berlin, Heidelberg: Springer Berlin Heidelberg, 137-142.

Johnston, A. C., & Warkentin, M. (2010). Fear appeals and information security behaviors: An empirical study. *Management Information Systems Quarterly*, •••, 549–566.

Judijanto, L., Hindarto, D., Wahjono, S. I., & Djunarto, A. (2023). Edge of enterprise architecture in addressing cyber security threats and business risks. [IJSECS]. *International Journal of Software Engineering and Computer Science*, *3*(3), 386–396.

Kalinin, M., Krundyshev, V., & Zegzhda, P. (2021). Cybersecurity risk assessment in smart city infrastructures. *Machines (Basel)*, *9*(4), 78.

Kamolov, S., Kaunov, E., & Lisov, A. (2023). Cyber readiness as an imperative for public governance in the digital age. MODERN APPROACHES IN ENGINEERING AND NATURAL SCIENCES: MAENS-2021, 2526(1), 030015.

Kannelønning, K., & Katsikas, S. K. (2023). A systematic literature review of how cybersecurity-related behavior has been assessed. *Information and Computer Security*, *31*(4), 463–477.

Karie, N. M., Sahri, N. M., Yang, W., Valli, C., & Kebande, V. R. (2021). A review of security standards and frameworks for IoT-based smart environments. *IEEE Access: Practical Innovations, Open Solutions*, *9*, 121975–121995.

Karpiuk, M., MELChIOR, C. L. A. U. D. I. O., & Soler, U. (2023). Cybersecurity Management in the Public Service Sector. *Prawo i Więź*, (4 (47)), 7–27.

Kaur, R., Gabrijelčič, D., & Klobučar, T. (2023). Artificial intelligence for cybersecurity: Literature review and future research directions. *Information Fusion*, *97*, 101804. DOI: 10.1016/j.inffus.2023.101804

Ke, G., (2017). *LightGBM: A highly efficient gradient boosting decision tree*. NIPS.

Ke, H., Xu, J., Wang, Y., Chen, H., & Shen, Z. (2025). Adversarial machine learning in cybersecurity: Attacks and defenses. *International Journal of Management Science Research*, *8*, 26–33. DOI: 10.53469/ijomsr.2025.08(02).04

Kelsey, J., et al. (2015). "Secure Hash Standard." NIST FIPS PUB 180-1.

Kerikmäe, T., & Pärn-Lee, E. (2020). Legal dilemmas of Estonian artificial intelligence strategy: In between of e-society and global race. *AI & Society*, *36*(2), 561–572. DOI: 10.1007/s00146-020-01009-8

Kern, M., Landauer, M., Skopik, F., & Weippl, E. (2024). A logging maturity and decision model for the selection of intrusion detection cyber security solutions. *Computers & Security*, *141*, 103844. Advance online publication. DOI: 10.1016/j.cose.2024.103844

Kerzner, H. (2023). *Project management metrics, KPIs, and dashboards: A guide to measuring and monitoring project performance* (3rd ed.). Wiley.

Kezron, I. E. (2024). Enhancing Cybersecurity Capacity in Small and Medium Enterprises: A Framework for Workforce Development. *Iconic Research and Engineering Journals*, *7*(10), 421–428.

Khader, M., Karam, M., & Fares, H. (2021). Cybersecurity awareness framework for academia. *Information (Basel)*, *12*(10), 417.

Khadka, K., & Ullah, A. B. (2025). Human factors in cybersecurity: An interdisciplinary review and framework proposal. *International Journal of Information Security*, *24*, 119. DOI: 10.1007/s10207-025-01032-0

Khaleel, Y. L., Habeeb, M. A., Albahri, A. S., Al-Quraishi, T., Albahri, O. S., & Alamoodi, A. H. (2024). Network and cybersecurity applications of defense in adversarial attacks: A state-of-the-art using machine learning and deep learning methods. *Journal of Intelligent Systems*, *33*(1), 20240153. Advance online publication. DOI: 10.1515/jisys-2024-0153

Khan, O. U., Abdullah, S. M., Olajide, A. O., Sani, A. I., Faisal, S. M. W., Ogunola, A. A., & Lee, M. D. (2024). The Future of Cybersecurity: Leveraging Artificial Intelligence to Combat Evolving Threats and Enhance Digital Defense Strategies. *Journal of Computational Analysis and Applications*, *33*(8).

Khan, S., (2022). A Systematic Analysis of the Capital One Data Breach: Critical Lessons Learned. *ACM Transactions on Privacy and Security*, *26*(1), 1–29. DOI: 10.1145/3546068

Khan, S., Luo, F., Zhang, Z., Rahim, M. A., Ahmad, M., & Wu, K. (2022). Survey on issues and recent advances in vehicular public-key infrastructure (VPKI). *IEEE Communications Surveys and Tutorials*, *24*(3), 1574–1601. DOI: 10.1109/COMST.2022.3178081

Khayat, M., Barka, E., Serhani, M. A., Sallabi, F., Shuaib, K., & Khater, H. (2025). Empowering security operation center with artificial intelligence and machine learning—A systematic literature review. *IEEE Access: Practical Innovations, Open Solutions*, *13*, 19162–19197. DOI: 10.1109/ACCESS.2025.3532951

Khedr, A., Hassan, H., & Eisa, S. (2024). Practical solutions in fully homomorphic encryption. A review. *Cybersecurity*, *7*, 37. DOI: 10.1186/s42400-024-00171-4

Kim, M., & Lauter, K. (2021). Privacy preserving machine learning using homomorphic encryption. *IEEE Security and Privacy*, *19*(4), 42–49. DOI: 10.1109/MSEC.2021.3075652

Kop, M., (2024). Navigating the quantum frontier: Examining the interplay of quantum computing, policy, and global security. *Technology in Society*, *77*, 102589.

Korine, R., & Hendler, D. (2021). DAEMON: Dataset/platform-agnostic explainable malware classification using multi-stage feature mining. *IEEE Access : Practical Innovations, Open Solutions*, *9*, 78382–78399.

Koskinen, J. (2023). *Organizational and cultural cloud adoption challenges: A case study of a SaaS data engineering team* (Master's thesis, Aalto University). Aaltodoc. https://aaltodoc.aalto.fi/bitstreams/3e4077de-6345-446d-a4dd-27d42f064e93/download

Kumar, D. (2024, December 13). *Basic of BGP routing protocol – A two napkin protocol – Part 1*. Cisco Learning Network. https://learningnetwork.cisco.com/s/article/Basic-of-BGP-routing-Protocol-A-Two-Napkin-Protocol-Part-1

Kumar, R. (2024). The role of human factor in cybersecurity: Behavioral insights and training strategies. *International Research Journal of Modernization in Engineering Technology and Science*, *6*(3), 2282–2290. https://www.irjmets.com/uploadedfiles/paper/issue_3_march_2024/51493/final/fin_irjmets1711953082.pdf

Lammle, T., Odom, S., & Wallace, K. (2001). *CCNP routing study guide*. Sybex.

Latifah, I. A., Rafrastara, F. A., Bintoro, J., Ghozi, W., & Osman, W. M. (2024). Comparative Analysis of Feature Selection Methods with XGBoost for Malware Detection on the Drebin Dataset. [Sistem Informasi dan Komputer]. *Jurnal Sisfokom*, *13*(3), 403–409.

Lee, I. (2021). Cybersecurity: Risk management framework and investment cost analysis. *Business Horizons*, *64*(4), 509–519.

Leo, W. W. C., Laud, G., & Chou, C. Y. (2023). Digital transformation for crisis preparedness: Service employees' perspective. *Journal of Services Marketing*, *37*(1), 102–116.

Lewis, A. D., & Groth, K. M. (2022). Metrics for evaluating the performance of complex engineering system health monitoring models. *Reliability Engineering & System Safety*, *219*, 108200.

Li, F., Yao, H., Liu, Z., & Chen, P. (2023). A survey on searchable symmetric encryption. *ACM Computing Surveys*, *56*(5), 131.

Liu, Y., Lu, Q., Yu, G., Paik, H.-Y., & Zhu, L. (2021). Defining blockchain governance principles: A comprehensive framework. *Journal of Information Technology. Operational Analysis*, *27*(3), 155–172. DOI: 10.1080/10580530.2020.1720046

Li, Y., & Liu, Q. (2021). A comprehensive review study of cyber-attacks and cyber security; emerging trends and recent developments. *Energy Reports*, *7*, 8176–8186.

Luo, M., Wang, Y., Xie, Y., Zhou, L., Qiao, J., Qiu, S., & Sun, Y. (2021). Combination of feature selection and catboost for prediction: The first application to the estimation of aboveground biomass. *Forests*, *12*(2), 216.

Maddux, J. E., & Rogers, R. W. (1983). Protection motivation and self-efficacy: A revised theory of fear appeals and attitude change. *Journal of Experimental Social Psychology*, *19*(5), 469–479.

Madi Odeh, R. B., Obeidat, B. Y., Jaradat, M. O., Masa'deh, R. E., & Alshurideh, M. T. (2023). The transformational leadership role in achieving organizational resilience through adaptive cultures: The case of Dubai service sector. *International Journal of Productivity and Performance Management*, *72*(2), 440–468.

Mahfuzhi, A. W., Reswan, Y., & Handayani, K. M. (2024). Network design using proxy-based BGP (Border Gateway Protocol) routing. *Jurnal Komputer, Informasi dan Teknologi*, *4*(1).

Mahlatje, N. (2022). The function of cyber-security awareness and training in shaping cyber-risk perceptions and resultant cyber behaviours. *Journal of Cybersecurity and Digital Trust*, *1*(1), 45–62.

Makkonen, H., Kask, T., & Vassil, K. (2022). Cryptography and transparency in the Estonian e-government ecosystem. *Government Information Quarterly*, *39*(3), 101702. Advance online publication. DOI: 10.1016/j.giq.2022.101702

Malviya, M. K., & Singhal, M. K. (2024). A Literature Survey on Different Data Encryption and Decryption Techniques. *JETIR*, *11*(9), 1–6.

Marchesi, L., Marchesi, M., & Tonelli, R. (2024). A survey on crypto-agility and agile practices in the light of quantum resistance. *Information and Software Technology*, *178*, 107604. DOI: 10.1016/j.infsof.2024.107604

Marotta, A., & Madnick, S. (2021). Convergence and divergence of regulatory compliance and cybersecurity. *Issues in Information Systems*, *22*(4), 25–31.

Marshall, R., Pardo, A., Smith, D., & Watson, T. (2022). Implementing next generation privacy and ethics research in education technology. *British Journal of Educational Technology*, *53*(4), 737–755. DOI: 10.1111/bjet.13224

Mashiane, T., & Kritzinger, E. (2021). Identifying behavioral constructs in relation to user cybersecurity behavior. *Eurasian Journal of Soil Science*, *9*(2), 98–122.

Mavroeidis, V., Hohimer, R., Casey, T., & Jesang, A. (2021, May). Threat actor type inference and characterization within cyber threat intelligence. In *2021 13th International Conference on Cyber Conflict (CyCon)* (pp. 327–352). IEEE.

Mbanaso, U. M., Abrahams, L., & Okafor, K. C. (2023). *Research techniques for computer science, information systems and cybersecurity*. Springer.

Melaku, H. M. (2023). A dynamic and adaptive cybersecurity governance framework. *Journal of Cybersecurity and Privacy*, *3*(3), 327–350.

Menezes, A. J., van Oorschot, P. C., & Vanstone, S. A. (1996). *Handbook of Applied Cryptography*. CRC Press.

Metin, B., Özhan, F. G., & Wynn, M. (2024). Digitalisation and Cybersecurity: Towards an Operational Framework. *Electronics (Basel)*, *13*(21), 4226.

Mia, M. R., Shahriar, H., Valero, M., Sakib, N., Saha, B., Barek, M. A., & Ahamed, S. I. (2022). A comparative study on HIPAA technical safeguards assessment of Android mHealth applications. *Smart Health (Amsterdam, Netherlands)*, *26*, 100349. DOI: 10.1016/j.smhl.2022.100349 PMID: 39086849

Mishra, J., Sahay, S. K., Rathore, H., & Kumar, L. 2021, October. Duplicates in the drebin dataset and reduction in the accuracy of the malware detection models. In *2021 26th IEEE Asia-Pacific Conference on Communications (APCC)*, 161-165.

Mızrak, F. (2023). Integrating cybersecurity risk management into strategic management: A comprehensive literature review. *Research Journal of Business and Management*, *10*(2), 65–75.

Moallem, A. (2024). Human behavior in cybersecurity privacy and trust. Human-Computer Interaction in Intelligent Environments, 77-107.

Mohammed, A. (2022). Cybersecurity in Smart Cities: Securing IoT and Smart Infrastructure. Available at *SSRN* 5066095.

Mohammed, A. (2024). Cybersecurity in Smart Cities: As cities become smarter, new vulnerabilities arise. Research can focus on securing IoT devices, smart infrastructure, and privacy concerns associated with smart city data. *Pioneer Research Journal of Computing Science*, *1*(1), 75–82.

Moore, T., & Ridley, A. (2022). Cryptographic key mismanagement in practice: Failures and lessons. *Journal of Cybersecurity*, *8*(1).

Moşteanu, N. R. (2024). Adapting to the unpredictable: Building resilience for business continuity in an ever-changing landscape. *European Journal of Theoretical and Applied Sciences*, *2*(1), 45–57.

Moustafa, A. A., Bello, A., & Maurushat, A. (2021). The role of user behaviour in improving cyber security management. *Frontiers in Psychology*, *12*, 725422. PMID: 34220596

Muniandy, L., Muniandy, B., & Samsudin, Z. (2017). Cyber Security Behaviour among Higher Education Students in Malaysia. *Journal of Information Assurance & Cybersecurity*, 1–13. https://doi.org/DOI: 10.5171/2017.800299

MUSHI. J. (2023). Examining the Factors Obstructing Cyber security Readiness in Public Sector (Doctoral dissertation, IAA).

Nagyfejeo, E., & Von Solms, B. (2020). Why do national cybersecurity awareness programmes often fail. *International Journal of Information Security and Cybercrime*, *9*(2), 18–27.

Nasir, S. (2023, July). Exploring the effectiveness of cybersecurity training programs: factors, best practices, and future directions. In *Proceedings of the Cyber Secure Nigeria Conference* (pp. 151-160).

National Institute of Standards and Technology. (2023). *Post-quantum cryptography standardization project*. https://csrc.nist.gov/projects/post-quantum-cryptography

Nedyalkov, I. (2023). Application of GNS3 to study the security of data exchange between power electronic devices and control center. *Computers*, *12*(5), 101.

Nifakos, S., Chandramouli, K., Nikolaou, C. K., Papachristou, P., Koch, S., Panaousis, E., & Bonacina, S. (2021). Influence of human factors on cyber security within healthcare organisations: A systematic review. *Sensors (Basel)*, *21*(15), 5119. DOI: 10.3390/s21155119 PMID: 34372354

Nisenoff, A., & Golla, M. B. U. (2023). *Measuring the Risk Password Reuse Poses for a University*. USENIX. https://www.usenix.org/publications/loginonline/measuring-risk-password-reuse-poses-university?utm_source=chatgpt.com

NIST. (2022). Guide to Test, Training, and Exercise Programs for IT Plans and Capabilities. https://nvlpubs.nist.gov/nistpubs/Legacy/SP/nistspecialpublication800-84.pdf

Nizich, M. (2023). Preparing the cybersecurity workforce of tomorrow. In *The Cybersecurity Workforce of Tomorrow* (pp. 117–146). Emerald Group Publishing Limited.

Nkosi, M., Gupta, K., & Mashinini, P. M. (2023). Assessing the Capacity for Change Prior to the Adoption of Human Factors Engineering in Power Plant Maintenance. *Systems*, *11*(10), 520. DOI: 10.3390/systems11100520

Nobles, C. (2022). Stress, Burnout, and Security Fatigue in Cybersecurity: A Human Factors Problem. *HOLISTICA–Journal of Business and Public Administration, 13*(1), 49–72.

Nwachukwu, U., Vidgren, J., Niemimaa, M., & Järveläinen, J. (2023). Do SETA Interventions Change Security Behavior?–A Literature Review.

Obelovska, K., Snaichuk, Y., Liskevych, O., Mitoulis, S. A., & Liskevych, R. (2025). Mitigation of risks associated with distrustful routers in OSPF networks—An enhanced method. *Computers, 14*(2).

Odom, W. (2010). *CCNP route 642-902 official certification guide* (Official certification guide series). Cisco Press.

Ohiri, U. W. (2024). Examining the Concept of an AI-Based Cybersecurity Awareness Training Aimed at Remodeling Employees' Behavior (Doctoral dissertation, National University).

Olaiya, O. P., Adesoga, T. O., Adebayo, A. A., Sotomi, F. M., Adigun, O. A., & Ezeliora, P. M. (2024). Encryption techniques for financial data security in fintech applications. *International Journal of Science and Research Archive, 12*(1), 2942–2949.

Olaniyan, R., Rakshit, S., & Vajjhala, N. (2023). Application of user and entity behavioral analytics (UEBA) in the detection of cyber threats and vulnerabilities management. In *Computational intelligence for engineering and management applications* (pp. 1–15). Springer. https://doi.org/DOI: 10.1007/978-981-19-8493-8_32

Oliha, J. S., Biu, P. W., & Obi, O. C. (2024). Securing the smart city: A review of cybersecurity challenges and strategies. *Engineering Science & Technology Journal, 5*(2), 496–506.

OWASP. (2021). OWASP Top Ten. https://owasp.org/www-project-top-ten/

Paar, C., & Pelzl, J. (2009). *Understanding Cryptography: A Textbook for Students and Practitioners*. Springer.

Paigude, S. D., Pangarkar, S. C., Dari, S. S., Patil, M., & Gujar, S. N. (2024). A Review of Cybersecurity Policies in the Public Sector: Challenges and Solutions. *Computer Fraud & Security, 2024*(7), 7–12.

Paliszkiewicz, J. (2019). Information Security Policy Compliance: Leadership and Trust. *Journal of Computer Information Systems, 59*(3), 211–217. DOI: 10.1080/08874417.2019.1571459

Parsons, C., McCormac, A., Butavicius, M., Pattinson, M., & Jerram, C. (2023). Determining employee awareness using the Human Aspects of Information Security Questionnaire (HAIS-Q). *Computers & Security, 123*, 102982. DOI: 10.1016/j.cose.2022.102982

Patel, M. D., & Sable, R. (2023). Leading with integrity: How leadership personality shapes cybersecurity behavior. In *The Interdisciplinary Nexus* (Vol. 299, pp. 120–135). Law, Humanities, and Management.

Paul, E., Callistus, O., Somtobe, O., Esther, T., Somto, K., Clement, O., & Ejimofor, I. (2023). Cybersecurity strategies for safeguarding customer's data and preventing financial fraud in the United States financial sectors. *International Journal on Soft Computing, 14*(3), 01-16.

Pektaş, A., & Acarman, T. (2020). Learning to detect Android malware via opcode sequences. *Neurocomputing, 396*, 599–608.

Pemmasani, P. K. (2023). National Cybersecurity Frameworks for Critical Infrastructure: Lessons from Governmental Cyber Resilience Initiatives. *International Journal of Acta Informatica, 2*(1), 209–218.

Pemmasani, P. K., & Osaka, M. (2021). The Future of Smart Cities: Cybersecurity Challenges in Public Infrastructure Management. *International Journal of Modern Computing, 4*(1), 72–85.

Piardi, L., Leitão, P., Queiroz, J., & Pontes, J. (2024). Role of digital technologies to enhance the human integration in industrial cyber–physical systems. *Annual Reviews in Control, 57*, 100934. DOI: 10.1016/j.arcontrol.2024.100934

Poláková, M., Suleimanová, J. H., Madzík, P., Copuš, L., Molnárová, I., & Polednová, J. (2023). Soft skills and their importance in the labour market under the conditions of Industry 5.0. *Heliyon, 9*(8), e18670. DOI: 10.1016/j.heliyon.2023.e18670 PMID: 37593611

Pöyhönen, J., & Lehto, M. (2020, June). Cyber security: Trust based architecture in the management of an organization security. In Proceedings of the 18th European Conference on Cyber Warfare and Security ECCWS2020, 25–26 June 2020, Chester, UK (pp. 304-313). Reading: Academic Conferences and Publishing International Limited.

Prümmer, J., van Steen, T., & van den Berg, B. (2024). A systematic review of current cybersecurity training methods. *Computers & Security, 136*, 103585. DOI: 10.1016/j.cose.2023.103585

Puhakainen, P., & Siponen, M. (2010). Improving employees' compliance through information systems security training: An action research study. *Computers & Security, 29*(5), 612–624. DOI: 10.1016/j.cose.2010.05.001

Quinn, S., Ivy, N., Barrett, M., Witte, G., & Gardner, R. K. (2024). *Staging cybersecurity risks for enterprise risk management and governance oversight.* National Institute of Standards and Technology.

Răceanu, D. N., & Marian, C. V. (2023). Cybersecurity Virtual Labs for Pentesting Education. *2023 13th International Symposium on Advanced Topics in Electrical Engineering (ATEE)*, 1–4. https://doi.org/DOI: 10.1109/ATEE58038.2023.10108187

Radu, C. (2023). Fostering a positive workplace culture: Impacts on performance and agility. In *Human Resource Management—An Update* (pp. 87–101). IGI Global.

Rahouti, M. (2019). Board 129: Facilitation of Cybersecurity Learning Through Real-world Hands-on Labs. *2019 ASEE Annual Conference & Exposition Proceedings.* https://doi.org/DOI: 10.18260/1-2--32228

Ramezanian, S., & Niemi, V. (2024). Cybersecurity Education in Universities: A Comprehensive Guide to Curriculum Development. *IEEE Access: Practical Innovations, Open Solutions, 12*, 61741–61766. DOI: 10.1109/ACCESS.2024.3392970

Rana, S., Biswas, S., & Mahato, B. (2023). A comprehensive survey of cryptography key management systems. *Journal of King Saud University. Computer and Information Sciences, 35*(7), 101594.

Rashid, T., & Chauhan, K. (2020). Cyber Security in the Public Sector: Awareness of Potential Risks among Public Policy Executives. In Security Analytics for the Internet of Everything (pp. 67-91). CRC Press.

Rasslan, M., Nasreldin, M. M., Abdelrahman, D., Elshobaky, A., & Aslan, H. (2024). Networking and cryptography library with a non-repudiation flavor for blockchain. *Journal of Computer Virology and Hacking Techniques, 20*(1), 1–14.

Redino, R., Iyer, R., & Suri, N. (2022). Zero day threat detection using graph and flow based security telemetry [Preprint]. arXiv. https://arxiv.org/abs/2205.02298

Ristenpart, T., & Yilek, S. (2020). The role of AI in cryptographic key management. *IEEE Security and Privacy, 18*(3), 54–61. DOI: 10.1109/MSEC.2020.2975045

Roe, M., Spanaki, K., Ioannou, A., Zamani, E. D., & Giannakis, M. (2022). Drivers and challenges of Internet of Things diffusion in smart stores: A field exploration. *Technological Forecasting and Social Change, 178*, 121593.

Rogers, R. W. (1975). A protection motivation theory of fear appeals and attitude change1. *The Journal of Psychology, 91*(1), 93–114. PMID: 28136248

Roseline, S. A., & Geetha, S. (2021, May). Android malware detection and classification using LOFO feature selection and tree-based models. In *Journal of Physics: Conference Series* (Vol. 1911, No. 1, p. 012031). IOP Publishing, 1-10.

Saeed, S., Suayyid, S. A., Al-Ghamdi, M. S., Al-Muhaisen, H., & Almuhaideb, A. M. (2023). A Systematic Literature Review on Cyber Threat Intelligence for Organizational Cybersecurity Resilience. *Sensors (Basel), 23*(16), 7273. DOI: 10.3390/s23167273 PMID: 37631808

Sáez-de-Cámara, X., Flores, J. L., Arellano, C., Urbieta, A., & Zurutuza, U. (2023). Clustered federated learning architecture for network anomaly detection in large scale heterogeneous IoT networks. *Computers & Security, 131*, 103299.

Safa, N. S., Von Solms, R., & Furnell, S. (2016). Information security policy compliance in organizations: A review. *Computers & Security, 56*, 70–82.

Salako, A. O., (2025). Securing Confidentiality in Distributed Ledger Systems with Secure Multi-party Computation for Financial Data Protection. *Journal of Engineering Research and Reports, 27*(3), 352–373.

Salem, M., Samara, K., Pray, J., & Hussein, M. (2024). Evaluating the Effectiveness of Online Cybersecurity Program in Higher Education. *2024 IEEE Global Engineering Education Conference (EDUCON)*, 1–9. https://doi.org/DOI: 10.1109/EDUCON60312.2024.10578833

Sallos, M.-P., Garcia Perez, A., & Bocanet, A. (2024). Organisational cyber resilience: A heuristic for bridging foundations and applications. *Journal of Enterprise Information Management, 37*(6), 1926–1952. DOI: 10.1108/JEIM-06-2023-0317

Sarker, I. H., Furhad, M. H., & Nowrozy, R. (2021). AI-Driven Cybersecurity: An Overview, Security Intelligence Modeling and Research Directions. *SN Computer Science, 2*(3), 173. DOI: 10.1007/s42979-021-00557-0 PMID: 33778771

Sasse, M. A., Brostoff, S., & Weirich, D. (2001). Transforming the 'weakest link'—A human/computer interaction approach to usable and effective security. *Computers & Security, 20*(3), 229–237. DOI: 10.1016/S0167-4048(01)00342-0

Sasse, M. A., Brostoff, S., & Weirich, D. (2021). Transforming the 'weakest link'—A human/computer interaction approach to usable and effective security. *Interacting with Computers, 33*(3), 239–260.

Savaş, S., & Karataş, S. (2022). Cyber governance studies in ensuring cybersecurity: An overview of cybersecurity governance. *International Cybersecurity Law Review*, *3*(3), 265–276. PMID: 37521508

Schlienger, T., & Teufel, S. (2002). Information security culture: The socio-cultural dimension in information security management. In *Security in the information society: Visions and perspectives* (pp. 191–201). Springer US.

Schmeelk, S. E., & Dragos, D. M. (2024). A Global Cybersecurity Embedded Course: Student Learnings and Curricular Design. *2024 IEEE Frontiers in Education Conference (FIE)*, 1–9. https://doi.org/DOI: 10.1109/FIE61694.2024.10893447

Seaman, J. (2023). Zero trust security strategies and guideline. In *Digital transformation in policing: The promise, perils and solutions* (pp. 149–168). Springer International Publishing., https://www.springerprofessional.de/en/digital-transformation-in-policing-the-promise-perils-and-soluti/23882432

Seneviratne, O., Kagal, L., & Berners-Lee, T. (2020). Cybersecurity and the evolving web: Threats and solutions. *IEEE Internet Computing*, *24*(1), 52–59. DOI: 10.1109/MIC.2020.2970638

Sepúlveda Estay, D. A., Sahay, R., Barfod, M. B., & Jensen, C. D. (2020). A systematic review of cyber-resilience assessment frameworks. *Computers & Security*, *97*, 101996. DOI: 10.1016/j.cose.2020.101996

Seth, B., Dalal, G., & Kumar, S. (2020). Integrating encryption techniques for secure data storage in the cloud. *Transactions on Emerging Telecommunications Technologies*, *33*(4), e4108. DOI: 10.1002/ett.4108

Sewak, M., Karim, R., & Pournaras, E. (2022). Deep reinforcement learning for cybersecurity threat detection and protection: A review [Preprint]. arXiv. https://arxiv.org/abs/2206.02733

Shah, C., Du, Q., & Xu, Y. (2022). Enhanced TabNet: Attentive interpretable tabular learning for hyperspectral image classification. *Remote Sensing*, *14*(3), 1–21.

Shamir, A. (1979). How to Share a Secret. *Communications of the ACM*, *22*(11), 612–613.

Shazeer, N. 2020. Glu variants improve transformer. *arXiv preprint arXiv:2002.05202*.

Shillair, R., Esteve-González, P., Dutton, W. H., Creese, S., Nagyfejeo, E., & von Solms, B. (2022). Cybersecurity education, awareness raising, and training initiatives: National level evidence-based results, challenges, and promise. *Computers & Security*, *119*, 102756.

Sholeha, E. W., Jaya, D. Y., Supriyanto, A., & Utomo, H. S. (2025). Komparasi fungsionalitas EVE-NG dan GNS3: Simulasi protokol jaringan. *Algoritma: Jurnal Ilmu Komputer dan Informatika, 9*(1), 1–8.

Siagian, R., Siahaan, L., & Hamzah, M. I. (2023). Human rights in the digital era: Online privacy, freedom of speech, and personal data protection. *Journal of Digital Learning and Distance Education, 2*(4), 548–558.

Sihag, V., Manu Vardhan, Pradeep Singh, Gaurav Choudhary, and Seiil Son. (2021). De-LADY: Deep learning based Android malware detection using Dynamic features. *Journal of Internet Services and Information Security, 11*(2), 34–45.

Sikolia, D., Biros, D., & Zhang, T. (2023). How effective are seta programs anyway: Learning and forgetting in security awareness training. Journal of Cybersecurity Education. *Research and Practice, 2023*(1), 4.

Silić, M., & Lowry, P. B. (2020). Using Design-Science Based Gamification to Improve Organizational Security Training and Compliance. *Journal of Management Information Systems, 37*(1), 129–161. DOI: 10.1080/07421222.2019.1705512

Singh, A. K., Anand, A., Lv, Z., Ko, H., & Mohan, A. (2021). A survey on healthcare data: A security perspective. *ACM Transactions on Multimedia Computing Communications and Applications, 17*(2s), 1–26.

Singh, A., & Kaur, R. (2024). The human factor in cybersecurity: An analysis of emerging trends and challenges. *International Journal of Advanced Computer Science and Applications, 15*(2), 112–121. https://www.researchgate.net/publication/384471305_The_Human_Factor_in_Cybersecurity_An_Analysis_of_Emerging_Trends_and_Challenges

Singh, S., & Supriya, . (2013). A Study of Encryption Algorithms (RSA, DES, 3DES and AES) for Information Security. *International Journal of Computer Applications, 67*(19), 33–38.

Singun, A. J. (2025). Unveiling the barriers to digital transformation in higher education institutions: A systematic literature review. *Discover Education, 3*, 22.

Siponen, M., Rönkkö, M., Fufan, L., Haag, S., & Laatikainen, G. (2024). Protection motivation theory in information security behavior research: Reconsidering the fundamentals. *Communications of the Association for Information Systems, 53*(1), 1136–1165.

Smith, E., Haustein, S., Larivière, V., & Siler, K. (2018). Author, publisher, and journal responses to open access and open data in scholarly publishing. *JASIST, 69*(12), 1475–1487. DOI: 10.1002/asi.24069

Sneha, R., Vasumathi, K., & Selvakani, S. (2024). Securing Data Using Cryptography and Steganography. *IJNRD*, *9*(3), 1–8.

Solomon, G., & Brown, I. (2021). The influence of organisational culture and information security culture on employee compliance behaviour. *Journal of Enterprise Information Management*, *34*(5), 1515–1533.

Sontan, A. D., & Samuel, S. V. (2024). The intersection of Artificial Intelligence and cybersecurity: Challenges and opportunities. *World Journal of Advanced Research and Reviews*, *21*(2), 1720–1736. DOI: 10.30574/wjarr.2024.21.2.0607

Souppaya, M., & Kent, K. (2006). Guide to Computer Security Log Management. NIST SP 800-92. https://csrc.nist.gov/publications/detail/sp/800-92/final

Springer. (2025). Artificial intelligence and machine learning in cybersecurity. *Knowledge and Information Systems, 101*(15). https://link.springer.com/article/10.1007/s10115-025-02429-y

Springer, J., & Haindl, P. (2024). Blockchain-based PKI within a corporate organization: Advantages and challenges. *Journal of Information Security and Applications*, *79*, 103648.

Stalin, K., & Mekoya, M. B. (2024). Improving Android Malware Detection Through Data Augmentation Using Wasserstein Generative Adversarial Networks. *arXiv preprint arXiv:2403.00890*.

Stallings, W. (2020). *Effective cybersecurity: A guide to using best practices and standards*. Addison-Wesley Professional.

Stallings, W. (2023). *Cryptography and network security: Principles and practice* (8th ed.). Pearson.

Stenalt, M. H. (2021). Digital student agency: Approaching agency in digital contexts from a critical perspective. *Frontline Learning Research*, *9*(3), 52–68. DOI: 10.14786/flr.v9i3.697

Stenberg, H. (2020). *The seven dimensions of security culture*. KnowBe4 Research. https://www.knowbe4.com/hubfs/CLTRe-The7DimensionsSecurityCulture-ResearchPaper.pdf

Stepanov, A., Kühling, J., & Rannenberg, K. (2021). GDPR compliance challenges for SMEs. *International Data Privacy Law*, *11*(1), 35–51. DOI: 10.1093/idpl/ipaa017

Streimikiene, D., Mikalauskiene, A., Digriene, L., & Kyriakopoulos, G. (2021). Assessment of the role of a leader in shaping sustainable organizational culture. *Amfiteatru Economic*, *23*(57), 483–503.

Subbiah, A. (2024). Enhancing Learner Motivation and Academic Achievement. In *Recent Trends and Future Direction for Data Analytics* (pp. 270–288). https://doi.org/DOI: 10.4018/979-8-3693-3609-0.ch012

Subbiah, A., & Ibrahim, O. (2011). Implementing affinity analysis in determining critical factors on e-service systems in Malaysia. *2011 International Conference on Research and Innovation in Information Systems*, 1–6. https://doi.org/DOI: 10.1109/ICRIIS.2011.6125747

Sudaryono, S., Pratomo, R., Ramadan, A., Ahsanitaqwim, R., & Fletcher, E. (2025). Artificial Intelligence in Predictive Cybersecurity: Developing Adaptive Algorithms to Combat Emerging Threats. *Journal of Computer Science and Technology Application*, *2*(1), 1–13.

Sulaiman, N. S., Fauzi, M. A., Hussain, S., & Wider, W. (2022). Cybersecurity behavior among government employees: The role of protection motivation theory and responsibility in mitigating cyberattacks. *Information (Basel)*, *13*(9), 413.

Sutton, A., & Tompson, L. (2025). Towards a cybersecurity culture-behaviour framework: A rapid evidence review. *Computers & Security*, *129*, 103212.

Syed, S. (2024, September). The human factor: Enhancing intelligence capabilities with people-centric knowledge management. In *AU Hybrid International Conference 2024 on "Entrepreneurship & Sustainability in the Digital Era"* (Vol. 4, No. 1, pp. 556–567).

Taherdoost, H. (2022). Understanding cybersecurity frameworks and information security standards—A review and comprehensive overview. *Electronics (Basel)*, *11*(6), 892.

Taheri, R., Ghahramani, M., Javidan, R., Shojafar, M., Pooranian, Z., & Conti, M. (2020). Similarity-based Android malware detection using Hamming distance of static binary features. *Future Generation Computer Systems*, *105*, 230–247.

Tambe-Jagtap, S. N. (2023). Human-centric cybersecurity: Understanding and mitigating the role of human error in cyber incidents. *SHIFRA Journal of Cybersecurity Research*, *2*(1), 88–101.

Tejay, G. P. S., & Winkfield, M. (2025). Does leadership approach matter? Examining behavioral influences of leaders on employees' information security compliance. *Information Systems Frontiers*, *27*(2), 321–338.

Tennant, J. P., Waldner, F., Jacques, D. C., Masuzzo, P., Collister, L. B., & Hartgerink, C. H. (2016). The academic, economic, and societal impacts of open access: An evidence-based review. *F1000Research*, *5*, 632. DOI: 10.12688/f1000research.8460.3 PMID: 27158456

Thangaveloo, R., & Jing, W. (2020, March). W., Kang Leng, C. and Abdullah, J. "DATDroid: Dynamic Analysis Technique in Android Malware Detection". *International Journal on Advanced Science, Engineering and Information Technology*, *10*(2), 536–541.

Thomas, G., & Sule, M. J. (2023). A service lens on cybersecurity continuity and management for organizations' subsistence and growth. *Organizational Cybersecurity Journal: Practice. Process and People*, *3*(1), 18–40.

Tofoni, T., Luciani, F., & Prado, A. (2023). *BGP (Border Gateway Protocol): From theory to practice*. Independently published.

Tolah, A. (2021). A Framework for Understanding and Establishing an Effective Information Security Culture.

Trenerry, B., Chng, S., Wang, Y., Suhaila, Z. S., Lim, S. S., Lu, H. Y., & Oh, P. H. (2021). Preparing workplaces for digital transformation: An integrative review and framework of multi-level factors. *Frontiers in Psychology*, *12*, 620766. PMID: 33833714

Triplett, W. (2021). Establishing a cybersecurity culture organization. Acta Scientific COMPUTER SCIENCES Volume, 3(8).

Triplett, W. J. (2022). Addressing human factors in cybersecurity leadership. *Journal of Cybersecurity and Privacy*, *2*(3), 573–586.

Tsap, V., (2020). The Estonian E-government ecosystem: A case study. *Procedia Computer Science*, *175*, 46–53.

Ünver, H. M., & Bakour, K. (2020). Android malware detection based on image-based features and machine learning techniques. *SN Applied Sciences*, *2*(7), 1299.

Ur, B., Segreti, S. M., Bauer, L., Christin, N., & Cranor, L. F. (2022). Measuring real-world accuracies and biases in password security metrics. *Proceedings on Privacy Enhancing Technologies*. https://doi.org/DOI: 10.2478/popets-2022-0012

Ur, B., Segreti, S., Bauer, L., Christin, N., Cranor, L. F., & Mazurek, M. L. (2022). Measuring real-world accuracy and use of password managers. *USENIX Security Symposium*, *31*, 397–414.

van Steen, T. (2022). *When Choice is (not) an Option: Nudging and Techno-Regulation Approaches to Behavioural Cybersecurity* (pp. 120–130). https://doi.org/DOI: 10.1007/978-3-031-05457-0_10

van Steen, T. (2025). Developing a behavioural cybersecurity strategy: A five-step approach for organisations. *Computer Standards & Interfaces*, *92*, 103939. DOI: 10.1016/j.csi.2024.103939

Vandercruysse, L., Buts, C., & Dooms, M. (2020). A typology of smart city services: The case of data protection impact assessment. *Cities (London, England)*, *104*, 102731.

Vaswani, A., Shazeer, N., Parmar, N., Uszkoreit, J., Jones, L., Gomez, A. N., & Polosukhin, I. (2017). Attention is all you need. *Advances in Neural Information Processing Systems*, •••, 30.

Velkes, R. (2019). GDPR: The right of access to personal data. *New York University Journal of International Law & Politics. New York University. International Law Society*, *51*(4), 1395–1433.

Venkatesh, V., & Davis, F. D. (2000). A theoretical extension of the Technology Acceptance Model: Four longitudinal field studies. *Management Information Systems Quarterly*, *24*(2), 115–143. DOI: 10.2307/3250955

Verizon. (2022). Data Breach Investigations Report. https://www.verizon.com/business/resources/reports/dbir/

Victor-Mgbachi, T. (2024). Navigating cybersecurity beyond compliance: Understanding your threat landscape and vulnerabilities. *Iconic Research and Engineering Journals*, *7*(2), 11–17.

Wang, G., Tse, D., Cui, Y., & Jiang, H. (2022). An exploratory study on sustaining cyber security protection through Seta Implementation. *Sustainability*, *14*(14), 8319.

Wang, H., & Song, Y. (2018). Secure Cloud-Based EHR System Using Attribute-Based Cryptosystem and Blockchain. *Journal of Medical Systems*, *42*(8). PMID: 29974270

Wang, L., Yang, J., & Wan, P.-J. (2020). Educational modules and research surveys on critical cybersecurity topics. *International Journal of Distributed Sensor Networks*, *16*(9), 155014772095467. DOI: 10.1177/1550147720954678

WeActis. (2022). *The human factor in cybersecurity: Turning weaknesses into strengths* [eBook]. https://weactis.com/wp-content/uploads/WeActis_The_Human_Factor_ebook.pdf

Welekwe, A. (2024, December 2). *BGP attributes and path selection*. Comparitech. https://www.comparitech.com/net-admin/bgp-attributes-and-path-selection/

Williams, L., Anthi, E., Cherdantseva, Y., & Javed, A. (2024). Leveraging Gamification and Game-based Learning in Cybersecurity Education. *Journal of The Colloquium for Information Systems Security Education, 11*(1), 8. DOI: 10.53735/cisse.v11i1.186

Willie, M. M. (2023). The role of organizational culture in cybersecurity: Building a security-first culture. *Journal of Research, 5*(3), 77–85.

Willie, M. M. (2023). The role of organizational culture in cybersecurity: Building a security-first culture. Journal of Research. *Innovation and Technologies, 2*(2 (4)), 179–198.

Winata, T. J., Souwiko, R., & Sutanto, J. (2024). Simulasi jaringan untuk sistem terdistribusi KOHA dengan GNS3. *Jurnal Ilmu Komputer dan Sistem Informasi, 12*(2).

Windarta, S., Suryadi, S., Ramli, K., Pranggono, B., & Gunawan, T. S. (2022). Lightweight cryptographic hash functions: Design trends, comparative study, and future directions. *IEEE Access: Practical Innovations, Open Solutions, 10*, 82272–82294.

Woodrum, T. D. (2003). 21 CFR Part 11: The Role of Predicate Regulations and Associated Internal Policies. *Drug Information Journal, 37*(2), 159–164. DOI: 10.1177/009286150303700205

Woon, I. M. Y., Tan, G. W., & Low, R. T. (2005). A protection motivation theory approach to home wireless security. *Proceedings of the Twenty-Sixth International Conference on Information Systems*, 367–380.

Xia, N., Xie, Q., Griffin, M. A., Ye, G., & Yuan, J. (2020). Antecedents of safety behavior in construction: A literature review and an integrated conceptual framework. *Accident; Analysis and Prevention, 148*, 105834. PMID: 33120185

Xue, J., Xin, X., Zhang, W., Zheng, M., Song, Q., Zhou, M., Dong, Y., Wang, Q., Mohaisen, D., Wu, H., & Lou, Q. (2025). Measuring Computational Universality of Fully Homomorphic Encryption. arXiv. Submitted 15 April 2025.

Yaacob, M. N., Idrus, S. Z. S., & Idris, M. (2023). Managing cybersecurity risks in emerging technologies. *International Journal of Business and Technopreneurship, 13*(3), 253–270.

Yaacoub, J. P. A., Noura, H. N., Salman, O., & Chehab, A. (2022). Robotics cyber security: Vulnerabilities, attacks, countermeasures, and recommendations. *International Journal of Information Security, 21*(1), 115–158. PMID: 33776611

Yang, Q., Ma, L., Tu, S., Ullah, S., Waqas, M., & Alasmary, H. (2024). Towards blockchain-based secure BGP routing, challenges and future research directions. *Computers, Materials & Continua*, *79*(2), 2035–2062.

Yan, J., Xu, T., Yu, Y., & Xu, H. (2021). Rainfall forecast model based on the tabnet model. *Water (Basel)*, *13*(9), 1–16.

Yaro, H. U. (2025). Phishing Susceptibility Metrics in Academic Environments: Simulation-Based Analysis at Federal Polytechnic Bali, Nigeria. *Asia-Pacific Journal of Information Technology and Multimedia*, *14*(01), 219–239. DOI: 10.17576/apjitm-2025-1401-13

Yeo, L. H., & Banfield, J. (2022). Human factors in electronic health records cybersecurity breach: An exploratory analysis. *Perspectives in Health Information Management*, *19*(2), 1i. PMID: 35692854

Yin, R. K. (2017). *Case Study Research and Applications: Design and Methods*. Sage Publications.

Yusif, S., & Hafeez-Baig, A. (2021). A Conceptual Model for Cybersecurity Governance. *Journal of Applied Security Research*, *16*(4), 490–513. DOI: 10.1080/19361610.2021.1918995

Yuvaraj, M. V. (2023). Performance analysis of Border Gateway Protocol (BGP) in multi-autonomous system network with OPNET simulator: A case study. *Cyber Security in Engineering Technology and Management (ICCETM-2023)*, 97.

Zaid, T., & Garai, S. (2024). Emerging trends in cybersecurity: A holistic view on current threats, assessing solutions, and pioneering new frontiers. *Blockchain in Healthcare Today*, •••, 7. PMID: 38715765

Zamany, M. A. Z., Supendar, H., & Wanda, S. S. (2022). Optimalisasi routing menggunakan satu autonomous system number (ASN) Border Gateway Protocol (BGP). *JEIS: Jurnal Elektro dan Informatika Swadharma, 2*(1), 48–56.

Zeadally, S., Adi, E., Baig, Z., & Khan, I. A. (2020). Harnessing Artificial Intelligence Capabilities to Improve Cybersecurity. *IEEE Access: Practical Innovations, Open Solutions*, *8*, 23817–23837. DOI: 10.1109/ACCESS.2020.2968045

Zengeni, I. P., & fadli Zolkipli, M. (2024). Zero-day exploits and vulnerability management. Borneo International Journal eISSN 2636-9826, 7(3), 26-33. https://majmuah.com/journal/index.php/bij/article/view/648

Zhang, X., & Jain, A. (2024). Apple Loquat: A SNARK-Friendly Post-Quantum Signature. Proceedings of Crypto 2024

Zhang, C., & Ma, Y. (2012). *Ensemble machine learning*. Springer.

Zhang, S., Su, H., Liu, H., & Yang, W. (2025). MPDroid: A multimodal pre-training Android malware detection method with static and dynamic features. *Computers & Security*, *150*, 104262.

Zhao, D. (2025). Compile-Time Fully Homomorphic Encryption: Eliminating Online Encryption via Algebraic Basis Synthesis. arXiv. Submitted 19 May 2025.

Zhao, D. (2025). Advances and Applications in Fully Homomorphic Encryption Research. [EWA Direct]. *Applied and Computational Engineering*, *135*, 39–48. DOI: 10.54254/2755-2721/2025.20959

Zolanvari, M., Teixeira, M., & Jain, R. (2021). Blockchain-based solutions for secure and transparent banking services. *IEEE Access: Practical Innovations, Open Solutions*, *9*, 17832–17845. DOI: 10.1109/ACCESS.2021.3054551

Zwilling, M., Klien, G., Lesjak, D., Wiechetek, Ł., Cetin, F., & Basim, H. N. (2022). Cyber security awareness, knowledge and behavior: A comparative study. *Journal of Computer Information Systems*, *62*(1), 82–97.

About the Contributors

Asif Iqbal Hajamydeen is a seasoned cybersecurity expert specialising in anomaly-based intrusion detection systems, computer security, and data mining within the expansive domains of cybersecurity and computer networks. With over 18 years of dedicated service at Management & Science University (MSU), Dr. Asif Iqbal has become a cornerstone of the Faculty of Information Sciences and Engineering, where he currently serves as an Associate Professor. Throughout his career, Dr. Asif Iqbal has made significant strides in both academic and applied cybersecurity, producing impactful research that addresses today's most pressing digital security challenges. His scholarly output includes numerous publications, book chapters, and collaborative research on advanced security frameworks, machine learning innovations, and IoT applications. His work is widely recognized, with 540 Google Scholar citations and an h-index of 15, underscoring his influence in the field. Dr. Asif Iqbal's dedication to academic excellence has earned him prestigious accolades, such as the ITEX medals and the TEA President's Award. As a committed mentor and educator, Dr. Asif Iqbal supervises postgraduate students at the Master's and PhD levels, guiding them in pioneering research across various subfields of computer security and network safety. His role also extends to curriculum development and hands-on training in cybersecurity, where he actively integrates practical knowledge into his teaching. Notably, he has contributed to SOC (Security Operations Center) management, implementing innovative AI-driven cybersecurity projects that blend theoretical frameworks with real-world applications. Dr. Asif Iqbal's dual commitment to research excellence and educational mentorship makes him a sought-after leader in the academic and professional cybersecurity communities.

Asma'a Alhakimi obtained her Diploma in Computer Programming in 2006 from the University of Science and Technology in Sanaa, Yemen. She earned her bachelor's degree in computer studies in 2008 from Northumbria University in

Newcastle, UK, followed by a master's degree in software engineering in 2011 from Staffordshire University, UK. She completed her Ph.D. in Software Engineering at Universiti Putra Malaysia. Dr. Asma'a has extensive experience in the networking field and served as a lecturer at Asia Pacific University (APU) in Malaysia for five years. She is recognized for her expertise in conducting industrial cybersecurity training. Her research interests encompass Cybersecurity, Reverse Engineering, Software Engineering, and Artificial Intelligence. In addition to her teaching and research responsibilities, Dr. Asma'a is an Editorial Board Member of the American Journal of Electrical and Computer Engineering (AJECE) and is affiliated with the Association for Computing Machinery (ACM) and IEEE Access. Currently, she is a senior lecturer and researcher at MSU University, where she leads a research group focused on cybersecurity and forensics. Dr. Asma'a is dedicated to her work and is known for her innovative contributions across various domains. She has a strong publication record in cybersecurity and smart cities and has participated in an international exhibition showcasing a cybersecurity project that received significant recognition. Her numerous publications highlight advancements in smart cities and cybersecurity.

Md Gapar Md Johar is Senior Vice President for System, Technology and Innovation of Management and Science University, Malaysia. He is a professor in Software Engineering. He holds PhD in Computer Science, MSc in Data Engineering and BSc (Hons) in Computer Science and Certified E-Commerce Consultant. He has more than 42 years of working and teaching experience in various organizations include Ministry of Finance, Ministry of Public Enterprise, Public Service Department, Glaxo Malaysia Sdn Bhd and Cosmopoint Institute of Technology as well as attachment at Staffordshire Hospital, UK. His proficiency in software engineering is complemented by a diverse research portfolios include learning content management system, knowledge management system, blended assessment system, data mining, RFID, e-commerce, image processing, character recognition, voice recognition, data analytics, artificial intelligent, brain-computer interface, Internet of Things and healthcare management system. He has managed the development of more than 35 computer applications, Notably, he spearheaded the groundbreaking Smart Poultry Farm Monitoring System, earning accolades at various international exhibitions, including a gold medal at ITeX 2024, ITeX 2022 and recognition at MTE 2022, PECIPTA'22, and SIIF 2022. This system revolutionizes IoT-based poultry farming by automating temperature, humidity, and ammonia gas monitoring, and poultry healthcare management showcasing his commitment to innovation and technological advancement.

I Wayan Budi Sentana is a senior lecturer at the Department of Information Technology, Politeknik Negeri Bali, specializing in Cyber Security and Blockchain technology. He received the prestigious LPDP scholarship in 2019 to pursue his PhD at Macquarie University, Australia, where his research focused on enhancing the security of internet routing protocols (BGP) and mobile applications. Dr. Sentana is also an expert consultant at DUCO Inc., California, and a member of IEEE. He holds certifications in Cisco DevOps and EC-Council CHFI, strengthening his expertise in cybersecurity. He was awarded the Research Bridging Program in Taiwan in 2018 and was a finalist in the 2022 Cyber Thesis Competition at UNSW Sydney.

***

Abdul Rahim Sadiq Batcha is a distinguished academician and researcher with over 35 years of teaching experience in Electrical and Electronics Engineering. Currently, he serves as the Associate Professor in the Faculty of Engineering, Built Environment, and IT at MAHSA University, Malaysia. He holds a PhD from Multimedia University, Malaysia, and degrees from India in Electronics and Communication Engineering. His research focuses on 5G wireless technology,, Artificial Intelligence and Internet of Things. As a researcher, he has secured various grants and conducted cutting-edge research in the field of 5G technology, particularly dielectric resonator antennas for small cell base stations.. A Chartered Engineer and member of multiple professional bodies, Dr. Sadiq is also an active trainer, journal editor, and keynote speaker, contributing significantly to advancements in engineering education and research.

Halima Abbas Assaied Ahmed, from Libya obtained an undergraduate degree in Computer Programming from the University of Benghazi in 2000. In 2016, they obtained a Master of Science in Networking Professional from Sheffield Hallam University, UK. They are currently pursuing a PhD in Information and Communication Technology at Management and Science University (MSU), Malaysia. Worked for 5 years as a head of Computer Science Department At Engineering Provision Higher Institute Almajory -Benghazi- Libya .Moreover they worked in networking field, they were a lecturer of computer networks and a supervisor for undergraduate projects and a lecturer at the School of Enginnering and Technology at the Libyan International University.Working in the financial department as software developer and lecturer at Higher Institute for Engineering Technologies Majori Benghazi-Libya and at Ministry of education Benghazi-Libya. Research interest includes Cybersecurity, and networking.

Balqees Alhaddad is a Master's student in Education Instructional Technology at Universiti Geomatika Malaysia, Malaysia, with a Bachelor's degree in Kindergarten from King Faisal University, Saudi Arabia (4.5/5 GPA). Experienced educational leader with a background in kindergarten management, curriculum development, and school administration. Passionate about integrating technology into education, with growing interests in cybersecurity, information security, and smart city innovations. Aspiring to bridge the gap between education management and advanced digital solutions to enhance learning environments and community development.

Srinivas Chippagiri is a technology leader, cloud computing expert, and published researcher with over a decade of experience architecting and delivering scalable, secure, and resilient software solutions. His professional journey spans multiple domains including telecommunications, healthcare, energy, and enterprise SaaS where he has consistently driven innovation at the convergence of cloud infrastructure, AI/ML applications, and distributed systems. Srinivas holds a master's degree from the University of Utah, where he was honored for his academic accomplishments. He has won numerous awards in recognition of his contributions to technology and engineering innovation.

G. Sofia serves as an Associate Professor in the Department of Computer Science at Lady Doak College, Madurai. She holds an M.C.A. from Manonmaniam Sundaranar University, Tirunelveli, an M.Phil. in Computer Science from Mother Teresa Women's University, Kodaikanal, and a Ph.D. in Computer Science from Bharathiar University, Coimbatore. She has actively contributed to the academic community by presenting numerous research papers at national and international conferences. She has published articles in reputed journals and authored book chapters in her areas of expertise. She has served as a resource person for various workshops and faculty development programmes, where she shares her knowledge and insights with academic peers and professionals. Her outstanding contributions to teaching and research have earned her accolades such as the Katie Wilcox Teacher of the Year Award and the Best Paper Award at the Virtual Conference on Smart Computing and Advanced Communication. She holds academic memberships in various institutions, serving as a subject expert and member of Board of Studies meetings, member of doctoral committees, and external expert for academic council meeting. Her areas of specialization include Image Processing, Data Science, and Virtual Reality.

Rajendra Mahanandia is the Assistant Professor at the VIT Business School Bhopal University, India. Dr. Mahanandia is a Doctorate from the School of Management Studies, University of Hyderabad. His Ph.D. thesis is entitled on the topic of "A Study on the Corporate Sustainability Reporting Practices in the Indian Context." He completed his M.Phil. and PG in Industrial Relations and Personnel Management (IR&PM) from Berhampur University, Odisha. Master of Business Administration (MBA- General) from Pondicherry University (D). Dr. Mahanandia has a total of 5 publications in various reputed National and International journals in Scopus, ABDC (C), and UGC care listed. During his doctorate journey, he has been associated with organizing International conferences and workshops. He has attended several FDPs and workshops from premier institutions in India and abroad. His area of interest is HR, OB, Sustainability, SHRM, Marketing and Labour Law.

Latha Manickam is the Senior Lecturer / PhD & DBA Program Co-ordinator in the Faculty of Business, Accounting, Finance, Law & Humanity, MAHSA University, Malaysia. She has over 20 years of experience in teaching. She has completed PhD from Madurai Kamaraj University in the area of Green Banking. She has presented numerous research papers at International Conferences, published articles in Scopus and authored book chapters in her areas of expertise. Her areas of specialization include Management, Accountancy, Environmental Sustainability in addition to Artificial Intelligence. She has been appointed as the Supervisor for Doctor of Philosophy in Management and at present guiding 8 Ph.D. Scholars from various countries like China, Nigeria, Middle East, Bangladesh and Malaysia. She is a Life Time Member (TN241) of Indian Commece Association (ICA). She is also a Professional QUVAE Member (QVP3340) with a professional commitment to research advancement.

Froilan D. Mobo, DPA, Ph.D. is a distinguished Filipino educator, researcher, and academic leader known for his outstanding contributions to education, public administration, and development studies. He currently serves as a Full Professor II at the Philippine Merchant Marine Academy (PMMA), where he has devoted over a decade of service in shaping future maritime professionals. In addition to his academic role, he is the Editor-in-Chief of the International Journal of Multidisciplinary: Applied Business and Education Research (IJMABER), a reputable international refereed journal. Prof. Mobo is a strong advocate of lifelong learning, having earned dual doctorate degrees—Doctor of Public Administration from Urdaneta City University and Doctor of Philosophy in Development Education from Central Luzon State University—as well as triple master's degrees, including a Master of Science in Computer Science, Master of Business Administration, and Master of Arts in Social Studies Education from Bicol University Open University. He also holds a Diploma in Social Studies Education from UP Open University and is a Licensed Professional Teacher with a specialization in Social Studies.

Nur Fasihah Mohd Esa is a Senior Lecturer at the Faculty of Information Sciences and Engineering, Management and Science University (MSU), Malaysia. She holds a PhD in Cryptography and has deep research interests in symmetric-key cryptography, post-quantum cryptography, and cybersecurity. In addition to her academic and research work, she actively teach students in programming, cybersecurity and cryptography.

Siavosh Haghighi Movahed MSc, BSc is a Senior Lecturer in Computer Systems and Networks, Course leader for MSc Advanced Computer Networks School of Computing and Digital Technologies Industry and Innovation Research Institute.

Sheena Christabel Pravin, Assistant Professor Senior Grade at Vellore Institute of Technology has over 14 years of Engineering teaching experience, with 4 years of research experience in disordered speech processing and one year of project experience at DRDO-Chennai on Acoustic and Vibration Signal Processing. She completed B.E. in Electronics and Communication Engineering, M.E. (Communication Systems) securing University rank under Anna University. During her Doctoral Program under Anna University, she had built hybrid deep learning models for disfluent speech categorization, phonation deviation assessment and speech resynthesis. She has published over 30 research papers in National and International Conferences and Journals. She has completed three funded projects under AICTE's Research Promotion Scheme, TNSCST and SEEE Grant-in-aid scheme. She has built several speech recognition systems for various disordered speech patterns. She continues her research in the field of disfluent speech processing, speech enhancement, Artificial Intelligence, deep learning and applies her knowledge in health analytics to bring low-cost health care devices and assistive aids for the ailing.

Manickam Ramasamy is a chartered engineer registered with Engineering Council United Kingdom. Currently working in UCSI University Malaysia. Vast experience in working with different ethnic groups gained through a career spanning 34 years working in countries like India, Malaysia and Singapore.

S. Anubha Pearline currently serves as an Assistant Professor (Senior Grade) in the School of Computer Science and Engineering at the Vellore Institute of Technology, Chennai campus. She was formerly associated with SRM Institute of Science and Technology, Vadapalani campus. She received her doctoral degree from Madras Institute of Technology, Anna University. She earned her M.Tech in Information Technology from Madras Institute of Technology, Anna University. She acquired her Bachelor of Engineering in Computer Science and Engineering from

Tagore Engineering College, affiliated with Anna University. Her research interests include Computer Vision, deep learning, machine learning, cybersecurity, and data analytics. She is a member of IEEE, IUPRAI, ACM, and ISTE.

Manisha Singh is an Assistant Professor at the Business School, VIT Bhopal University, Madhya Pradesh. She holds a Doctorate in Management from Maulana Azad National Institute of Technology (MANIT), Bhopal, with a specialization in Human Resource Management. Her doctoral research focused on the "Impact of Employer Brand on Employee Retention." Dr. Singh also holds an MBA with dual specializations in Finance and HRM from Punjab Technical University and an M.Com. from Barkatullah University, Bhopal. With 18 years of diverse experience in both industry and academia, she has established herself as a distinguished academician. Her research expertise includes Employer Branding, Employee Retention, Organizational Behavior, Human Resource Management, and Finance. Dr. Singh has a prolific publication record in renowned international and national journals, including SCOPUS-indexed works. She has also contributed chapters to books published by leading publishers and actively participates in national and international conferences. In addition, Dr. Singh has organized short-term courses, serves as an external paper setter, and is a reviewer for several esteemed journals. She holds design patents, reflecting her innovative approach and commitment to research excellence.

Sonali Srivastava is presently working as an Assistant Professor (Senior Grade) at Jaypee Business School, JIIT, Noida. She is a doctorate in Finance from Dayalbagh Educational Institute, Agra. She has an academic experience of more than 8 years with several reputed institutions i.e. Symbiosis Centre for Management Studies, (SCMS) Nagpur, VIT Bhopal University, MNNIT Allahabad, IIM Ahmedabad, Ministry of Finance and Amity University. She has published a number of research papers in peer reviewed international and national journals indexed in Scopus and WOS. She has also presented research papers in international and national conferences, seminars and conventions. Dr Sonali has organized a number of Conferences and Short-term courses. She is appointed as an external paper setter in many universities. She has authored books titled "Advanced Auditing and Recent Advances in Accounting, Taxation & Auditing". She has also published design patents with grants under controller Department for promotion of industry and internal trade, Government of India. She is a member of various professional bodies and Member of the Reviewer Board of Various Journals.

Ahgalya Subbiah is currently a Research Coordinator & Group Leader, as well as a Senior Lecturer with the Faculty of Information Science and Engineering (FISE) at the Management and Science University (MSU). She has many years of experience teaching System and Data Science courses such as System Analysis and Design, Database System, Project Management, Software Engineering Design, and Strategic IS, IS Infrastructure and Data Mining, etc. She graduated from Universiti Teknologi Malaysia (UTM) with a PhD degree in Information System. Her research focuses on Smart City, Transportation, Service System Value, Healthcare Informatics, HCI, e-Government, Public Policy, Health Informatics, Gerontology and IoT. She worked in Citibank Singapore for eight years and gained plenty of industry experience through different functions and been in education & training for the past seventeen years and helped many young students to GOT. Her research in the last decade has revolved around the following theme: Service Innovation & Co-Creation of Value between the computational complexity of various computational problems, particularly lattice problems. Some of her recent research centers around improving construction of such extractors in various settings, and their applications.

Index

www.ingramcontent.com/pod-product-compliance
Lightning Source LLC
LaVergne TN
LVHW062324300926
849161LV00007B/1563
* 9 7 9 8 3 3 7 3 4 1 5 4 5 *